Assessing English on the Global Stage

Assessing English on the Global Stage

The British Council and English Language Testing, 1941–2016

Cyril J. Weir and Barry O'Sullivan

equinox

SHEFFIELD UK   BRISTOL CT

Published by Equinox Publishing Ltd.
UK: Office 415, The Workstation, 15 Paternoster Row, Sheffield, South Yorkshire
        S1 2BX
USA: ISD, 70 Enterprise Drive, Bristol, CT 06010

www.equinoxpub.com

First published 2017

© Cyril J. Weir and Barry O'Sullivan 2017

All rights reserved. No part of this publication may be reproduced or transmitted in any form or by any means, electronic or mechanical, including photocopying, recording or any information storage or retrieval system, without prior permission in writing from the publishers.

British Library Cataloguing-in-Publication Data

A catalogue record for this book is available from the British Library.

ISBN-13 978 1 78179 491 3   (hardback)
         978 1 78179 492 0   (paperback)

Library of Congress Cataloging-in-Publication Data

Names: Weir, Cyril J. | O'Sullivan, Barry. | British Council. English
    Language Services Department.
Title: Assessing English on the global stage : the British Council and
    English Language Testing, 1941-2016 / Cyril J. Weir and Barry O'Sullivan.
Description: Sheffield, UK ; Bristol, CT : Equinox Publishing Ltd, [2017] |
    Includes bibliographical references and index.
Identifiers: LCCN 2017002035 (print) | LCCN 2017027397 (ebook) |
    ISBN 9781781796016 (ePDF) | ISBN 9781781794913 (hb) |
    ISBN 9781781794920 (pb)
Subjects: LCSH: English language–Ability testing–Evaluation. | English
    language–Globalization. | Second language acquisition–Testing. |
    Language and languages–Testing.
Classification: LCC P118.7 (ebook) | LCC P118.7 .A77 2017 (print) | DDC
    428.0076–dc23
LC record available at https://lccn.loc.gov/2017002035

Typeset by S.J.I. Services, New Delhi
Printed and bound by Lightning Source Inc. (La Vergne, TN), Lightning Source UK Ltd. (Milton Keynes), Lightning Source AU Pty. (Scoresby, Victoria).

Contents

List of Tables   vii

List of Figures   viii

Acknowledgements   xi

Section 1: Spreading Influence around the World through the Promotion of English, 1935–2016

1. A global, promotional agenda, 1935–2016: Exporting British culture and language   3

2. Developing English language testing around the world, 1982–2016: Exporting British expertise   40

Section 2: Developing Academic English Tests for University Gatekeeping and Selection Purposes, 1954–2016

3. Testing the academic English of overseas students coming to Britain, 1954–1982: The British Council interview and the English Proficiency Test Battery   105

4. The English Language Testing Service: The first communicative test, 1975–1989   136

5. The International English Language Testing System, 1989–2016   208

Section 3: Developing Language Tests for Other Purposes

6   Language test development in the 21st century: The return to a product centred approach   257

7   Conclusions and the future   331

Appendix 1 Overview of the Aptis Test Papers   338

Appendix 2 British Council Assessment Research Awards and Grants, 2013–2016   344

References   348

Subject and Key Personnel Index   374

Tables

2.1	Examples of British Council overseas testing projects	46
3.1	Students coming to the UK, 1945–1975	108
3.2	Composition of original EPTB Form A	116
5.1	Details of the final formats of the Academic modules introduced for IELTS in 1995	245
5.2	IELTS candidature	251
6.1	Development of the ILA papers	266
6.2	Levels of localisation in the Aptis test system	280
6.3	Brief overview of key parameters (Reading)	296
6.4	Brief overview of key parameters (Writing)	300
6.5	Language functions in expected responses (Writing)	302
6.6	Reliability estimates 2015 – Core, Reading, Listening	303
6.7	Mean correlations for Writing tasks	307
6.8	Mean correlations for Speaking tasks	308
6.9	Mean inter-rater correlations across all tasks	308
6.10	Aptis variants used in 2015/16	309
6.11	Published Assessment Research Grants (2013–2016) and their impact	321
6.12	British Council sponsored award at the LTRC, 2013–2016	324
6.13	British Council LAL project elements	326
6.14	English Impact Project evidence bases	329
7.1	British Council involvement in English language testing, 1941–2016	333

Figures

3.1	Overseas students coming to Britain, 1981–1996	109
6.1	Original design suggested for the ILA	264
6.2	British Council Exams Strategy: Key initiatives for 2009/10	271
6.3	Initial theoretical Aptis test development model	282
6.4	Actual Aptis test development model	283
6.5	Aptis validation model	291
6.6	Operationalisation of the Khalifa and Weir (2009) Reading model	294
6.7	Reading Task 4 specification	295
6.8	Writing Task 4 specification	299
6.9	Aptis rating model	305
6.10	Aptis rating scale for Speaking Task 2 (extract)	305
6.11	Aptis Control Item (CI) rating quality assurance system	306

Acknowledgements

Many people have shared their professional experiences with us and thereby helped illuminate various aspects of the long history of the British Council's involvement in language testing. Their voices are in themselves an important historical record that has been documented for future generations.

The authors wrote to a large number of people who had been associated with the British Council sponsored projects examined in Chapter 2 and, with only one notable exception, they were all willing to write a short piece on the objectives of the project(s) they had been involved in, synthesise what each project achieved and reflect on the wider impact the project had in the host country. These vignettes are reported in Chapter 2 against each project. We are grateful to: Eszter Benke, Mark Crossey, Ildiko Csépes, Les Dangerfield, Alan Davies, John Gildea, Rita Green, Liz Hamp-Lyons, Roger Hawkey, Arthur Hughes, Tony Lilley, Susan Maingay, Alan Moller, Nick Saville, Ian Seaton, Richard Smith, Alexander Urquhart, Dianne Wall, Gill Westaway, Barbara Wickham, Yan Jin and Shen Zou for their help in enriching this chapter.

During the period 2013–2016 extended interviews were carried out with people who had featured prominently in the history of the British Council's involvement in language testing. A real debt is owed to Roger Hawkey who carried out many of the interviews in his own engaging, idiosyncratic and emergentist fashion. The taped recording of these interviews provided a rich data source for writing Chapters 3 to 7 and it is intended that these interviews should be archived for the benefit of future researchers.

We are grateful to the following people for participating in the interviews and allowing us to record their voices for posterity: Brendan Carroll, Nick Charge, Anne-Marie Cooper, Les Dangerfield, Alan Davies, Peter Falvey, Tony Green, Roger Hawkey, Liz Hamp-Lyons, Roland Hindmarsh, John Gildea, Beth Kerrison, Mike Milanovic, Alan

Moller, Caroline Moore, John Munby, Jenny Pugsley, John Reddaway, Nick Saville, Ian Seaton, Susan Sheehan, Anne Staniforth, Paul Sweeney, Lynda Taylor and Mark Walker.

Numerous people have commented on the drafts of the manuscript itself, providing useful additional information and correcting any occasional misinterpretations on our part. Richard Smith and Roger Hawkey provided insightful early feedback on Chapters 1 and 2; Alan Davies on Chapter 3; Alan Davies, Liz Hamp-Lyons, Mike Milanovic, Nick Saville and Ian Seaton on Chapter 4; and Nick Charge, Les Dangerfield, Tony Green, Mike Milanovic, Nick Saville, Lynda Taylor and Gill Westaway on Chapter 5. The following British Council and former British Council staff contributed to the ILA section of this book in Chapter 6: Barbara Hewitt, Martin Lowder, Caroline Moore, Paul Sweeney, Richard Sunderland and Mark Walker. Vivien Berry, Jamie Dunlea, John Knagg, Martin Lowder, Andrew Mackenzie, Mark Robson, Liz Shepherd and Mark Walker contributed to the Aptis and British Council Tests section in Chapter 6.

Two external reviewers provided insightful and detailed comments on the final draft of the whole book. We are particularly grateful to Richard Smith and Roger Hawkey for all their efforts in reviewing the manuscript so carefully and helping to make this a better book.

Two members of the British Council Assessment Advisory Board, Jin Yan and Christine Coombe, closely edited the final version of the manuscript and corrected our many slips of the word processor. Any faults that remain are of our own making.

Last but not least we need to thank Melissa Downing, Joanna Rosenzweig, Geoffrey Browell and Joanna Loxton, in the British Council History of Assessment Project Team, for their sterling work in locating resources relevant to the project and keeping us on track; Jennifer Le for her help in making arrangements for the interviews; and Shigeko Weir and Angela Mugomezi for their help in proof reading, accessing relevant books and articles, and getting the rather long set of references sorted out.

We are grateful to OUP and Merrill Swain for permission to use an extract from p. 34 of Michael Canale and Merrill Swain's 'Theoretical Bases of Communicative Approaches to Second Language Teaching and Testing' in *Applied Linguistics*(1980), 1(1).

Section 1

Spreading Influence around the World through the Promotion of English, 1935–2016

> The English language is travelling fast towards the fulfilment of its destiny… is running forward towards its ultimate mission of eating up, like Aaron's rod, all other languages.
> (De Quincey 1907: 109)

Chapter 1

A global, promotional agenda, 1935–2016: Exporting British culture and language

The birth of the British Council: A cultural dimension for British foreign policy

The 1930s proved a difficult period for British foreign policy. The government was faced with growing threats to stability in Europe and increasing unrest in its Empire in other parts of the world. The 'Pact of Steel' between Germany, Italy and Japan meant three potential enemies to defend against, each in a different sphere of war and each with considerable military might. Economic, military and international factors would oblige the British government to try to avoid war with these countries at all costs.

The 1920s had witnessed a heavy disarmament programme in Britain and as a result the country was badly placed to fight another war. The situation worsened in the 1930s as the adverse economic effects of the Great Depression meant scant funding was available for rearmament, let alone further conflict (Hughes 2004). Britain was faced with the daunting task of defending an Empire covering over a quarter of the globe's surface with inadequate military resources (Self 2005 and 2006). Its lack of armed strength was compounded by the absence of any real support for military attempts at combatting international aggression. The League of Nations did not prove to be the check on bellicosity that it was intended to be; the USA was following an overtly isolationist policy and could not be relied on to intervene on the British side; neither could much be expected from a politically weak France. Problems with Empire in the form of incipient nationalism were already tying down a majority of Britain's overstretched armed forces and the Dominions as a whole were strongly against involvement in another war. The British public too were in no mood for further conflict, with memories of the horrors of WW1 still fresh in many people's minds.

In this climate peaceful diplomacy, based on a strategy of taking every opportunity to influence international events and cultivate support in foreign circles, became the pragmatic policy of choice. Cultural propaganda or, from a British Council perspective, 'cultural promotion', would provide a new dimension to British foreign policy in this period. Kessel (2011: 220), in her seminal work on cultural policy, concludes that by the 1930s Britain was forced to face up to the fact that it had to win the hearts and minds of people abroad through the promotion of its culture and national language in order to at least maintain international political power. 'The wolf in sheep's clothing', as Kessel so neatly described it, entered the realm of British foreign policy.

The Foreign Office was in fact one of the few government departments that saw the need for the promotion of British culture, education, science and technology in other countries, along the lines of existing French, German and Italian cultural organisations. Kessel (2011: 3) describes how these other countries had been involved in cultural diplomacy ever since the end of the 19th century: in Germany through the Allgemeiner Deutscher Schulverein zur Erhaltung des Deutschtums im Ausland (1881–), in France through the Alliance Française (1883–) and in Italy too, through the Società Dante Alighieri (1889–).

While other European governments routinely spent public money to project their respective language, arts, literature or science, hitherto there had been minimal commitment to the cultural promotion of Britain (TNA, FO 431/1, Cultural propaganda, introductory memorandum). Nicolson (1939: 171–172) comments on how little was spent on 'propaganda' through grants to the British Council as compared with the amounts paid by other European governments for propaganda purposes. Whereas Germany spent £4,000,000 to £6,000,000 annually on foreign propaganda, France £1,200,000 and Italy £1,000,000, in Britain comparatively small grants were made available to the British Council, for example £5,000 in 1935, £15,000 in 1936, £60,000 in 1937 and £100,000 in 1938.

Outside of the Foreign Office, many people considered government involvement in cultural propaganda as unnecessary at a time when the

British Empire still covered a large portion of the globe, and many saw it as rather disreputable, given the excesses of the often-mendacious propaganda used by the British in the First World War. A voluntarist approach was seen as preferable in a liberal tradition, where culture was regarded as something better left to individuals than government.

Attitudes were to change in some parts of government. In 1919 Lord Curzon, the Foreign Secretary, had appointed a committee to investigate how the government could support British communities abroad and make British values known to foreign nations. This investigation into British communities abroad resulted in the Tilley Report (1920), which represented a significant shift in attitude, in certain quarters, towards the cultural promotion of Britain overseas. Among its recommendations, Haigh (1974: 35–36) reports that the committee felt assistance should be made available to enhance the experience of foreign students coming to study in Britain and that British Institutes and libraries should be created in various foreign capitals. These plans were, however, ultimately unsuccessful as Lord Curzon's initiative was turned down by the government. Nevertheless, Donaldson (1984: 15) refers to the Tilley Report as 'a blue-print for the British Council'. Though funding was not made available for these purposes at the time due to opposition from the Treasury, the report nevertheless mapped out some of the key areas the British Council would in time take responsibility for.

White (1965: 5–19) chronicles in great detail the events leading up to the formation of the British Council. He emphasises (1965: 3) the importance of the work of a Joint Committee of the Board of Trade and the Board of Education established in 1933 under the chairmanship of Sir Eugene Ramsden to consider the education and training of students from overseas. Its report would eventually provide the blueprint for the student activities of the British Council. White argues that the report produced by the committee pointed to (ibid.):

> ...the wider problem of the ignorance overseas of British achievement in the fields of education, culture, science and technology. The Committee recommended as a matter of the greatest urgency the setting up of a body to deal with the problem. This support from the two Departments of State concerned with this Committee was a most useful reinforcement for the efforts of the Foreign Office to get something done.

Kessel (2011) draws attention to the importance of economic factors in generating the political goodwill that would make the genesis of the British Council possible. She provides (2011: 52) detail of three important economic missions abroad: the D'Abernon British Economic Mission to South America (1930), Ernest Thompson's British Economic Mission to the Far East (1930–1931), and Sir Alan Anderson's Trade Mission to Scandinavia (1933), each of which provided evidence for the government and the civil service of the need to prevent trade being affected by an absence of cultural propaganda.

Kessel (2011: 319) concludes, however, that in the event it was political developments in the Mediterranean region rather than commercial exigencies that proved pivotal in convincing the British government to recognise cultural influence as an essential part of foreign policy. In November 1933, the British High Commissioner in Egypt, Sir Percy Loraine, sent a despatch to the Foreign Office (TNA, FO 371/17034, J 2790/2790/16, Sir Percy Loraine to Sir John Simon, 9 November 1933) that expressed his grave concern about Britain's weak cultural influence in Egypt and about the growing competition for influence in that country from France. Kessel (2011: 197) identifies Loraine's despatch as an important catalyst in the formation of a body to channel and disseminate cultural policy. Donaldson (1984: 21–22) concurs and sees Loraine's despatch as important for the future creation of an 'institution to undertake cultural relations' in the early 1930s.

As well as the wider social, economic and political forces in play, individuals also had their part to play in the events leading up to the creation of the British Council in 1934. Lord Bach, Parliamentary Undersecretary of State in the Ministry of Justice, 2008–2010, and chairman of the All-Party Parliamentary Group on the British Council, when speaking in the 2012 debate on British Council funding in the House of Lords, identified two men who had made a significant contribution:

> Anyone who has read about the long, drawn out beginning of the council itself, way back in 1934, will know that, if it had not been for the persistence and will power shown by some, particularly Sir Reginald Leeper and Lord Lloyd, the council might never have come into existence.
> (House of Lords Debate, 19 July 2012, c452)

During the First World War Leeper had served in the Foreign Office's Political Intelligence Department. He entered the British Foreign Office in 1920, and in 1929 he joined the News Department, which was responsible for information work overseas. Convinced of the importance of what he termed cultural promotion, he persuaded Foreign Office colleagues to fund this work. In 1931 Leeper arranged lecture tours and book donations to nearly 30 countries and in 1933 contributed to the setting up of a Cultural Relations Committee – with the support of the Board of Education and the Department of Overseas Trade. According to Kessel (2011), Leeper was known to have an excellent relationship with Robert Vansittart, Permanent Undersecretary to the Foreign Office from 1930 to 1938, and Anthony Eden, Undersecretary of State for Foreign Affairs from 1931 to 1934, then Foreign Secretary until February 1938 (later serving as Prime Minister of the United Kingdom from 1955 to 1957). The support of such high-profile contacts was certainly useful in a wider climate that distrusted any overt cultural propaganda/promotion. Leeper continued to promote the British Council within the Foreign Office until 1938, when he was appointed to head the Political Intelligence Department. He held the office of the Honorary Vice President of the British Council till his death in 1968.

In 1934 the Cultural Relations Committee became the *'British Committee for Relations with Other Countries'*; the British Council was born. Initially the Committee's work focused on two areas: support for English education abroad and the promulgation of British culture through lecture tours, musical troupes and art exhibitions. The creation of the Committee brought together a coalition of interests – from government departments, industry, the arts and science – to actively promote an understanding of Britain across the world. The name was changed to the *'British Council for Relations with Other Countries'* in 1935 when advisory committees for books, fine art, music, lectures, Near East and Latin America were set up; the first Foreign Office grant of £5,000 was agreed and support provided for the British Institutes in Florence, Paris and Buenos Aires. The aim was to spread and strengthen influence through encouraging cultural, educational and other interchanges between the United Kingdom and countries abroad.

At the inauguration of the British Council on 2 July 1935, the Prince of Wales (later King Edward VIII) outlined the goals of the new organisation and the particular importance that should be attached to disseminating English around the world:

> The basis of our work must be the English language.... Our object is to assist the largest number possible to appreciate fully the glories of our literature, our contribution to the arts and sciences, and our pre-eminent contribution to political practice. This can be best achieved by promoting the study of our language abroad.
> (Speech reproduced in White 1965: Appendix B, pp. 121–122)

Haigh (1974: 41) singles out the critical importance of Lord Lloyd's contribution to the survival of the fledgling British Council. Lloyd was a former Governor of Bombay and High Commissioner in Egypt, who had become the British Council chairman in 1937 (see Atherton 1994 for further details of his career). As Secretary of State for the Colonies and Leader of the House of Lords in 1940, he fought for and obtained a Royal Charter for the British Council, which gave it independent, permanent status for the first time. The move was strategically astute as it assured the organisation of recognition as a legal body, and made it harder for it to be disbanded. Lloyd subsequently prevented the British Council from becoming part of the wartime Ministry of Information and won governmental support for the British Council in its unofficial role as the cultural department.

The Royal Charter begins:

THE BRITISH COUNCIL
Charter of Incorporation granted by His Majesty King George VI 1940
Whereas it has been represented to Us by Our Principal Secretary of State for Foreign Affairs that for the purpose of promoting a wider knowledge of Our United Kingdom of Great Britain and Northern Ireland and the English language abroad and developing closer cultural relations between Our United Kingdom of Great Britain and Northern Ireland and other countries for the purpose of benefiting the British Commonwealth of Nations and with a view to facilitating the holding of, and dealing with, any money provided by Parliament and any other property, real or personal, otherwise available for those objects and with a view to encouraging the making of gifts and bequests in aid of the said objects, it is expedient that the voluntary association now existing and known as the British Council should be created a Body Corporate.

Kessel (2011: 54) details how, in the early period of its history, the British Council assiduously promoted the teaching of English language and literature in schools, colleges and universities in countries around the world by: setting up British Institutes which engaged in the direct teaching of English alongside cultural activities (25 Institutes by 1940 in areas of strategic importance); providing subsidies for existing Institutes (e.g. the *Culturas* in Brazil); supporting lecturer posts and chairs in foreign universities; cooperating closely with nearly 200 Anglophile societies through the provision of lecturers, books, newspapers, gramophone records (Donaldson 1984: 20–21 and 60–62); helping with sponsored speakers, and donating library resources. The British Council's additional role in assisting overseas students with scholarships to come and study in Britain is of particular relevance to our discussion of the British Council involvement in testing the proficiency of overseas students in English for Academic Purposes (EAP), which we turn to in Section 2.

The British Council was always careful to distance itself from the notion of its being involved in cultural propaganda, speaking instead of cultural promotion or the transmission of information in order to achieve a better international understanding. In the words of Rex Leeper:

> Publicity, as opposed to political propaganda, is the attempt to make known abroad the main features of our political, economic and cultural activities, to give an accurate picture of this country and to refrain from criticizing the activities of other countries....
> (TNA, FO 800/396, Memorandum by R.A. Leeper, 22 October 1938. Enclosed in Leeper to Cadogan, 22 October 1938)

The British Council thus became an important conduit for the cultural promotion of Britain – in other words for the creation of *soft power* (see Phillipson 1992: Chapter 2, Martens and Marshall 2003, Nye 2004, Melissen 2005 and Fisher 2009: 2–3). In a debate on British Council funding in the House of Lords in 2012, the former European Commissioner, Labour Party leader and past Chairman of the British Council, 2004–2009, Neil Kinnock, made reference to the importance of soft power and the British Council's contribution to it:

> ... lessons have been arduously learnt about the necessity of developing convincing and effective public diplomacy – so-called soft power. In the wise words of a US general, international strategy, which neglects that, is *'trying to put out a fire with a hammer'.*
>
> But soft power is not a soft option. It requires investment, long-term patience and consistency, candour and transparency in relationships. It must have esoteric and practical usefulness to those who are the objects of soft power. It must manifest mutuality in the development of understanding – the ability to be good listeners as well as trustworthy communicators.
> (House of Lords Debate, 19 July 2012, c456)

In the same debate Lord Howell of Guildford (Minister of State, Foreign and Commonwealth Office; Conservative) reinforced the point:

> ...cultural diplomacy, the promotion of values and attitudes, will be as powerful, if not more powerful than, ranges of carrier fleets, rockets and heavy military equipment....
> (House of Lords Debate, 19 July 2012, c467)

Key aims for the British Council were to foster the wider appreciation of Great Britain and the English language abroad. The contributions to this process which we examine in this and the following chapter involve consideration of: how English became a global language in the 20th century; the British Council's extensive English language teaching operations abroad; its participation in the worldwide delivery of well-respected English language proficiency examinations through its close working relationship with the University of Cambridge Local Examinations Syndicate from 1941 onwards (this Chapter); and its setting up and management of British government sponsored English language testing development projects around the world from the 1980s onwards (Chapter 2).

The rise of English as a global language

A combination of economic, political, social and technological factors contributed to the global spread of English in the 19th and 20th centuries (British Council 2013a, Brutt-Griffler 2002, Crystal 1997, Graddol 1997 and 2006, Howatt 1997, Howatt and Widdowson 2004 and Phillipson 1992).

A recent British Council publication *The English Effect* (2013a: 5) sheds light on some of the early drivers of this growth:

> The momentum was originally provided by the political, military, religious and merchant classes. Through colonisation, ship-borne trade with the Americas, North Africa, the Indies and China, and the attendant role of Christian missionaries, the English language was exported worldwide.

The evolution of English towards world language status is explained by Crystal (1997) as the result of British military and political imperialism and economic strength in the 19th century, as well as English being the best means at the time for societies and individuals to access new knowledge. The survival of English as a global language in the 20th century, Crystal (1997) puts down to American economic supremacy and Phillipson (1992: 7) to United States military and technological leadership.

Crystal (1997) expands in detail on the variety of contributory factors which led to the increasing dominance of English as a world language in the 20th century. He identifies its widespread use in: accessing knowledge, conducting international relations, the press, advertising, broadcasting, motion pictures, popular music, international travel, international safety, international business, education and communication. Howatt (1997: 263) points out that people no longer tended to stay in one place and that English became the requisite *lingua franca* 'to meet the needs of international communication'.

Most recently in *The English Effect* (2013a: 5) the British Council has suggested that it was technological developments that critically impacted on the reach and significance of the English Language in the latter part of the 20th century:

> If English took hold due to the historic factors of trade, empire, military and industrial might in earlier centuries; technology has enabled it to jump the fence and to thrive without the physical contact, which had previously been necessary. The growth of English and the emergence of the internet as a global communication channel are mutually reinforcing trends.
>
> This lack of boundaries is important. Previously, the spread of language was governed by those physical encounters, then by the circulation of printed materials, then by radio, television, cinema and other mass media. The arrival of the internet and social media, with the potential for even wider reach, has meant that those languages with the greatest momentum and the most attractive characteristics and attributes, such as widespread usage, immediate applicability, well-regarded cultural ambassadors or accessible teaching and learning, have become the most successful channels of online communication and exchange.

External economic, political, social and technological forces have all undoubtedly played a major part in bringing this linguistic hegemony about, but the evolution towards a global language may not have been entirely inevitable. In the quotation above, the reference to the importance in becoming a global language of possessing 'the greatest momentum and the most attractive characteristics and attributes' is significant. The English language benefited from a number of attendant sociolinguistic dimensions, not least the role fulfilled by the British Council of a 'well-regarded cultural ambassador' for over 80 years, successfully promoting and offering 'accessible teaching and learning' of English worldwide, as well as providing global opportunities to take reputable examinations in English as a foreign language (EFL) from the 1940s onwards. The birth of the British Council and its subsequent investment in the teaching and testing of English in many countries around the world might thus be seen to have played a relatively small but nevertheless significant part in the systematic globalisation of the English language.

Phillipson and Pennycook suggest that the British Council was indeed interested in 'spreading English'. Pennycook (1994: 134) interprets efforts to spread English around the globe as part of a wider focus on cultural and linguistic expansion in preference to earlier material exploitation by the western powers. For Pennycook, the 'search for new means of social and political control in the world' saw 'the prodigious spread' of English in the post-war [WW2] era. This globalisation of English would not be universally acclaimed and a number of critics have seen it as a result of ulterior economic and political motives on the part of government (see Phillipson 1992: Chapter 8, and Pennycook 1994: Chapter 5). As we will see below, the spread of English was indeed not entirely serendipitous (Kessel 2011).

Phillipson (1992: 144, 150–152) argues that in the British government's support for the spread of English, political and economic interests were paramount. He sees the post-war spread of the English language as one of the key means for acquiring influence for Britain out of all proportion to its size. Phillipson points to the availability of massive government and private foundation funds especially from 1960 onwards to support the propagation of the language and identifies the importance of the British Council as a driver in this spreading of the English language around the world. He links this self-interested English language expansionism to the foreign policy objectives set out in the *Drogheda Report on the Overseas Information Service*, a key post-war foreign policy statement completed in 1953 (Committee on the Drogheda Report on the Overseas Information Services: Papers 1–15, CAB 130/98, 1953 Dec 3–1954 June 1). Martin (2014) concurs and notes how the Drogheda Report recommended that the British Council should seek more political and commercial goals. One manifestation of this would be the development of English language teaching programmes, with the British Council targeting its activities at influential elites with the express intention of creating a climate of opinion that favoured British interests.

Exporting English to the world: The British Council and Cambridge English language examinations, 1941–1993

English language examinations and soft power

One can in fact find earlier examples of English linguistic expansionism that pre-date those offered by Phillipson (1992) and Pennycook (1994). Bernard Spolsky (1995: 305) reveals how Jack Roach, Assistant Secretary at the University of Cambridge Local Examinations Syndicate (UCLES), 1925–1945, for both ideological and personal reasons, seized on the Cambridge Certificate of Proficiency in English (CPE) when he joined UCLES after the First World War. Roach hoped for 'the reaffirmation and spread of British influence' (Roach 1929) through the export of Cambridge English examinations, believing international English language tests would realise his 'modest ambition of making English the world language' (Roach 1956: 2). He was aware that exporting Cambridge tests would act as a direct method of transmitting the English values and culture that he was such a strong advocate for.

Roach had started working at the Syndicate in 1925 after a career in the Indian army. He left the army, went up to Cambridge, gained a First in French and German and then joined the Syndicate. In 1929 he was asked to take responsibility for English exams. Spolsky (1995: 75) notes how Roach intended to spread Cambridge English examinations as widely as possible around the world and argues that Roach was probably one of the first people to understand clearly how English tests could be an important source of influence globally.

This influence of English tests is explored further in the subsection on *National examination reform projects* in Chapter 2. Shohamy (2008: xiv) provides a wide-ranging account of 'the societal role tests perform' and 'their central functions in education, politics and society'. Shohamy (2001) offers a seminal account of the 'power of tests'.

Richard Smith of the Centre for Applied Linguistics, University of Warwick, provides additional evidence of other early proactive attempts to assure the status of English as a world language (Smith 2004: 229–231). He describes a new, politically motivated focus on simplified lexical content in British English language teaching from the 1930s until the end of the Second World War:

> Discussions in the emerging United Kingdom 'centre' from the mid-1930s until the end of World War II had focused quite explicitly and narrowly on needs to propagate English as a world language via simplification of the lexical contents of instruction. ... Along with Basic, the other main 'systems' considered by the British Council Advisory Committee in the wartime years – West's 'New Method' series, Eckersley's *Essential English* and the Oxford English Course, with Palmer and Hornby's *Thousand-Word English* being increasingly seen as a major rival – were essentially all sets of materials and/or proposals for limited vocabularies.

Weir, Vidakovic and Galaczi (2013) argued that the politically motivated agenda behind simplification in English language teaching in the 1930s helps explain why Roach introduced a new EFL examination at UCLES, the Lower Certificate in English (LCE) in 1939. Developing a test at a lower level than the UCLES Certificate of Proficiency in English (CPE), with a much larger potential candidature, sat well with the expansionist goal described above and with Roach's own aspirations for the English language. Cambridge would be aided by the British Council in this endeavour.

Both the British Council and the University of Cambridge Local Examinations Syndicate would play a proactive role in exporting English through their joint, worldwide activities designed to foster both the teaching and the assessment of the English language. In 1941 the British Council entered into a formal alliance with the UCLES, with Sir Stephen Gaselee (the Librarian at the Foreign Office) presiding at this meeting, strongly suggesting the link was favoured by government.

The fortunes of Cambridge English Language Examinations and the British Council would thereafter be inextricably linked for most of the second half of the 20th century. From 1941 to 1993 the British Council would be a close partner in the development and export of Cambridge English examinations, providing important advice to Cambridge, based on the British Council's growing experience and expertise in English language teaching around the world, actively promoting the examinations in its teaching operations abroad, and making their teaching centres available for the administration of Cambridge English examinations (see Hawkey and Milanovic 2013: Chapters 2 and 3 for a full description of a number of these centres and the work they carried out). This fitted in well with Roach's avowed intent to spread English around the globe in line with the concept of developing soft power for the UK described above. Cambridge was the leading EFL Examining Board at the time, and this together with the prestige associated with the Cambridge University branding, made it the obvious candidate for such cooperation, although the Council would also, as part of its institutional neutrality with regard to UK examinations from many sources, 'administer English language exams for a whole range of awarding organisations' in addition to Cambridge (http://www.britishcouncil.org/exam/uk-boards-overseas/english-language).

The positive influence of the British Council on Cambridge English language examinations from the 1940s right through to the early 1990s was due in no small part to a limited but critical mass of expertise in English language teaching (ELT), arising from its global cultural mission, that resided in the British Council ELT staff; initially through individuals such as Hornby and Gattenby in the 1940s–1950s and then through a wider cadre of ELT expertise in the 1960s. In contrast, Hawkey and Milanovic (2013) make reference to Raban (2008: 7) to illustrate how for most of the period in Cambridge there was only a handful of staff to handle the testing of English, with UCLES EFL very much a cottage industry until the professionalisation and growth of an English language testing cadre from the late 1980s.

The Joint Committee of the British Council and the University of Cambridge Local Examinations Syndicate, 1941–1993

The Joint Committee: Early years

Weir (2013) describes how the March 1941 agreement between the British Council and UCLES (see box) laid out the close working relationship between the two organisations in running the Cambridge English examinations until the mutually agreed expiry of this agreement in 1993. The British Council, by virtue of its global mission, would come to possess not inconsiderable knowledge and expertise in the area of Teaching English as a Foreign Language, and as a result would play an important role in the development of English language tests at Cambridge. In addition, it would promote and deliver Cambridge examinations around the world through its network of offices overseas. From the late 1980s the situation would change and as the British Council dismantled its own professional cadre of experts in English language teaching and testing, Cambridge under the inspired leadership of John Reddaway (see further

The 1941 agreement

BRITISH COUNCIL AND THE UNIVERSITY OF CAMBRIDGE LOCAL EXAMINATIONS SYNDICATE

Agreement to collaborate in the conduct of examinations in English, drafted at a Conference of representatives of the British Council and the University of Cambridge Local Examinations Syndicate held on Saturday, 29th March 1941, for submission to the Council and the Syndicate.

1. A joint committee of the British Council and the Cambridge Local Examinations Syndicate, three members to be appointed by each, shall be set up for the general supervision of these examinations.
2. This committee shall make recommendations as to the syllabus and the conduct of the examinations, subject to the understanding that the ultimate responsibility for the appointment of Examiners, the marking of papers, the assessment of standards, and the issue of certificate shall rest with the Syndicate.
3. Where the establishment of new centres for the examinations is proposed the Syndicate shall act, through the committee, on the advice of the British Council, who will consult, where necessary, with the Foreign Office, with His Majesty's Missions, and with the local Representative of the British Council.
4. It is understood that in the conduct of the examination the Syndicate will co-operate in every possible way with the Institutes of the British Council and with other centres in which the Council are interested.
5. The regulations issued by the Syndicate for these examinations shall state that they are conducted by the Syndicate in conjunction with the British Council.
6. The British Council shall consider with the Syndicate year by year what grant, if any, should be made by the British Council towards the cost of conducting and advertising these examinations.
7. Nothing in this agreement shall be regarded as restricting individual Institutes of the British Council, or other centres in which they are interested, from conducting their own examinations.
8. This agreement may be terminated at two years' notice on either side and may be reviewed at any time at the request of the Syndicate or of the British Council.

(British Council Archives)

below) invested heavily in building a professional EFL Evaluation Unit of its own. The balance of influence in terms of professional expertise would eventually shift to Cambridge, as we will see in Chapter 5.

After the agreement was signed in March 1941 the inaugural meeting of the Joint Committee was held at the British Council in London later that year. An extract from the minutes of that meeting reads:

> The first meeting of the Committee was held at the headquarters of the British Council, 3 Hanover Street, London, on 22 July 1941 at 3 p.m.
>
> Minutes
> Formal cognizance was taken of the agreement to collaborate in the conduct of examinations in English, drafted at a conference of representatives of the British Council and the University of Cambridge Local Examinations Syndicate held on Saturday, 29 March 1941, and since confirmed by both Bodies. It was agreed that a copy of this document should be placed in the formal records of the Committee, whose official title should be the 'Joint Committee of the British Council and the Cambridge Local Examinations Syndicate'.
> ...
> 4 (a) The preparation of syllabus and regulations
> It was agreed that the following statement should appear in small type beneath the date in the centre of the first page of the regulations for 1942: 'The examinations for these certificates are conducted by the Syndicate in collaboration with the British Council'.

The minutes of the July 1941 Joint Committee meeting illustrate the significant professional input British Council representatives were making *ab initio*. First, in respect of CPE:

> Professor Daniel Jones [a representative of the British Council on the Joint Committee] mentioned criticisms of the examination, which had been made at a Committee of the British Council, and Professor Evans promised to send to the Syndicate's representatives, copies of the syllabus of an examination as drafted by that Committee. Mr Roach mentioned that a substantial modification was being made in the syllabus this year for British Council pupils who might take a special examination for the Certificate of Proficiency in English in August. Instead of a paper on prescribed texts, these students would offer a second language paper, and the draft of this paper had already been prepared by a British Council teacher, suggested to the Syndicate by the British Council. ... It was agreed that concrete suggestions for modification in the plan of the examinations should be made at

the autumn meeting, and Professor Daniel Jones agreed to visit Cambridge for a preliminary discussion.

The importance of the Cambridge examinations for encouraging the take up of English globally was emphasised in the following memorandum:

> Memorandum on a discussion on 21 January 1943 between Mr Seymour and Mr Orton, representatives of the British Council, and Mr Bennett and Mr Williams, representatives of the Local Examinations Syndicate.
> In the course of a preliminary survey of the present position it was agreed that the Syndicate's examinations were a valuable incentive to the study of English not only in the Council's Institute abroad, but also for other educational organisations and for private students both at home and abroad.

The same memo evidences the financial support provided by the Council to Cambridge in addition to its professional input:

> The representatives of the British Council agreed that a fair proportion of the overhead expenses in connection with the examinations [LCE and CPE] ought to be met by the Council….

Such financial help was no doubt welcomed by Cambridge and enabled it to support the development of its EFL examinations at a time when candidature, and resultant income, were relatively small. Support for Cambridge examinations in English for foreign students through annual grants from the British Council would continue until 1955 by which time candidate numbers were reaching reasonable levels and the examinations became more self-supporting.

Weir (2013) records how in the early years there were a number of high-level academic representatives of the British Council on the powerful Joint Committee. Their presence added to both the status of the examinations and to the quality of their content. The British Council representatives included:

- Professor F. Clarke the Director of the Institute of Education of the University of London and member of the British Council Committee on the Overseas Teaching Service.
- Professor Ifor Evans, Education Director of the British Council during the war and Provost at University College London (UCL), 1951–1966, a well-known writer, literary critic and broadcaster.

- S.H. Wood, representative of the Board of Education of the British Council who was involved in helping refugees from Germany in particular in the 1930s and helped set up the Resident Foreigners Committee, later the Home Division of the British Council.
- Professor Daniel Jones, Head of the Department of Phonetics at University College London, was a further addition to the British Council representation in the July 1941 committee meeting.
- A.S. Hornby, an English grammarian, lexicographer and pioneer in the field of English language learning and teaching, the founder and first editor of the *English Language Teaching Journal* (published by the British Council from 1946 onwards), had joined the British Council in 1942 and was then posted to Iran as Acting Director of the Anglo-Persian Institute in Teheran; he became the first linguistic adviser to the Education Division of the British Council 1945–1950 and a member of the Joint Committee in November 1945.

The work of the Joint Committee would be supported by the *UCLES Executive Committee for the Syndicate's examinations in English for foreign students* which was set up in November 1957 as a sub-committee of the Joint Committee. Hawkey and Milanovic (2013) detail how:

> This committee was expected to do business as well as direct it, 'to conduct under the general direction of the Joint Committee, the detailed business arising out of the examinations'. The Executive Committee would be supported by a new Syllabus Sub-committee 'responsible for drafting syllabuses and considering suggestions for modifications' (both citations from UCLES Cambridge Examinations in English Survey for 1957, p. 7). The committees were often influential in their own right because their decisions took account of the academic and professional views and actions of members from outside the Examinations Syndicate.

Weir (2013) reports that the Executive Committee included a small number of syndicate members (up to four), two representatives of the British Council to be nominated by the Controller, Education Division for each meeting, two representatives of Local Education Authority schools, one Local Education Authority official, one university teacher of English to Foreign Students, one or two examiners, occasional centre representatives, plus the chair of the Joint Committee (normally a British Council representative) as an ex officio member.

The British Council's wider involvement in ELT

Between 1941 and 1993, the British Council provided major input into Cambridge examinations through the knowledge and global experience in ELT of its specialist officers. Other developments in the wider ELT field signalled the growing importance of the British Council contribution. In 1946 the British Council helped set up the journal initially called *English Language Teaching* [later *ELTJ*, the *English Language Teaching Journal*]. The first issue was produced under the editorship of its founder A.S. Hornby. British Council officers and affiliates were major contributors to the journal in these early years. Behind the instigation of *English Language Teaching* in 1946, were events which indicated a growing status in the UK context for the teaching of English as a foreign language.

Richard Smith (2005: xviii–xix) describes the role of *ELT*:

> In the area of English teaching, the Council's focus at this point was firmly on its own centres overseas, and *English Language Teaching* – Hornby's own brainchild [...] – was perhaps intended, or at least justified as being intended mainly as a way for teachers in these centres to keep in touch with one another and with headquarters. The journal may also have been conceived partly as a form of ongoing teacher-training for the Institutes. [...] In the first few years of its existence, the journal also served as a way to inform the world of further developments in the UK that were signalling a new status and new institutional foundations for the teaching of English as a foreign language, namely at the University of London Institute of Education [...], BBC English by Radio [...], and the University of Cambridge Local Examinations Syndicate.

In the area of English Language Teaching (ELT), the British Council was a leading player in this period as a number of conferences and other publications testify (British Council 1950, Wayment 1961 and Smith forthcoming). The British Council was largely responsible for helping to set up the first British department of Applied Linguistics at Edinburgh University in 1957 with the express aim of providing a theoretical basis for EFL teachers. It was also closely involved with the setting up of a one-year course for overseas teachers from the Colonies at Moray House Training College, Edinburgh, founded in 1959. Enhancing the professional expertise of those involved with ELT overseas was yet another way of spreading influence through the promotion of English around the world.

The British Council established its English Teaching Information Centre (ETIC) in London in 1961, which housed the world's largest collection of ELT resources. Richard Smith (forthcoming) notes:

> ETIC was founded in London, with George Perren as its first Director, to serve as an archive and to produce bibliographies of research and of published materials. In 1967 a Language Teaching Library was also established and opened to the public in conjunction with CILT (the Centre for Information on Language Teaching), which had itself been established in 1966. For a time, ETIC and CILT shared offices, although with separate Directors. [...]
>
> One of ETIC's first activities was to establish a series of *English-Teaching Abstracts* in July 1961. In 1968 the title was changed to *Language Teaching Abstracts* and publication taken over by Cambridge University Press (but with editing still the responsibility of the British Council, under Valerie Kinsella). Still later this turned into the journal *Language Teaching*. [...]
>
> From 1971, ETIC began to issue 'ELT Documents', first as a mimeographed bulletin and later, from 1978, as a book series [...]. ETIC was to serve British Council staff and the wider profession for twenty-five years until 1986.

The Joint Committee: 1960s onwards

Returning to the Joint Committee, Weir (2013) describes how it continued to be an influential body, and in the 1960s it is revealing to see leading lights in the United Kingdom English Language Teaching/Applied Linguistics field, some British Council officers, some not, serving as the representatives of the British Council on that Committee, including:

- Professor Bruce Pattison, the first Chair in the Teaching of English as a Foreign Language, University of London, 1948–1976;
- H.A. Cartledge, a prolific English Language Teaching author; and
- George Perren, Director of the British Council English Teaching Information Centre (ETIC) London, one of the first specialists in English language testing (see Chapter 3 for details his contribution to the English Proficiency Test Battery (EPTB), the first international English for Academic Purpose (EAP) test) and training of teachers of English as a second language in the United Kingdom, and author of *Linguistic Problems of Overseas Students in Britain* (1963).

Weir (2013) details how later representatives of the British Council on the Joint Committee were to include:

- Dr W.R. ('Bill') Lee, editor of *English Language Teaching (Journal)*, 1958–1981, and Chairman of the International Association of Teachers of English as a Foreign Language (IATEFL), 1967–1984;
- B.M. Lott, Controller of the British Council English Language Teaching Division in the late 1960s;
- Roland Hindmarsh, author of the 1980 *Cambridge English Lexicon: A graded word list for materials writers and course-designers*, who would be seconded from the British Council to UCLES for a year;
- Arthur H. King, Controller of the Education Division of the British Council in the 1960s, a poet and an English literature specialist;
- R.A. 'Roddy' Cavaliero, future Deputy Director General of the British Council;
- Brendan Carroll, lead developer of the English Language Testing Service (ELTS) test;
- Alan Moller, British Council Senior Consultant in Testing and Evaluation from September 1979 to mid-1984, Director of ELSD (English Language Services Department) from mid-1983 to mid-1984;
- Peter Hargreaves, Senior Consultant to the Testing and Evaluation Unit after Moller, who would leave the British Council in 1989 to head English Language Testing at Cambridge; and
- Sir John Lyons, an eminent linguist at Edinburgh then Cambridge Universities, who chaired the Joint Committee from 1986 to 1993, after which the Committee was dissolved, the minutes of its meeting of 8 July 1992 explaining that 'many of the functions formerly undertaken by the Joint Committee could be performed in other more efficient ways'.

Weir, Vidakovic and Galaczi (2013: 421) note that the brief of the Joint Committee of the British Council and Cambridge Local Examinations Syndicate was *inter alia* to collaborate in the actual development and conduct of UCLES EFL exams; make decisions on policy and regulations; prepare examination syllabi and the 'general plan of the examination'; and cooperate in publicity and finance. The knowledge and expertise in English language pedagogy and the standing of the high-ranking professionals who served as British Council representatives on the Joint Committee made a significant contribution to the development of Cambridge English examinations (see below). The Joint Committee was testimony to a close and mutually beneficial working relationship between the British Council and Cambridge in promoting the spread of Cambridge English examinations abroad.

The Joint Committee: Some key episodes

We next examine a number of important events and developments that took place under the auspices of this Joint Committee, which exemplify the close cooperation in examination development and language testing research that took place between the British Council and Cambridge in the period 1941–1993. In the main the relationship was a positive and harmonious one, but occasionally, as in our first example, there was some slight discord.

Concerns over the use of 'Basic English' in Cambridge Examinations

The first Cambridge LCE examination in 1939 had initially only been offered 'at centres outside Great Britain'. Jack Roach (1983: 6) claimed that the exclusion of UK centres was because the British Council at first opposed the introduction of the LCE in the UK itself. One can tell from the minutes of the Joint Committee below that the British Council's objections stemmed from a concern that an English exam at a level below that of the CPE might suggest an acceptance of lower target standards in the language. One of the key issues was the British Council's reservation about the use of Basic English in the LCE examination. Hawkey and Milanovic (2013) describe how Basic English was developed in the 1920s by the linguist Charles Ogden working with the literary critic Ivor Richards. It was an attempt to abstract from Standard English a minimum grammar and vocabulary for everyday communication, e.g. a minimal syntax, a fixed word order and a reduced vocabulary of 850 words. Phillipson points out (1992: 130) that the goals of Basic English were to provide a 'universal second language for general communication and science' as well as encouraging the uptake to wider forms of English.

British Council concerns were raised at the first meeting, on 22 July 1941, of the Joint Committee of the British Council and the Cambridge Local Examinations Syndicate:

> Professor Daniel Jones drew attention to the fact that books in Basic English were among those prescribed for the Lower Certificate in English and suggested that the British Council could not associate themselves with an examination in something which might not be English. [...] Professor Jones said that he would rather see the words 'simple English' in the regulations in place of 'simplified English' and it was agreed that this whole matter would need further discussion.

The problem surfaced again at the next meeting in October 1941:

> There was some discussion of the principle of setting Basic texts containing phrases, which are not current English. Professor Evans read some examples of such phrases, which had been culled by Professor Daniel Jones from the Basic texts prescribed by the Syndicate for the Lower Certificate. ... It was quite clear from the discussion that the British Council could not lay themselves open to the criticism of approving texts which were not current English throughout, and it was agreed that if Basic texts read 'naturally' there is no objection to their being prescribed for an examination although labeled 'Basic'.

Differences between the British Council and Cambridge were resolved by 1943 when the LCE was introduced in Britain. Weir (2013: 35) describes how the Syndicate and the British Council had agreed on the need for the LCE examination in the light of the growing demand for an examination at a lower level than CPE level to be offered at United Kingdom centres to cater for servicemen stationed here during the war, as well as overseas.

A speech delivered by Winston Churchill, the British wartime Prime Minister, at Harvard in 1943 (Churchill 1943: 713–715), in which he advocated the use of Basic to spread English globally as an international language, led to pressure being put on the British Council to endorse Basic English following a 1944 White Paper. The speech serves as another reminder that there was a clear intention at the highest levels of government to spread influence through the promotion of the English language as widely as possible around the world, albeit with an initial focus on reaching elites in countries overseas. By the 1960s, the clear target was the wider masses.

The Diploma of English Studies 1945: A British Council inspired Cambridge test

As well as offering advice on their existing examinations (LCE and CPE), the British Council took a proactive role in encouraging Cambridge to add an innovative new examination, the Diploma of English Studies, to the Cambridge 'Main Suite' of English language examinations for overseas students in the 1940s. The origins for this exam can be found in the demand for an advanced, specialist examination in English Literature and background studies at post-Proficiency level in the British Institute in Cairo, Egypt. The Diploma was first offered in December 1945 to 16 candidates, eight in Egypt, at the British Institutes in Cairo and Alexandria, two at the Cultural Institute in Montevideo, Uruguay, and six at the Polytechnic in Regent Street, London.

The Joint Committee minutes of April 1942 record:

> Higher literary studies in British Institutes.
> ...Professor Evans said that some of the British Council teachers in Cairo had been considering the possibility of more extensive studies in English Literature, to follow after the Proficiency course. It was agreed that a statement should be sent to the British Council setting out the possibilities of holding a test, by means of the December Higher School Certificate question papers in English Literature, for candidates who had already gained the Certificate of Proficiency in English; Professor Evans undertook to consult certain representatives abroad. It was thought to define the standard of work for such an examination as e.g. that of English 'specialists' in the 6th forms of secondary schools and for London Intermediate.

The minutes of the Joint Committee meeting December 1942 provide further detail of the special nature of the relationship between the British Council and Cambridge with regard to examination provision and development and the part played by the British Council in financing such:

> Advanced examinations in English studies.
> Special provisional arrangements for Cairo. It was agreed to hold a temporary examination of local character, as already promised by the Syndicate, for a certificate with some such title as the following: 'Special Certificate of Advanced Studies in English for Students of the British Institute, Cairo.'
>   Request from the British Council for a 'Diploma in English Studies'. Mr Grose pointed out that the Syndicate's representatives had no authority to pledge the Syndicate to a 'further substantial commitment' until the

> general matter of finance was settled. Subject to that over-riding consideration, the committee agreed in principle that plans ought to be made for holding an advanced examination, which would be available in various parts of the world. It was agreed that the British Council should consult Professor Evans further on the subject and it was understood that Professor Entwistle and Mr Orton [acting Educational Director of the British Council] would put forward further suggestions for a syllabus....

The meeting of the Joint Committee in April 1943 established that the Diploma should be a Cambridge examination, and thereby part of the prestigious Cambridge Main Suite, not an examination for the British Council by Cambridge, and the British Council would defray the cost:

> ...Professor Entwistle...said it was very much to be hoped that the Syndicate would be able to establish the examination, not as a piece of work undertaken for the British Council, but as a responsibility of the University. In reply to his enquiry, the Syndicate's representatives re-affirmed their readiness to recommend the establishment by the Syndicate of an advanced examination in English. ...
>
> Professor Entwistle asked for some indication of the probable cost to the British Council of the establishment of an advanced examination. A rough estimate of £100 was given as the probable cost of preparing a syllabus and of setting and printing question-papers on one occasion; this took no account of the fees to be received from eventual candidates. ...
>
> Dealing with the draft syllabus prepared by himself and Mr Orton, Professor Entwistle said that they assumed this would be used as a convenient basis for discussion when the Syndicate themselves set to work to prepare a scheme of examination. It was understood that further experts would have to be consulted and that the drafting of a scheme would be the task of a sub-committee.

The British Council, as per usual, were also concerned with the wider picture:

> Professor Entwistle referred to cultural treaties, which were being negotiated between this country and allied and friendly counties and to the need for an examination of high standard and repute which would give an officially recognised qualification for teachers of English in such countries. He therefore emphasised the advantage of obtaining permission if possible for the use of the word Diploma. It was understood that the Syndicate would not feel able to use this term without the authority of the University. The Vice-Chancellor had promised to bring the matter before the Council of the Senate....

Exporting British Culture and Language, 1935–2016   27

At the July 1943 meeting the contents of the new Diploma examination were agreed:

> The scheme of tests for the Diploma examination.
> It was agreed that there should be two separate oral examinations. One would be a test of the candidate's spoken English and the other would be an oral examination of the candidate's course of studies for the Diploma.
>
> It was agreed that there should be a paper, compulsory for all candidates, on 'The Grammar and Structure of Spoken English'. It was agreed that the syllabus and scope of this paper should be considered in close relation to the test of spoken English, that it should include the writing of a dialogue, and that it should require a sufficient acquaintance with phonetics for the purpose of this paper.
>
> It was agreed that there should be a paper entitled English Essay.
>
> It was agreed that there should be separate translation papers from and into English. The suggestion was made that the two papers together should only carry the same weight of marks as any other test. It was agreed that the papers should test a variety of style and should therefore include both continuous prose and dialogue. Mr Orton recorded his misgivings concerning translation from English as a part of this examination.
>
> It was agreed that there should be a paper of English Language consisting essentially of passages for comment and understanding chosen from a list of books, which the candidates would be expected to read.
>
> It was agreed that there should be three papers on the content of the candidate's course of study, apart from the list of reading for the English Language paper, and that each candidate should be required to offer any two of these. The papers would be General English Literature, Contemporary English Literature and Thought, English Life and Institutions. The titles of these papers were not finally settled. It was agreed that the papers on General English Literature and on Contemporary England should each be set in connection with a list of prescribed texts: a list of reading would be suggested as a guide for English Life and Institutions. The original suggestions placed before the Committee as a basis of discussion had proposed to make Contemporary English Literature and Thought compulsory and Mr Grose recorded his disapproval of a scheme which, while not making some study of the best English authors compulsory, forced candidates to study Contemporary England through second-rate literary material. Mr Grose accepted the compromise suggested by Mr Bennett whereby candidates will now have an equal chance to select the paper on General English Literature. Mr Orton said that it might well be the policy of British Institutes to lay stress on the study of present day life and institutions in England.
>
> It was agreed that there should be an optional paper, which intending teachers would be recommended to take, on the phonetics of English. The

time allowed for this paper, as for each other written test, would be three hours; this would include the time needed for phonetic transcription.

It is interesting to see that, in common with CPE and LCE, there is a spoken language examination in this paper at such an early date, as well as an essay (few spoken examinations appear in the USA until the 1950s). In the end the Diploma was similar in structure to the other main suite examinations LCE and CPE, although there was a greater focus on content such as Literature and British Life and Institutions. Phonetics has also reappeared (dropped from CPE in 1932) perhaps indicative that the Diploma was now seen as the exam for teachers whereas CPE was now intended for a much broader demographic. By 1947 CPE was:

> ...open to all candidates whose mother tongue is not English and it is designed not only for prospective teachers but also for other students with a wide range of interest within the field of English studies.
> (CPE Regulations 1947)

The British Council was keen for the Diploma 'to be regarded abroad as a valuable qualification for foreign teachers of English' (letter to UCLES from the British Council Secretary-General A.J.S. White dated 23 March 1945). In the January 1945 Joint Committee minutes, it is clear that the British Council (in the chair at this meeting) was also pushing for the inclusion of a paper on the teaching of English in the Diploma examination. Although there was a reluctance to embark on a test specifically for English language teachers at this stage, this was an area of Cambridge's work which would eventually increase dramatically, in spite of this early reticence (Wilson and Poulter 2015):

> British Council request for a paper on the teaching of English.
> ...The Chairman pressed the need, not only for a practical test, but also for an adequate record of a candidate's teaching practice over a period. It was agreed to refer the matter to an expert Committee to be called together for the purpose. It was understood that Mr Potts would be invited to assist in this Committee's work and that among its members might be, in addition to Mr Orton and Mr Reach, Professor Hamley of the Institute of Education, Mr Colline, H.M.I., and two or three other experts. It was agreed that a letter of 22 September 1944 from Professor Daniel Jones concerning the oral side of the Diploma examination should be referred to this special Committee.

The issue of a paper on Teaching Methods was raised again at the July 1948 meeting following the 1947 UCLES/British Council conference but a decision was again postponed:

> Min. 5(d) Proposal for a Diploma paper on Teaching Method.
> There was further discussion on the proposal for the inclusion in the Diploma examination of an optional additional paper on the teaching of English as a foreign language. It was pointed out that, irrespective of the desirability of such a paper from the candidates' point of view, it was doubtful whether, in view of the present lack of a recognised body of doctrine, it was a suitable subject for examination. The subject would be taken up again at a future conference.

In a sense this was an opportunity missed and it would be over 40 years before Cambridge became actively involved in offering ELT teaching qualifications as the global spread of English caused the demand for qualified ELT teachers to soar round the world. Even by the 1960s, the climate with regard to ELT qualifications had clearly changed and International House and the Royal Society of Arts began offering English language teaching qualifications driven in the main by practical considerations rather than theoretical.

Weir and Saville (2015: x) describe how in 1988 the well-established and respected Royal Society of Arts (RSA) English language teaching qualifications moved to Cambridge under the guidance of Lynette Murphy O'Dwyer, who transferred from the RSA to UCLES at the same time. The training of English language teachers and the assessment of their competence (knowledge, skills and ability) were increasingly seen as an important part of ELT in general and the Cambridge landscape in particular. The 1990s saw further changes to the former RSA examinations leading to the new CELTA and DELTA (Certificate/Diploma in Teaching English to Speakers of Other Languages) and the addition of a separate Teacher's Knowledge Test in 2005. These new additions to the Cambridge suite proved far more attractive to teachers than the older Diploma of English Studies, conceived in an era before the communicative language teaching and testing paradigm, especially as the latter examination was pitched at a very high proficiency level, i.e. beyond the C2 level of the CPE exam.

The Diploma in English Studies examination in the event was to last over 50 years, but as the influence of the British Council on Cambridge examinations waned in the late 1980s there was less willingness to continue with the Diploma because of continuing low candidate numbers and the availability of more popular alternatives in the Cambridge family of tests. Hawkey and Milanovic record (2013: 166) how in 1996 it was removed from the examinations made available to the public by Cambridge. This saw the demise of the only international English language examination ever offered at a hypothetical D level (i.e. above the A1 to C2 range of proficiency of the Common European Frame of Reference (CEFR)).

A shift in focus from culture to language

After the Drogheda Report to the government in 1953, the British Council was encouraged to focus on the instrumental use of English in its operations abroad rather than viewing English as a means of spreading British culture; a move to an educational rather than a cultural focus became the order of the day.

Richard Smith in *The British Council and ELT: Milestones, 1946–2016* (forthcoming) notes that in the 1960s, in particular, there was an

> overall shift away from British Council cultural diplomacy via its own Institutes and towards ELT as 'development aid' (with a focus on teacher-training for the former colonies).

Smith (ibid.) sees the change as enabling Britain to forge stronger relationships with former colonies:

> The apparent success of constructive, neutral-seeming (because linguistically- not literature-focused) efforts in post-Independence India, combined with the establishment of applied linguistics as a discipline in the UK (a move which was strongly encouraged and facilitated by The British Council), both contributed to the way British ELT expertise was confidently promoted abroad during the 1960s. [...] Through ELT, it must have appeared, relationships and a benign influence could be maintained with the newly emerging 'Commonwealth' nations.

Indeed, as Smith (2005: xli) records, the linguist J.R. Firth had reported in 1957 to the British Council on a trip to India and Pakistan, underlining

> the central problem there, that of freeing English studies from their old literary trammels in order to provide scientific and technical workers with a clear and efficient type of English suited to their needs. The Indians and Pakistanis themselves were of the opinion that they could look after

literary studies, but they did need help with the English language, which would have to be their medium for both teaching and research for many years to come.
(Minutes, Linguistics Panel of English Studies Advisory Committee, 9 December 1957, BW 138/1, in Public Records Office, Kew)

Smith (2004: 241), in his doctoral thesis on the work of Harold Palmer and the roots of ELT, charts the demise of literature studies and the growth of a more utilitarian approach to language learning:

In 1960, at the beginning of a new era of 'intense cultivation of ELT' (Phillipson 1992: 113), [Bruce] Pattison reported somewhat regretfully that 'Literature had tended to be pushed into the background in recent years by the rapid development of language teaching' (Minutes, British Council English Studies Advisory Committee, 9 November 1960, BW 138/1, in Public Records Office, Kew). The clearest (and most paradoxical) sign of this was the transformation in the views of Arthur King [...] who between 1959 and 1969 exerted considerable influence as the Controller of the Education Division of the British Council (Donaldson 1984: 218).

Smith argues that Arthur King (paradoxically also a poet, a writer and an expert in literary stylistics) was the man most responsible for the British Council's shift *away* from literature and 'cultural promotion' *towards* language in the 1960s. Donaldson (1984: 218) also stressed the importance of King in bringing about a mind shift in the Council's approach to English Language Teaching. King was aware that not everybody saw English as the means to access our culture through literature.

The presence of King as one of the British Council representatives on the powerful UCLES/British Council Joint Committee, from June 1960 through to 1969, and the new direction the British Council was taking in its approach to teaching English abroad as a result of macro-political influences, help explain the important changes that took place in English language examinations at UCLES. In the 1960s, we can see the beginnings of a significant shift in Cambridge's approach to its English examinations towards a view that language might be divorced from testing literary or cultural knowledge. The Joint Committee in 1962 discussed recent developments in the field of English teaching and their relevance to the syndicate's examinations. It was felt that:

...the policy at present followed in the Certificate of Proficiency examination, whereby candidates are expected to have some familiarity with English background and culture, should not be altered, but that enquiry

should be made about the extent of the demand for a more purely linguistic type of examination. Mr Cartledge [a British Council representative] was asked to obtain information from Teheran about proposals, which have been made there, and it was agreed that the Secretary, in consultation with the British Council, should send out an exploratory circular to Local Education Authorities in this country.
(Joint Committee of the Local Examinations Syndicate and the British Council 1962)

Weir (2013) records how the eventual decision for CPE to offer a more language focused route from 1966 onwards was ground-breaking, and reflected a developing interest in the *use of English* among the language teaching profession and applied linguists. It again signified the increased importance accorded to English as a global means of communication rather than an object of study for accessing British culture.

The British Council's contribution to research and development at UCLES

From the inception of the Joint Committee in 1941, the British Council was involved not only in promoting and delivering Cambridge examinations abroad but also in assisting in their development through a range of activities including joint research with UCLES, British Council sponsored research, validation studies utilising British Council personnel and centres round the world, and even secondment of Council English Language Officer (ELO) staff to UCLES itself to work on test research and development, e.g. Roland Hindmarsh in the 1970s and Peter Falvey in the 1980s.

So, as well as being involved in the development of new examinations, the Joint Committee minutes of 17 October 1941 record how the British Council was active in encouraging research on the Cambridge examinations:

Research in the technique of oral examination.
Professor Clarke and Professor Evans thought that this was necessary and that it might be a matter for financial and other help from the British Council. It was agreed that Professor Evans should consider later whether British Council financial help should be made available for the experimental tests proposed for December.

Its involvement in the ground-breaking standardisation of marking for the oral test was of particular note, as can be seen in this minute from the July 1942 meeting:

> Use of gramophone records.
> Reference was made to the apparently successful attempt at coordination of standards by Mr Parker, Mr Orton and Mr Roach, who had met at Nottingham and 'marked' the reading and conversation tests of certain foreign students which had been recorded for the gramophone by Mr Parker, thanks to a grant made to the Institute of Education by the British Council. Professor Clarke expressed his conviction that carefully made records of this kind, if sent out to Overseas Centres with comments made by a small committee of examiners in the United Kingdom, might be of real value as a guide to oral examiners. Eventually, Overseas Centres might in their turn record the reading and conversation of certain candidates and send the records to England for discussion and comparison. The need was stressed for high technical quality in the recording, and it was agreed to consult Professor Jones concerning the method of reproduction to be used if it became possible to make records for this purpose.

Realising that individual judgement cannot serve as an absolute measure, Jack Roach of UCLES had emphasised the importance of examiner standardisation (Roach 1945: 39):

> Two hundred candidates at various levels were presented in September by the R.A.F. Polish Initial Training Wing.... Advantage was taken of this to conduct certain experiments in the standardisation of marking. Four examiners were sent, including a British Council phonetician from Cairo, and the R.A.F Education Officers also took part. The Engineer-in-Chief of the General Post Office very kindly lent a Mobile Recording Unit and the services of his engineers without charge, and several gramophone records were made (UCLES 1944, minute 8),

and concluded that:

> gramophone recordings of candidates at various levels should assist examiners, not only to reach agreement on standards among themselves, but also to assimilate standards officially approved by the central examining body.

Reliability continued to be a concern in the Diploma oral examination. Over 25 years before the idea was taken up in Main Suite Examinations, it was recommended in the July 1948 Joint Committee meeting that oral input to candidates should also be standardised:

> Mr Butlin and Mr Roach stated that in their opinion it would be desirable to use in the examination a recording of one of the passages for dictation or reproduction, which would make for standardisation of the reading of the set passage. The Committee welcomed a proposal by Professor Searls that the British Council should conduct a controlled experiment along these lines under the guidance of Mr Butlin and Mr Roach. It was suggested that the Ministry of Education should also be consulted. Mr Roach and Mr Butlin were asked to consider the technique, which it was desirable to adopt in giving a dictation, as well as the implications of giving a dictation to a large number of candidates simultaneously by means of a loudspeaker. It was understood that the British Council would be responsible for the costs of the experiment, up to a maximum of £50.

The Executive Committee attended to what we now refer to as scoring validity (see Weir 2005: 177–206 for discussion of this) on a regular basis over the years. We may note the apparently balanced roles of Council and Cambridge members in efforts to achieve this aspect of validity:

> 10. Oral Examination
> The need for a review of standards and procedure was discussed, and it was decided to form a sub-committee for this purpose. Miss Platon [a British Council English Language Officer] agreed to serve on this, and it was decided to ask Mr Cartledge to do so, together with Mrs I.T. Tenant and other experienced oral examiners at Home and Overseas centres who might be available, and also Mrs C. McCallien.
>
> The sub-Committee will be asked to consider the following matters, and report to the next meeting of the Committee:
>   (i) Methods of instructing and co-ordination of oral examiners
>   (ii) Range of prepared conversation topics in L.C.E.
>   (iii) Possible new elements in C.P.E. conversation tests.
> (Executive Committee 19th Meeting, October 1967)

The Joint Committee minutes in 1944 provide evidence of a commitment to ensuring the examinations were marked as reliably as possible, as the following reference to an early experiment in double marking shows:

> We found time to make a preliminary survey of certain problems, to conduct some interesting experiments, and to prepare a first report. This has had an immediate influence in causing certain modifications of the

oral tests to be held in 1945, and we hope that it will stimulate discussion wherever the examinations are taken. The chief experiments in joint examining took place at the Polish Initial Training Wing, R.A.F., and at the Polytechnic, Regent Street, London.

There is other evidence of the British Council's contribution to the development of sound examination practice in these early years that was critical for establishing scoring validity. For example, piloting of tests in British Council operations abroad appears at an early stage:

> Mr Burton reported that questions from the specimen 'Use of English' paper had been worked by a small number of students in Portugal and London, and were also being worked by a group of students in Paris. The results of the first two sets appeared to be satisfactory....
> (Quoted in Weir and Milanovic 2003: 13).

The British Council used research, based on Cambridge examination scripts, to provide data for use in teaching:

> Minute 8.
> Use of scripts for research work. The Secretary reported that scripts had been supplied to Dr Lee on the terms agreed. Mr Cartledge asked for C.P.E. and L.C.E. scripts to be supplied also to the English language Unit of the Education Division of the British Council on the same terms. The intention was that the scripts from a specified area should be used to prepare a report on linguistic characteristics, which would be used by the Council for the training of British teachers of English about to be seconded to the area. The scripts, from which only extracts would be used, would be returned to the Syndicate and a copy of the report would be submitted to the Syndicate. It was agreed to make scripts available for this purpose.
> (Executive Committee 6th Meeting, May 1960)

This foreshadows later work in the English Profile Project (www.englishprofile.org) in the 21st century, a global research programme to help teachers, curriculum developers, course-book authors and test writers understand which aspects of English are typically learned at each Common European Framework of Reference (CEFR) level of English. In English Profile research, Cambridge English Language examination scripts from a specially constructed corpus have been used to look more closely at linguistic progression across levels (see Hawkins and Buttery 2010 and Green 2012).

The British Council also carried out important surveys in the field, which fed into the work of Cambridge examination development. The Executive Committee 17th Meeting, October 1966 makes reference to early attempts in gathering evidence on the washback/impact of the Proficiency examination by the Education Division of the British Council conducting a survey in its overseas teaching centres.

The Executive Committee 27th Meeting, October 1971 records an investigation of the value of introducing an examination at a lower level than LCE (later FCE):

> (iv)(71/10 and 70/15) Examination at elementary level
> The outcome of the British Council's consultation with overseas teaching centres regarding the possible demand for a locally based preliminary testing service, following a suggestion that the Syndicate might act in an advisory capacity or provide material for such a service, was reported.

Roland Hindmarsh's attachment to Cambridge

The Joint Committee minutes of 3 July 1970 provide further evidence of the closeness of the working relationship, with Roland Hindmarsh, an experienced British Council English Language Officer, actually being seconded to Cambridge from the British Council for a year:

> ...the Syndicate had recently received a request from the British Council for collaboration in connection with the appointment by the Council of Mr R.X. Hindmarsh to undertake research on Examination Syllabuses, with particular reference to English as a second and/or a foreign language.... The English Examinations would benefit from any such investigation and collaboration between Mr Chaplen and Mr Hindmarsh might be most fruitful....

The arrangements were confirmed at the Executive Committee 25th Meeting in October that year, and the minutes provide interesting detail of the broad spectrum of research Hindmarsh was to carry out during his time at Cambridge:

> ...Mr Hindmarsh explained that his research programme...will include investigation of the aims of candidates and the uses made of qualifications in English, and consultation with teachers and examiners on the most useful way in which more detailed knowledge of the requirements of the examinations might be provided....

Further discussion covered the following points:
(i) The need for research on the oral tests, which might not come sufficiently within the scope of the current review.
(ii) The relation between teaching and examining methods, bearing in mind the responsibility hitherto felt for encouraging good teaching by the form of the examinations.
(iii) The possibility of including in the research programme some investigation of proposals to collaborate with the British Council over special tests for use at overseas centres. These might be locally administered objective tests for special purposes at various levels, or preliminary tests which might provide a basis for local certificates of attendance and attainment, thus providing an incentive in the early stages of a course. These proposals, about which the British Council is at present consulting teaching centres, would not involve awards by the Syndicate, but it is felt that the regular provision of standardised test materials might be a valuable service.

Point iii is an early harbinger of the direction in which British Council/Cambridge relations would develop in the 1970s (see Chapter 4). Cambridge would be asked in 1975 to produce a test for use by the British Council in its centres abroad for screening overseas applicants wishing to be considered for UK government scholarships to study at tertiary level in the UK.

The minutes of the Executive Committee 26th Meeting, May 1971, evidence two further dimensions of Hindmarsh's work at Cambridge: an early attempt by Hindmarsh to identify the lexico-grammatical content of the Cambridge Exams at different levels (see Khalifa and Weir 2009 for the most recent attempt to do this) and the first attempts at Cambridge to develop syllabuses for English language examinations.

70/3 Research and Development
(ii) A report by Mr Hindmarsh on the visit to teaching centres in Italy, Switzerland and Germany undertaken as part of his programme of research on syllabuses was received, together with further details of the progress of his investigations with specimen analysis of the vocabulary and structural content of examination material. Work done on the possibility of issuing a...syllabus for the Proficiency and Lower Certificate examinations was noted with interest.

This research foreshadows work that would be done for the Council of Europe by Jan Van Ek and John Trim to develop descriptions of English language proficiency at different levels that eventually, via *Waystage*,

Threshold and *Vantage*, resulted in the CEFR 'blue book' (Council of Europe 2001).

Hindmarsh made a valuable contribution to Cambridge English Examinations and his secondment to Cambridge, as that of Peter Falvey from 1984 to 1988, is further testimony to the close working relationship between the two organisations aimed at improving the quality and the reach of the examinations. Such input was valuable given the limited expertise in English language examining in Cambridge pre-1989. In an interview for this history project (May 2015), Peter Falvey describes how John Reddaway, the Secretary of UCLES, came to Hong Kong to set up Falvey's attachment to Cambridge to help improve testing practice there:

> he then said he'd like me to come on secondment, and it was a fairly open brief, and he basically just said get to grips with it, because it was a one man and a dog [show]….

As we will see in Chapter 5, Falvey played an important role in increasing the professionalism of the Cambridge EFL examination board and was instrumental in bringing a critical mass of expert testers to Cambridge in the late 1980s.

Endnote

The minutes of the Joint Committee and the Executive Committee meetings cited above provide many examples of the breadth and depth of the British Council's close involvement in language testing research and development with UCLES over an extended period of time. They show that the British Council was prepared to invest both financial and human resources in test research and development to work with Cambridge to improve the quality of the examinations that it was helping to deliver around the world and thereby encourage increasing numbers of people to sit them. Aiding and abetting the global spread of British influence through the promotion of English was the not so hidden agendum.

As well as a continuing contribution to the research, development and export of Cambridge English language examinations, the British Council was increasingly involved from the 1980s onwards in a new role: it became the global facilitator of British government sponsored ELT projects abroad. This new role had its roots in the British Council's increasing involvement in developing countries and the building of a close relationship with the Overseas Development Association from the 1960s.

In the next chapter we look briefly at some of the projects that had a clear assessment focus, which the British Council helped set up, manage, support and monitor from the 1980s onwards, and examine their impact. They reveal the British Council's increasing involvement with the management of international English language testing projects as a further means of promoting the universal spread of the English language and British influence, that took place in the latter part of the 20th century.

Chapter 2

Developing English language testing around the world, 1982–2016: Exporting British expertise

> Tell me, Muse, of the man of many devices, who wandered far and wide… and saw the towns of many men…. – *The Odyssey* 1, l. 1

In the previous chapter we examined the British Council's leading role in the development, promotion and delivery of Cambridge English examinations around the world. The British Council further contributed to spreading British influence by promoting English in its global direct English teaching activities overseas; through its support for English Language Teaching (ELT) development projects and in the later part of the 20th century through its use of British government funding to support the spread and development of British approaches to English language *testing* in many countries around the world.

From the 1970s onwards, there were indeed hundreds of Overseas Development Agency (ODA) (later Department for International Development (DFID))/British Council supported ELT projects around the world and details of many of these are available in the Warwick ELT Archive website (http://web.warwick.ac.uk/fac/soc/CELTE/eltarchive/Archive/overview_bydate.php). Though each one evidences the proactive role of the British Council in facilitating the global spread of influence through the promotion of the English language, over-emphasising them in this narrative would only serve to divert us from our main focus on testing. However, as we shall see, the Council's EL assessment activities are often quite closely associated with its EL teaching role (for details of some of these ELT development projects see: Abbott and Beaumont 1997; Alderson 2009; Bowers 1983; British Council Dunford

House Seminar Reports between 1978 and 1993; British Council 1996; British Council 2013a; Brumfit 1983; ODA 1985; Pincas 1995b; http://englishagenda.britishcouncil.org; Tribble 2012 and United Kingdom Trade and Investment (UKTI) Education 2014).

We will focus instead on a number of the myriad of English language projects which had *testing* as a major theme, and where the British Council, on behalf of government, was involved in funding, administering, managing, participating in or otherwise supporting British initiatives. Like the ELT projects, these testing projects demonstrate a continuation by other means of one of the British Council's central aims: to spread British influence by promoting and facilitating the reach and significance of English around the world. They illustrate how, in the latter part of the 20th century, British Council activities went far beyond the earlier professional support for the research and development of Cambridge English language examinations in the UK, and the promotion and administration of Cambridge English language examinations (as well as examinations provided by other Boards) in its teaching centres abroad (for detail of this see Chapter 1 of this book and Hawkey and Milanovic 2013: Chapters 2 and 3). In this later period the British Council became an international catalyst facilitating the development of indigenous English language tests by national bodies worldwide, as well as contributing to the professional upgrading of local expertise in English language assessment in many countries.

Early indications of this expanded role appear in the 1970s with the growth of a professional specialised ELT cadre based at the British Council headquarters in Spring Gardens in London. In an interview with Roger Hawkey (10 December 2014), an expert in EFL and a former British Council Officer, he pointed out that the British Council set up an in-house English Language Consultancies Department (ELCD) in Spring Gardens in 1976 (renamed English Language Services Department (ELSD) in 1978), from which British Council Officers made frequent visits to English language related projects abroad, often on particular pre-negotiated course design, test development or staff training contracts. Advice on testing was often a vital part of these projects as in the King Abdul Aziz University (KAAU) Communication Skills in English (CSE) Project in Saudi Arabia in the 1970s (Carroll 1980). Vivien Berry, Senior Researcher, English Language Assessment, English and Exams British Council, who was involved in this project, commented (personal communication March 2016):

> Under the guidance of Alan Moller from the British Council, the College of Medicine and Allied Sciences, the College of Engineering and the Institute of Meteorology and Arid Land Studies at KAAU all developed their initial placement tests from the British Council's Mini Platform test. They also developed subject specific Band Scales for their final assessments, which were similar to the original ELTS scales. These scales ranged from Band 3, which was the minimum acceptable level for entry, to Band 7.5, Band 6 being the target exit band.

In the 1980s, however, there was growing concern on the part of certain sections of UK academia that British Council consultancies were being delivered on a *pro bono* basis and as such they were depriving UK universities of valuable revenue. This resulted in a decrease in such consultancy activities on the part of British Council staff and the employment of specialists mainly from British universities to fill this role.

Alan Moller was the British Council Senior Consultant in Testing and Evaluation from September 1979 to mid-1984 (when Peter Hargreaves took over) and for the last year of his tenure he was also the Director of ELSD. In a personal communication (December 2015) Moller confirmed this direction of travel:

> During the early and mid 1980s British Council specialist staff facilitated the transition from sending their own consultants on testing projects overseas, to identifying specialists from UK universities to initiate or support testing projects, and finally to enabling UK institutions to enter into arrangements directly with overseas institutions.
>   ...this was the period when English testing was burgeoning, the Council was consequently obliged to devolve much of its work in the field to the increasing number of highly qualified individual consultants and then later to academic institutions and departments themselves. As ever with the Council it was not articulated policy but its pragmatic response to a rapidly developing situation, which could not have been – or at least wasn't – foreseen.

This chapter will record the hitherto somewhat under-publicised, yet rather significant contribution to the field of language testing made by these UK university based testing specialists on the behalf of the British Council in the period 1982–2016.

Outsourcing indeed became a necessity when the British Council's own in-house cadre of specialist advisers on assessment at its headquarters in Spring Gardens was scaled down in the 1990s. By 1997 Roger Bowers, Clive Bruton, Brendan J. Carroll, Roger Hawkey, Roland

Hindmarsh, Arthur McNeill, Alan Moller, Ian Seaton, Richard Webber and Gill Westaway had either left the Council or in a few cases transferred to managerial roles in British Council offices abroad. As we discuss later in Chapter 5, the British Council policy in the 1990s was to focus on the management and administration of projects, and testing activities such as IELTS rather than actually carrying them out themselves. Overseas the emphasis for the permanent career service was placed on the growing British Council Direct Teaching of English Operations. These were managed by staff that might previously have been English Language Officers (ELOs) with a more specialist focus, but were now expected to be generalists.

British language testing experts, including Clive Criper, Alan Davies and Liz Hamp-Lyons (Edinburgh University), Rita Green, Tony Green, Arthur Hughes, Keith Morrow, Don Porter, Cyril Weir, Eddie Williams and Tony Woods (Reading University), Charles Alderson, Caroline Clapham, Pauline Rea and Dianne Wall (Lancaster University), Richard West and Pat McEldowney (Manchester University), and Brian Heaton (Leeds University), were increasingly employed by the British Council as external consultants, both short term and long term, to provide professional input to ODA/British Council sponsored testing projects around the world. Many of these consultants had already completed their PhD studies in the area of language testing in the UK and thus possessed an expertise in assessment that was lacking in most other parts of the world.

This individual specialist expertise was enhanced by the setting up in the early 1980s of units/groups devoted to language testing at a number of universities, most notably Reading (The Testing and Evaluation Unit) and Lancaster (Language Testing Research Group), where small but critical masses of staff carried out research and ran professional courses in testing up to MA and PhD level from the early 1980s onwards.

We will discuss the 'British' approach to English language testing in more detail in Chapters 3 and 4 when we focus on the British Council's involvement in test development in the UK. These chapters will demonstrate the singular contribution the people above made to the development of communicative and English for Specific Purposes (ESP) language testing in the UK from the late 1970s to the 1990s, whilst at the same time carrying out consultancies for the British Council abroad. They were at the forefront of the research and scholarship underpinning modern communicative approaches to language testing which put the emphasis on *what* should be tested, informed by an analysis of the real-world use of the language, as compared to the American psychometric approach which at that time was mainly concerned with the *how* of language testing and post-test statistical validation (see Weir 2013 for an extensive discussion of the two different approaches in the 20th century). The presence of this critical mass of state-of-the-art expertise in British universities and the uniqueness of the British communicative approach to language testing was what enabled the British Council to facilitate its export so well.

At the same time as making valuable contributions to their field, these UK academics gained valuable practical experience of high-stakes test development in these consultancies abroad, often at a national level, which helped considerably in their own professional progression. Perhaps most tellingly, many of the theoretical advances made by UK *academia* in the language testing field in the period 1985–2015, for example in formulating a comprehensive and systematic approach to language test development and validation, addressing the washback validity of tests, and the development of a socio-cognitive approach, had their roots in ODA/British Council sponsored testing projects. We draw attention to these impacts in the discussion below.

As well as these short-term visiting UK consultants and the long-term British Council career officers posted to a country, Hawkey reminds us (interview 10 December 2014) that in many countries key roles were played in language assessment by ELT professionals recruited by the British Council in London and paid jointly by the British Council and the in-country educational institution to which they were posted. These British Council 'contract specialists' promoted and helped develop the teaching and/or testing of English as part of the daily responsibilities of their British Council connected posts. They were often invited to get involved with the development and improvement of indigenous national examinations in English in the countries they were serving in, e.g. Hawkey, while serving as a British Council 'Teacher of English Overseas' (TEO) in Thailand, worked regularly with teams of test developers to produce the national school-leaving examination in English, on which, among many other decisions, the selection of students to study in the UK was based.

This experience was repeated in many countries. In Sri Lanka British Council officers Raymond Brown, Ian Pearson and Richard Webber contributed to the reform of English examinations in the 1980s (see accounts of Sri Lankan NCE and 'O' Level below). Arthur Hughes spent two years in the early 1980s as a Key English Language Teaching Officer

(KELT) at Boğaziçi University in Istanbul, helping to develop an innovative EAP test and setting up a testing unit for this English-medium university (see the subsection below: *Boğaziçi University, Turkey, EAP test development project*). Similarly Tony Lilley, who spent 16 years at the British Council sponsored ESP Centre in Alexandria University, was heavily involved in the development of an academic English reading proficiency test for Egyptian universities (see below, *Egyptian Universities' National Academic Reading Test*). Rita Green spent two years at Shanghai International Studies University in Shanghai (SISU) helping validate the Test for English Majors (see below, *Test for English Majors Validation Study, PRC*) and two years (1991–1993) at the Department of Technical and Economic Co-operation (DTEC), Bangkok Thailand on an ODA/British Council project. More recently, Professor Charles Alderson spent two years in Hungary, on secondment from Lancaster University, advising on the reform of national English examinations (see below, *Examination Reform Teacher Support Project, Hungary*). Supporting the development of indigenous English language testing expertise and localised English language examinations helped establish the importance of learning English in these countries at both a government and an individual level.

Indigenous language testers from many of the overseas testing projects subsequently came on British Council sponsored attachments, or attended courses in a UK university, often working closely with the consultants who had been involved in their domestic projects. In a number of cases overseas personnel who had participated in British Council supported testing projects, were funded by the British Council to continue their assessment studies to doctoral level in Britain.

A selection of the testing projects the British Council has been involved in managing are listed chronologically in Table 2.1, and these will be examined below with particular reference to their impact. The final selection was made from an initial set of 29 testing focused projects we had managed to identify, with one key criterion being the availability and willingness of project participants to provide personal reminiscences of what objectives had been achieved and the project's impact in the country concerned.

For the most part these projects came about in response to national or local institutions requesting support from the British Council/British government (ODA, then DFID). In general, the projects described below may be seen as following the Council's traditional brief of spreading global influence through the promotion of English. Given the many millions of individuals that were touched by these projects, this core aim has almost certainly been realised.

The selection of projects are initially itemised in chronological order to show the historical span of such activities. These projects were sometimes concerned with *national curriculum renewal and exam reform*, e.g. in the Baltic States, Hungary, Mozambique, Russia, Sri Lanka and Uzbekistan. There were also projects that targeted particular *English for Specific Purposes (ESP) activities* such as: tests for civil servants in Thailand and in Malaysia; tests for the military in Europe; and English for Academic Purposes (EAP) tests at university level in China, Egypt, Mexico, Sri Lanka and Turkey.

Before examining each project in detail, it is relevant to this history to note the various roles played by British Council personnel in their delivery.

Table 2.1 Examples of British Council overseas testing projects

Boğaziçi University English Proficiency Test, Turkey, 1982–1984
Sri Lankan National Certificate in English Evaluation, 1986–1987
Sri Lankan O Level English Language Evaluation Project, 1989–1991
Egyptian Universities' National Academic Reading Test, 1990–1995
College English Test (CET) Validation Project, China, 1991–1995
Test for Civil Servants, Thailand, 1991–2015
Test for English Majors Project, China, 1993–1996
Year 12 English Examinations Project, Baltic States, 1994–1997
Advanced English Reading Test Project, China, 1995–1998
St Petersburg Examination Project (SPEX) Russia, 1996–2001
UK Peacekeeping English Project, 1996–2010
English Language Assessment System for the Public Service, Malaysia, 1998–2000
Secondary and Technical Education Project (STEP), Mozambique, 1997–2002
Examination Reform Teacher Support Project, Hungary, 1998–2002
University Entrance Test Development Projects, Uzbekistan, 2004–2009
The EXAVER Project, Mexico, 2000–2010
English for Tourism Project, Venezuela, 2007

The British Council's role: Project management

Rea-Dickins and Germaine (1993: 173) identify three main functions in good management practice for promoting development in ELT projects:

- leadership
- communication
- ability to organise

and (1993: 166) they identify areas where the ability to organise and administer ELT undertakings is criterial:

- planning
- staffing
- setting up systems
- budgeting and financial planning for the future
- meetings/briefings (link with communication and leadership)
- monitoring (plans in action, budget, routine admin, staff)
- crisis handling (resolving)
- managing change (transitions)
- evaluation.

These areas of responsibility most often fell to the local British Council career service officers in ELT projects abroad. Apart from its funding of the individual UK ELT testing specialists recruited to lead the work on the projects listed in Table 2.1, the British Council played an invaluable role in project-managing these initiatives. We approached a number of British Council officers who had been connected with these testing projects and asked them to reflect back on the role played by the British Council in delivering project objectives.

Gill Westaway, who joined the British Council in 1982 as an English Teacher at the Language Centre in Bogotá, Colombia, was by 2002 the Council's Country Director in the Philippines, having, in the intervening 20 years, worked at the Council in London developing the IELTS test, in Kenya managing development projects and establishing a Teaching Centre in Nairobi, and in Indonesia as Deputy Director. In her post as British Council Country Director in Sri Lanka from September 2006, Gill played a major role in Council supported projects and services in further and higher education. This career path is fairly typical of current Council officers who start as EL teachers at BC Direct Teaching Operations (expanding rapidly from the mid-1970s) and gradually broaden their career focus through other EL posts to what used to be called more 'generalist' duties as they advance in their careers.

Responding to the invitation to characterise the British Council's various roles in delivering EL-related educational projects, Gill Westaway (personal communication November 2015) wrote:

> The designated Project Managers were in many cases British Council Officers with an ELT background, who although not required to make direct specialist interventions, could through their understanding of the ELT field provide appropriate management interventions and help maximise the project inputs and outputs and build sustainability with the host country government.

Westaway (1993) describes the way in which she worked as a Project Manager to support her ELT specialist consultancy teams in Kenya. This includes consideration of the importance of accountability and good, flexible, financial management; providing an interface between the project team and the funding agency, freeing up the ELT specialist consultants from unnecessary administrative involvement so that they can focus on the professional tasks at hand; facilitating access to the decision-makers and developing effective relationships with the host government, crucial to real acceptance of the project and long-term sustainability; objectivity, offering professional support to the Project team without becoming too close to the specialist detail; and overview: as manager of a number of different ELT projects and as the holder of the more general brief of promoting English in the host country, the British Council Project Manager has a good overview of all activity in this area. He/she can see the transferability of a successful idea on one project to another, thus avoiding the reinvention of too many wheels. He/she is also able to determine how small amounts of the British Council's own funds can be effectively used to underpin donor project work in the interests of achieving maximum impact in a given context.

Barbara Wickham, former Director, British Council, Shanghai, China, who started her professional career in 1978 as an English Language teacher in Cairo, was also British Council Country Director in Venezuela and Ethiopia, and a Regional Director of Sindh and Baluchistan, Pakistan, before joining the Dhaka office as Director, Bangladesh in January 2015.

Wickham (1995: 2 and 10) offers a detailed overview of the British Council's project work in China in the 1990s. Note the complex administrative and managerial procedures that were a necessary part of such work by the British Council's permanent career service:

As the number of projects increased during the decade, the need for more standardised administrative systems became apparent. In April 1988 the Cultural and Education Section of the British Embassy (the British Council) and the Foreign Affairs Bureau of the State Education Commission agreed and signed the 'Administrative Guidelines for the Sino-British Programme of ELT Projects'. This provided the basis for the terms and conditions of service for the British specialists on the programme. Further documents, agreed between the two sides, set out in detail the structure within which the ELT programme operates. These specify the following: procedures an institution must follow in applying for a project; a standard job description for the specialists; a specification for counterpart selection, UK training, and pre/post training involvement in the project; regulations for the provision of equipment and materials; and the responsibilities of the two sides for consultancy visits.

...The fact that there are some thirty projects in the programme at any one time, covering a wide range of professional areas, with a variety of inputs, means that the programme is complex to manage. Professionally, the managers need a wide range of experience and expertise to be able to design appropriate projects and then monitor the products of these. Monitoring (through regular visits and progress reports), which is essential to ensure the quality of the product, is time-consuming as is the administration of the various inputs.

Susan Maingay, formerly Director, British Council in the Baltic countries (personal communication November 2015) commented:

> The British Council was ideally placed to identify and scope such projects. It had a physical presence in each country, with a team of local staff who brought with them knowledge of the local context, as well as a network of professional contacts at all levels of the education system – from the Ministry of Education through to universities and training colleges down to the teachers in schools. This meant that we were attuned to the local socio-political context and how this played out in government policy on education. In the early days of the newly independent Baltic countries we had particularly good access to the newly appointed ministers of education as they faced massive reform agendas. Along with representatives of other EU countries, we were seen as a potential partner and as such, participated in many face-to-face discussions with ministers about current needs and future plans for reform.
>
> At the same time – both directly and through ELT colleagues in London – we had a professional overview of the range of potential UK partners for the provision of training and the exchange of expertise.

Tasks typically undertaken by the local British Council office in the delivery of such projects would include:

- Project identification in consultation with key stakeholders – including, where relevant, the drawing up of Memoranda of Understanding.
- Project planning and design – development of project documentation, setting out aims and objectives, inputs and outputs, and including timelines and financial plans.
- Recruitment and management of key project personnel – including BC contract staff dedicated to project management and implementation.
- Recruitment of local experts for a range of project roles.
- Identification of potential UK partners to bid for training and development inputs.
- Financial management and reporting.
- Project monitoring, quality assurance and evaluation.

Mark Crossey, currently British Council Director in Uzbekistan, commented (personal communication December 2015) on the impact the British Council experience of project design, management and evaluation could have on the British government as well as government in other countries. He reflected on the Council's influence on high-level decision-making processes arising out of the Peacekeeping English Project (PEP) on which he was a manager and later director (see subsection below, *UK Peacekeeping English Project*):

> The British Council has also been well placed at various points to actively influence and even shape British government approach to best practice in project design, management and evaluation. This was arguably because the Council's own methodologies and understanding of impact evaluation and audiences are developed and updated very much by its on-the-ground experience and daily work with partner country experts.
>
> This influence was particularly evident in comparatively new areas of project intervention, such as the Peacekeeping English Project ('PEP'), which commenced in Central and Eastern Europe in the mid-1990s. Here, the Council lobbied PEP's government funders (MoD, FCO and DFID) to work together on a Steering Group platform; this resulted in a better understanding of the needs of the funders and their intended audience and outputs. Concrete developments from the Council's 'facilitation' role here were better methodologies, evaluating the direct impact the programme had on the effectiveness of peacekeeping missions, as well as on the careers of PEP 'graduates'. This steering group approach also eventually resulted in the significant achievement of a three-year, instead of annual, project

planning cycle. So a major success of British Council's management of the PEP was in developing government thinking on project planning so that it became more strategic, better anticipated the needs of all stakeholders and thus appeared less overtly 'political'.

Similarly, project aims and outcomes as specified by government departments, often resulting from direct requests from partner states, could be articulated and qualified by the British Council. This is particularly important in the case of language testing, and again the example of the Peacekeeping English Project is salient. In the early days of the PEP, UK was lobbied by aspirant NATO member states for project interventions which would focus on the introduction of entirely new national testing systems according to 'NATO standards' – it was British Council's already longstanding experience of working in such areas which allowed us to articulate the potential risks of too dramatic interventions here.

The British Council designed, managed and evaluated ELT projects with the support and help of: local partners in the countries concerned (e.g. Ministries of Education, national associations and educational institutions); the experts it employed for the projects from the UK and in-country; and the Council's own relevant expertise in its country offices and headquarters in London (see Pincas 1995b). Expertise for a project was required not just in the specialist area of language testing itself but often in designing and bidding for the project, building in a system for evaluation, recruiting and managing a team, and ensuring that the project has a sustainable future after the experts left.

We approached a number of people who had been frequently employed by the British Council on these projects to comment specifically on the role of the British Council in their management.

Rita Green, a free-lance language testing consultant is one of the most experienced and valued testing experts recruited by the British Council, who contributed to five of the projects examined in this chapter and to numerous others. She listed the following many and varied facilitating activities by the British Council in respect of the projects she was involved in (personal communication November 2015):

- Responding to local requests for support in setting up a project. Or initiating said project.
- Drawing up and signing MoUs with local partners to facilitate the project work.
- Integral part in helping to develop the necessary terms of reference for a project so that the right person(s) are ultimately appointed as well as conditions for the project to succeed.

- Being part of the selection process for identifying the appropriate trainer(s)/consultant(s) in consultation with local bodies where relevant.
- Drawing up contracts for the appointed consultants ensuring that appropriate finances are available.
- Facilitating the drawing-up of viable timelines with local partners.
- Providing appointed trainers/consultants with in-country notes, background information relevant to the project.
- Facilitating visa requirements.
- Meeting and briefing appointed personnel on their preliminary visit to the country and facilitating initial meetings with stakeholders.
- Providing in-country support for the project by attending crucial stakeholder meetings.
- Supporting projects through local financial contributions for travel costs, material preparation, the provision of equipment (OHP, laptop etc.), the printing of handbooks, item writing etc.
- Acting as the point of contact between the trainer/consultant and the project team members in between country visits.

Dianne Wall, formerly of the Institute for English Language Education, Lancaster University, UK was also involved in five of the projects we address below. She commented on the British Council's contribution as consisting of:

- Establishing initial contacts within ministries, universities, training institutions, boards of educations and other relevant organisations.
- Working with stakeholders to identify language education priorities.
- Maintaining relations and communications with key individuals and institutions during stable times and in times of change.
- Managing current budgets, and planning and lobbying for future funding.
- Identifying suitable candidates for professional development.
- Identifying suitable partners, both in-country and in-UK, to provide relevant training and support.
- Providing professional input and feedback, both to in-country teams and outside specialists.
- Ensuring the smooth running of projects via appropriate communication with all parties, monitoring, contributing to discussions.
- Evaluating projects in formative stages and at project end.
- Keeping abreast of developments in relevant academic areas to inform all other activity.

British Council language testing projects, 1982–2007

We next provide a short detailed account of each of the language assessment projects listed in Table 2.1 above. These descriptions are intended to:

- clarify the aims of the project with regard to assessment;
- provide a summary of the project's main achievements;
- demonstrate any immediate impact in the host country;
- identify any wider impact on the language testing field.

Wherever possible, we made contact with people involved in these projects and invited them to add their own voices to the narrative. They are quoted extensively in the text below.

We group our discussion of the projects into two subsections, each organised chronologically:

- national examination reform projects;
- projects with an English for Specific Purposes (ESP) assessment focus.

National examination reform projects

The UK Government publication, *English Language Education and Training Capability* (UKTI Education 2014: 10–12) sets out clearly the critical importance of designing and delivering valid English language assessment in educational settings overseas and the hallmarks of success in doing this:

> Assessing starting point, progress and achievement in student and teacher English language proficiency is a fundamental requirement for education systems worldwide, with high stakes for all involved. Individual students seeking entry to the next stage of their education, employers seeking to recruit high-caliber staff, and policy makers seeking to evaluate the impact and success of their policies all need robust and reliable assessment.
>
> …Key considerations in the design and delivery of high quality, appropriate English language assessment include:
> - Ensuring that the language and skills assessed are the language and skills needed for work, life or further study and not just the language and skills that are easily tested

- Understanding the powerful impact that examinations can have on what happens in the classroom, where typically what gets tested gets taught, with skills that are not tested rarely being taught
- Appreciating that the equity of the assessment process that enables progression from one level of the education system to the next, for example from secondary school to university, is especially crucial to a nation's management of its human capital.

The benefits to recipients of such inputs in English language testing are well-documented. Accurate language certification through accredited language tests has played an important role in generating economic prosperity (British Council 2013a). In the developing world, English language proficiency underpins the growth of national and individual wealth and helps drive economic development. Governments in the developing world view the improvement and certification of English language skills at all levels as an essential part of achieving growth, not least because it gives domestic companies a competitive edge in the global economy. Such language skills are a significant factor in attracting inward Foreign Direct Investment (FDI). Coleman (2010) provides empirical evidence of the benefits of English language proficiency: increasing individual employability; enabling international collaboration and cooperation; providing access to research and information; facilitating the international mobility of students, tourists, workers etc. He concludes that English impacts positively on individuals, on particular industrial sectors (especially service economies) and at a national level. Valid certification of English proficiency through language tests plays an important role in this.

The projects detailed below are likely to have led to more valid, dependable and fair English language measurement tools. For millions of successful candidates such enhanced English tests have improved job prospects, increased transnational mobility and opened doors to educational and training opportunities. Accurate proficiency tests have contributed to better-informed and more equitable decision-making processes in society.

Sri Lankan National Certificate in English (NCE) Evaluation, 1986–1987

The British Council first facilitated visits from UK curriculum reform and testing consultants to the National Institute for Education (NIE) in Colombo in the early 1980s. Cyril Weir paid a visit to Sri Lanka in

1982 to discuss English examinations with senior officials M.A. de Silva and Nihal Cooray at the NIE and, through focus groups and meetings with the Ministry of Education, possible changes to the then-current national examinations were explored. British Council support for developing English language assessment continued in the mid-1980s, when Sri Lankan teachers sponsored by the Council were sent to Lancaster University for training in examination design and administration. Their first target was to develop a new National Certificate in English (NCE), which was intended to serve as a measure of proficiency for the adult population. Their second target was to revise the O Level examination in English Language, which assessed the proficiency of students completing the final year of compulsory schooling in the state education system.

There was a good deal of support for the NCE examination from the British Council English Language Teaching Officer (ELTO) Ian Pearson who worked with visiting experts from Lancaster University in an evaluation of the examination from 1986 to 1987. Ian Pearson from 1964 until 2004 worked mostly with the British Council on English language projects in Bosnia and Herzegovina, Ukraine, Russia, Tanzania, Sri Lanka, Thailand, Spain, Norway and Finland, and held university teaching posts in Edinburgh, Khartoum and Trondheim. Dianne Wall, a language testing specialist from Lancaster University, acted as one of the consultants (with colleagues Charles Alderson and Caroline Clapham) for the British Council on the project and provided the following description (personal communication 17 March 2015) of it:

> **National Certificate in English (NCE)**
> The NCE was first administered in 1986. It represented a significant innovation in the Sri Lankan setting. Part 1 attempted to incorporate notions of authenticity and relevance into tasks for reading and writing, and to assess language knowledge in context via gap-filling and c-tests. Candidates who met the demands of Part 1 were able to register for Part 2, which measured listening and speaking abilities. More than 17,000 candidates took Part 1 the first year it was administered, of whom some 2,300 were allowed to register for Part 2.
>
> This was the first time that listening and speaking had been measured on such a large scale in Sri Lanka. The methods chosen (dictation, reading aloud, response elicitation and picture description) were deliberately quite controlled but they presented major challenges for exam delivery and for the training and monitoring of interlocutors and markers.
>
> In addition to measuring the language proficiency of the adult population, the NCE served as a proving ground for assessment methods that

were being considered for the revised O Level examination, due to be introduced in 1988. Both the NCE and the O Level were high-stakes examinations so it was important to determine whether the NCE came up to standard in terms of validity and reliability. The British Council provided considerable support to the examination design team through the work of ELTO Ian Pearson. The Council also commissioned Lancaster University to evaluate the first and second administrations of the NCE, in 1986 and 1987 respectively. The Lancaster team consisted of Charles Alderson, Dianne Wall and Caroline Clapham. The 1986 evaluation provided a thorough look at both the content of the examination and its statistical properties, paying special attention to rater reliability. The immediate impact of this evaluation was to provide guidance for improving the design of the 1987 examination and associated procedures. It also established a model for evaluation that the Sri Lankan team could use as they carried out their own validation exercises in years to come. The 1987 evaluation focused not only on investigating the qualities of the examination but also on training the Sri Lankan team in evaluative methods, data analysis and report writing. This training would enable team members to evaluate their own work not only on the NCE, but also on the O Level Examination, which was to follow shortly, and on other examinations they would be involved in designing in the future.

The findings of the 1986 evaluation were reported in detail in Alderson, Wall and Clapham (1987) and a full account of the methodology used was published in Wall, Clapham and Alderson (1991). The findings of the 1987 evaluation were reported in Goonetillike, Samarasinghe, Senaratne and Sinhalage (1988).

The framework for evaluation provided by the Lancaster team was an interesting early attempt to develop a rigorous and systematic approach to language test construction, delivery and validation, which had been noticeably absent in many national and international ELT examinations in this period. Alderson, Clapham and Wall (1995) would draw on such valuable experiences in the field to formulate their taxonomy of assessment considerations ELT examining boards needed to address.

Sri Lankan O Level English Language Evaluation Project, 1988–1991

Wall and Alderson (1993: 42–43) provide detail on the consistently low pass rate (c. 20%) in the traditional English O Level examination in Sri Lanka. It was questionable whether, even for those who passed, it actually prepared students for the demands of real-life communication (spoken or written) given its focus on grammatical structures and general reading abilities. The exam gave students little opportunity to engage in everyday communication, either orally or in writing.

Given these limitations, an effort was made in the 1980s to make English language learning more communicative and the Ministry of Education, with the help of the British Overseas Development Administration (ODA), developed a new textbook series written for secondary schools, which focused on reading and writing for a purpose, and oral skills. Related training courses aimed to equip teachers with the skills to deliver these new materials. In order to get teachers to take the changes seriously it was decided to introduce a new examination in 1988 when the first students to go through Years 9, 10 and 11 of the textbook series would come to the end of their studies. The examination would reflect what was supposed to be taught through the materials.

In 1988 a research team from Lancaster University was commissioned by the British Council on behalf of ODA to investigate the impact of the new O Level examination in English as an international language on English language teaching in secondary schools in Sri Lanka. Wall (1990: 15) describes how the project was intended to evaluate the validity of the new examination and to determine its impact on classroom practice. Though there was evidence of considerable impact on the content of English lessons and on the teacher-designed classroom tests, little impact was found on the methodology employed by teachers in the classroom.

Dianne Wall (personal communication 19 March 2015) provided further detail on the project and its achievements, and reflected on the impact of the new exam:

> **O Level in English as an International Language**
> In 1988 the British Council, on behalf of the ODA, commissioned a research team from Lancaster University to provide an external evaluation of the new O Level examination in English as an International Language and to analyse its impact on English language teaching in secondary schools in Sri Lanka. The examination had recently been revised as part of an 'innovation package' to upgrade English language teaching country-wide and to make it more relevant to learners' modern-day communicative needs. New textbooks had been introduced in primary and secondary schools, and training programmes had been devised to help teachers to cope with new approaches to teaching. It was realised, however, that these changes might not be taken seriously unless there were also changes in the O Level examination administered at the end of compulsory schooling. Students who wished to continue in education needed good O Level results in order

to secure a place in the next level of schooling; students who were leaving education needed good results to secure a place in employment. Pearson (1988) used the term 'lever for change' to represent the power that important examinations like the O Level could have over the type of teaching and learning that led up to them. It was generally accepted that teachers and learners would focus mainly on the language and the skills they believed would appear in the examination. In the language testing literature this phenomenon is referred to as 'washback' (Alderson and Wall 1993).

The evaluation project was to last four years, from 1988 to 1991. The terms of reference included investigating the validity and the reliability of the examination, and measuring its washback on classroom teaching. The analysis of the examination itself was straightforward and the results can be found in Alderson and Wall (1992). The analysis of the exam's washback was more challenging, both at a theoretical level and in actual practice. The theoretical challenge involved a critical review of previous claims about the relationship between assessment and classroom practice, and a discussion of the types of methods that would produce convincing evidence of whether the teaching and learning that took place after the introduction of a new examination were due to the power of that examination or to other factors in the educational context. These discussions were recorded in a series of publications on the nature of washback, chief amongst which were Alderson and Wall 1993, Wall 1996a, and Wall 2005.

The practical challenges involved organising a large-scale and long-term observation programme in about 60 schools across the country. The observations were carried out by a team of Sri Lankan teachers who were trained in research methodology at Lancaster University and who made repeated visits to schools in their region over a period of two years. In-depth interviews were carried out at the end of the observation study. The research revealed that the examination had had both positive and negative washback on the content of classroom lessons and the tests that teachers prepared for their pupils, but there was little to no impact on the techniques they used when they managed their classes or on the way they responded to their pupils' test performance. The research made it clear that the examination was only one of the factors at play when teachers planned and delivered their lessons.

We now believe an exam on its own cannot reinforce an approach to teaching that the educational system has not adequately prepared its teachers for. Factors which may prevent the implementation of the new approach, and which may make the task of reinforcement by an examination (washback) difficult, include frequent turnover in teaching staff, lack of material resources, management practices within schools, insufficient exam-specific teacher training, inadequate communication between those responsible for the exam and its users, inadequate understanding of the philosophy of the textbook or the examination, and teachers' beliefs that a particular method is more effective than those represented by the text book or implicit in the examination.

Until the educational system is able to coordinate the efforts of material designers, exam designers, teacher trainers, and those inspecting classes and advising teachers, the mere setting into place of an examination will not reinforce materials and approaches to teaching that may not be well enough understood in the first place. By the same reasoning, the mere existence of an examination which is in conflict with textbook content, methodology, or philosophy, or with teacher beliefs and practices, will not necessarily 'force' teachers into teaching a particular content, or using a particular methodology.

The O Level evaluation project had the desired effect in the local context, through its analysis of the examination itself and its discussion of factors that were facilitating or inhibiting beneficial washback (Alderson and Wall 1992). It also had an impact on the field of language testing by exploring the notion of examination washback more fully and by emphasising the need to incorporate insights from other disciplines, principally educational innovation, into washback investigations.

The innovative research of Dianne Wall, Charles Alderson and Caroline Clapham, together with their Sri Lankan colleagues in this British Council funded project was to result in a number of seminal publications on test washback, which subsequently proved of great value to the language testing field (Alderson and Wall 1992 and 1993, Wall and Alderson 1993, Wall 1996a and 2005). Their work provided language testing with a deep and comprehensive understanding of the concept of test washback and perhaps more importantly, they provided a feasible and plausible methodology for its investigation.

British Council funded research into the washback of examinations is also evidenced in the later investigations carried out by Tony Green of the University of Bedfordshire on the IELTS examination (Green 2007), out of which grew a model for washback research that is widely used by researchers in this area.

Year 12 English Examinations Project, Baltic States, 1994–1997

Phillipson (1992: 10) observed that with the move away from communism in Eastern Europe the British government seized the opportunity to strengthen the case for English as a possible alternative to Russian as the second language throughout Eastern Europe. With the break-up of the Soviet Union, English did indeed become the new additional language of choice for many of the newly independent governments in the region (see Pincas 1995b).

Susan Maingay, formerly Director, British Council in the Baltic countries (personal communication November 2015) commented on the British Council's involvement in this process:

> In the early 1990s the British Government established the *Know How Fund*, a source of funding available to support reform agendas in post-Soviet countries with aspirations to EU membership. The British Council was asked to manage a significant tranche of the fund, especially in relation to education reform, and played a key role in identifying opportunities for the UK to participate in joint projects. Many, though by no means all, of these projects were in the area of English language teaching and focused largely, though not exclusively, on teacher training both in- and pre-service. In the Baltic countries this also included examination reform projects, such as the Year 12 project.

The part played by new English language examinations in this linguistic revolution was significant. At an early stage in the Baltic States project, Dianne Wall (1996b: 15–17) commented:

> The purpose of the Baltic States Year 12 Examination Project has been to support national teams in Estonia, Latvia and Lithuania in their attempts to design, administer and evaluate new school-leaving examinations in English as a Foreign Language. All three countries have experienced major social and economic changes since gaining independence from the former Soviet Union, and English has quickly replaced Russian as the most widely-taught foreign language in schools. This change has been accompanied by a revision of the foreign language curriculum in each country, the appearance of new teaching materials, and the creation of several new pre-service and in-service training programmes to equip teachers (many of whom were ex-teachers of Russian) to respond to the countries' changing needs. An analysis and possible re-design of the school-leaving examinations for English seemed a logical and appropriate next step in this process of reform.
>
> The school-leaving examination in all three countries followed the same pattern: general guidelines for assessment were issued by the Ministry of Education, and panels of teachers within each school administered individual oral tests to each candidate. Although the same general procedures were followed in all schools it was up to each panel to decide the length and exact nature of each test they gave, the texts they would use, and their own criteria for marking. There were no means of guaranteeing that students from different schools had been faced with the same types of challenges, or that the marks that they received were comparable. This meant that universities and other institutions of higher education could not rely

on these marks for admissions purposes, and felt it necessary to run their own examinations for entry and placement.

The Year 12 Project was begun in June 1994, the product of agreements between The British Council and the Ministry of Education in each country. The goal in each country was to design a new Year 12 examination, which would be fully functional by June 1997.

The training and advising was carried out in both the UK and in the Baltics. The programme components provide insights into the depth of training needed to set up a rigorous system for the delivery of valid national examinations (see Wall 1996b: 15–17 for details). In all, 11 training courses were delivered between 1994 and 1996, ranging from three days to three weeks. Additionally, Lancaster provided an online support service, to enable Project teams to ask for advice or feedback throughout the year.

Twenty years later Dianne Wall (personal communication 23 March 2015) reflected on the experience of being involved in such an important project which she noted had a dramatic effect on the professional lives of all those involved. She and many of her colleagues regarded it as 'one of the highlights of their careers'.

The Baltic States Year 12 Project

British Council offices were opened in all of the Baltic States – Estonia, Latvia and Lithuania – in 1991, soon after the countries gained their independence from the former Soviet Union. Amongst the Council's early priorities was supporting these countries in their attempts to improve English language teaching and assessment. All the countries had experienced social and economic changes since Independence and English quickly replaced Russian as the most commonly taught language in schools. New curricula were being developed and new teaching materials were being introduced in the classroom. New teacher training programmes were also needed, and the Council responded by supporting projects to (1) help former Russian teachers to re-qualify as English teachers and (2) develop a cadre of in-service trainers to design and deliver courses suitable to the countries' emerging English language needs.

A third project was launched in 1994, to develop valid and reliable English language examinations for Year 12 – the end of secondary schooling. The project was called 'The Baltic States Year 12 Project' but there were actually three parallel projects, one in each country. The goal was to develop examinations that were appropriate for each country's own educational context. Three national teams were formed, each consisting of a representative of the Ministry (an advisor or inspector who would understand political and organisational possibilities and constraints), a representative from a university or teacher-training organisation (who would guide academic developments and represent the interests of tertiary-level institutions) and three secondary or tertiary teachers (who would provide insights 'from the chalk face' and communicate with school heads, teachers, students and parents). The new Year 12 examinations would replace the school-based examining that was common in the former Soviet Union and much of Central and Eastern Europe. They would ensure that the grades awarded to students were comparable across all schools and that universities could rely on the results for their own admissions purposes.

Lancaster University was invited to provide training and consultancy services over the course of three years, both in the UK and in the Baltics. It was decided at the start of the project that the teams needed not only input and practice in examination design but also support in integrating their new examinations into established educational structures. It was important that the examinations complemented newly evolving language teaching curricula and that they were understood and accepted by all stakeholders. It was also important to create systems for the production and delivery of the examinations, the marking of objective and subjective components, the processing of results, and the reporting of outcomes and their implications to all relevant parties. The teams received training not only in language test construction and evaluation but also in aspects of project management such as planning, decision-making, budgeting, negotiating, and communicating with the media. The management training was provided by John McGovern from the British Council, who went on to offer similar support to many English language development projects worldwide.

The Year 12 project represented three important innovations in testing support from the Council:

1. the idea of designing not only examination papers but also systems to support the design, administration and evaluation processes (e.g. secure printing and delivery of exam papers, efficient registration procedures, statistical analysis of results);
2. the idea of providing training in management skills as well as testing skills; and
3. the idea of a long-term relationship between national teams and the UK trainers/consultants, with nearly a dozen opportunities for working together over the three years of the project.

The impact of the Year 12 project was impressive, both by the time of its completion and in the long term. All three teams produced innovative multi-skills examinations from scratch, designing specifications, items and tasks, level definitions, rating scales, and procedures for marking and statistical analysis. They devised training programmes for all participants in the examining process, including item writers, interlocutors and markers, and they produced publications and conducted seminars to help teachers to understand the new requirements and to prepare their students for the examination. They cooperated with teams from the teacher training projects the British Council was supporting, and formed networks for wider dissemination of the ideas embodied in their examinations. The examinations encouraged changes in approaches to teaching (e.g. a new focus on the skills of writing, which had been neglected in earlier times) and influenced perceptions of the type of methods and materials that were effective. The shape of the English examinations influenced the design of examinations in other languages, including the national languages, and the procedures for item writing, marking etc. were taken on by other subjects in the curriculum. Further impact included the spread of Year 12 ideas to examinations in earlier years of schooling (e.g. Year 9 or Year 10) and the eventual acceptance by universities of the Year 12 examinations for admissions purposes.

The original teams worked together for many years, contributing to assessment policy in their own contexts, providing valuable input to newly established national examination bodies, and running seminars, workshops, and in-service and pre-service courses related to the examinations they had designed and to testing principles and practice more generally. They developed new projects, securing funding from sources such as the European Union, to consolidate the work they had already done and extend it further. Individual team members were able to disseminate their ideas about good assessment practice through posts they held during and after the project (in ministries, examination boards, universities, and other educational institutions) and through the guidance they provided to other teams who were trying to establish their own examination systems elsewhere in Europe.
(Acknowledgements are due to Year 12 team members Ulle Turk [Estonia], Vita Kalnberzina [Latvia], and Zita Mazuoliene and Stase Skapiene [Lithuania] for their input to this description via personal communications, March 2015.)

This project, like the NCE project in Sri Lanka discussed above and the CET project in China discussed below, is a good example of steps taken, strongly supported by the British Council, towards the professionalisation of English language testing that began to emerge in the UK during the 1990s. To be considered professional it was necessary to develop a rigorous comprehensive testing system that covered: test specifications, extensive trialling, conducting validation studies, psychometric analysis and monitoring test washback and impact, as against just creating a test instrument per se. Alderson, Clapham and Wall at Lancaster University were leading lights in the movement to establish language testing as a more professional, scientific endeavour in contrast to the more cottage industry type approach that had hitherto been the norm in the pre-scientific days of British language testing in the first half of the 20th century (see Weir 2013 for a detailed discussion of this shift to professionalism). Similar changes were taking place at the same time at UCLES in Cambridge in the 1990s, a key British Council partner under the leadership of Mike Milanovic and Peter Hargreaves, both former British Council officers, and these are detailed in Chapter 5 in connection with the International English Language Testing System (IELTS) test.

St Petersburg Examination Project (SPEX), Russia, 1996–2001

During the first phase of the project, a joint initiative of the St Petersburg City Department of Education and the British Council, a new model of school-leaving exam for English was established in St Petersburg. The purpose of the original SPEX project was to create an exam for St Petersburg, not for the whole of Russia.

Yelena Belyaeva (2001: 32–33) described the initial project in St Petersburg:

> The project's purpose was to change the school leaving examination system from being totally school based to being centrally directed. The idea was to develop a valid and reliable system, which would improve the quality of English language teaching and learning. The project management team and the development team have successfully delivered the agreed objectives.... The newly developed examination in English allows for effective and efficient assessment of both receptive and productive skills.... The SPEX examination allows for meaningful comparisons of language proficiency and academic achievements in language learning as its level corresponds to Waystage and Vantage levels in the European examination system and KET and FCE in the UCLES scheme.

After the SPEX exam was up and functioning, the work on the national exam began with the intention of introducing a valid and reliable school-leaving examination system for English for Russia as a whole: SPEX-D (D for dissemination). Dianne Wall, working closely with John McGovern, served as a trainer and advisor to the project. John McGovern was Director of Lancaster University's Institute for English Language Education; prior to that, he held the post of English Language Officer in a number of countries while serving as a member of the British Council's Overseas Careers Service. He is currently a member of the British Council English Language Advisory Group (ELAG).

Dianne Wall comments on SPEX and the later national project SPEX-D (personal communication 25 March 2015):

SPEX and SPEX-D
The seeds were sown for the St Petersburg Examination Project (SPEX) in the mid-1990s, during discussions between the Education Committee of St Petersburg and the British Council. A full baseline study was carried out in 1995, to investigate the feasibility of such an undertaking and to provide a measure against which impact could be measured if decision-makers decided to take it forward. The study looked at areas such as the political and educational context, the social and economic context, the current policy regarding foreign languages teaching, the curriculum, existing assessment practices and the current language teaching situation. A full list of contents can be found in Wall 1996a.

The project was officially launched in 1997, when a team of ten highly qualified and experienced teachers were sent to Lancaster University for training in test design and evaluation and in project management. As was the case with the Baltic States Year 12 Project, the agreement with Lancaster included several UK training courses and a number of consultancy visits to St Petersburg. As was also true with the Baltic States Project it was clear from the beginning that the team would need to develop not only examination papers and guidelines for all stages of the design and delivery process, but would also need to create an infrastructure to support the examination in a context where there had been no centralised examining before. They were instrumental in creating the educational standards (the curriculum) upon which the examination would be based. They also created procedures for enrolling candidates, ensuring the security of the examination, printing and delivering papers to schools, and analysing and interpreting the results so that the exam informed decision-makers as well as individual candidates and schools.

By 2001 the team had succeeded in designing a workable examination system for St Petersburg and in liaising with representatives from a number of other regions in Russia to disseminate SPEX ideas and make possible the administration of the new examination further afield than just the St Petersburg region. It was around this time that the national Ministry of Education decided to develop a Unified National Examination (UNE), which would serve both school leaving and university entrance purposes. The SPEX team won the competition to design the English language component of the UNE, and thus began the second phase of the SPEX project, which came to be known as SPEX-D (D for dissemination). The British Council provided support to this development. The brief for the UNE project was similar to the brief for the original St Petersburg project but 'scaled up' multi-fold: to design a valid and reliable test for the UNE and to create, in cooperation with other educational partners, a sustainable infrastructure at regional and federal levels. Key to the achievement of these targets was the SPEX team itself – mainly the original team members, who had by now developed a great deal of expertise in testing, training and stakeholder communications, but also colleagues (many of whom were members of other Council-supported projects) they had trained in other regions of the country.

Yelena Prokhorova, the head of the SPEX and SPEX-D teams, identifies three main types of impact: impact on English language teaching, impact on the development of language testing in Russia and impact on higher education in the country. The impact on English language teaching included:
- The influence of SPEX test specifications on language teaching goals, e.g. there is now a focus on all four language skills.
- SPEX programmes for training examiners and teachers influenced the nature of professional development for English teachers, so that it is now more practical and trainee-oriented.
- Under the SPEX-D framework more than 300 examiners gained qualifications in 45 regions of the country.
- More than 1,000 English language teachers became familiar with the main concepts of external assessment.

The impact on language testing included:
- The development of a valid and reliable examination and set of procedures which was approved for all regions of the country, and adopted for the French, German and Spanish languages.
- Many of the procedures developed with the SPEX project – test design, item writing, approaches to marking writing and speaking, statistical analysis, and training of examination personnel – have been adopted by other examinations in the curriculum, including the Russian language.

The impact on higher education has occurred through the transfer of most of the original SPEX specialists to tertiary-level assessment. They are now working with one of the leading universities in the Russian Federation to design an in-house quality examination system with evidence-based links to the Common European Framework of Reference.

(Yelena Prokhorova's contribution to the above retrospective account is gratefully acknowledged.)

In 2002 the Ministry of Education and Science conducted a tender for a new model of a Unified National Exam (UNE) for English. The British Council jointly developed product won the tender. In SPEX-D, the SPEX team applied their expertise to developing a national exam, based on their experience of working on the regional exam they had produced for St Petersburg. The St Petersburg team worked directly with the Ministry in designing and rolling out the new national exam. At the request of the Ministry and the Federal Testing Centre the British Council continued supporting the training of Russian examiners and item writers and was consulted by the Ministry on further development of the exam.

The project achieved the following outputs: a valid and reliable examination system in English for use throughout Russia, which was rolled out in 2009 by the Ministry; a skilled team of item writers and teacher trainers; an exam support system developed: training programmes for examiners, interlocutors, and test administrators, and a teacher training programme. The number of regions taking the exam grew year by year. The team trained by the British Council provided ongoing expertise, assisting with further revisions of the exam and delivering teacher training.

Walter, West and Millrood in their review of ELT projects in Russia (2006) concluded:

The project was successful both in meeting its original goals and in its wider impact during the dissemination process and its gradual adoption across a growing number of regions. Not only has the team created an examination format which has largely been adopted for the UNE in English and other foreign languages, and created teams of trained personnel to develop and support the examination as it has spread to more regions, but the syllabus of the exam seems to be having a wide impact on the approach to language teaching across Russia. The feedback that the reviewers received from Russian beneficiaries at all levels was overwhelmingly positive.

Contributing to the modernisation of national English language examination systems, especially in the case of global superpowers such as Russia (SPEX), China (CET and TEM) and India (CBSE project India 1988–1997: see CBSE-ELT 1997 and Mathew 1997), is a good example of the creation of the soft power we discussed in Chapter 1. The creation of English language examinations at a national level clearly helps fix the study of English into a school system and has other spin-offs, not least the acknowledgement of British expertise and British ways of doing things in EL testing.

Secondary and Technical Education Project (STEP), Mozambique, 1997–2002

The British Council, in partnership with the Mozambique Ministry of Education and the University of London, managed a major five-year British government funded project to improve the quality of English language teaching and learning in secondary and technical schools, at national level in Mozambique (Bentall 2003). The project had considerable impact on secondary English provision in the country. It successfully developed a team of well-qualified managers in the Ministry of Education and Provincial Directorates of Education; revised secondary English syllabuses for Grades 7 to 11 and commissioned suitable textbooks adapted to the Mozambican content; set up a certificated Diploma Course validated by the Institute of Education, University of London and an Access Course for less-qualified teachers; and established English Language Resource Centres, connected to the internet, in all ten provinces of the country.

By the end of the project approximately 150 teachers had been trained to diploma level and over 300 had benefited from the Access Course. A series of secondary-level textbooks was adapted by the British ELT publisher Macmillan to fit the new syllabuses, and for the first time all students at secondary level had access to the books and materials they needed to achieve success in English.

In the area of assessment Rita Green, a leading testing expert sponsored by the British Council, provided consultancy expertise in 2000–2001 to assist in the creation of instruments and a methodology for obtaining data on the English language performance of secondary school students across the ten provinces of Mozambique. This was followed by analyses of the gathered data, the findings from which were summarised in a handbook (Angela Martins and Rita Green 2001) targeted primarily at secondary school teachers of English. In addition to test specifications for Grades 10 and 12, guidelines for assessing both written and oral performance including the provision of sample scripts and sample oral activities, were provided.

The aims of the handbook were to:

- increase awareness of the procedures used to assess students' English language abilities at the 10th and 12th grades
- report on students' English performance during the years of 1998–2000
- describe the rationale behind English examinations by providing examples of the types of tasks students in grades 10 and 12 will meet
- provide information regarding the types of skills/strategies that students at Grades 10 and 12 should be able to exhibit
- give guidance on how the written composition should be graded (BC, http://www.teachingenglish.org.uk/elt-projects/step-project-mozambique).

Rita Green (personal communication 31 March 2015) commented:

The Secondary and Technical English Project (STEP), Mozambique
The Secondary and Technical English Project (STEP) was initiated in 1997 between the National Directorate of Secondary Education under the Ministry of Education and the Department for International Development (DFID), UK with a view to bringing about quality improvements in education in the country as a whole. The five-year project included work on teacher training, syllabus development for secondary schools (Grades 8–12) and established a network of Resource Centres run by Provincial English Advisers (PEAs).

During the course of the project, it became clear that the Ministry of Education had little, if any, reliable data on the performance of secondary school students on the final examinations at the end of the 10th and 12th years. As a consequence, work started in 2000 on creating a database using results from the 1998, 1999 and 2000 test administrations. With the help of the PEAs, 7,000 cases were collected from across Mozambique's ten provinces, detailing students' performances on the final reading, writing and oral tests as well as their continuous assessment grades. Further information about the type of student, gender, school location and teachers' qualifications was also gathered.

Findings from the database were subsequently shared with teachers throughout the country in the 'Examination Handbook' publication (see below). One of the most important results showed that the writing test appeared to be far too difficult with most students scoring 1 or less. Feedback from teachers' questionnaires supported this conclusion and also revealed requests for guidelines on how to mark and create both writing and speaking tasks. In light of the data collection it was recommended that new writing and speaking scales be constructed and guidance on how to develop appropriate tasks should be provided.

The 'Examination Handbook', published by the Ministry of Education and developed in the later stages of the project, focused on making the examination system clearer and more accessible to all. It did this by describing in detail the rationale behind the examinations and by providing examples of the types of tasks students in those grades would meet. It also discussed the types of skills/strategies that students at these grades should be able to exhibit.

Until the project began, secondary school teachers in Mozambique had received little guidance in how to devise and grade writing and speaking tasks for the final examinations. As a consequence many had to rely purely on their own ability and experience. In order to standardise this situation, the handbook provided a range of sample speaking and writing tasks together with newly developed rating scales. Guidance on how to use

70 *Assessing English on the Global Stage*

the scales using a range of sample scripts showing which bands had been awarded together with justifications were provided in the handbook.

A concrete product from a project is an outcome much favoured by funding agencies. In this case it took the form of an examination handbook, so that, even when personnel moved on, the wisdom generated survived. Carefully documented procedures made the initial investment worthwhile and additionally benefited future cohorts of language teachers.

Examination Reform Teacher Support Project, Hungary, 1998–2002

Karmen Pizorn and Edit Nagy (2009: 193–202) describe the problematic situation as regards school-leaving examination results prior to this British Council supported exam reform project. One criticism had been that it was not possible to compare the English language examinations locally, regionally or nationally. Pizorn and Nagy also felt the existing focus on grammar and translation did not accord with current good practice in language teaching and had poor washback in the classroom. Teachers were not trained in how to rate examination performance or how to carry out the oral examinations. In addition Pizorn and Nagy were concerned with the lack of external monitoring and the absence of any analysis of test results.

In May 1998 a British Council funded project to support the Ministry of Education was officially launched with the aim of developing a multilevel, standardised, valid and reliable school-leaving examination in English for the Hungarian School-leaving Examination Reform project. Lancaster University was once again involved, with a leading role played by Professor Charles Alderson, who was seconded to the project from 1998 to 2000 as the British Council Adviser, Budapest (see http://www.lancaster.ac.uk/fass/projects/examreform/Pages/Publications.html, Alderson et al. 2000 and Alderson et al. 2004).

The British Council's own project website clearly reflects not only the priorities of the Hungary Examination Reform Teacher Support Project, but also the importance the Council attaches to language assessment that is appropriate to its users and in its impacts:

> The ultimate goal of examination reform was to encourage, to foster and to bring about change in the way English is taught and learned in Hungary.

Project Philosophy: Testing is about ensuring that those tests and examinations which society decides it needs, for whatever purpose, are the best possible, that they represent the best in not only testing practice, but in teaching practice, and that the tests reflect the aspirations of professional language teachers. Anything less is a betrayal of teachers and learners, as is a refusal to engage in testing….

The Project produced the following documents before 2002, when they were handed over to the Ministry of Education. The documents are available as research materials.

- Detailed Requirements and Test Specifications (for research purposes)
- Guidelines for Item Writers: Reading and Use of English l Speaking l Writing l Listening
- Scales for the assessment of Speaking and Writing
- Interlocutors' Frame

The Lancaster University website provides more detail of this British Council project (www.lancaster.ac.uk/fass/projects/examreform/Pages/Projects.html), which could well serve as a comprehensive blueprint of objectives for British Council projects of this kind. It lists how project members were trained by internationally recognised experts in:

- modern testing principles and techniques including test construction
- item writing
- evaluation
- basic statistics.

The project developed:

- a rigorous algorithm of Item Production (item commission, revision, item vetting, piloting, calibration) to ensure the quality of the tasks
- procedures for test development and test administration
- trialling procedures for tasks administered to large samples of secondary school students all over the country with results statistically analysed
- training materials and courses, for raters of spoken and written performance, for Interlocutors and Assessors (Speaking exam)
- benchmarking and standardisation sessions in order to set the levels of the tasks

- a useful resource for those interested in testing, by publication of the three-volume study *English Language Education in Hungary* (1999–2001) that documents its developmental work
- testing procedures that met modern European standards, and a large number of piloted and calibrated tasks.

The website also describes how the British Council, true to its mission, decided to make these calibrated tasks (tested in about 250 Hungarian secondary schools with 4,000 students nationwide) available to a wider public in the book series *Into Europe: Prepare for Modern English Exams* in order to help teachers and students understand the levels and demands of modern European examinations. There are four books covering the four skills, listening, reading, speaking and writing. They contain:

- tasks with keys
- explanations of basic principles of testing and good practice
- guidance on modern test task design
- insight into modern assessment practice
- useful guidelines for designing tests for classroom usage and exam preparation.

However, Pizorn and Nagy (2009: 195–202) express some reservations about the project. They argue that although the project achieved its technical objectives: training teams of test developers in core activities, establishing an item production system, developing an item bank across the proficiency range and developing courses to help teachers prepare for new tests, because of micro-politics, the project's achievements were not implemented by the system. Their view is that individuals in positions of political power, who perhaps lacked the expertise to make the major changes they did to the proposed examination system, vitiated the manifold achievements of this testing project.

Evaluation of the micro-politics of individuals in each project we refer to is clearly beyond the scope of this chapter (see Alderson 2009 for such dedicated micro-analysis). Our history operates, in the main, at the broader macro-level in our description of the Council's global involvement in English language testing. Nevertheless this Hungarian example provides a useful caveat that the micro-politics of relationships have the potential to impact negatively as well as positively on a project's success. Social and political factors can indeed determine the impact of a project. It has thus always been part of British Council project planning, implementation and evaluation to attempt, calling upon its usually comprehensive background knowledge and experience of the country, institutions and key individuals involved, to predict and take account of key aspects of the social and political context.

Examination Reform Teacher Support Project participants we consulted were at pains to stress the positive outcomes of this project and its impressive technical achievements. Ildikó Csépes was from 1998 to 2006 a member of the Hungarian Examinations Reform Teacher Support Project of the British Council (item writer, Core Team member, materials developer and trainer at the Oral Examiner Training Course). In a personal communication (15 February 2014), she shared her experience of the project, including her positive view on the British Council's contribution to the project and its longer-term effects:

> **The Hungarian Exams Reform Teacher Support Project**
> This British Council project was a unique endeavour as it managed to achieve something more fundamental than it was originally launched for. At the outset, the main goal of the project was to design a new, two-level school-leaving examination in English that was expected to meet the highest professional standards by rigorously monitoring all the stages of test development, which was masterminded by the project advisor, Professor Charles Alderson. Unfortunately, this goal was only partially met as only the test specifications were adopted by the Educational Authority in the end, but all the other materials (test items and examiner training materials) were published in the form of a series of books called Into Europe. The four volumes are now available online for free downloading, thus anyone can benefit from the expertise and resources of the project. Although the school-leaving examination in English that the British Council project was linked to has been in operation for ten years, it is probably not this aspect for which the project created its landmark. Without doubt the most beneficial outcome of the whole project was that it functioned as a catalyst. Thanks to the extensive training and experimental nature of the project, language testing as a field became professionalised in Hungary, and a cadre of testing specialists were trained to become responsible later for all kinds of language testing related activities across the country, ranging from test development for accredited language examination providers to teacher training in language assessment at tertiary level. Besides a few academics, those who joined the project at its early stages were mostly newcomers to the field of language testing, relatively young and motivated teachers, therefore the British Council provided ample opportunity for them both to develop practical skills in test development and to gain insights into the principles and the theoretical background to language testing. The expertise they were offered at that time was highly appreciated and cutting-edge.

The project members got trained as item writers, item moderators, raters, assessors as well as test analysts. Furthermore, with careful guidance from external advisors, the project members were allowed to develop an examination model from scratch, which meant that they could learn invaluable lessons from all the trials and errors that they would hardly have been able to experience in their own home contexts. The strong commitment and good team spirit helped the project members bond and several other research projects were set up later thanks to the professional network that had been created. Some of this network is still alive, as many of the former team members' friendships have lasted ever since. While the project was still running, the expertise in test development and examiner training was disseminated among Hungarian secondary school teachers of English at summer schools and teacher development events organised by the British Council and even on an international scale at the EALTA conference in Kraków in 2006 and in Sitges in 2007 in the form of pre-conference workshops. Some project members wrote test preparation materials for the school-leaving examination in English, while some others saw testing as a new avenue for professional development and started publishing on testing and even did their PhDs on testing. Some project members became members of the Hungarian Accreditation Board for Foreign Languages, which in turn led to increased professional standards prescribed for state accredited language examinations too. Many of those who run language testing courses in English teacher training courses at universities nowadays were once linked to the project in one way or another, which probably means that the British Council project still gets mentioned for its role in the development of the school-leaving examination and for other achievements, reflected mainly in its publications. The Into Europe series has been firmly acknowledged as a useful resource and is reported to be used outside Hungary as well, especially for training purposes in language assessment. For assessing Speaking and Writing, the Handbooks are an exceptionally rich resource that illustrate good practice and highlight pitfalls in task design. The sample performances in the form of recorded mock exams as well as students' scripts provide unfailing evidence for the claims made about task design principles, ratings or levels.

As with many other British Council sponsored testing projects, a clear commitment to the training of indigenous cadres to become specialists in the field meant the legacies of such projects were often just as important as, if not more important than, any achievements during the lifetime of the project itself. The series of handbooks produced by the project were also a valuable legacy in Hungary and beyond.

Projects with a specialised language purpose: English for Specific Purposes tests

In the second half of the 20th century there was considerable expansion in international scientific, technical and economic activity conducted through the medium of English. This was matched by a growing interest in the linguistic aspects of the English associated with these specific domains of use (Hutchinson and Waters 1987: 6). The 1960s are generally viewed as the dawn of interest in English for Specific Purposes (ESP) approaches, though there were clearly traces in earlier centuries (Halliday, McIntosh and Strevens 1964, Swales 1988, Dudley-Evans and St John 1998: 19, and Howatt and Widdowson 2004).

Dudley-Evans and St John (1998: 4–5), identify three 'absolute' characteristics of these ESP approaches to language teaching:

- meet specific needs of the learner
- make use of the underlying methodology and activities of the discipline it serves
- focus on the language, skills, discourse, and genre appropriate to these activities.

They see the late 1970s and early 1980s as the period when the ESP approach was consolidated. Hutchinson and Waters (1987: 7) identify how the Oil Crises of the 1970s resulted in oil-rich countries especially in the Gulf region opening their doors to western knowledge. As it was mainly scientific and technical knowledge that had to be transferred, ESP emerged as the most appropriate discipline to facilitate this. *The ESP Journal* was first published in 1980, confirming ESP's coming of age as an academic discipline.

The areas addressed by an ESP approach would continue to grow and ESP came to be seen as embracing the English used for academic purposes (EAP) as well as for occupational purposes (EOP) (Dudley-Evans and St John 1998: 5, Hutchinson and Waters: 1987: 6, and Robinson 1991).

The remainder of this chapter deals with how the British Council sought to spread British influence abroad by supporting indigenous ESP test development projects in both academic and occupational English, from the heyday of ESP in the early 1980s right up till the present day.

Improving university-level academic English assessment

Academic English language skills are essential if students are to perform effectively in English-medium university/college contexts, and to engage in study with relative independence and adequate comprehension. Greater precision in academic English tests enables academic institutions to target their resources in ways that bring maximum benefit to students, both pre- and post-entry.

All students need appropriate English language skills to benefit fully from English-medium tertiary-level education. Furthermore, if students with inadequate language proficiency are admitted, the economic costs to the institutions and the negative social and personal impact on the students can be enormous (Banerjee 2003 provides empirical data on the severity of these costs). Soundly conceived Academic English tests provide accurate and valid information to universities for making access decisions and determining the length and nature of any remedial language instruction required.

Boğaziçi University, Turkey, EAP test development project, 1982–1984 et seq.

Arthur Hughes was appointed as a Key English Language Teaching (KELT) Officer on a two-year British Council contract from 1982 to 1984 (originally as a consultant to the project but later Director of the Testing Office and a member of the Academic Council of YADYOK). He was to help develop a new EAP test at one of the premier English-medium state universities in Turkey. Hughes spent these two years helping to set up a testing unit there, on secondment from Reading University. He worked with Turkish colleagues to produce a new criterion referenced proficiency test (reading, listening and writing components) that would be used on entry to determine whether remedial help for English was needed in a foundation year set up for this purpose. The test would also be employed at the end of Foreign Languages School training to determine whether students possessed sufficient English for academic studies in Boğaziçi University (see Hughes 1988).

The Boğaziçi University test was a seminal early example of a new breed of criterion referenced communicative tests (see ELTS discussion in Chapter 4, and on TEAP in Weir 1983) which was based on target situation needs analysis, i.e. it was modelled on those academic study skills activities students would have to cope with in the first year of their studies (see Chapter 3). The 'real-life' approach was mocked by American testers at this time who were heavily constrained by the US psychometric tradition (see Bachman 1990: Chapter 8). Ironically the pursuit of such situational and interactional authenticity has now become the approach of choice of leading American testers as in the new TOEFL iBT (https://www.ets.org/toefl/ibt/about).

A seminar supported by Boğaziçi University and the British Council was held at the University in 1984 and the proceedings were published as *Testing English Beyond the High School* edited by Arthur Hughes and Selma Bozok (Bozok and Hughes 1987).

An account of the EAP test development project can be found in Hughes (1988), a volume based on the proceedings of the conference at Boğaziçi University on tests developed for use in assessing academic English.

Consultants were subsequently regularly funded by the British Council to visit Boğaziçi University to help maintain and develop the testing system. Cyril Weir paid several visits and Arthur Hughes has also been a frequent visitor there over the years on British Council sponsored visits.

Arthur Hughes (personal communication July 2014) provided the following information:

Boğaziçi University, Turkey, EAP Test Development
1. Students were [and still are, I believe] accepted by BU regardless of their English ability. The *test is first administered on arrival*. Those who fail it enter a preparatory year of English training, at the end of which they take the test again. At the time of my arrival the current testing procedures allowed entry to undergraduate and graduate courses for ever increasing numbers of students with insufficient English. Much teaching was being carried out in Turkish.
2. The test *did not include a speaking* component. Practicality was the problem.
3. The test caused the *curriculum to be completely revised and more appropriate materials written* [backwash].
4. The *prep year was extended* for weaker students, giving them a better chance of reaching the necessary standard of English.
5. The test in essentially the same form is *still in place more than 30 years later*.
6. Many subsequent *visits have been funded by BU* [sustainability].

Egyptian Universities' National Academic Reading Test, 1990–1995

The Testing Unit of the ESP Centre in Alexandria University was founded under the inspirational leadership of Tony Lilley OBE, a British Council Key English Language Teaching (KELT) Officer with EFL experience in the Czech Republic, Portugal and Libya, who worked extensively in Egypt as head of the British Council Aid project based in the University of Alexandria. The project aimed at developing teacher qualifications and expertise in the area of English for specific purposes at university level throughout the country, and led to the establishment of several autonomous ESP centres at Egyptian universities. During his 16 years in this post Lilley helped develop the English for Specific Purposes (ESP) Centre at Alexandria University to become the leading centre for ESP in the Middle East.

Lilley and his team were responsible for the development and validation of a prototype for a national, university entrance, reading test. Several members of the Testing Unit there were subsequently sponsored by the British Council to undertake doctorates in testing and evaluation in the UK supervised by Weir, one of the consultants to the project. One of these students, Hanan Khalifa, in later life Director of Research at Cambridge English Language Assessment, based her doctoral thesis on the development and validation of this national reading test (Khalifa 1997).

Tony Lilley wrote as follows (personal communication, January 2014):

> **Egyptian Universities' National Academic Reading Test**
>
> ...the important thing is that the Egyptian University regulations were changed as a result of the project and precedents were established. Following on from the Alexandria model, other Egyptian universities were able to set up (and did) their own ESP centres and programmes and tests. By the end of the project in 1996, thousands of Egyptian students had benefited from ESP programmes, and a large number of Egyptian ESP teachers had been given both practical and academic training up to MA level. Much of this happened in situ, but many also were funded (by the ODA/BC) to go the UK universities for both MA and PhD studies.... These were high calibre people who would not otherwise have had the chance to realise their full potential. A lot of goodwill accrued at the highest levels towards the project and towards the UK (despite the fact the British effort was much smaller than the USAID one). Many of those trained now occupy senior positions in Egyptian universities and other tertiary institutions

such as the Arab Maritime Academy. Some of them occupy senior positions elsewhere. Accordingly, I believe that the objectives were realised.

The test was an early example of a *real-life* approach to testing where, like Arthur Hughes' work in Turkey, target situation needs analysis informed the specification of operations and conditions for academic reading in Egyptian university settings. Later Khalifa and Weir (2009) would update this approach in *Examining Reading,* but the cognitive processes (Chapter 3) and the contextual parameters (Chapter 4) of this later publication are essentially more well-informed versions of the operations and performance conditions they had sought to address in 1995 in the Egyptian National Academic Reading Test. This was another project, like those in China that we turn to next, which informed the development of the socio-cognitive approach to language testing (see Weir 2005).

The College English Test (CET) Validation Study, PRC, 1991–1995

Barbara Wickham (1995: 3), formerly the Director of the British Council Shanghai office in the PRC, describes the extent of the British Council's involvement in ELT projects in China during the 1990s:

> During the 1993/94 academic year, there are thirty ELT projects in twenty-four institutions in sixteen cities, employing thirty specialists.... The typical project life is three to five years and as some finish others come on line, producing a rolling programme. In addition to a maximum of two specialists at any one time, project inputs typically include training or attachments in Britain for Chinese counterpart lecturers to enable them to take over the running of the project after British inputs have finished, and consultancy visits as necessary.

The British Council in China played a major role in securing funding for these projects from DFID/ODA and helped administer and manage the professional inputs from the UK (see above). They provided support for British experts involved in working in situ over extended periods of time.

From 1991 to 1995 the British Council provided assistance to the College English Test (CET) developers based in Shanghai Jiao Tong University (SJTU) to carry out a validation study of this important test now taken by over 18 million students each year in the PRC. The CET was taken at two levels (Band 4 and Band 6). These bands reflect the number of semesters a student has studied English (i.e. Band 4 is taken at the end of the second year of the undergraduate programme, and Band 6 at the end of the third year). The Band 4 test had become the main accepted indicator of college students' English proficiency. Students had to obtain a pass at Band 4 in order to graduate from university.

The first test validation project was accompanied by a second research project in SJTU looking at other aspects of CE teaching: syllabi, textbooks and teaching methodologies. The results of the projects provided a broad-based curriculum development specification for the first two years of the non-English major undergraduate programme (Wickham 1995: 4).

Jin Yan, the current Head of the CET Committee and a leading member of the validation team, described the CET study as follows (personal communication May 2014):

The College English Test (CET) Validation Study

The CET was designed in the mid-1980s and launched in 1987 by the CET Design Group (the CET Committee since 1994) for tertiary institutions in China with a view to promoting the implementation of the national college English teaching syllabus. By the early 1990s, the CET had established a system of item development, test delivery, scoring and score reporting. To prove the accountability of the test and improve its quality and services, the CET Design group proposed a joint validation study with the British Council.

In the 1990s, test validation was a new area of research in applied linguistics in China, which came out of the need for improving the accountability of large-scale standardised tests. The British Council's major contribution to the CET validation project was the professional input it provided in the form of multiple visits by specialist testing experts from the University of Reading, including Cyril Weir and Tony Woods, to help local partners with the research design, data collection, data analysis, and writing up the project report. The local project team, i.e. the CET Design Group, also benefited from the professional training they received during the process of the validation project, especially during their numerous visits to the UK sponsored by the British Council. Dr Jin Yan, the current head of the CET Committee, spent a year at the Testing and Evaluation Unit, Centre for Applied Language Studies (CALS), University of Reading, working on the project, and other CET board members such as Professor Yang Huizhong from Shanghai Jiao Tong University, former Chair of the CET Committee, Professor Liu Hongzhang from Shanghai Jiao Tong University, and Professor Zhang Yanqiu from Beijing University, came on several extended visits to CALS to work on project related matters.

The study paid attention to all aspects of test validity and collected various types of evidence, providing the basis for proving that the test was a valid and reliable measure of college students' listening, reading and writing proficiency in English. The study made suggestions for improvements in task type, score reporting, and the minimum requirements for writing. The study also suggested that new tests be designed for tertiary institutions in China to assess oral proficiency and advanced competence of reading in English for Academic Purposes. This validation study was the first of its kind in China since large-scale standardised language tests had come into being in the mid-1980s. Through collaborative research, the study contributed significantly to the growth and development of professional language testing expertise in China. A full history of the validation project can be found in Yang and Weir (1998).

As with many other British Council sponsored testing projects, a clear commitment to the training of indigenous cadres to become specialists in the field meant the legacies of such projects were often just as, if not more important than any achievements during the lifetime of the project itself.

The Test for English Majors (TEM) Validation Study, PRC, 1993–1996

As well as the validation study of the CET used with undergraduates, from 1993 to 1996 the British Council sponsored and supported a similar study on a test designed specifically for English major students at Shanghai International Studies University (SISU). The object of this substantive project was to validate the Test for English Majors (TEM) and to improve it where necessary. The immediate purpose was to review the existing TEM 4 and TEM 8 English language tests in terms of content, construct, predictive and concurrent validity and to establish their reliability through statistical analysis of the test data. By developing enhanced procedures for item writing and marker standardisation, it was hoped that future tests would better reflect the English language performance of the test takers. The project's long-term aim was to improve the positive washback effects on ELT teaching and learning in Chinese universities.

The Final Report on the TEM project (Zou, Green and Weir 1997) describes how:

> ...the two national ELT syllabuses for English language majors, which were drawn up under the auspices of the State Education Commission of China (SEdC), were published in 1989 and 1990 respectively. They were the first of their kind in P.R. China. The former related to the foundation stage, i.e.

the first two years of a degree programme in English language and literature; the latter was for the third and fourth years of the same programme.

Their primary purpose was to serve as guidelines for educational decision-makers and teachers alike when it comes to the development of ELT curriculum, ELT programmes and ELT materials in various universities across China. To serve this end, the two teaching syllabuses established specific teaching requirements and English language proficiency standards for each of the four years in an ELT undergraduate programme for language and literature majors. It was hoped that by standardizing teaching across China, English language teaching would be enhanced, and that this, in turn, would result in the improvement of the English language proficiency of the students.

As TEM 4 and TEM 8 were originally regarded as a means to check the implementation of the national teaching syllabuses, it was agreed that the test content should reflect the requirements in the syllabuses. In view of this consideration, test content included listening, reading and writing for TEM 4 and listening, reading, writing and translation for TEM 8. Although speaking is given equal importance in the teaching syllabuses, it was decided to defer the testing of this skill for practical reasons.

The objectives of the TEM test were: to evaluate English language teaching and learning at the end of the foundation stage and at the end of a four year undergraduate programme...and to bring about beneficial washback effects on teaching and learning (Zou et al. 1997: 1). TEM 4 was first administered in 1990 and TEM 8 in 1991. By 1995 13,675 candidates were taking TEM 4 and 6,325 TEM 8.

Although TEM 4 and TEM 8 were welcomed by universities across China as a means of assessing ELT teaching and learning, the tests were by no means free from imperfection. It was felt that they fell short of standards required by international tests, which were expected to demonstrate sound validity and high reliability. For example, investigations had not been conducted into the validity of the tests; no statistical measures had been taken to ensure the reliability of the tests; there was insufficient marker training; a team of item writers with experience and expertise had not been established. These problems rendered the tests vulnerable to both public and professional criticism, and therefore posed potential threats to the validity, reliability and sustainability of the TEM tests.

In view of the above situation, at the annual meeting of the National ELT Committee, which came into existence in the autumn of 1992, it was decided that measures should be taken to validate the TEM tests so as to build up their strength and profile. As both TEM 4 and TEM 8 had, by then, come to be based in Shanghai International Studies University (SISU), SISU was nominated to carry out the validation work. It was hoped that through a series of validation measures, the TEM tests would improve their image as national tests, and establish their authority as a means of assessing the English language proficiency of the test takers.

A visit was paid to SISU in Oct. 1992 by Dr C.J. Weir, who was then consultant on the College English Test (CET) validation project in Shanghai Jiao Tong University, to discuss matters related to test validation. During the discussions, it became clear that due to the existing conditions of the TEM tests and their predicted future roles, it was imperative that TEM undergo the necessary procedures of validation, and that a formal proposal should be made to the British Council for a test validation project so as to enlist the required expertise of British testing specialists crucial to the forthcoming validation study. Following Dr Weir's visit to SISU in Oct. 1992, a project framework was drawn up and submitted to the British Council office in Beijing. The project framework spells out both the immediate and long-term objectives of the project, its interim and final outputs, the proposed monitoring procedures, and resources required. The proposal for the TEM validation project was approved by the British Council in April 1993. It was scheduled to start in September 1993 and finish in June 1996.

Rita Green was the BC-funded resident specialist from the UK on the project from September 1993 to June 1995, and as the account of the project above shows, the Council was involved both through HQ in London and through its Beijing Council office. Rita Green was based at Shanghai International Studies University (SISU) where TEM was run. She performed a valuable role in helping to create efficient systems for the development, analysis and monitoring of TEM and in producing the instruments for the validation study, collecting and analysing the data and writing up the research report on the project.

As a result of the project activities, full specifications for TEM were produced; sample tests were written; item writer training packs were established; a test development system was put in place; appropriate mark schemes were developed, standardisation and monitoring procedures were evolved, administrative procedures for running the test were introduced; a computer-based system for statistical analysis was constructed; an annual report became the norm; test certificates were now available; in-house expertise in test development and statistical analysis was developed. None of these features were present in TEM in 1993 but all were in place by 1996. In all, a full test production system was set up. The validity study has indicated both teachers' and students' general satisfaction with the TEM tests, in particular TEM 4.

The project bears comparison with what was happening in Cambridge in the 1990s where Mike Milanovic and his colleagues were making similar efforts to professionalise a language testing system (see Chapter 5 for details). Those responsible for Cambridge examinations had rather neglected the demands of test validity before the arrival of Peter Hargreaves and Milanovic in the late 1980s. The TEM project was a clear reminder to the field that one did not need to be an industrial-scale enterprise to address validity demands in test production. Rita Green and eight Chinese colleagues were able, with various forms of support from the British Council, to operationalise robust procedures that were an example to other countries in the region. The validation instruments were also of use to others wishing to monitor or evaluate their own tests.

In addition to the resident expert, Rita Green, the project had two external BC-sponsored consultants: Cyril Weir and Tony Woods, both from Reading University. Weir visited the project in 1993, 1994 and 1995, and Woods in 1993 and 1995. Shen Zou the project leader (1996) and her colleagues Zhu Yanhua and Li Huilin (1993), Chen Hansheng, Zhang Yixing and Huang Suhua (1994), Li Jian and Zhang Yanli (1995) visited Reading University for periods up to several months during the project, under the auspices of the British Council, to participate in specific courses that were designed for them in various aspects of testing and to work with their British counterparts on the validation study, including the final writing of the report in 1996.

The final TEM Test Validation Project Report was produced by Shen Zou in 1996 and published the following year (Zou, Green and Weir 1997).

Shen Zou wrote as follows (personal communication May 2014):

The Test for English Majors (TEM) Validation Study
Nearly 20 years have passed since the completion of the TEM validation project (1993–1996), which was supported by the British Council and was based in Shanghai International Studies University (SISU). Looking back on the years in between, I feel very pleased that the language assessment expertise the Chinese counterparts acquired during the project has enabled us to move further in test construction and research. Some of the original members of the project team are still active in test development and research. Perhaps I myself am a typical example. I was then the head of the BC-SISU project, and I am now responsible for developing and researching into TEM 4 and 8 tests, which have reached an annual test population of 260,000 and 210,000 respectively. The professional know-how gained during the days of the project has proved extremely useful in our persistent efforts to improve test validity and maintain relatively high quality standards. For instance, in 2005 we began another round of TEM

test validation ourselves, using the experience gained from the TEM validation project. This year, we have started another TEM revision project and I believe the knowledge and skills learned from the BC-SISU project will, once again, be of enormous help in our current validation endeavours.

In addition, the impact of the project can also be felt in teaching and research. My university (SISU) is now one of the few universities in P.R. China, which can offer a PhD programme in language assessment. In the past 15 years or so, more than 30 PhD students have studied on the programme, whose doctoral research has covered a wide range of assessment related topics in the Chinese context, and has thus contributed to the growing body of language testing research in China. Some of them have, after completing their doctoral study, become teacher-researchers in language assessment in their own universities or have gone abroad for post-doc study. They also actively participate at national and international conferences on language testing. Thus, the original small project team has grown into a big one, and what is more important is these people help disseminate the language testing know-how which was originally obtained during the project.

The TEM validation project is over, but we believe its impact continues in our test construction, teaching and research.

Rita Green (personal communication 9 April 2015) added:

Before this project started, test development work aimed at university students majoring in English was not wholly based in Shanghai. Teams had been established in such places as Luoyang's PLA Institute and in Guangzhou's Foreign Language University amongst others. Once SISU was given the sole responsibility these teams continued to contribute and regularly sent teachers to take part in the grading exercises (writing and translation tasks). This network of test developers made the TEM Development Project a truly national initiative and proved very useful in both disseminating information and spreading expertise thus creating a national testing network. This inclusive approach is, I feel, a crucial factor in the potential success (and acceptance) of a project's objectives and is a practice I have tried to emulate wherever feasible in other test development projects.

... During my current visits to China, the TEM 4 and TEM 8 tests are quoted when comparing the difficulty level of other examinations or to define a student's ability.

Note in the retrospective comments of the project head Shen Zhou, as well as in those of Rita Green, the *longer-term* value of such projects as TEM, as the expertise they help develop spreads its influence to later related projects and programmes. This kind of impact is a key aim of the British Council in most of its ELT project support.

The Advanced English Reading Test Project, PRC, 1995–1998

One recommendation arising from the CET validation study reported above was the need to examine further the possibility of developing a specialised English test of reading for academic purposes. Cyril Weir was appointed by the British Council as the Senior UK Consultant to the Advanced Reading Test in English for Academic Purposes (AERT) project, China, in 1995. The British Council sponsored and supported the project, which was again based in Shanghai Jiao Tong University under the auspices of the CET committee. The project resulted in a publication for Cambridge University Press (Weir, Yang and Yan 2000).

Jin Yan, the current head of the CET, describes the project and the part she played in it (personal communication May 2014):

> **The Advanced English Reading Test**
> In tertiary institutions in China, students who have completed their compulsory English education at the foundation stage, i.e. the first two years of English courses, are required to further improve their ability to read in English for Academic Purposes (EAP). To encourage the teaching of EAP reading, the CET Committee proposed a joint project for developing assessment procedures to measure EAP reading with the British Council. During the project, the British Council provided substantial professional and financial support to help local partners with test design, item development, piloting and revision, and test validation. A number of staff from the Testing and Evaluation Unit, Centre for Applied Language Studies (CALS), University of Reading (Green, Porter and Weir) worked on the project with the Chinese members of the development group. Two doctoral candidates from Shanghai Jiao Tong University were sponsored by the Council to spend one year at CALS for the development of test specifications and the prototype test. Under the joint supervision of their Chinese supervisor Professor Yang Huizhong and the Council sponsored project consultant Cyril Weir, the candidates completed their doctoral dissertations successfully based on the research conducted for the project.
>
> These empirical studies have lent support to a componential view of the construct of reading and produced evidence supporting the claim that the AERT was a valid and reliable EAP reading test which was fair to all students and did not discriminate against anybody whatever their discipline. What's more important, the AERT has provided a blueprint for the development of academic reading in English in China because the development

of the test has led to a clear specification of what is involved in EAP reading both in terms of activities and in terms of the performance conditions that must be addressed in text selection and test administration. This is a major step forward and has facilitated the preparation of course materials for teaching EAP reading, not only in China but also in other countries where English is taught and learnt as a foreign language.

The socio-cognitive framework, first comprehensively elaborated in Weir's (2005) *Language Testing and Validation,* has its roots in earlier academic monographs by Weir (see *Communicative Language Testing* (1990) and *Understanding and Developing Language Tests* (1993)), which arose out of this earlier collaborative work by Weir in China, first as senior UK consultant on the national College English Test (Yang and Weir 1998). It developed further in his work on the Test for English Majors (Zou, Green and Weir 1997) and the Advanced English Reading Test (Weir, Yang and Yan 2000). Working with Chinese colleagues on these tests involved developing a clearer specification of the operations and performance conditions underlying language test performance. These provided the conceptual basis for the cognitive and contextual validity parameters that appear in Weir (2005) for reading, listening, writing and speaking, which were then further developed in the constructs volumes in the SiLT series (Shaw and Weir 2007, Khalifa and Weir 2009, Taylor 2011 and Geranpayeh and Taylor 2013).

State Testing Centre, University Entrance Test (UET)/University Entrance Test Extension (UETX) Projects, Uzbekistan, 2004–2009

The University Entrance Test (UET) is a high-stakes examination affecting thousands of students across Uzbekistan every year. This joint project, between the British Council and the State Testing Centre (STC) under the Cabinet of Ministers, witnessed improvements in the validity and reliability of the test scores being awarded to its test takers. This was accomplished through the training of a small team of experienced English teachers in the principles and practice of test design, and the extensive trialling and statistical analysis of the test items before use in the live test administration.

Rita Green was the senior British Consultant on these projects. Her website http://test-development-training-analysis.com/language-testing-projects describes the work involved:

88 *Assessing English on the Global Stage*

UET Project, 2004–2006
- Reviewing existing UET papers and presenting recommendations for the improvement of the validity and reliability of the test scores;
- Training a team of test developers to develop and analyse a series of stakeholder feedback questionnaires;
- Developing Reading and Use of English test specifications and tasks;
- Trialling and statistical analyses;
- Assisting the team to develop a UET handbook (Reading/Use of English);
- Providing advice on the incorporation of the new generation of test items into the 2006 and 2007 UET.

UETX Project, 2007–2009
- Training experts from six subject areas (maths, physics, chemistry, history, Uzbek language and literature, and Russian language and literature) in the development of valid and reliable multiple-choice items for the annual UET test taken by approximately 400,000 candidates;
- Developing test specifications, tasks, administration guidelines and a UETX handbook;
- Trialling of all tasks and delivery of feedback questionnaires.

Rita Green adds (personal communication 29 March 2015):

University Entrance Test (UET)/University Entrance Test Extension (UETX) Projects (2004–2009)
An extensive needs analysis and questionnaire survey at the beginning of the project in 2004 formed the basis for the development of the reading and language in use test specifications and test items for the university entrance test in Uzbekistan. The items the team members produced were instrumental in bringing about qualitative changes in the English language component that in turn enhanced the validity and reliability of the resulting test scores. As one of the team commented, the use of the project's items enabled 'a lot of school leavers […] to become university students thanks to their knowledge'. Another added:

> …new types of (reading) test items were introduced, which were accepted well by both teachers and students. Grammar tests also improved eliminating many concerns during the appeals procedures. Test specifications became more precise and useful to cover

the domain of knowledge, and also to take into account the nature of entrance tests in terms of time and content.

In addition to the regular team members, the thrice yearly workshops were also attended by several members of the State Testing Commission, and this ultimately led to the desire for an extension project which involved the training of test developers from other subject areas (see below). Two members of the original English language team (an Uzbek L1 and a Russian L1 speaker) became the facilitators for this extension project (UETX) whose language medium was Uzbek and Russian. This new role had the beneficial effect of consolidating the knowledge of the team members. In addition, UET team members gave frequent workshops to school teachers both in Tashkent and other regions of the country, presented their work at the annual Uzbekistan Teachers' Conference (UzTEA) and produced a handbook on language testing for teachers.

The project raised awareness in Uzbekistan of the complexity of the testing process. This was the case not only for the English language component of the UET (2004–2006) but also for the other subject areas such as history, geography, maths, chemistry and physics as well as Uzbek and Russian languages (2007–2009). The crucial importance of working together in the UETX workshops with colleagues, not only from the same field but also from others, underlined the significance of not creating test items in isolation which had been the procedure prior to the initiation of the project. In addition, the vital need for trialling and statistical analyses became an accepted fact and an integral part of the project's work.

Prior to the start of the project, the statistical analyses carried out by the State Testing Centre had focused on reliability and due to the sheer numbers and items involved this was consistently high (.9 and above). Little attention had, however, been paid to the validity side of the equation and initial analyses of the items used before the beginning of the project revealed that many were related more to historical, geographical and cultural knowledge rather than to linguistic knowledge. The project successfully highlighted this issue and was instrumental in bringing about a change in the focus of the items.

The development of test specifications in all subject areas had a major impact on the item writing procedure as they clarified the importance of a standardised approach to task development rather than one based on the test developer's own knowledge or what they individually felt the test takers should know.

The project left behind a group of trained test developers (one of whom subsequently completed an MA in language testing) in a range of subject areas who in turn have gone on to train others. In terms of professional development, one team member stated:

> The project helped me to understand essential issues about testing and assessment, for example, the role statistics play in the analysis of test items, the importance of trials, the effectiveness of teamwork, to name but a few. And the most important thing is probably the understanding that we must be fair to test takers and not try to 'catch' them (out) using tricky questions.

With regard to the country's gain, two further comments revealed:

> Overall, the UET Project was a success which brought a valuable positive change to the language testing and assessment practices in the country, and a common belief among those who were involved in it at different stages and levels.

and

> Some of the techniques, such as trials and statistical analyses of test items, are (now) being used in tests evaluating English teachers and their certification. Also, some of the experts trained in the UET/UETX projects are using their skills to develop good quality test items in academic institutions.

As with many projects, the issue of sustainability is ever present. The system in Uzbekistan is that teachers are only permitted to write items for a period of around three years before other colleagues must replace them due to perceived concerns with security. (The UET/X is a high-stakes test with scholarships and reduced fees in the balance for successful candidates.) This means that those who were trained through the project were not allowed to submit items to the UET/X after a period of time, though they were able to share and use their newly gained knowledge in other ways.

This is yet another example of the British Council helping to professionalise indigenous language testing systems at a national level overseas by sponsoring professional input from a British expert with a proven track record in the area.

The issue of sustainability raised by Green once again suggests the importance of long-term collaboration between the British Council and the host country, though the issue of cost is clearly a factor that works against this ideal. However, the production of clear procedures for test specification, development, administration, scoring and analysis which are then closely documented in a written form are still of great value even when individuals move on. Such a tangible product from projects, as in this case and that of the STEP project in Mozambique, can be of considerable long-term value.

The EXAVER Project, Mexico, 2000–2010

Abad et al. (2011) describe the context and conduct of the EXAVER project: from an initial dependence in 2002 on foreign expertise to develop the test papers; to a later realisation that local appropriateness was not being addressed; and finally to a change in the project approach to one closely involving local staff in the test development. From 2005 to 2009 with the benefit of British Council sponsored consultancy from Barry O'Sullivan, then of Roehampton University, UK, now British Council Head of Assessment Research and Development, the foundations of EXAVER test development were revised by the team using, and in the process helping to refine, Weir's (2005) socio-cognitive framework. The project represented one of the first practical applications of the socio-cognitive framework as a basis for test design and development. Another innovative aspect of the project was the decision of the team to link the three tests in the EXAVER suite to the CEFR (a first for the Americas).

In addition to developing professional quality tests, the project aimed to train a group of local teachers in language testing theory and practice so that they would guide the design and development of the final test papers and ensure the sustainability of the project. In addition to the training in language testing, a range of additional work was undertaken in order to deliver the project. Most notably:

- Recruitment and training in classical and IRT [item response theory]-based test data analysis of a team member (Luis Alejandro Santana Martinez) who remains the test's chief statistician.
- The creation of a set of wordlists for the different levels based on research carried out by one team member (Roger Dunne, test writer and vocabulary researcher).

The research was significant in two ways. Firstly, the tests were made culturally appropriate for the people of Central and South America, an early example of localisation (see Chapter 6 for a discussion of this in relation to the British Council Aptis testing system), and secondly, they cost less than one-fifth of equivalent assessments, making them much more accessible to local people.

David Ryan (test writer and assessment researcher), Adriana Abad Florescano (a former EXAVER coordinator) and Verónica Ruiz (the current EXAVER coordinator) helped construct the following account of the project (26 March 2015):

The EXAVER Project, Mexico
The EXAVER project was instigated in 1999 by the then Rector of Universidad Veracruzana in Xalapa, Mexico. The development of the project itself began the following year. The aim of the project was to create a suite of three English language tests, at CEFR level A2, B1 and B2, that would be locally appropriate and produced. They would also be affordable, a critical expectation, and would be used initially across the institution, but with a longer-term goal to spread across the state of Veracruz and across Mexico itself. The support provided by the British Council lasted for 11 years, from 2000 to 2010. The Secretariat of Public Education in Mexico now accredits the tests for national use.

The impact of EXAVER
The impact of the EXAVER Project has already been substantial, both internally at the Universidad Veracruzana and in Mexico. Internally, the university now has a highly skilled exams development, validation and administration team, which feeds into other internal English examinations development projects. This growth in professionalism within the EXAVER team has been highlighted by the fact that two members of the team completed their PhD studies on the project, while a third completed an MA in Language Testing, again based on his work on the project. Team members have presented papers at a series of four national conferences initiated by the EXAVER team (Abad et al., 2011: 239) and at international conferences in South America and Europe. In addition, papers have been published in a national journal (Dunne 2007) and have appeared in two books (Abad et al. 2004 and Abad et al., 2011).

The establishment of a dedicated and professional team has meant that the project has shown real sustainability and remained significant across Mexico since the EXAVER exams were included in the national project for the certification of English language proficiency (CENNI) in 2007. In fact, the EXAVER tests have remained the only exams produced by a Mexican institution to have achieved this recognition. From an initial test population of just a few hundred candidates (all students of the Universidad Veracruzana) the test gradually grew to over 3,000 in 2014. At the time of writing (March 2015) all aspiring postgraduate students at the Universidad Veracruzana now have to sit an EXAVER exam, to demonstrate their language knowledge. A number of other institutions in different parts of the state now use these examinations as part of their official certification processes.

We next examine a number of ESP projects outside of academia where British Council testing projects had a social and economic impact on society in Europe, the Far East and South America.

ESP test projects with impact on wider society

Test for Thai civil servants, 1991–2015

Rita Green, who was involved in a number of testing projects with the British Council in the 1990s, regularly acted as a consultant working closely with local staff, often over an extended period of time. She was the lead consultant on the Department for Technical and Economic Cooperation (DTEC) Test, Thailand 1991–1993, designed to develop a test for civil servants in Thailand in which Ian Stewart, British Council English Language Officer, Thailand 1988–1992, and later Director, British Council English Language Division, UK, was also involved in a managerial role (see discussion of the British Council's critical role in project management above). Rita Green personal communication (29 March 2015) shared the following information on the project:

> **DTEC Test, Thailand**
> The main achievement of this ODA-funded/British Council managed project was to develop a new suite of tests to replace the bank of earlier tests used for deciding which Thai candidates should be put forward for consideration for academic or practical overseas scholarships. The new tests still referred to the candidates as 'academic' or 'practical' but this distinction was now made on the grounds of the *content* of the proposed course of study rather than on *length*. The new tests retained the same level of difficulty and pass-mark(s) but some distinction was made in the types of tasks, which the 'academic' and 'practical' candidates were asked to perform. Only 20%–25% of the items should focus on grammar while the rest would focus on testing reading and listening skills.
>
> All new tasks were extensively trialled on a minimum of 200 candidates from a range of different Ministries in Thailand thus reflecting the target test population. All data were analysed and where necessary the tasks revised and re-trialled. To help with this work, the project appointed a Thai counterpart who was trained in all aspects of language testing including item writing, trialling, statistical analysis and the production of sample tasks. Workshops in the basics of language testing were also provided for members of the DTEC staff and the Thai testing team were trained and monitored in the marking of the new tests.
>
> In light of the new test formats used, the project also impacted on EAP curriculum development within DTEC, one of whose purposes was

94 *Assessing English on the Global Stage*

to provide preparation courses for the DTEC Test. In addition, a completely revised version of the DTEC Testing Handbook was written which included a complete set of sample tasks; mock test materials were also made available.

The tests developed during the project have been used for a period of 22 years (1993 to 2015). A new set of tests will be launched in July 2015. Feedback from stakeholders during the development of this new set of tests (2015) indicated that they have been pleased with how the (1993) tests have worked over the 20 years but appreciate that with new knowledge about how skills can be tested, that it is time for a new test to be rolled-out. In addition the new (2015) test will offer writing and speaking components, while the language in use element will be dropped.

A clear lesson to be drawn from this project is that it once again indicates the importance of training a local counterpart(s) who can carry on the work once the project has finished. The project's Thai counterpart, Khun Wantanee Saipimpan, was still in post in 2010 when I was approached to help in revising the test once more.

The value of a long-term relationship between the British Council consultant(s) and the local project team is once again shown here (see Tribble 2012 on this). Trust and a close professional relationship can be built up over time and the external consultant can be made fully aware of the local context and ensure that the expertise they provide is fit for purpose in that context. The various stages of the project(s) 1991–2015 also show how approaches to testing do change over time and tests need to be revisited to bring them in line with developments in the field.

English Language Assessment System for the Malaysian Public Service (ELPA), Malaysia 1998–2000

The English Language Assessment System for the Malaysian Public Service (ELPA) was a collaborative project involving the English Language Unit of INTAN (the National Institute of Public Administration) and the British Council, Malaysia. The British Council recruited Rita Green from the University of Reading's Testing and Evaluation Unit and Don Porter the Director of the Unit to provide support in professional testing expertise. The aim of the ELPA project was to train a team from the English Language Unit (ELU) to develop a battery of English language tests specifically aimed at the proficiency needs of public service employees. The team was also trained to carry out trials, to analyse the resulting statistics, and to revise the tasks and related documents in light of these findings.

Rita Green commented (personal communication May 2015):

English for Malaysian Civil Servants (EMCS) Project (1998–2000)
The main achievement of this British Council-Malaysian Government Project was the setting up of the EMCS testing system at the National Institute of Public Administration (INTAN) in Kuala Lumpur. Amongst other things, this involved the development of a proficiency test for Malaysian civil servants at the M2 and M3 levels. A team of test developers, taken from amongst INTAN's teachers, was identified and a number of workshops led to the development of test specifications and appropriate tasks to measure the prospective candidates' reading, writing and spoken language skills. Team members were also trained in the procedures to be followed during field testing, the interpretation of statistical data and the revision of the test and related documents such as feedback questionnaires.

Further workshops provided advice on a range of testing aspects such as how to carry out concurrent validation measures, the development of the test rationale document, test familiarisation sessions, the interpretation of the EMCS test bands, the production of practice test materials, the development of the EMCS Handbook and finally the feasibility of streamlining the ECMS test, known as ELPA (English Language Proficiency Assessment).

The testing system, which was first launched 15 years ago, is still very active. Indeed recent feedback suggests that it will be developing new versions, for example to assess officers who have been identified for fast-tracking strategic posts in the public service.

After the project the small-scale ELPA, which was designed for a particular service, was extended to assess officers across multiple services and grade levels. Kadir, one of the core members of the development team, (personal communication May 2015) describes:

…how the scope of the assessment has widened since first administered in 1998 to the time the data for this study was collected in 2007, the number of officers tested rose from 300 per year solely from the PTD service to more than 4,000 officers from various schemes of services and grade levels at the end of 2006.

Project outputs were impressive and included detailed test specifications, rating instruments for the assessment of writing and speaking skills and a handbook for stakeholders. As a result of involvement in the project, Kadir used the English for Malaysian Civil Servants (EMCS) testing system as the basis for her PhD (*Framing a Validity Argument for Test Use and Impact: The Malaysian Public Service Experience*, 2008).

Kadir's thesis was a valuable addition to the literature on test validation. Her comprehensive validity enquiry investigated whether there might be support for the administration of the ELPA across different services in terms of usefulness and impact, and provided an impressive case study of an argument-based approach to evaluating an extended large-scale testing use.

UK Peacekeeping English Project, 1996–2010

In the British Council's *The English Effect* (2013a: 2), Mark Robson describes how English is often used as a 'language of convenience, facilitating dialogue and building trust where an understanding of diverse positions is crucial – notably in peacekeeping and conflict resolution, where security forces and other uniformed services increasingly speak to each other in English'.

According to the British Council website, from 1996 until 2010 the British Council managed the Peacekeeping English Project (PEP) programmes on behalf of the United Kingdom Foreign and Commonwealth Office, the Ministry of Defence and the Department for International Development, with the aim of providing assistance in more than 20 countries in the areas of curriculum design, materials and resources development, teacher training and testing. The support for testing included:

- advice to national testing teams;
- regional seminars and workshops on test construction and evaluation;
- international training opportunities, including specialised postgraduate studies;
- a regional network of qualified testers, for discussion of problems and the sharing of experience.

The aim of PEP was to reduce, resolve and prevent conflict worldwide through improved English language communication. English was needed for 'interoperability' to:

- enable multinational forces involved in NATO, EU and UN peace support operations to communicate effectively with each other for humanitarian purposes;
- allow military and other security forces to interact with non-governmental agencies in conflict and post-conflict situations;

- enable border guards and police to combat drug smuggling and human trafficking;
- serve as a tool for promoting democratic values and respect for human rights.

The Peacekeeping English Project was a major initiative involving a range of English language development work. Since it began in 1996, the PEP has designed and set up an impressive number of programmes across the globe in:

> Albania, Angola, Armenia, Azerbaijan, Bosnia and Herzegovina, Belarus, China, Colombia, Democratic Republic of the Congo, Croatia, Czech Republic, Estonia, Ethiopia, Georgia, Hungary, Indonesia, Kazakhstan, Kyrgyzstan, Latvia, Libya, Lithuania, Macedonia, Moldova, Mongolia, Mozambique, Poland, Romania, Serbia and Montenegro, Slovakia, Slovenia, Tajikistan, Turkmenistan, Turkey, Ukraine, Uzbekistan, Vietnam.

PEP worked closely with ministries in participant countries in order to establish secure and impartial English language testing systems for the military, border guards and police. One of the main objectives was to foster a common understanding of military testing to NATO STANAG 6001 standards. The Project also provided training for testers and established national language testing teams. From 2003 to 2009 the Peacekeeping English Project organised three major international testing conferences.

Green and Wall (2005: 396) concluded that despite much progress in the areas of test construction and development, and regional communication and cooperation, there were still pressing issues on the theoretical and practical sides with regard to the more explicit specification of the target language use domain at targeted levels of proficiency. On the political side, they argued that there was a need for a review of whether the Supreme Headquarters Allied Powers Europe (SHAPE) Test functions effectively as a measurement tool and how best to carry out training. They also expressed concern that within NATO it was not clear where the responsibility lay for dealing with such testing matters, as there was no single body responsible for these.

Crossey (2009: 147–165) was similarly uncertain as regards the possibility of achieving a common language training and assessment policy because of macro-political constraints for example in achieving standardisation of proficiency levels in certification across member states. He pointed to a number of potential stumbling blocks including lack of comprehension of language proficiency assessment at upper levels in the military command structure and no clear channels of communication between educators and those responsible for military education policy implementation (ibid.: 150–151).

On a more positive note, Dianne Wall (personal communication 1 March 2015) provided the following retrospective on her work for the project:

Peacekeeping English Project (PEP)

The Peacekeeping English Project (PEP) grew out of a smaller programme called the Baltic Battalion ELT Project, which was established in 1994 in the three Baltic States and five other countries in the Central and Eastern Europe (CEE) region. Both the earlier programme and PEP were funded by the UK Ministry of Defence (MOD) and the Foreign and Commonwealth Office (FCO). These agencies were later joined by the Department for International Development. The original aim of the project was:

> to improve the English language skills of the armed forces so as to involve them in NATO peacekeeping operations and other areas of co-operation, thereby enhancing political and military stability.

The project has expanded in the two decades since its establishment, now operating in countries well beyond the original CEE setting. The aims have also expanded, now including:

> the provision of specialised English language testing relating to human rights, counter-narcotics work and, first and foremost, democratic peacekeeping according to the United National charter to military and police forces worldwide. (Crossey 2008: 207)

This brief account covers only the first ten years of the project, up to when the PEP focus began moving away from the CEE region and to other parts of the globe.

PEP objectives were determined on a country-by-country basis, through negotiations between the British Council and the local Ministry of Defence or Interior. These negotiations could be quite lengthy and complicated, but the resulting objectives commonly included the design of an English language curriculum, course and/or materials, the training of teachers in military English, and the creation of a valid and reliable testing system. It was important to create systems which could assess whether military and relevant civilian personnel had sufficient English language proficiency to perform their duties in multinational contexts where English was the common means of communication. It was up to each country to measure this proficiency, in accordance with levels stipulated in the NATO's Standard Agreement (STANAG) 6001. STANAG 6001 had in the NATO context functions similar to those of the Common European Framework of Reference in today's Europe – to encourage a common understanding of language requirements and to enable mutual recognition of tests across the region. A country's interpretation of the STANAG descriptors could have other effects within its educational setting, in terms of curriculum goals, textbook choice and advice given to teachers at all levels of training.

There were initially two types of British Council input into the building of these testing systems, both of which depended on the skills and interests of the Council-appointed PEP managers in the different countries. The managers' testing responsibilities differed from context to context but generally included activities such as advising on testing policy at ministerial level, recruiting teams of testers and giving them initial training, providing working space and other resources, and contributing to teacher training activities and sometimes to test production.

The second type of input was provided by a handful of PEP managers working in consortium through the Testing Research Unit for Military Purposes (TRUMP) Working Group in 1999. TRUMP had a number of testing-related objectives, including learning more about the testing situation at NATO's Supreme Headquarters Allied Powers Europe (SHAPE – the SHAPE testing operation had a powerful effect on many of the PEP-supported testing teams), surveying and critiquing tests being produced in the CEE region, and organising special testing materials and summer schools to develop the expertise of testers in the countries where they were advising and across the PEP context. TRUMP members also lobbied funders for further testing support, including professional development possibilities for themselves and key members of their national teams.

In 2000 the British Council commissioned a review of the testing operations in a sample of PEP countries, and an assessment of the training needs of PEP Managers and national test developers (Wall 2001). The review recommended high-level training in testing. The next four years saw approximately 30 PEP testers receiving intensive training in testing at Lancaster University, most receiving an MA in Language Testing and others gaining a Postgraduate Certificate in Language Testing. A significant feature of the MA training was the research the participants carried out for their dissertations, which required a critical look at testing issue in their home setting and the application of ideas from language testing to improve the situation.

The impact of this training naturally depended on the practical and political conditions in each of the countries where the project was active. The practical issues included matters such as the size of the testing population in each military setting, the amount of time the teams could devote to testing rather than other duties, and general resourcing. The political issues included the status and power of the teams (who were almost exclusively civilians) within the military structures they worked in, and the inability of many policy-makers to understand or respect the amount of time and resourcing necessary to ensure proper test construction and validation. A discussion of these problems can be found in Green and Wall (2005). A fuller discussion of the challenges of project implementation in a highly political and multilateral context can be found in Crossey (2008, 2009 and 2012).

Despite the challenges faced by some teams the investment in training had positive impact within their countries and across the PEP project. Crossey (2009: 61), a former PEP manager who later became PEP Director, writes that

> The pool of testers developed remained largely influential with their MODs and also effected impressive changes in generally low-resourced testing environments…. Moreover, a key political success for the UK government as sponsors of this work was the recognition of valid and transparent testing procedures as a positive product by many MODs, and therefore as a potent enabler of effective and potentially improved contribution to international peace support operation missions.

Impact beyond the original context was also impressive, including
- Cooperation between teams in neighbouring countries on test design and pre-testing projects (in later years this included collaboration between teams in countries whose governments were hostile to each other).
- Expansion (and re-labelling) of the original TRUMP Working Group to include national testers, resulting in fresh insights in debate and decision-making in regional meetings and workshops.
- The cascading of expertise from the new national testers via the presentations and training they gave at multi-national seminars and conferences, and through international consultancies.
- Contributions to high-stakes testing projects in other sectors, including tests of aviation and maritime English, national school-leaving examinations, university examinations, and tests for international publishers.

This is a good example of a multinational project in an area of strategic importance where the British Council, working in conjunction with British experts, played a leading role in a project leading to the successful training of participants in how to develop English language tests fit for military purposes.

The English for Tourism Project, Venezuela, 2007

Our final case study looks briefly at a further distinctive area of English for Specific Purposes, namely that of *English for tourism*. English is the primary language of global tourism given that most tourism authorities and others use English to interact and engage with foreign tourists. Good oral and written communication skills are a key requirement for working at all levels in the tourist industry.

In an effort to improve the national tourist industry, the Venezuelan Ministry of Tourism decided to award certification to personnel who meet its established standards of service. As part of this policy, in 2007 the Ministry, doubtless informed by its long experience of British Council cooperation on ESP and other English language teaching and assessment related matters in Venezuela (for example see Abbott and Beaumont 1997: 23–24), asked the Council to advise on a project creating a national system for certification of the English language level of tourism personnel. The project was highly innovative in its approach. It comprised these elements: the selection and training of a committee of 40 evaluators for the production of the test instruments, to be used initially to test 750 tourism workers; monitoring of the testing and certification process; and the subsequent cascading of the training to a further group of evaluators. The project is a key component of the Venezuelan government's plans to stimulate tourism, by ensuring that existing and future employees in the sector have adequate English language skills (British Council http://www.teachingenglish.org.uk/elt-projects/english-tourism-project-venezuela).

Section 1 Endnote

In Chapter 1 we examined the closeness of the long-term working relationship, whereby the British Council helped Cambridge English Language Assessment to become the leading global provider of EFL examinations in the second half of the 20th century. As well as promoting and administering Cambridge examinations in its centres abroad, the British Council was a continuing source of professional input into Cambridge EFL examinations such as LCE (later FCE), CPE and the Diploma in English from 1941 to 1989. In exploring the partnership established by the 1941 agreement, we identified the British Council's role in building soft power for the British government through its involvement in spreading English teaching and testing around the world.

In Chapter 2 we have seen how, in the latter part of the 20th century, the British Council enhanced this role through its work for British government (ODA/DFID) and other agencies in commissioning and managing indigenous, national, English language testing projects around the world; by providing training in English language assessment in numerous countries overseas using British consultants; through its teachers of English and ELOs delivering support on the ground in these countries for national English language test development; and by bringing local personnel from the assessment field to the UK for study and consultation. These projects had an immediate impact on locally developed national English curricula and examinations overseas, and more widely on important areas of society such as tertiary education, the civil service, tourism and the military. The work carried out in a number of these projects also contributed substantively to the development of language testing theory and practice, thereby enriching the language testing field as a whole.

In Section 2, our story takes a different turn. We examine how the British Council became directly involved in English language test development in its own right. An increasing responsibility for government sponsored overseas students coming to Britain in the 1960s would lead to British Council involvement in the important area of assessing academic English proficiency. Between 1963 and 1989, British Council staff in Spring Gardens became directly involved in test development projects such as the English Proficiency Test Battery (EPTB) (Davies 1965a and 2008, and Chapter 3 below) and the innovative English Language Testing Service (ELTS) test (Carroll 1978, 1980 and 1981, and Chapter 4 below). Through its significant involvement in these projects, the British Council became a leading world authority in this period on how to assess the English proficiency of overseas students wishing to study through the medium of English at tertiary-level institutions. This marked an important adjunct to its long-term facilitative role in helping spread English examinations and British communicative approaches to language testing round the globe.

Section 2

Developing Academic English Tests for University Gatekeeping and Selection Purposes, 1954–2016

Chapter 3

Testing the academic English of overseas students coming to Britain, 1954–1982: The British Council interview and the English Proficiency Test Battery

> Each year over 600,000 international students from 200 countries come to study at universities, colleges and boarding schools in the UK and a further 600,000 come to do a short English language course. In 2011, they contributed the lion's share of the UK's £17.5 billion education-related export market helping institutions, cities and communities throughout the UK to thrive. Analysis by London Economics suggests that the value of that market might be approximately £21.5 billion in 2020 and £26.6 billion in 2025 (both in 2008–09 prices).
> (British Council, *The English Effect* 2013a:16)

A changing role for the British Council

With the entry of Britain into the Second World War in 1939, the government at first considered amalgamating the British Council with the newly formed Ministry of Information, which was responsible for propaganda. However, the British Council Chairman (1937–1941), Lord Lloyd, successfully argued for the value of the British Council as an independent organisation, responsible for building long-term relationships (Adam 1948). Although its information work was transferred to the new ministry, the government encouraged an expansion of the British Council's cultural and educational work.

In response to the fallout from events in Europe a new role opened up for the British Council. A Resident Foreigners Division (RFD) was set up in 1939 to take responsibility for work in the UK with refugees, overseas students and servicemen from Allied countries. Nancy Parkinson, on joining the British Council in 1939, had been asked by the chairman, Lord Lloyd, to set up the RFD, which, in cooperation with the Home Office, the Admiralty, the War Office and the Air Ministry, was to be responsible for organising educational and cultural facilities for refugees and Allied forces based in Britain during the Second World War. The RFD would eventually become the Home Division of the British Council. Centres were set up across the country to provide the necessary physical, pedagogical and administrative support (see Roach 1945 for detail of the provision of English language assessment for allied service personnel in WW2, also Hawkey and Milanovic 2013 and Weir 2013).

Richard Smith (forthcoming) describes how Parkinson:

> ...oversaw an increasingly large-scale regional UK operation to promote social and cultural relations with refugees and allied soldiers in the UK, including English teaching. [...] Lessons were held in locations of every kind from ballrooms to billiard salons. A regional network of British Council Allied Centres for refugees, exiles and overseas service personnel was also developed, including the Allied Centre in Liverpool, opened in 1941. English lessons were an important part of planned activities in these Centres. There was further direct work with allied forces, for example Polish forces in Scotland, where a great many of the teachers had to live in close proximity to the units they were teaching. Some did their teaching aboard destroyers and submarines, and occasionally went to sea with their pupils, in order that the continuity of their studies should not be interrupted.

The first centre was the Polish Hearth in London, which opened in July 1940 for Poles who were regrouping in Britain when Poland fell to the Nazi invasion. It was also the meeting place of the Polish government in exile. By the end of the war there were British Council assistance centres in London, Liverpool, Manchester, Birmingham, Oxford, Stratford-on-Avon and Wilton in England, Edinburgh and Leith in Scotland, and Cardiff in Wales. The government provided the British Council with a separate vote for this support and the work became a unique feature of the British Council during the war. After the war, Parkinson expanded the work of the Division – now renamed the Home Division – to cater for the increasing numbers of overseas visitors and students coming to the UK. The regional offices would provide valuable support to overseas students and invited visitors coming to Britain right up until many of them were closed for financial reasons in the 1980s. The ones in Oxford, Edinburgh and Cardiff, however, survived into the 21st century.

Eastment (1982: 51) identifies the important educational role the British Council was to play in wartime and singles out the part played by Professor Ifor Evans of London University who became British Council Educational Director in December 1940, working to four main objectives:

- the creation of a permanent overseas teaching service;
- the provision of the most effective system for teaching English as a foreign language;
- the encouragement of other English studies abroad;
- the introduction of foreign students to Britain.

Our concern is with the last of these, as the growth in numbers of overseas students coming to study in British universities from the 1940s onwards would lead directly to the British Council's unique involvement in testing their English language proficiency for such study.

White (1965: 21–22) provides detail on the start of government scholarships for overseas students wishing to study in the UK and argues that the administration of these awards would become an important focus for British Council activities:

> ...it was decided to offer one year post graduate scholarships, in a very limited range of subjects, the selection to be made by H.M. Missions and the places in British universities to be found by the Committee of Vice-Chancellors. An increased budget of £20,000 was earmarked for the Students Committee for 1938–9 and this enabled a scholarship scheme to start which has ever since been of all the Council's activities perhaps the soundest investment.

Eastment (1982: 60–62) traces the British Council's remit for foreign students coming to Britain, which would be the catalyst for its future involvement in assessing the language ability of students who wished to study through the medium of English worldwide (see below). She describes how the British Council spent £350 in 1935 for the most part on European students, climbing to £35,000 by 1938/39. After 1940 students from the United States, Turkey and Latin America were supported by the British Council and in 1943 around 50 came from China. In total by 1944 there were 165 foreign students on British Council scholarships, rising to 250 a year 1945–1950 (see Dunlop 1966). From 1950 the British Council was additionally responsible for 4,000 colonial students studying in Britain.

Government policy, economic prosperity and growing air travel all contributed to the general increase in numbers of students coming to the United Kingdom after the Second World War (Howatt and Widdowson 2004: 242). The exponential growth in the number of these students can be seen in the figures below. First from the *British Council Annual Reports* 1945–1996 we provide the figures for ten-year periods 1945–1955, 1955–1965 and 1965–1975 in Table 3.1; from 1980 onwards these ten-year totals are dwarfed by the annual intakes shown in the chart (Figure 3.1).

Table 3.1 Students coming to the UK, 1945–1975

Years	1945–1955	1955–1965
Colonies	2,411	4,411
Commonwealth	3,099	16,660
USA	1,943	252
Latin America	1,864	4,224
Middle East	3,064	10,346
Far East	1,890	6,007
East Europe	3,413	13,069
North and West Europe	9,926	11,345
South Europe	3,465	1,791
Total	**31,075**	**68,105**

Years	1965–1975
Commonwealth	47,041
Middle East and Africa (Foreign)	16,336
SE Asia and Far East	8,715
Latin America	11,609
Europe (including Soviet Union)	86,450
USA	289
Total	**170,440**

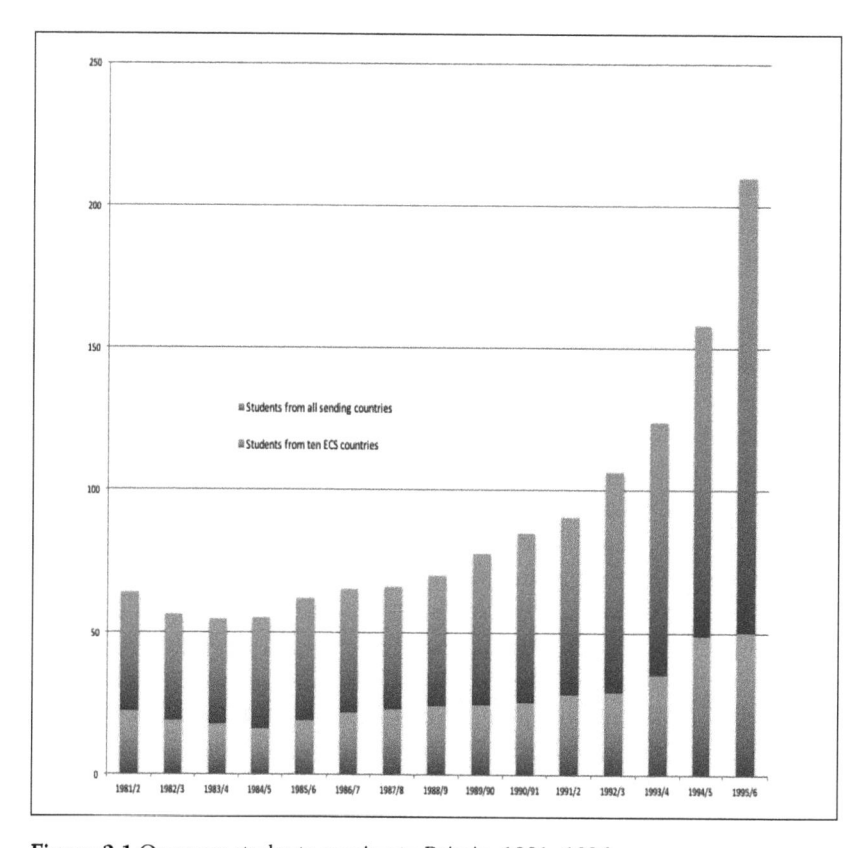

Figure 3.1 Overseas students coming to Britain, 1981–1996

Post-war economic imperatives

The objective of *introducing foreign students to Britain* was part of a general shift in post-war direction for the British Council. Pennycook (1994: 48) singles out the *Drogheda Report*, presented to the British government in 1953, as being a clear directive to the British Council to move from a cultural to an educational focus and henceforward concern itself with 'developing' rather than 'developed' countries. The report triggered a move away from a relatively elitist focus on culture towards a more instrumentally oriented ELT. Haigh (1974: 126) expands on the suggested directions of travel and argues that the government wanted the British Council to cut down on its work in Europe and seize the great opportunities available in Asia and Africa. This required a shift from cultural work overseas (e.g. art exhibitions and theatrical and orchestral tours) to educationally focused work particularly in the area of English language. The report expressed considerable satisfaction with the current work of the British Council in taking responsibility for overseas visitors and students and advised an increase in the number of scholarships and bursaries awarded.

The clear change in emphasis to educational work, especially the teaching of English, and praise for the British Council's success in looking after visitors and students within the United Kingdom are germane to our story. They help contextualise the direction the British Council's work took in the 1960s, particularly in relation to increasing the number of overseas students coming to the UK, and the British Council's own involvement in EAP testing to ensure that these students had sufficient language proficiency to cope with and benefit from their studies.

The view of English as a means of access to British culture all but disappeared from the corridors of power in the 1950s, as more materialistic considerations gained precedence. Exporting British educational, commercial and technological services together with British products would loom much larger in the minds of government in the post-war world than cultural promotion. Pennycook (1994: 154–155) refers us to a key Ministry of Education document published in 1956, the *Report of the Official Committee on the Teaching of English Overseas* (para 10), which established clearly the government's view on the promotion of English:

> English is a commodity in great demand all over the world; it is wanted not only for reasons of friendship and trade with the English-speaking countries but also for other reasons not necessarily connected with any desire to imitate British ways or to understand British history and culture. We are, therefore, looking at the language mainly as a valuable and coveted export, which many nations are prepared to pay for.... English is, moreover, an export, which is very likely to attract other exports – British advisers and technicians, British technological or university education, British plant and equipment and British capital investment. There are clear commercial advantages to be gained from increasing the number of potential customers who can read technical and trade publicity material written in English.

Richard Smith (personal communication August 2016) additionally drew our attention to the 1957 *Hill Report* and the White paper that implemented it (Cmnd 225). He notes: 'The White paper (UK government statement of decisions taken) as a result of a review by Dr Charles Hill, Minister responsible for co-ordinating the "information services" (including BBC as well as British Council), laid special emphasis on the teaching of English and the care of overseas students.' Martin (2014: 13) describes how plans for development in the Hill Report included the introduction of a scholarship programme whereby key students from abroad would be brought to Britain for training in English as a foreign language (see also Donaldson 1984: 205–207).

In 1961 the Department for Technical Cooperation (DTC) was set up with a responsibility for British aid to developing countries. From 1962 the Department tasked the British Council with responsibility for trainees and students coming to Britain from overseas. The hope was that one day these visiting students would reach a position of influence in their own countries. Through the rest of the 1960s and up until the 1990s, the British Council would have a direct responsibility for education programmes and student training schemes in the developing countries of Africa and Asia, and received a substantial proportion of its government funding from this new Department.

With the growing educational (and indeed economic) role of facilitating access to British Higher Education came responsibilities for ensuring that applicants met the required standard in language ability. This was not a new concern for the British Council as the following subsection shows.

Assessing the language proficiency of the growing numbers of overseas students coming to Britain: The subjective interview

On 7 October 1953 the Deputy Controller of the Home Division, R.A. Phillips had written to all British Council overseas representatives (GEN 320/2, Circular Letter No 53/8) expressing concern over the situation as regards student language proficiency and offered a way forward:

> Dear Representative,
>
> *Knowledge of English*
>
> There have been some cases recently of visitors and bursars arriving without the knowledge of English, which they were reported (on the proposal form) to possess. You will appreciate that this may seriously affect the whole programme for the visit etc., as well as reflect on the Council's good name and good sense.
>
> We realise that the problem is a tricky one but, after discussion with Education Division, we feel that the use of the attached questionnaire should help to solve it. The questionnaire, which is self-explanatory, will

be particularly useful where you have to rely on others, e.g. Consular staff, to interview candidates. As from the date of receipt of this letter therefore will you please use this form for all visitors and bursars.

So in 1953 an attempt was made in British Council operations abroad to regularise pre-departure language testing procedures by the introduction of the *Knowledge of English 4 Point Scale* for use in determining proficiency in each of the four skills (see box).

Knowledge of English 4 Point Scale

Put tick in appropriate boxes in Sections* (1), (2), (3), (4)

(*Delete numbers of Sections which may be irrelevant)

(1) <u>Understanding of Spoken English</u>

    (a) Understands without difficulty when addressed at normal speed ☐

    (b) Understands almost everything if addressed slowly and carefully ☐

    (c) Requires frequent repetition and/or translation of words and phrases ☐

    (d) Does not understand spoken English ☐

(2) <u>Speaking of English</u>

    (a) Speaks fluently and accurately and is easily intelligible ☐

    (b) Speaks intelligibly, but is not fluent or altogether accurate ☐

    (c) Speaks haltingly, and is often at a loss for words and phrases ☐

    (d) Does not speak English ☐

(3) <u>Understanding of Written English</u>

    (a) Reads fluently, with full comprehension ☐

    (b) Reads slowly, but understands almost everything he reads ☐

    (c) Reads with difficulty, and only with frequent recourse to the dictionary ☐

    (d) Cannot read English ☐

(4) <u>Ability to Write English</u>

    (a) Writes with ease and accuracy ☐

    (b) Writes slowly, and/or with only a moderate degree of accuracy ☐

    (c) Writes with difficulty and makes frequent mistakes ☐

    (d) Cannot write English ☐

This 'test instrument' was used to measure the adequacy of the English ability of overseas students competing for official awards in the country. Concerns about its reliability (Davies 2008: 9) would result in an amended version the *Overseas Spoken Interview (OSI)* in 1958, using a ten-point scale, the addition of a sheet of instructions about procedures, suggestions to the examiner about materials, together with instruction about the level of proficiency necessary for eligibility to study in Britain. In 1961/62, this rating form was administered to over 2,000 applicants but considerable dissatisfaction with it was expressed by British Council officers (Davies 2008: 10 and Perren 1963b).

Details of how the interviews were conducted are unavailable, but one can only assume that untrained staff in British embassies carried out this job in a fairly informal fashion, as once again seems to be happening in the 21st century in order to provide additional pre-departure checks on the language proficiency and motivation of applicants to enter the UK prior to granting visas.

The rapid growth in student numbers noted above prompted concerns over the adequacy of these instruments for the assessment of the proficiency in English of students wishing to commence academic study in the UK (see below for discussion of study related language problems). Where numbers of sponsored students had been small, this traditional, impromptu, subjective, British Council interview by a local officer was tolerated (though not without reservations) as a quick and easy solution to the problem. But this approach became untenable as numbers swelled and more importantly the composition of the students changed, with the balance swinging towards foreign rather than Commonwealth students. The students from countries where English was a *foreign* language were likely to have a lower level of proficiency in English, the target language, as compared with students from countries in the Commonwealth. Whereas many of the latter had been educated in English, the foreign-country students had not.

Developing a more suitable and efficient English proficiency test for screening students coming to study in Britain under the British Council's Scholarship programme became an operational necessity. The cost of selecting candidates who subsequently were unable to cope with the language demands of English-medium tertiary-level study was viewed as unacceptable.

The Davies Test/English Proficiency Test Battery, 1965–1980

From 1965 until 1980 the British Council would employ a new English language proficiency measure, the English Proficiency Test Battery (EPTB), as a qualification for overseas students entering higher education in Britain. EPTB was the innovative product of Alan Davies' doctoral research at Birmingham University and would be administered to as many as 5,000 students a year over this 15-year period. The British Council would promote, pay for and oversee the operation of EPTB for the whole of the life of the test from 1965 to 1980, when the English Language Testing Service (ELTS) came in to replace it, but the two ran in tandem until ELTS became fully operational. EPTB was finally retired in 1982 (Davies 2008: 29).

Here, over half a century back, was the British Council identifying, specifying, recruiting for, monitoring, evaluating and implementing a major English language testing project, with implications not only for its own objectives and programmes, but for many other organisations and potentially influential individuals round the world. It helps explain why the British Council felt 'expert' enough to manage testing projects around the world (as detailed in Chapter 2).

In 1963, the EPTB project, funded by the British Council, was set up in the University of Birmingham (see Davies 1965a). Davies described the genesis of the project in his interview for this history (January 2015):

> I moved into the Faculty of Education with a man called Peel who was very much interested in testing. That was his specialism, not language, but just testing generally. That was a British Council project which paid me for three years to write the test for the British Council which was to replace the subjective type of measure that had been in use. They felt they had to have something more reliable and so I produced this test – 'The English Proficiency Test Battery'.

Davies wrote his doctoral thesis as part of the EPTB project from 1963 to 1965 under the joint auspices of the British Council and Birmingham University (Davies 1965a). He was appointed by the British Council as Senior Research Associate on the project under the direction of Edwin Peel, a leading pyschometrician and Head of the School of Education at Birmingham University, with research design and statistical support from George Burroughs and Phillip Levy from the Psychology

Department. George Perren provided advice from the British Council side. Perren had previously worked for a number of years in teacher training in East Africa and was the first Director of the British Council's English Teaching Information Centre (ETIC), founded in 1961 in London. Davies' 2008 book on testing academic English is dedicated to the memory of George Perren, clear testimony to his influence. Davies in his interview (30 January 2015) noted: 'I found him a great source of both knowledge and inspiration.'

Perren had previously carried out research into the reliability of the British Council interview test (see above) because it was not proving satisfactory to the receiving institutions, particularly in the case of students only staying for one year, where there was very limited time for improvement for those with an English language deficit (see discussion of overseas students' language problems below and Perren 1963b: 28).

Davies (2008: 9) emphasised the importance of Perren's earlier work for the field and for his own doctoral work and saw it as the basis for the future testing of academic English in the UK. Perren (1963a: 2) provides detail of his involvement in one of the earliest EAP tests:

> It was desired to construct and administer tests of English ability to West and East African students in Britain in order to discover:
> - to what extent their work in technical or academic courses in Britain was significantly handicapped by weaknesses in English;
> - in which aspects of English such weaknesses are most prevalent;
> - how weaknesses might best be overcome either by different teaching overseas, by preliminary courses in Britain, or by remedial courses which could be taken concurrently with other studies.

Perren developed a battery of six tests:

1. A test of articulation (ability to produce the primary phonemes of English).
2. A test of phonemic discrimination (ability to distinguish between English phonemes).
3. A test of auditory comprehension of prosodic features (stress and pitch in a recorded dialogue).
4. A test of reading comprehension (single sentences).
5. A test of hearing (combining the features isolated in Tests 1–3).
6. A test of reading comprehension (two texts).

He achieved high concurrent validation estimates for his tests in relation to teacher estimates and advised that Tests 3 and 5 were worthy of further consideration and the addition of a test of reading speed might be considered.

Practical considerations in developing the EPTB

Davies (2008: 13) makes the practical constraints on this British Council EPTB development project clear. He argues that what was needed was a group-administered test that could, if necessary, be delivered in a short space of time by unskilled and untrained examiners. The original intention was to include two test types: linguistic categories tests and work sample (performance) tests based on what overseas students had to use their English for. There would be separate tests of phonology (phonemic discrimination, intonation and stress) and grammar for the former, whereas the work sample should include listening to lectures and reading textbook type material. In the event, because of practical difficulties (especially with the listening tests 4a–4c in Table 3.2), work sample tests for science and non-science students were abandoned early on and the reading and listening multiple-choice question (MCQ) comprehension tests were removed from the operational short form version A.

Table 3.2 Composition of original EPTB Form A

Test	Items	Content	Skill	Aspect
1	65	Phonemic Discrimination: words in isolation	Listening	Linguistic
2	25	Phonemic Discrimination: words in context	Listening	Linguistic
3	50	Intonation	Listening	Linguistic
4a	8	Listening Comprehension: general	Listening	Work sample
4b	5	Listening Comprehension: specialised science	Listening	Work sample
4c	5	Listening Comprehension: specialised arts	Listening	Work sample
5	196	Reading Speed	Reading	Work sample
6a	49	Reading Comprehension: general	Reading	Work sample
6b	50	Reading Comprehension: specialised arts	Reading	Work sample
6c	50	Reading Comprehension: specialised science	Reading	Work sample
7	50	Grammar	Reading	Linguistic

A Short Form A of EPTB was trialled in 1964 on around 1,000 students (496 overseas students in Britain, 238 students in their home countries and 267 native English students) with the following sub-tests:

Listening
Test 1 58 items Phonemic discrimination
Test 2 38 items Intonation and stress (in conversation).

Reading Comprehension
Test 3 49 items Gap filling selective deletion
Test 4 47 items Grammatical structure

Optional
Test 5 196 items Reading speed (Rates of reading emerged as important in the needs analysis so in addition to tests of reading comprehension it was decided to include a test of reading speed)
(See Davies 2008: 16–23 for more detail on the individual EPTB sub-tests and pp. 120–133 for test examples.)

In all, there were four forms of EPTB: Form A 1964 and Form B 1965 produced by Davies, Form C 1973 produced in cooperation with Alan Moller, and Form D 1977 developed with Charles Alderson. Hughes (1987) provides a useful critique of the later Form D of the Davies test in Alderson, Krahnke and Stansfield's (1987) edited volume *Reviews of English Language Proficiency Tests*. Hughes notes that: '…discussion will concentrate on Form D, as Davies (1984: 55–59) regards the Listening components of earlier versions to be inferior' whilst D retained the strengths of the reading comprehension parts (see also Davies and Alderson 1977). Form D contained a listening test, a multiple-choice grammar test and a rational deletion cloze (exact word). Hughes (op cit.: 31) describes the kinds of skills the listening tasks covered:

- understanding of sentence stress (25 items),
- recognition of appropriate responses in discourse (25 items),
- identification of written notes correctly summarising points made in an interview (17 items).

The reading tasks contained:

- a single modified cloze passage (containing 50 syntactic deletions with the first letter supplied),
- a multiple-choice grammar test (50 items).

Hughes commented that the reading comprehension passages and a vocabulary section had been dropped from the original trial version due to length constraints. Perhaps most critically, performance on some of the tasks that the student would be engaged in at a university, e.g. reading into writing tasks or oral interaction in seminars, were not directly measured.

Hughes (1987) quoted the following Kuder-Richardson 21 (KR21) reliability estimates for EPTB based on a sample of 189 UK students as: Listening Comprehension 0.79; Modified Cloze 0.91; Grammar 0.82; Reading Speed 0.92. No data were available on the reliability estimate for the whole of the test or on the standard error of measurement.

Scores were converted to assign candidates to one of three levels:

1   sufficient English,
2   requires 4–12 weeks of EAP instruction before course,
3   requires minimum of 6 months' full time tuition.

Hughes details how supplementary tests (reading speed, essay and interview) were available to help distinguish between the first two levels in borderline cases and to determine length of tuition necessary for those assigned to level 2. The British Council took a lead role in advising institutions how much English would be necessary for its sponsored candidates.

The initial extended battery was considered too long for practical use in British Council offices overseas. The realities of running a speaking test were considered problematic, as was a test of writing. Although the EPTB developers acknowledged the importance of writing and speaking skills, the practical problems of testing these skills (e.g. the requirement for skilled examiners), combined with the British Council's need for a test which could be taken in a short period of time, meant that tests of speaking and writing were not included in the EPTB battery. EPTB concentrated instead on the receptive skills which leant themselves to a group-administered test and could also be overseen by untrained examiners. Thus EPTB, in the event, became mainly a traditional set of standardised tests in a multiple-choice format, focusing on the receptive skills of reading and listening together with knowledge of grammar and pronunciation. (Facsimile test material for the original EPTB Form A can be found in Davies 2008: 120–135, Appendices 2.1–2.3.)

Davies (2008: 14) explains that the dilemma facing the original EPTB designers was whether they could predict success on an English-medium academic course on the basis of tests of reading and listening alone. It was not that he thought speaking or writing in any way less important than reading and listening but that these productive skills were, practically, more problematic and time-consuming to include. In his interview for the British Council History of Testing Project on 30 January 2015, Davies reflected on the eventual pragmatic choice of content for the operational version of EPTB:

> It just wasn't sort of available or appropriate for people across the world to do speaking tests. So it didn't happen anyway.... I mean in a way it was a cop out I suppose, but it seemed to me to be the only thing to do, and it was accepted. Having said that, it still seems to me even now, that academic proficiency is largely about the written word, not about the spoken. You know, if you think what it is that students do in studying their subject, much of the time what they're doing is reading, and trying to understand difficult texts and so it was I think, not inappropriate, not altogether a cop out to test only the receptive skills.

Thus in the end it was the less subjective EPTB *micro-linguistic* tests of reading and listening comprehension that constituted the primary measures of students' English language proficiency via their implied relationship to students' ability to follow a university course and to pass the associated examinations at the end of the course.

Growing dissatisfaction with the EPTB: The demand for a 'real-world' test in English for Academic Purposes

> Although we would agree that language is a complex behaviour and that we would generally accept a definition of overall language proficiency as the ability to function in a natural language situation, we still insist on, or let others impose on us, testing measures which assess language as an abstract array of discrete items, to be manipulated only in a mechanistic way. Such tests yield artificial, sterile and irrelevant types of items, which have no relationship to the use of language in real life situations.
> (Rea 1978: 1)

In the 1970s, as the number of the overseas students in the UK rose rapidly, there was growing evidence of a demand for a more 'appropriate' English language entrance test which would relate closely to the communicative needs of students in an academic context. Wingard (1971: 55) had expressed the view that it was: '...partly because of the lack of firm agreement as to the skills actually needed by students pursuing university courses in a second language, that English proficiency testing designed to establish levels of competence for this purpose has so far proved rather disappointing', and this still appeared to be the case six years later, when Cowie and Heaton (1977: 8) in a SELMOUS publication noted:

> Before effective action can be taken on a national scale to overcome the many language problems of overseas students in Britain, there is first an urgent need for a reliable proficiency test in English, capable of identifying and accurately assessing the language needs of each student, in terms of his prospective course of study in Britain.

There was obvious discontent in this period with the wide variety of English language examinations acceptable as evidence of language proficiency for entry purposes to institutions in the tertiary sector. A survey of the contemporary literature indicates widespread dissatisfaction with both the nature and the amount of information that the then current English examinations were able to provide concerning the academic English proficiency of the candidates who sat them (cf. Chaplen 1970, Laing 1971, Wijasuriya 1971, Holes 1972, Morrison 1974, Moller 1977 and 1982, Cheung 1978, Kelly 1978, Ryan 1979, Taylor 1979, Pickett 1980, Barnes and Seed 1981).

Note that this list of professionals involved at the time in EL assessment for academic studies includes previous British Council ELOs such as Alan Moller, Doug Pickett (in the late 1970s Deputy Director of the British Council's English Teaching Information Centre) and Clive Holes (1971–1983: British Council overseas career service).

University of Cambridge Local Examinations Syndicate (UCLES) examinations (i.e. LCE and CPE) were among the best tests available for non-first language English users, but even these did not have separate papers for reading and listening until 1975 and still included tests which could be considered of limited relevance to university study through the medium of English, e.g. translation into and out of a foreign language, reading aloud, an impromptu knowledge telling essay writing task, and an English literature paper.

Although the Davies test did have separate papers for reading and listening it also came in for some criticism. Roger Hawkey (personal communication May 2015) notes that the annual meetings of tutors of Commonwealth Fellows were dissatisfied with the inadequacy of information provided by EPTB and wanted a more satisfactory and reliable service. The tutors felt the test was far too general and did not give a clear indication of how students would cope with the communicative demands of their courses of study. Hawkey followed up on these matters in his doctoral dissertation (1982) which identified the study problems of such students, sponsored by the British Council at the Institute of Education, London.

While there was clearly a connection between a student's proficiency in English and the degree to which s/he would benefit from and contribute to the course of study, it was felt it might be difficult to predict academic problems caused by weakness in English, if there was not available a more accurate picture of the *communicative* demands made upon the student in his/her course of study than any so far established, and a profile of the student's language ability with respect to these. An analysis of the student's target study situation and of the language involved in the exercise of roles in that situation would enable test developers to identify more closely the communicative skills required for study purposes (cf. Munby 1977, Price 1977b and Ryan 1979).

Measuring Academic English proficiency

English proficiency, as far as receiving institutions were concerned, was often simply reduced to a binary question of whether a student possessed adequate English to be able to cope with his/her chosen course of study or not (Moller 1977). All too often administrators wanted a clear-cut yes/no decision and EPTB had provided them with a predictive estimate of this, but one heavily based on indirect measures of academic English proficiency.

A number of questions arise when we talk of a student having adequate proficiency to cope with an academic course of study. What is 'adequate proficiency' in this academic context? And thinking in more *communicative* terms (see below), what are the tasks a student has to cope with in English, and what are the underlying *enabling skills* that a student has to use, receptively and productively, in the chosen course of study? Does s/he have what Davies himself (1965a: 11) called 'control of English on all levels in appropriate situations'?

Hitherto, language proficiency had been mainly defined in terms of performance on tests of *linguistic* competence such as in the operational versions of the EPTB, which assessed the ability to produce grammatical sentences or utterances through knowledge of linguistic rules. The more balanced developments in approaches to language testing in the 1970s regarded proficiency as a matter of *communicative* as well as linguistic competence, because the effective control of English in an appropriate situation required command of *use*, as well as *usage* (contextual as well as linguistic competence).

Davies (1977: 62), harking back to his earlier interest in work sample EAP tests (1965a), argued that proficiency considerations were a design influence involving an assessment of what test candidates needed to do with the language and the varieties they had to employ in the contexts in which they found themselves. Heaton (1975a: 164) similarly saw a proficiency test as being concerned with measuring the student's control of the language in the light of what s/he would be expected to do with it in his/her future performance of a particular task in a future course of study or job. For Kelly (1978: 218) the term *proficiency test* denoted a test constructed to measure a candidate's ability to use the 'target' language in certain specified communication situations. Alan Moller (1981a), likewise, advocated a sociolinguistic/communicative approach, where proficiency is seen as the ability actually to use the language in valid, sociolinguistic situations (cf. Morrow 1977 and 1979; Carroll 1978 and 1980).

In the case of a foreign student being taught on an academic course through the medium of English, a circumscribed definition of proficiency was called for, as concern here was with proficiency in an academic context, rather than general English proficiency. Pat McEldowney (1976: 5), responsible for the Northern Universities Joint Matriculation Board (JMB) test of academic English, argued that neither the English of social interaction nor the English found in literature was required for successful English-medium study. What students needed was the more expository, neutral, transactional type of English that is the medium of education in English-speaking countries. She argued that, in order to be proficient in English-medium study, students needed to control this academic 'expository' English in the following ways: they needed to be able to understand the spoken mode for listening to lectures and discussions, to understand the written mode for reading textbooks and other sources of information; to produce adequate written English in their set work and examinations; and to produce adequate spoken English when necessary, e.g. in discussions, asking questions and presentations.

Problems encountered in the various study modes in tertiary-level education in the UK in the 1970s

To help understand the paradigm shift that took place between the construction of EPTB in 1963–1965 and ELTS in 1975–1980, it is useful to examine in more detail the target learning situation these tests were addressing, i.e. what language related study skills were considered necessary by those involved in the teaching and testing of Academic English *in the 1970s*. Drawing heavily on the literature on EAP published in the 1960s and 1970s, we describe below an emerging consensus on what needed to be tested and, thus, taught, in terms of the language related study skills students would need to cope with tertiary-level education in Britain at the time.

Studies of overseas students in Britain date back to 1907 with the report of the Lee Warner Committee on Indian students. The point emerging clearly from this and subsequent studies was that language is only one, albeit the most important one, of a number of problems overseas students face on entry to this country. This point was emphasised in Singh (1963), Burns (1965), Davies (1965a, 1977), Political and Economic Planning (P.E.P.) (1965), Dunlop (1966), Morris and Ajijola (1967), Holes (1972), Daniel (1975), Walker (1978) and Geoghegan (1983). Weir (1983) provides comprehensive coverage, as does Hawkey (1982), of the social and cultural factors affecting performance in the academic context, but we will limit ourselves here to those language related problems which are capable of being measured in a language proficiency test.

Alan Davies (1965a: 12) was clear on the centrality of language proficiency to successful academic study:

> English proficiency itself may well be affected by a number of variables such as sex, age, home language and country, as well as by intelligence. From a theoretical point of view such influences could be highly important; but from the practical point of view of a receiving institution in this country what matters is not the biographical history of an overseas student but whether his English is adequate for the course he wants to take.

In the first issue of the *Journal of English for Academic Purposes*, Robert Jordan (2002: 70) described the beginnings of EAP provision in Britain in the 1960s, when language support for overseas students was very much dealt with on an *ad hoc*, part-time basis as and when problems emerged. This sometimes led to the development of short *induction* courses; Birmingham University's, for example, was one of the first in 1962. On this course students' problems were investigated, teaching materials developed, and an attempt made to utilise a diagnostic test to identify areas in need of support.

In view of the many difficulties in English for academic purposes faced by overseas students, the Special English Language Materials for Overseas University Students (SELMOUS) group was set up in June 1972 and would provide valuable feedback on the development of ELTS in the late 1970s. The SELMOUS aim was to share experiences in dealing with overseas students' English language difficulties on the basis of investigation of language needs and the production of relevant teaching materials for use in any necessary remedial work. This group was very much aware of the extent of the language problems involved. One of its members, Bob Jordan (1977a: 13), stated that however weak a student's English was, she/he was seldom required to delay a course of study and attend a full-time EAP programme. According to SELMOUS members, about 30% of the students they looked after were in need of full-time English tuition ranging from 3 to 12 months.

SELMOUS was prominent in highlighting the particular language needs of overseas postgraduate students and Price (1977a) described how its members had been instrumental in setting up pre-sessional courses to try to improve the language performance of students before their academic studies got under way. Given that university language entry requirements varied between institutions and were not uniformly applied, and that attempts to assess student language ability were considered not wholly satisfactory, there was still uncertainty over the remedial teaching, either pre- or in-sessional, that would be necessary because of a shortfall in some overseas students' language abilities. There was a felt need for better testing procedures, which would point to areas where remedial work was needed. Language shortfall did not necessarily entail failure for the overseas students, but it was likely that the more proficient they were in the language, the more they would benefit from their chosen courses of study.

Roger Hawkey (personal communication November 2015) sheds some light on the British Council's involvement in EAP:

> A further insight into EAP and the influence of the British Council at Spring Gardens comes from R.R. Jordan of the University of Manchester, cited in Garcia Sanchez (2001: 181):

> It is of interest to note when the term 'EAP' was first used. Tim Johns recalls first using it at a meeting with two British Council officers, Keith Jones and Peter Roe, in October 1974. By spring 1975, it was being used generally by the Council.

From an early stage, the British Council involved itself with UK academics such as those in the SELMOUS group in establishing the nature of English for Academic Purposes. For example, in 1975 the British Council English Teaching Information Centre (ETIC) produced *English for Academic Study with Special Reference to Science and Technology* as an ETIC Occasional Paper. This was the outcome of a joint British Association of Applied Linguists (BAAL)/SELMOUS seminar organised in 1975 at Birmingham by Brian Heaton and Anthony Cowie. As well as papers on English for Science and Technology (EST) by Henry Widdowson, Keith Jones, Peter Roe, the latter two both Council ELOs, and James Ewer, the ETIC volume contained an important paper by Chris Candlin, Michael Kirkwood and Helen Moore on 'Developing Study Skills in English'. Candlin et al. provided a useful analysis of the range of study skills required for academic study. In 1976, the British Council English Teaching Division Inspectorate in London organised a training seminar on EAP for its ELT staff. The British Council publication ELT documents 109 *Study Modes and Academic Development of Overseas Students* (Greenall and Price 1980), the edited proceedings of the Special English Language Materials for Overseas University Students (SELMOUS) Easter seminar in April 1979, contained numerous articles relating to the study requirements of various academic subject areas, to students with particular cultural profiles (including papers by British Council officers Roger Bowers on the background of students from the Indian subcontinent and Roger Hawkey on Thai students) and to research into factors affecting academic development.

A composite picture of the overseas student's situation had been presented by Sen (1970) who carried out by questionnaire, English test and interview, a study of 2,367 overseas students and 553 nurses from 130 countries, studying in Britain from 1964 to 1966. Amongst other things, Sen investigated their academic and language difficulties and the problems they encountered in adjusting to English society. In her study over a third of the students found writing essays difficult and a large number had difficulties in following lectures and tutorials. If one examines Sen's relative figures for different national groupings, however, they point to what was an even greater cause for concern, namely the worse plight of the foreign as compared to Commonwealth students. She notes (ibid.: 58) that the Middle Eastern students, who scored less than the other groups in the Davies test, on the whole seem to find most difficulty with their studies. Only few expressed no difficulty with lectures, tutorials and in contacting their teachers, and a high proportion found writing essays and reference reading very difficult.

A majority of the students in Sen's survey were from the Commonwealth and in terms of their previous use of English as a medium of instruction, the earlier age at which they had begun to learn English, and their use of English at home, Sen found they had had considerably more exposure to the language than their foreign counterparts. This was a real cause for concern, as the balance between foreign and Commonwealth students coming to study in the UK changed in the early 1970s and subsequently there would be considerably more foreign than Commonwealth students. By 2014 less than 30% of all overseas students would come from Commonwealth countries (Anderson 2014). The English ability of the foreign students was, in all probability, lower than that of the Commonwealth students because of a much more limited exposure to the language, and it might be reasonable to infer that these students were likely to encounter more language difficulties proportionate to this in their academic courses.

Davies (1977: 36) mentions his concern regarding how serious a problem language was, on the basis of his findings in a survey completed for the Scottish Education Department on the English proficiency of foreign students in the non-university sector in Scotland (see Davies and Moller 1973). He found that students ranked English language as being the most serious problem, followed by academic status, social contacts and accommodation. The view that language was an important factor in academic progress was also indicated by the National Association of Foreign Student Advisers (NAFSA) (1961) survey and subsequent studies. Hawkey (1982) refers to the British Council's 1981 *Survey of the Factors affecting the Performance of Overseas Development Agency (ODA) Sponsored Study Fellows*, the main finding of which was that the 'unsatisfactory' performance of 30% of the sample was due mainly to inadequate language proficiency and motivation and a failure to adapt successfully to the new academic and social environment. The majority of studies reviewed indicated that serious language problems existed for a number of overseas students.

Although many of the problems overseas students faced in this country in the 1970s could be attributed to social and other factors, there is no doubt, from the EAP literature of the time, that for many students the problems arose through the relationship between their ability in language and the requirements of their study. Thus, as Davies (1965a: 12) pointed out in his doctoral thesis:

> ...while English proficiency may not be the most important factor for all overseas students, it is one important factor for them all, one that it may be possible to isolate for testing purposes, perhaps, indeed one – the only one! – that can be radically improved when revealed.

Adequate proficiency in English may not have guaranteed a student success in an academic course and lack of it may not have entailed failure. It was, as we noted above, only one of the factors involved. It did, however, mean that a student would be able to compete on a more equal footing with native speaker counterparts and have the opportunity to derive the maximum benefit from a course of instruction in this country.

In the 1970s the language proficiency of some overseas students could not be described as adequate when they started courses in this country. The inadequacies detailed below might well have been merely the tip of the iceberg as, for the most part, evidence of them emerged from the work done in those institutions that were fortunate enough to have language servicing facilities which could provide remedial English language tuition. In examining the EAP literature of the period, it soon becomes clear why a new test, which more closely identified shortfall in language proficiency for study purposes, was essential.

The language demands of the target situation and the problems encountered by overseas students in coping with these are further detailed in subsections below. This is intended to serve as an outline of the construct that needed to be measured by a more direct EAP test that would be beneficial to universities wishing to have a clearer picture of a student's ability to cope with the language demands of academic study.

Such a development would be of considerable relevance to the British Council, of course, with its crucial investment in students from around the world coming to Britain, for studies conducted in English, to develop their expertise in key areas vital to their own and their countries' futures.

Lectures

Jordan (1977a) described how postgraduate students at the Universities of Manchester and Newcastle heard most spoken English in a passive listening role, i.e. in situations where they were not called upon to respond at all, for example, listening to lectures, where no check is made on comprehension. In his study, 70% listed understanding spoken English as their biggest difficulty on arrival in the United Kingdom. Edwards (1978) found a similar pattern in her study of overseas nurses coming to study in the UK, and concluded that the overseas learners' language problems lay mainly in the field of spoken English. She describes how in both understanding and speaking, over 78% admitted to having difficulties of some kind with this. Sen (1970) had found that 25% of the students she surveyed admitted to having listening comprehension difficulties. It would seem possible, therefore, as Morrison (1974) argued, that lack of exposure to natural spoken British English accounts for the initial difficulty that many overseas students experienced on arrival.

Wijasuriya (1971) found overseas students had difficulties in lectures due to a complex of factors. At the phonological level, both he and Morrison (1974) refer to the difficulties caused by the speed at which lectures are delivered. They also detail evidence of the difficulty occasioned by a variety of native speaker accents, as do Sen (1970), Jordan and McKay (1973), UKCOSA (United Kingdom Council for Overseas Student Affairs) (1974), Edwards (1978) and Walker (1978). Candlin et al. (1975) also refer to difficulties with phonology (elision, reduction, intonation and regional accent). James (1980) notes the difficulties many overseas students have in decoding a lecturer's utterances because of unfamiliarity with English stress-timed rhythm and sometimes arbitrary lexical stress.

At the level of lexical meaning, the difficulties met by students were as relevant to the reading and writing study modes as they were to lectures, seminars and practicals. Chaplen (1970), Wijasuriya (1971), Morrison (1974) and Candlin et al. (1975) all cite lexis as a source of difficulty, and Hutchinson and Waters (1981) report a specific difficulty when there is a lack of precision in the vocabulary used instead of standard technical terms.

Holes (1972) cites register switching as a serious cause of difficulty in the lecture mode. He draws attention to the fact that: '...the distinctions between formal and informal language may be blurred in a lecture situation where there may be drastic change from formal to informal language when giving explanations...it could be disastrous for the foreign student who may have been taught English in a combination of literary and formal English' (1972: 33).

Sen (1970), Holes (1972), UKCOSA (1974) and Jordan (1977a) all refer to the difficulty of comprehending lectures in general and taking notes. Johns and Johns (1977a) were concerned more specifically with the difficulty overseas students had in grasping the basic argument and relating it to the framework of the subject under discussion. The study skill of note-taking was seen by James (1980) as a problem involving four main activities for the student: understanding the message; identifying the main points; deciding when to write them down and writing them down quickly, so that comprehension of the ongoing lecture is not interrupted, and clearly so that they will be understood at a later date.

In our discussion of ELTS in Chapter 4 we describe the listening test that was included in ELTS in 1980. It is worth noting again that prior to 1975, listening had never been tested in its own right in a test paper by Cambridge English language examinations, and only a short dictation was used in the speaking test (see Weir, Vidakovic and Galaczi 2013: Chapter 5). EPTB did not test meaning construction in listening in the operational version. The attempt to measure the student's ability to comprehend seminars and monologue in ELTS (see subsection *The testing of reading and listening in ELTS* in Chapter 4) would fit well with students' observed difficulties in this area when they first enter a UK university from abroad.

Seminars

The perceived areas of difficulty referred to above in connection with the lecture mode nearly all apply to the seminar study mode as well. There is however, evidence of additional problems occurring in the seminar mode.

Rogers (1977: 37) discovered in the courses he ran for postgraduate students in science and technology that despite much previous work in the language, students could not participate effectively in academic discussion and tended to be unable to take part in social activities with native speakers. Mackenzie (1977: 41) also found that, for the Latin-American students he taught, lack of oral fluency often proved an insuperable obstacle to effective participation in seminars and tutorials. It seemed to be mainly in the production of coherent discourse that seminars put an additional burden on the overseas student, though Johns and Johns (1977a) refer to problems in understanding the varying realisations of functions and Hawkey (1982) to problems associated with topic switching. Edwards (1978: 316) instanced occasions where students:

'... had difficulty in remaining linguistically coherent when attempting to answer at length or when joining in discussions'. She commented (ibid.: 321) that if one adds to this difficulty the problems with accent, more general difficulties in understanding the teaching staff and '... the indigene [home student] learners' near total ellipsis when answering questions and the speed at which they do so', one had some idea of the factors which might inhibit participation. Edwards concluded that: 'what learner-initiated participation there was in the classroom activities was dominated by indigenes'.

Holes (1972) and Jordan (1977a) noted overseas students' difficulties in communicating functionally, especially in asking questions for appropriate purposes. Similarly the UKCOSA (1974) survey found: 'a reluctance to ask questions due to a fear of using English. This contributed to the formation of nationality groups where students hardly ever speak in English.' Rogers (1977) and Jordan (1977a) both found that overseas students did not take an active part in discussions and gave restricted answers when questioned, due to problems with fluency and self-expression. Rogers indicated that some also had problems because they were too formal and polite; they had difficulty with conversational 'openers', 'closers' and 'topic change'; they had difficulty with humour of all kinds or did not understand the various conventions of non-verbal behaviour.

In the ELTS test (see subsection *The testing of writing and speaking in ELTS* in Chapter 4), spoken interaction would be tested in an oral component where the candidate took part in discussions with the examiner much as s/he would with a course tutor. This matched Weir's (1983) finding that most of the interaction in seminars was dyadic between student and tutor. In one task in the ELTS listening test, candidates would also listen to and answer questions on an academic seminar.

Reading

Jordan (1977a) recorded a general inability on the part of the overseas student to read quickly or understand the complexities of academic prose. He found that the average student had only one speed (i.e. slow) for silent reading – about 150–160 words a minute. Edwards (1978) noted similar difficulty with reading comprehension, and UKCOSA (1974) mentioned 'difficulty in reading effectively' as a common problem, as was 'difficulty in understanding examination questions'. Holes (1972) referred to slow reading as a universal complaint. He had the impression that the cause of low reading speeds was that many overseas students regarded books with great reverence and felt they had to spend a long time summarising the whole of the book rather than search-reading it to extract criterial information for their assignments (ibid.: 66).

At the level of lexical meaning, Johns (1980) noted the problems caused by density of unknown vocabulary and metaphorical usage. Holes (1972: 66) echoed this when he pointed out that it was not the actual level of syntactic difficulty in the text which caused reading problems, but rather the terminological difficulties in new subjects causing many students to resort to dictionaries while reading textbooks. Ryan (1979) and Templeton (1973) also recorded difficulties encountered in mastering the technical register of a subject area.

There was a lot of evidence that problems were also serious at the study skills level. Brew (1980) instanced the problem of sorting out the main points from supporting details and Wallace (1980) abstracting the organisational pattern and main ideas from a text. Johns (1980) referred to problems in surveying for gist and scanning for information and Wallace (1980) to those in surveying and referencing.

Reading would be extensively tested by ELTS (see subsection on reading and listening in Chapter 4). Not only would ELTS test careful reading, but expeditious reading, central to academic performance, was also addressed (see Urquhart and Weir 1998). In addition, a passage in the reading paper would be used as stimulus material in the writing paper just like writing in the real-world academic context.

Essays, report writing, dissertation

Jordan and Mackay (1973) and Jordan (1977a) argued that as academic courses developed, writing skills become more important and would generally, according to Jordan (1977a: 18) '...supersede understanding as a cause of major difficulty' as written work had to be submitted. Particular difficulties in this area may of course only surface even later in the course when writing had to be done under the pressure of time constraints as in examinations; by then it may well be too late for remedial action. Jordan (1977a) likewise noted an acute problem in writing quickly.

There were close links between the problems overseas students faced in the reading mode and their own attempts at written production (Johnson 1981). At the phrase structure level, Greenall and Price (1980) pointed to additional problems in the use of the article, spelling, passivisation, relativisation and complex nominalisation, and Johns and Johns (1977b) to problems in the use of determiners.

At the language *coherence* as opposed to *cohesion* level, Kaplan (1966) and Johnson (1977a) noted difficulties students from different cultures had in achieving a coherent discourse structure in English, what Bruner (1975) terms 'analytic competence' (the ability to structure thought in linguistic terms). Jordan (1977a) and Rogers (1977) referred to difficulties in writing concisely, and Greenall and Price (1980) to evidence of a possible tendency on the part of the overseas student to aim at minimal content.

The study skill of organisation (Wallace 1980) and the researching of a piece of writing (Johns 1980) would seem to have presented great difficulty. Wallace (1980) referred to difficulties in organising essays and Price (1980) to difficulties in organising a dissertation. Weir (1983) found organisation and the relevance and adequacy of content to be the most criterial aspects of writing for almost all university staff.

As we note in Chapter 4 (see subsection on writing and speaking) ELTS would in many ways be unique as a writing test in the 1980s as it would involve the candidate making use of a reading text provided/used previously in the reading module, to produce a written product. Most other examinations after EPTB resorted to impromptu writing tasks which normally only involve knowledge telling abilities whereas ELTS would get closer to knowledge transformation, the hallmark of academic writing.

Summary of Academic English requirements from our review of the 1970s EAP literature

This brief survey of the EAP needs of tertiary-level students, and the language related problems faced by overseas students in particular, indicates that it was the difficulties caused by the 'higher-order' language skills at the meaning building and discourse construction levels in all the four language skills: listening, reading, writing and speaking, together with study skills and study attitudes and habits, which received most attention in the English for Academic Purposes literature of the 1970s. Less attention was paid to 'lower-order' language skills at the phonological, morphological, lexical and phrase structure level and there seemed to be an implicit assumption (correct, as later research in cognitive psychology was to suggest, see for example, Geranpayeh and Taylor 2013: Chapter 3) that ability in lower-order processing was largely subsumed within ability in higher-order processing. This emphasis on understanding, responding to and conveying meaning, increasingly seen as part of 'the communicative approach', was in vogue at the time in language teaching and to an increasing extent in language testing in the 1970s.

The British Council's operational versions of EPTB were tests, which for the most part focused on lower-order language skills at the decoding level rather than on the higher-order skills of meaning construction or discourse representation. The operational version contained no tests which focused on speaking, or writing, and the tests of reading and listening were mainly targeted at lower-level micro-linguistic processing. As we have shown in this review of academic study modes, it became clear in the 1970s that what was needed was a test which focused on the higher-order reading, listening, writing and speaking language related study skills which were necessary to operate successfully in the academic context.

The importance of early identification of inadequate language proficiency

Cowie and Heaton (1977: 7) noted, in their introduction to the SELMOUS report entitled *English for Academic Purposes*, that very few tertiary-level institutions required formal English language qualifications for those admitted at the postgraduate level. Most critics were in agreement with James (1980: 12) in his conclusion that some standardised policy should be developed to determine those students in need of remedial help with their English.

There was a pressing need to identify those overseas students, particularly if they were on one-year postgraduate courses, who might underachieve because of a shortfall in their English ability. The problem was a serious one because, without some means of identifying very early on in which study modes difficulty might occur, it could well be late in the first term before academic staff had sufficient evidence to make any decisions on a student's need to have remedial help with his English. Chaplen (1970) and Morrison (1974) drew attention to the fact that the departmental tutor was by no means certain to realise the extent of a student's problems immediately and that academic English inadequacy could remain hidden for some time. If students carefully controlled their linguistic output by limiting themselves to the structures they had confidence in utilising, their tutors may well have been left with a false impression about their spoken English and might mistakenly have inferred a lack of any problems on the part of the student in comprehending spoken discourse or producing written work based on extensive reading. Of course, the student might not help matters by choosing to affect complete comprehension for various reasons, for example, from a desire not to lose face. It might also happen that it was not until the students had to produce written work at a later stage in the course that they became fully aware of the extent of their own problems.

This was a disturbing state of affairs, especially for those students on nine-month postgraduate courses for, given the short length and heavy demands of these courses, it was likely that they would have very little time to spare for remedial English, which was often seen as extra-curricular study. This pressure was likely to be even greater in the spring and summer terms and, as Jordan and McKay (1973: 46) concluded in their survey of overseas postgraduate students at the Universities of Manchester and Newcastle, once a student fell behind with English language improvement, (s)he rarely caught up, especially on a one-year postgraduate course. Given the proliferation of one-year Masters and Diploma courses in most universities and the trend for non-Commonwealth and thus non-English-medium educated postgraduates to attend them, Davies' warning in his thesis (1965a: 117) that many of the more serious language problems are faced by the overseas postgraduates studying on courses in Britain for one year or even less was a wake-up call indeed.

Often students felt that their acceptance on to a UK university course implied, in the eyes of the receiving institution, the possession of adequate English to cope with the demands of the course. In a sense they were right and acceptance would seem to impose an obligation on the receiving institution to ensure that the student's progress was not impaired by inadequate linguistic ability. An early identification of students with a shortfall in their English proficiency was essential. If they were to be accepted on to programmes of study, both they and the academic staff involved would need to be apprised of any language problems and provision made for remedial language work as early as possible in the course, or even before it began.

The situation with regard to the identification of overseas postgraduate students at risk as a result of language deficit was therefore acute in the 1970s, particularly for those on one-year courses. The heterogeneity of the tests available was worrying for those concerned with test equivalence. The appropriateness of existing instruments, including the EPTB, for measuring academic English proficiency was clearly in question given the very different constructs they were measuring and the impoverished relationship of these to the language abilities required for the various courses of academic study at tertiary level. The communicative competence construct was beginning to attract far more attention and support than the linguistic competence construct targeted by tests such as the operational form of the EPTB.

There was now a clear case for a standardised test battery which could be administered efficiently and reliably overseas, and which could provide consistent, comprehensive and relevant communicative competence-focused information on student English abilities at entry to their tertiary-level studies in the medium of English. The ELTS test would attempt to fill this vacuum.

Chapter 4

The English Language Testing Service: The first communicative test, 1975–1989

Iacta alea est (The die is cast) – Julius Caesar, 10 January 49 BCE, as he led his army across the Rubicon river in northern Italy
(Quoted in Suetonius, *Vīta Dīvī Iūlī* (The Life of the Deified Julius), 121 CE, par. 33.)

A paradigm shift in language testing

Approaches to the testing and teaching of English were to change radically in the UK in the 1970s as a result of a burgeoning interest in the 'communicative approach', which focuses on how language is used in real-life situations. Richard Smith (forthcoming) identifies the signal contribution the British Council made to the general development of this communicative approach in English Language Teaching (ELT) in the 1970s:

> The British Council carried out and assisted ground-breaking research into ELT and methodological innovation in ELT in the 1970s. The communicative philosophy of language teaching, which gained currency in the 1970s, became a key component of the Council's English teaching programmes across the world.

In the 1970s and 1980s it is possible to discern a shift in the United Kingdom away from traditional *structural* approaches to language teaching. The concern in teaching was no longer with gradually equipping students with the grammatical structures of the language in a systematic, ordered fashion. This approach had been popular since the time of the German linguist Johann Christian Fick (1793) and was usually accompanied, in post-WW2 structural approaches, by a methodology based on presentation in context, pattern practice and other forms of relatively controlled production. The change was to an approach, which prioritised using language as a means of communication (see Weir 1990, Weir, Vidakovic and Galaczi 2013: Chapter 1 for a full account of this).

Cyril Weir (1983), in his doctoral thesis on the development of the Associated Examining Board's EAP test for university admission purposes (TEAP), exemplifies how the communicative approach was influencing language testing as well. Advocates of testing communicative language ability felt that earlier approaches to language testing, for example the EPTB discussed in Chapter 3, had paid insufficient attention to the importance of the productive and receptive processing of discourse arising out of *the actual use of language in a social context* (see Morrow 1979, Moller 1982).

In the eyes of many critics, the earlier 'discrete point' approach, as embodied in many of the sub-tests in the operational form of EPTB (see Chapter 3), suffered from the defects of the *construct* it sought to measure. Bernard Spolsky (1968) had argued that rather than measuring a person's knowledge of a language in terms of a percentage mastery of grammar and lexis, we would be better employed in testing that person's ability to perform in a specified sociolinguistic setting.

Kelly (1978: 350) identified the crucial characteristics of the communicative approach within testing:

> To take part in a communicative event is to produce and/or comprehend discourse in the context of situation and under the performance conditions that obtain. It is the purpose of a proficiency test to assess whether or not candidates are indeed capable of participating in typical communication events from the specified communication situation(s).

These views were expanded on in a seminal article written by Canale and Swain (1980: 34), which is seen by many as the catalyst for the communicative revolution in language testing:

> ...communicative testing must be devoted not only to what the learner knows about the second language and about how to use it (competence) but also to what extent the learner is able to actually demonstrate this knowledge in a meaningful communicative situation (performance).

In justifying the communicative approach adopted in the design of the Associated Examining Board's Test in English for Academic Purposes (the TEAP test, later rebranded as the Test in English for *Educational Purposes*, the TEEP test), Weir (1983) refers to the ground-breaking influence of Keith Morrow in the development of communicative approaches to language testing in the UK, particularly arising out of his work in the late 1970s on the Royal Society of Arts (RSA) *Communicative Use of English as a Foreign Language (CUEFL)* examinations. Morrow spoke from long experience in EL teaching, testing and management roles at university level and in the UK private sector. He was editor of the *ELT Journal* for 17 years (until 2012) and Chief Inspector for Accreditation UK, the language provider quality assurance scheme managed by the British Council. Morrow, a leading light among testers advocating the communicative approach, suggested (1979: 145) that if we are to assess language proficiency adequately, knowledge of the elements of the language would be worthless unless the user could combine these elements in new and appropriate ways in those contexts of situation they found themselves in. Morrow (1979) argued that although indirect measures of language abilities might lay claim to high levels of reliability and concurrent validity through *post hoc* statistical analysis, their claim to other types of validity remains suspect. He cites as evidence for this the fact that none of these testing procedures offers the possibility for oral or non-controlled written production and argues that since both the oral and written skills are generally held to be highly important, some means of assessing them reliably in communicative situations should be found.

Other researchers demonstrated that although earlier discrete and integrative measures appeared to correlate highly with similar measures of general language proficiency, there was evidence that they correlated only moderately with tests of written production and with spoken production (see Vollmer 1981a and 1981b). It was now felt that, provided valid and reliable tests of the kind of spoken and written English communication candidates would actually need in the target situation could be developed and validated, proficiency in these areas could and should be measured, in preference to discrete-point micro-linguistic indirect tests of overall proficiency.

Weir (1983) argues that concerns about the type of information provided by the 'discrete point' items in the earlier psychometric-structuralist approach led practising testers, in the UK in particular, to look to the 'communicative paradigm' to see whether this approach might prove more satisfactory. By the early 1980s the communicative perspective could be found in the work of language testers generally supportive of a broadly based model of communicative language ability with a marked shift in emphasis from the linguistic to the communicative dimension. The emphasis was no longer on linguistic accuracy, but on the ability to function effectively through language in particular contexts of situation. As Pauline Rea (1978: 4) succinctly put it, the focus shifted to: 'the ability to communicate with ease and effect in specified sociolinguistic settings'.

In the United Kingdom the spread of communicative language testing was encouraged by the work of British Council ELOs with testing knowledge and experience, including Clive Bruton, Brendan Carroll, Peter Hargreaves, Roger Hawkey, Roland Hindmarsh, Arthur McNeill, Alan Moller and Ian Seaton, all of whom served during this period in the English Language Consultancies (later Services) Department (ELCD). The communicative language testing movement was supported by university academics and other experts such as: Charles Alderson, Chris Candlin, Frank Chaplen, Caroline Clapham, Liz Hamp-Lyons, Andrew Harrison, Brian Heaton, Arthur Hughes, Graham Low, Pat McEldowney, Keith Morrow, Don Porter, Pauline Rea, Peter Skehan, Sandy Urquhart and Cyril Weir. The 'new' communicative approach to language testing was extensively discussed and critically evaluated at the inaugural meeting of the United Kingdom Language Testing Forum (LTF) in Lancaster in 1980. The discussion was recorded and written up along with the discussion papers and accompanying critiques in Alderson and Hughes, *Issues in Language Testing* (1981), an influential British Council publication.

The ELTS test: Origins

The English Language Testing Service (ELTS) test (Carroll 1978, 1980 and 1981, Moller 1981a and 1981b, and Seaton 1981) was developed within this communicative paradigm. It was created in response to a growing demand from test stakeholders for more detailed information concerning the ability of applicants for English-medium tertiary-level education to cope with the language related study demands of that context (see Chapter 3 above for discussion of these study demands).

Cambridge English Language Assessment (then known as the University of Cambridge Local Examinations Syndicate (UCLES)) and the British Council worked together from the mid-1970s to develop a replacement for the EPTB (see Chapter 3), the ELTS test, which took account of the significant changes that had taken place in the 1970s in approaches to language learning and teaching. Alan Davies (2008: 77) describes the EPTB as typifying the structuralist approach in its sampling of grammar and lexis. He argues that EPTB was 'swept away' by the communicative revolution, which ELTS embraced through its inclusion of real-life examples of specific language use. Reflecting on the EPTB, Davies (2008: 108), concludes that its structural model was too far removed from actual acts of everyday communication and that neither teaching nor testing the discrete structures of the language helped test takers prepare for the communicative interactions they would encounter in the target situation.

The design of the new ELTS battery by the British Council would embody the shift in emphasis in language teaching from an atomistic approach to a broader sociolinguistic one (cf. Carroll 1978 and 1980, Munby 1978, Clapham 1981, Moller 1982 and Seaton 1981) and take account of developments in English for Specific Purposes (ESP) where, by definition, the emphasis was no longer on catering, in a single test, for the needs of all users regardless of the purposes for which the language is required. Given the focus on the actual communicative needs of the learner groups being taught or tested, one size was not considered to fit all.

Ian Seaton, who, from the late 1970s, worked with a language-testing brief in ELCD (later ELSD) at the British Council, provides valuable insight into the drivers for change (personal communication September 2014). Note here, the warning tone, as the EPTB is seen as no longer in tune with the more communicative testing times and facing strong potential competition from a rival US test:

> In the late 1970s it became increasingly clear that the British Council needed a new way of testing the English language ability of the wide range of students and trainees coming from all over the world for tertiary study in Britain. The English Proficiency Test Battery, often known as the Davies Test, had gone through several versions in its lifetime and had simply 'run out of road' for further development. Its design, content and administration were no longer able to cope with the demands the Council and British universities and colleges placed on it. The Council also used an informal language assessment, mainly spoken, called the 'Subjective Test' in its smaller offices without any form of monitoring let alone validation studies to control its performance. Taken together it all resembled a cottage industry no longer fit for purpose. Even worse, major testing institutions

in the United States such as ETS Princeton could point to the absence of any central administrative supervision, the lack of any real longitudinal validation studies and the inadequate provision of alternate versions for heavy and repeated testing situations, and then begin to suggest with some justification that its TOEFL system should be widely adopted by British universities and colleges, as in the United States. Clearly a new beginning and a new test system were needed.

Before delving more deeply into the nature of the communicative construct underlying the new ELTS test, we will first trace the history of the ELTS test development. This will serve to illustrate the British Council's continuing involvement in academic English testing in the 1970s and 1980s, following on from its sponsorship of Alan Davies to develop the EPTB for the British Council in the 1960s (see Chapter 3).

What is clear in this part of our history (1975–1989) is that, post-EPTB, the British Council continued to make a significant contribution to the testing of EAP in the UK and overseas. In the 1970s and 1980s it still possessed a critical mass of staff with expertise in both ELT and assessment, including Brendan Carroll, Peter Hargreaves (until 1988), Roger Hawkey (until 1984), Arthur McNeill, Alan Moller, Ian Seaton and Gill Westaway. Cambridge did not have this degree of expertise until the arrival of Peter Hargreaves from the British Council in London in 1988 and of Mike Milanovic, formerly of the British Council in Hong Kong (the first teacher to be appointed specifically to be responsible for all testing in a British Council ELT operation), who joined together with Nick Saville in 1989 to form the UCLES Evaluation Unit. Lynda Taylor and Neil Jones closely followed them in the early 1990s, when the balance of expertise in testing would shift towards Cambridge as the British Council's ELT cadre was run down (see Chapter 5 for details of the institutional rationale for this). But in the 1970s and the 1980s the British Council was still the driving force in key EL assessment areas in the UK.

The genesis of the ELTS test is not clearly established in the language testing literature, but from the various sets of minutes held in the Cambridge and British Council archives, we were able to piece together the stages of its development. We first outline these stages and then we will look more closely at the constructs the new test attempted to measure.

Clive Criper and Alan Davies (1988: 3) report how, in 1975, the then Director General of the British Council, Sir John Llewellyn, 'requested the University of Cambridge Local Examinations Syndicate (UCLES) to form a joint consultative group with the British Council to initiate the

142 *Assessing English on the Global Stage*

setting up of the English Language Testing Service'. They also note that the UK Committee of Vice Chancellors and Principals had expressed as an urgent priority the need for a more effective monitoring of the language ability of non-native speaking overseas students and welcomed the British Council/UCLES plans for such a test.

In his interview for this history in January 2015, Alan Davies remembers there being discussions between the British Council and Albert Pilliner in Edinburgh, then a consultant to the British Council, UNESCO and other bodies, on the exam systems of various countries, about setting up a *testing service* in Moray House:

> So that was a possibility and the other possibility of course was Cambridge, and Cambridge eventually won out. It was bound to I think because it was a much larger better well known organisation, so they took it on and so it went to Cambridge....

From a minute of the British Council/UCLES June 1975 Joint Committee meeting, it is clear that the British Council initially hoped the Syndicate would provide them with a *testing service* to relieve the administrative load on its teaching operations around the world:

> Further to discussion about testing needs at British Council offices overseas both at scholarship screening level and at more elementary levels, it was reported that the British Council would now be formally asking the Syndicate to set up a testing service, which it will guarantee to use in the selection of potential award holders. The service would relieve Council officers of the burden of directly testing very large numbers (over 10,000 in 1974), and would provide on demand tests to be taken on a series of given dates. There would be no formal certification and the results of tests would not be published, but would be a matter of report by the Syndicate to the centre concerned, for its own use and for passing on to universities or other sponsors, at its discretion.

The UCLES Executive Committee 36th meeting, May 1976 minutes confirm that progress was being made on the setting up of such a service by Cambridge and that the special appointment of a new research officer, Andrew Harrison, had been made expressly for the purpose of developing materials for ELTS:

> 76/18 English Language Testing Service
> Progress was reported on the preparation of specifications for a series of tests for assessing competence in English for a variety of purposes,

from advanced academic study to industrial training. A Development Committee has been established, and a research officer (Mr A. Harrison) appointed from January 1976 to work with the Test Development and Research Unit as the co-ordinating body. Following trials this summer and the development of actual test material, tests will be available in December 1977, and will be both of general scope and designed to test fitness for particular activities involving linguistic skill. The progress made in the direction of testing English for special purposes was noted with interest....

The Test Development Research Unit (TDRU) annual report 1976 (3) refers to the leading role Cambridge was playing in the development of ELTS in 1976:

> After discussions with the British Council, the University of Cambridge Local Examinations Syndicate has undertaken to set up an English Language Testing Service, which will assess the competence in English of potential students and trainees from overseas who aim to attend courses in the United Kingdom. The Syndicate commissioned the Unit to develop the necessary tests, and in January 1976 Mr. A.W. Harrison joined the staff of the Unit principally to carry this work forward under the guidance of a Test Development Committee of specialists. The committee has met three times during 1976, and set up a Working Party to give detailed consideration to the content and form of possible tests. A small scale experiment to establish the viability of four test types was conducted in April. A larger programme of trial testing was carried out at centres in Britain between July and October. The tests were also tried out overseas, and the results are still being processed. The trial tests consisted of twelve booklets in over-lapping series designed to test general English for all candidates and English for Special Purposes in three categories according to candidates' special interests: two forms of 'Language for Science Study', two forms of 'Language for Non-Science Study', and a variety of tests for trainees. Commissioning is now in progress for pre-tests in spring 1977, preparatory to the compilation of operational tests for use in January 1978 onwards. It is intended to continue trial testing with other forms and contents of test during 1977.

The content of the initial version of the test had been mapped out by the January 1977 meeting of the British Council/UCLES Joint Committee. Initially, as with the EPTB, there was to be a version for science students, one for non-science students and one for non-academic students, but with plans for widening the range of modules available and developing parallel forms of existing versions. The minutes of the meeting record the intended structure of the test:

144   *Assessing English on the Global Stage*

> The recommendations of the Test Development Committee were accepted, and the following structure for the Test Service in 1978 agreed:
> Four tests will be available, being a test of the vocabulary and structure of everyday English, and a selection of three tests designed for (a) trainees, (b) students of science, (c) non-science subjects.
> Each candidate tested will normally take the general test and the equivalent subject-related test.
> Each test will be of 30–50 minutes, and consist of a variety of question types of objective forms, normally marked in Cambridge.
> There will be at least two alternative forms of each test.
>
> Development
> It was agreed that further development work should be undertaken, with the aim of establishing a system of renewal of the initial tests, revising their structure and content as necessary, and adding further subject-related tests at various levels according to requirements. The proposed further range, it was noted, includes diversification of the science/technology area, probably at post-graduate level, a test more specifically for humanities (literature, history, law) also at post-graduate level, and diversification of the general test. Development through 1978 and 1979 will, nevertheless, be cautiously undertaken, making use of maximum feedback from the current tests and further information about users' needs.

However, by the Executive Committee 38th meeting in May 1977 it seems that serious differences between Cambridge and the British Council had arisen with regard to the content of the test:

> 77/3 Matters arising out of the Minutes
> 2. English Language Testing Service
> Progress made towards the introduction of a range of tests on behalf of the British Council, for the screening of overseas applicants for study or training or various fields, was reported by Mr Otter [a syndicate representative] and Mr Hindmarsh [a British Council officer previously seconded to Cambridge]. It was noted that a programme of pretesting of material is in hand, together with detailed consideration of administrative arrangements. *Reservations expressed about the agreed range of content of tests may however mean that a pilot scheme only will operate during 1978* [emphasis added].

The UCLES Test Development Research Unit (TDRU) annual report 1977 (p. 11) is more informative:

The programme of trial testing initiated in 1976 was continued in the early part of the year. The plan had been to launch a modest form of the Service as early as possible in 1978, and materials for trainees and both for science and non-science students were brought to an advanced stage of preparation. Pre-tests were held both in the United Kingdom and overseas, with a view to drafting reliable test instruments for the various purposes.

Early in the year, however, the British Council, who had commissioned the work and been closely involved with its day to day progress, decided that the programme should be suspended pending an analytic review of language needs of trainees and students along lines recently being developed within the Council.

In the interview with Roger Hawkey (September 2014), co-author of a history of Cambridge EFL examinations (Hawkey and Milanovic 2013), he suggests that part of the problem may have been that Cambridge were intent on developing a test largely in the mould of their existing examinations (CPE and FCE):

> I think, as far as I could see, Cambridge would have automatically started as if they were expected to produce that kind of test. They would automatically start from their existing set of tests, so they would think, well, is this FCE or is it CPE, as a starter, rather than is this ESP or EAP or a Munby model? …the orthodox way of thinking of tests…'It would be like the other ones'.

Alan Davies confirms Hawkey's hypothesis in the interview we held with him as part of our History project:

> So the Council set up a committee with Cambridge and they said Cambridge would do development and the Council would be, as it were, consultants on this…. But because of Munby and Brendan [Carroll], fairly soon they decided that Cambridge and the other people, the other usual suspects on the committee, including me, were as it were too dyed in the wool in the past and they wanted something very different, and so the Council took it over completely. … They were paying for it, they were paying for the test and so they reckoned that they had the right therefore to develop it in their own way.

Sponsored by the British Council, John Munby had written a doctoral thesis (1977) entitled *Designing a Processing Model for Specifying Communicative Competence in a Foreign Language* at the University of Essex under the supervision of Professor Peter Strevens, then Professor of Applied Linguistics at the University, formerly Chair of Contemporary

English at the University of Leeds and later Director of the Bell Education Trust. Munby's thesis was published in 1978 as *Communicative Syllabus Design*, and as we shall see below it would have an important influence on the design of teaching materials and test development in ELTS and beyond (see for example Weir 1983).

The interviews conducted as part of this history project suggest a noticeable buoyancy on the part of the English language staff of the British Council at this time which may have encouraged them to pursue matters in their own way. Hawkey refers several times in his interview to a 'gung ho' spirit pervading the English Language Consultancies Department (ELCD), 'a period of huge optimism and belief in itself', with great enthusiasm and no fear of being controversial. According to Hawkey they thought they were at the cutting edge and best placed to develop a new communicative approach and drive the new test. Peter Falvey in the interview for the project also described a similar situation:

> It was seat of the pants flying. It was gut instincts, and the feeling, because they had through association and through osmosis come to terms with Munby's instrument, and the communicative movement, so they had that in them.

Thus, by the meeting of the Joint Committee in July 1977, the British Council were playing a more proactive role in relation to the test's development, with Brendan Carroll (a member of ELCD specialising in language testing) and Jo Barnett (as Controller English Language Division) proposing changes in the direction of an ESP (English for Specific Purposes) approach for determining the content of the test, in line with a 'Munby-based' needs analysis of the academic context.

Mike Milanovic, in his February 2015 interview for this history project, suggested it was a combination of factors that led to the British Council taking over responsibility for the test:

> Well, the British Council had previously commissioned what's commonly referred to as the Davies Test [EPTB] and prior to that had engaged in less formal types of assessment for foreign students coming to this country. During the sixties, seventies the number of foreign students coming to the country was starting to grow and at the same time the type of assessment that the Davies test represented was felt to be inappropriate because it wasn't very direct and at the same time John Munby had been working on his book on communicative language skills etc. Those things all came together and at the time the British Council had a more substantial

professional body of staff and so it was natural in some ways for the British Council to ask one of its own specialists to head the project.

Also, I think it's fair to say that Cambridge was probably understaffed in relation to English and it would not have had the capacity; in fact did not have a proper research function or a test development function beyond what it did for school exams. Although one or two universities were somewhat active, primarily Edinburgh, in assessment and Edinburgh was involved subsequently in the validation etc. the other universities which then became more interested in language testing such as Lancaster and Reading were still not really functioning at full strength. So it made sense for the project to be run from within the British Council in that regard.

The 10 August 1977 Minutes of the ELTS Management Committee record the new direction of travel for the test:

> 5.3. Mr Hindmarsh stated that the description provided by the Council on the characteristics of the test as seen in late 1975 had not constituted a specification in any strict sense, but only provided a context of work for the professional exploration to take place. The issue of test specification had from the outset been the most difficult one to make progress in. Now that the model developed within the Council by John Munby was coming into use, the Council believed that a new and practical instrument existed to assist with test specification.
>
> 5.4. It was agreed to recommend that the task of test specification should fall to the Council, which would undertake to process specifications for two learner stereotypes at the tertiary level by the end of October 1977, as well as several more by the end of December 1977. It was estimated that from three to five man-days are needed to process the first stage of a learner stereotype to the point of a language specification, and that a further three to five days (probably longer initially) will be required to produce a test specification deriving from this language specification.
>
> Roles and Responsibilities
> 6.1. Mr Barnett stated that the Council was prepared to produce the test specification and design (and initially the test items) and looked to Cambridge to administer the testing service.

The minutes of the Joint Committee meeting in October 1977 confirm there had indeed been a change in direction, with the British Council now taking responsibility for test specification and design. A paper tabled at the meeting by Joe Barnett signalled that the British Council was introducing its own approach to test development, based on an analysis of the needs of tertiary-level students using the theoretical model provided by Munby (1978).

Given the British Council's pioneering role in the development of the communicative approach in the UK and overseas (see above); the ELT and language testing expertise then present in the newly formed English Language Consultancies Division; the Council's growing global involvement in the tuition in English of candidates who had an interest in studying in the UK; and its consequent responsibility to establish that their English language levels were appropriately tested for that target context, it should perhaps come as no surprise that the Council would be so closely involved in the development of ELTS. Indeed, uniquely in the UK at that time, it had the expertise and wherewithal to do this.

Other British Council testing activities at the time of ELTS development

Alan Moller (personal communication December 2015) was keen to stress that besides EPTB and ELTS, the British Council was in fact closely involved with a wide variety of other testing activities in the late 1970s and early 1980s:

> In addition to the ongoing promotion of the Cambridge exams overseas the British Council was involved in the early development and monitoring of new tests within its own expanding teaching operations, seminal developments within the UK, and in emerging ELT situations overseas.
>
> Within British Council operations, widespread training of ELTS examiners and administrators was undertaken, a placement test was developed, known as the Platform test which was trialled and presented in Italy, Spain, Hong Kong and Jordan among others. This included the training of local teachers. Where individual teaching operations did not adopt the test, advice was given as to how they might improve existing procedures. Within the UK the Council responded to requests to send a representative [usually Alan Moller or Ray Underwood] to contribute to the advisory committees for the ARELS Oral Tests, for the new Communicative Use of English Test developed by RSA (this test was subsequently taken over by Cambridge), and for the Graded Tests of English being developed by the then University of London Schools Examination Board. ULSEB subsequently went through various changes of name and ownership and is now part of the Pearson Group. The Pearson Tests of English (PTE General) today are recent modifications of the original graded tests.
>
> One of the major projects overseas was the project in King Abdul Aziz University in Jeddah, Saudi Arabia, where a series of tests of achievement

in English in the Faculties of Engineering and Medicine were developed over a number of years, using a similar approach to that of ELTS. The first ELT (ODA/British Council) delegation to China led by Matt Macmillan in 1982 deliberately included the Council's Senior Consultant in Language Testing (then Alan Moller) since language testing was discussed at all points of call. In particular, the visit to Jiao Tong University in Shanghai marked the beginning of what was to become a very important and lengthy UK/Chinese cooperation in the TEM and CET projects [see Chapter 2 for details]. One more example of this transitional process was the University of Tsukuba project in Japan. The University requested a consultancy to aid them develop a series of tests for use with undergraduates in all faculties. The final test was to represent a level of English that every undergraduate was expected to attain. A week's visit by the Council's consultant resulted in agreeing a blueprint. Then Brian Heaton (University of Leeds) made further visits to develop and trial the tests, which subsequently provided a model for the Cambridge PET.

Richard Smith (forthcoming) provides detail of the significant expansion of the British Council's Direct Teaching of English Operations (DTEOs) from 1975 onwards which would necessitate involvement in language testing for placement purposes. Smith notes:

> The mid-1970s were a time of austerity and cuts in public services in the UK. In this climate, Sir John Llewellyn (Director-General, 1972–80) visited the two Institutes in Madrid and Barcelona in 1975 and found they were earning large surpluses through English teaching. Institutes and direct teaching of English were also still flourishing in Lisbon, Oporto, Naples and Athens. On his return to England he ordered an immediate investigation into revenue-earning potential of the direct teaching of English. A Study Group visited 13 centres in Southern Europe and the Middle East, establishing that there were great possibilities of increasing revenue. DTE almost immediately became a central part of Council activities there.

The British Council's active involvement in language test production as well as promotion and distribution in the late 1970s–early 1980s, can be seen in the development of the British Council's Mini Platform test for these DTEOs (see Moller, Seaton and McNeill 1982). Mini Platform was the forerunner of the 21st-century International Language Assessment (ILA) we deal with in Chapter 6.

At the European DTEO managers' conference in 1979 held in Lisbon, one of the frequently raised problems was the unsatisfactory state of placement procedures in the DTEOs. One of the recommendations to emerge from the meeting was 'that HQ design new, more satisfactory procedures'. As a result of this the English Language Services Department led by Alan Moller initiated the placement test project in December 1979. It was first used in 1980 and continued as the placement test of choice at many British Council teaching centres until the launch of the ILA in 2009. In fact, it remained popular with some schools even after that date.

In terms of level, it was felt that the tests should be aimed 'at a level approximately midway between no English and FCE level English'. They referred to this as the Platform level since they felt 'it represents an understanding of and ability to use features of the basic grammar of English and to establish meaning from oral communication' and offered the learner a platform from which to build on either their general or specific purpose language ability. The name of the test was then derived from the additional fact that the actual language element targeted the maximum information in the minimum length.

It was decided that the most appropriate way to collect candidate-related information would be through a questionnaire (to be delivered in the candidates' L1) and a test of English, which would be designed to assess a candidate's formal control of the grammar and their ability to communicate in spoken English. Candidates were asked to respond to the questionnaire, which focused on their education, experience of learning languages, precise language needs and finally a self-assessment. This was delivered in the learners' L1.

The main body of the test consisted of two parts, presented in any order:

Written (MPW)   30 minutes long
                Gap-filling and transformation-type items
                Clerically marked using Key
Interview (MPI) Short conversation (6 to 8 minutes)
                Based on test taker responses to a questionnaire
                Scored using a set of Performance Band Descriptors

Detail on the process of delivery, scoring and interpretation was provided in the Guide (Moller et al. 1982). The outcome of the test was two separate measures of the candidate's language ability. The first was the MPW. This was a score derived from performance on the Written paper. The second measure was the MPI derived from the Interview performance band descriptors.

Final placement decisions were made by a senior teacher at the DTEO. This involved creating a profile of the learner based on their MPW and MPI, which was then compared with a placement table. The placement table came in a standard form and, where needed, in a form modified for a specific DTEO, as was the case with the MPW transformation table.

The final piece of the jigsaw was the Questionnaire (the MPQ) which could be consulted by a senior teacher when making the final placement decision. This level of individualisation was highly valued as it was seen to be very accurate and very learner-centred albeit quite time-consuming.

Preliminary validation work found that the test was both reliable (the MPI was found to range from 0.8 and 0.92 depending on the centre; no MPW reliability estimates were reported) and accurate, with a reported 98% accuracy of placements reported for Milan and Lisbon in the first year of use.

However, in time, as the size of the overall DTEO increased and more pressure came on senior teaching staff, this individualisation was to prove to be too resource intensive and led to the Mini Platform losing its lustre with many Teaching Centres. However, it would not be finally replaced until nearly 30 years later by the ILA (see Chapter 6).

British Council Personnel and ELTS

Roger Hawkey (interview July 2014) describes internal developments in the British Council, which indicated how well placed it was in terms of personnel and capacity to develop a new EAP test itself in the late 1970s:

> ...the British Council opened the English Language *Consultancies* Department (in 1978 ELS (*Services*) D) at Spring Gardens, with its staff of 'Consultants', initially, from c. 1976 John Munby (Director), Patrick Early (Consultant ELT methodology), Roger Hawkey (ESP), Brendan Carroll (testing) and Ian Seaton (testing).

Brendan Carroll, a long-serving British Council ELO before his posting to Spring Gardens in the British Council's new English Language Consultancies Department, would lead the design of the ELTS test (see Carroll 1978, 1980 and 1981). Interviews with his former colleagues Roger Hawkey and John Munby confirmed Carroll's singular role in its development. Hawkey in his interview emphasises the small-scale nature of the team supporting the development of ELTS in the British Council and suggests that Carroll quite often enjoyed only limited informal support from his colleagues:

It is clear though that Carroll did not have a huge team at his disposal; initially one assistant [Malcolm Johnson?], later replaced by Ian Seaton, and the help of administrative assistants such as Jenny Pugsley and Ros Richards in the ELSD office…the decency and charisma of Brendan Carroll, who battled through all kinds of difficulties, having been told, 'Look, you've got to make the new tests,' that's really what it was, and he kept a good humour throughout the buffeting he sometimes took. There wasn't a huge coherent team, at that stage anyway. Isn't it strange?…the number [of people] I mentioned here, it's very small, and half of it is goodness of your heart, help when asked. However, Munby was there, with his, as he used to say, with his model over his shoulder, he was the Director, and he was a very high profile person, and…they were going to 'go ESP' in the test, as they did, EAP, and here was a man with a communicative needs profile, usually based on some kind of student…. People say, 'Why was ELTS based on that kind of model?' Well, it's clear cut. So, without much question, even though Brendan was never that enthusiastic about Munby's model, we *were* actually, and [Munby] was a very charismatic character, delightful to work with; he was very *gung ho*, and in the end Brendan went along with it, but there wasn't a 'straight' [i.e. long-term, exclusive] team and a huge coordinated plan.

The Minutes of the 3rd ELTS Management Committee of 22 February 1978 provide detail on how the test was subsequently developed by Carroll when the British Council took over responsibility for this from Cambridge:

> 5 It was agreed to proceed with actual test construction, by setting up a workshop for the purpose. The production team would work under Mr Carroll and, in addition to other British Council officers, representatives would be invited from UCLES, NFER, SELMOUS, and some assistance from postgraduate students of London University would be sought. The following action schedule for construction of preliminary tests and formulation of administrative procedures was agreed:
>
> March 1978
> - briefing of participants in item construction practice.
>
> April
> - item construction as assigned and small-scale trial
> - coordination of tests.
>
> May
> - drafting of pretest package (including all rubrics, instructions for administration, answer sheets and marking sheets).
> - typing and distribution to Management Committee members.

June
- meeting of the Management Committee, to consider pretest material.

September
- pretests.

June 1979
- final report to Joint Committee of the Syndicate and the British Council.

Autumn 1979
- first range of tests available.

It was envisaged that the Syndicate's role will be to receive the first range of pretested material in agreed form, issue this with all necessary instructions to the testing centres, then commission and supply further material as necessary. All tests will be marked locally.

In the *English Language Testing Service First Report* 1982 detail is provided on the piloting and pre-trialling:

- Materials were prepared by small teams of writers and subjected to a pilot test on approximately 950 students in 34 centres in the United Kingdom.
- They were subsequently edited and pretested on a total of 603 students in 19 countries overseas before being cast into their final form for administration to candidates in 1980.

The Test Development Research Unit (TDRU) annual report 1978 (p. 10) signals the direction of travel:

> The first forms of the test are being prepared within the offices of the British Council, but when the Service becomes operative it is the intention that subsequent forms should be produced by the Unit. With this in mind, the Unit has been represented at several meetings between the Council and the Syndicate during the year, and it is expected that during the coming year the staff of the Unit will be increased to commence work immediately on this development.

In the 1979 TDRU annual report, this working relationship with the British Council was confirmed:

> There was during the year an unusual increase in the test development demands made on the Unit. Preparations for the English Language Testing Service, which commences in January 1980, were officially in the hands of the British Council until September 1979, but in practice the Unit staff and that of the Syndicate worked continuously and in close collaboration with Council officers throughout the year.

The shaping of ELTS

Carroll's earlier published work provides useful insight into his communicative approach to testing, and how communicative needs analysis helps inform communicative test design. His book *Testing Communicative Performance* (1980) is about how the Munby (1978) model suited English Language Test Development (with examples).

Carroll had spent six years as an ELO in India earlier in his career in the 1960s and his work there, in the area of English for Academic Purposes (EAP), was to stand him in good stead in the development of ELTS. He had written a textbook (Carroll 1969) for students wishing to improve their English for university studies. In his interview for the history project he makes reference to this:

> We did the Bridge course. The whole of India was taken over by English-medium universities. The universities were desperate to learn English.... So, I was in charge of English medium with six universities in South India.

In many ways this made him a good choice to develop ELTS for use with overseas students wishing to study in the UK through the medium of English. His experience gave him a clear idea of the language related study skills students needed to cope with tertiary-level education.

Roger Hawkey, a Council ELT contemporary of Brendan Carroll in Spring Gardens, makes reference in his interview for the history project to other valuable EAP experience Carroll had before joining ELCD in Spring Gardens in the late 1970s:

> ...he had been director of ELTI, the English Language Teaching Institute, up the road, so he had a constant body of overseas students who were learning English there to help with the studies the British Council was going to give them in the university, so he could use that.

In *Testing Communicative Performance* Carroll (1980: 1–3) also provides detail of how extensive consultancy work by the British Council in testing in the 1970s laid the groundwork for the development of ELTS. He refers to three other major EAP testing projects the British Council was already involved in during the 1970s:

- Venezuelan students on a one-year preliminary course in English and Science before undertaking full-time tertiary studies.

- Two sizeable projects in the Middle East over a period of four years [e.g. the King Abdul Aziz University project; see Moller quote above], language tests developed for several major disciplines.
- A project in an East African university, where students in a number of faculties were assessed as to their study-skills competence to determine if remedial programmes were necessary....

Carroll's published work (1978, 1980 and 1981) illustrates the escalating interest in needs analysis, functional syllabus specification (Stern 1983: 109) and a communicative 'real-life' approach to English language teaching and ESP testing in the UK (Weir 1983). Members of the British Council's professional ELT cadre were at the forefront of this paradigm shift in approaches to language teaching and assessment in the 1970s and early 1980s. Their professional expertise and experience in assessment, English for academic purposes and needs analysis would contribute to the development of the ELTS test for determining proficiency in English for academic purposes.

The ELC/SD team at Spring Gardens thus had the capacity for new test development, while its partner organisation at Cambridge, perhaps with the exception of Andrew Harrison, did not, especially after the departure to Kuwait in 1975 of Frank Chaplen, Cambridge's first professional English language tester. As we noted above it would not be until the late 1980s that a professional testing cadre would be built in Cambridge.

Ian Seaton (personal communication 2015) regards the British Council as being in a strong position to develop ELTS as a result of the:

> ...vast experience of highly qualified ELQ [ELT-qualified] staff at home and abroad in their running of one of the biggest direct teaching operations [DTOs] in the world, as well as in administering, and developing a critical view of, the existing procedures to assess the language competence/performance of students coming to Britain for academic and vocational study.

Despite John Munby being in charge of ELCD, it appears that it was Carroll along with Jo Barnett, then Controller of the Council's English Teaching Division, rather than Munby himself, who were leading on the development of the new English Language Testing Service (ELTS). In his interview for this history in May 2015, Munby made it clear that he himself never pushed his model within the British Council as a basis for test development and, in any case, he left ELCD in 1978 for a new Council post in Kuwait, so was never involved directly with the development of

ELTS. Munby, reflecting back on his doctoral studies, considered that: 'The drive and impetus of that (Munby) model was never to produce a test. It wasn't even to produce a model for testing.' During his doctoral studies at Essex, Munby had developed a model for establishing what should be taught leading on to materials production rather than for testing. Nevertheless, Munby's own specification for a student of agriculture, academic discipline: biological science (1978: 205), provided one of the six profiles used by Carroll at the design stage of ELTS.

Brendan Carroll, though not necessarily a great believer in the *minutiae* of the Munby model, was able to use target situation analysis successfully for testing purposes (1980) as did Weir (1983) not so far away at the Associated Examining Board (AEB) in Aldershot. The presence of John Trim as first Director of CILT (the Centre for Information on Language Teaching) in his office on the same floor as Carroll and Munby at Spring Gardens, London from 1978 onwards probably added further weight to the perceived value of a needs analysis approach. We should note that Trim was also chosen to be the chairman of the ELTS Management Committee at its first meeting in August 1977. The seminal work Trim had been carrying out for the Council of Europe (the Threshold Level, and so forth) would eventually contribute greatly to the Common European Framework of Reference (the CEFR) (Council of Europe 2001). Later attempts, in the 1986–1989 ELTS revision project, to find an alternative approach that could improve on the use of needs analysis as the springboard for developing language tests, would meet with little success (see this chapter and Clapham and Alderson 1997).

Another original member of ELCD, Roger Hawkey, went on to carry out research into the problems experienced by government sponsored overseas students coming to the UK. Sponsored by the British Council, Hawkey (1982) completed a doctoral thesis entitled *An Investigation of Inter-Relationships between Cognitive/Affective and Social Factors and Language Learning*. His research provided a wealth of detail and insight concerning the demands made on overseas students in the UK and their study skills requirements, together with the problems they encountered with these.

Alan Moller, who worked with Hawkey and Carroll in ELSD in Spring Gardens, was similarly supported by the British Council in his doctoral studies (1982). Doing research for his PhD under the supervision of Professor Alan Davies at Edinburgh University, his thesis, entitled *A Study in the Validation of Proficiency Tests of English as a Foreign Language*, focused on existing tests that had served to evaluate student proficiency in English for Academic Purposes. Moller would bring an in-depth knowledge of previous attempts to test EAP (Cambridge CPE, ELBA, Michigan test, EPTB and TOEFL) to the development of ELTS and an awareness of contemporary developments in communicative language testing (see Moller 1982).

A further member of ELSD, Ian Seaton, who was Head of the ELTS Liaison Unit from 1980 to 1983, describes (personal communication 2014) its contribution to the early development of the first ELTS test:

> This Unit was set up in the Council to complete the supervision of all the item and test writers working on the initial subject specific modules as well as the introductory general modules, to organise all the pretesting of the multiple-choice format tests, to complete the design and writing of the two written and spoken modules including descriptors for the nine bands used to score and report the five sub-test profile 'scores', to liaise with The Syndicate's Test Development and Research Unit under Dr David Shoesmith, which carried out all the reliability studies, and then to lead the implementation and roll-out in Council offices worldwide. A crucial responsibility in the roll-out was to train both test administrators and assessors overseas in the new system and at home to continue the consultation with, and preparation for, British universities and colleges to process ELTS profiles for all the students/trainees under their consideration for admission. Much work had to be done to encourage, cajole and if necessary simply require all overseas offices to make staff, time and space for a test system quite different to the previous tests. Certain countries whose ministries of education exercised central control over their students, such as PR China, needed extended visits and even negotiation to explain how the new system would work. Consultation with British universities and colleges had from the start revealed widely differing practices and priorities for assessing the language ability of prospective students and trainees from overseas which again entailed much discussion, especially over cut-off band scores, both for individual sub-tests and overall profiles – what scores indicated straight acceptance, what indicated varying lengths and type of pre-course language training and what indicated rejection. And finally the Unit scoped out longitudinal studies to validate these individual module and overall profile bands as well as comparability studies to try to establish some form of equivalence with other international tests.

Peter Hargreaves was also involved in the ELTS revision in the 1980s. Before leaving the British Council to head ELT testing at Cambridge as Director of EFL in 1988, he had a career spanning 21 years with the British Council with whom he served in Africa, Asia, the Middle East and London. His final post with the British Council, before moving to

UCLES, was as Senior Testing and Evaluation Advisor based at Spring Gardens in London. Hargreaves played a prominent role in the annual Dunford House meeting of ELOs from the first meeting in 1978 when the Munby model and its implications were introduced (Abbott and Beaumont 1997).

As well as developing the test, the British Council was responsible for helping receiving institutions in the UK to interpret the results. Jenny Pugsley, when interviewed for this history, recalled:

> From 1985 to '89, I was head of something called the English Tuition Coordination Unit, and it was our job to look at the ELTS test results for the placement of the many, many TCTD (Technical Cooperation Training Department) scholars who were coming to the UK for pre-sessional courses before going on to post-graduate work. So we reviewed the tests and we worked out fairly tight guidelines for what kind of test result resulted in what length of EAP (English for Academic Purposes) training before the post-graduate course. It was part of my job to liaise with the schools and universities offering pre-sessional courses and to talk to them about the kind of work they should do with our scholars.

However, it must be remembered that the British Council, though possessing the advantage of extensive in-house expertise suitable for test design and interpretation purposes, was clearly *not* an examination board with the necessary infrastructure to support the operational validation of ELTS on its own. Cambridge may not then have had equivalent ELT teaching and testing expertise (with the possible exception of Andrew Harrison who had joined specifically for the ELTS development in 1975), but the Board did have the administrative capability required to deal with test validation because of the many other areas of examining it was and had been involved in for over 60 years.

Ian Seaton (personal communication 2014) noted that:

> only the University of Cambridge Local Examinations Syndicate had the necessary resources, reach and reputation to be the British Council's partner in all this, both short and long term.

At the Joint Committee meeting in July 1979 demarcation of certain scoring responsibilities were clarified:

> (ii) It was probable that there would be a dual system whereby in some case marking would be done locally overseas, subsequently moderated by the

Syndicate, in others all scripts would be sent with the results of the Oral interview to Cambridge for marking and the issue of results.

(iii) The Syndicate will be responsible for control of standards and results, the Council for any interpretation which they may require e.g. of profile results in terms of definition and length of courses.

Responsibilities were further specified at the Executive Committee meeting in June 1982:

82/4 Validation
...While any actions would be taken jointly – if necessary by meetings of those involved – responsibility for initiating and maintaining activities would be as follows:
N.B. For convenience, 'Cambridge' is used for those activities for which the Syndicate and/or the Test Development and Research Unit will be responsible.

Cambridge
(i) Check on mechanical accuracy of scoring tests and calculating and recording bands (normally a 10% sample). (The Council would be informed of any problem and would communicate directly with those concerned.)
(ii) The identification of Centres where assessment of M2 [see ELTS modules below] was inaccurate. (The Council to notify the Centres concerned.)
(iii) Item analysis of new tests.
(iv) The establishment of a complete computer record of candidate performance, including module chosen and any other information deemed necessary.

British Council
(v) Preparation of a description of the content (texts, tasks, items) of the general and modular sub-tests to be made available to item-writing teams.
(vi) Receipt and analysis of all comments on the face validity of tests.
(vii) Initiating action, to be co-ordinated with Cambridge, on performance descriptions.
(viii) Overall validation programme involving a follow-up of those candidates placed in tertiary education institutions in the UK.

The ELTS story is thus in essence a continuing manifestation of the broader narrative, which unfolded in Chapter 1, where the British Council, by virtue of its global involvement in ELT over a 50-year period from 1941, was able to provide significant professional input, in cooperation with Cambridge, into the English language testing field.

We now turn from the wider institutional context to consider the nature of the construct being measured by the ELTS test itself.

ELTS test: Validity

In the changing EAP climate of the 1970s, it was seen as essential to assess the writing and speaking skills of students coming to study in the UK through the medium of English. The inclusion of these core Academic English productive skills presented test developers with considerable theoretical and practical challenges. It is perhaps not surprising therefore that some testing agencies at the time (e.g. TOEFL) avoided using a direct approach for one or both of these skills. However, Weir (1983) demonstrated that with considerable time and effort it was possible to include direct tests of both, albeit in a lengthy test. He details the development of the communicative TEAP test, which included both written and spoken testlets as well as dedicated reading and listening papers which were also integrated with writing tasks. Similarly, from 1980 onwards, ELTS and later IELTS chose to include mandatory writing and speaking components on the grounds that these were fundamental components within the overall EAP language proficiency construct and that a direct approach to their assessment offered the best approach for assessing written and/or spoken ability.

ELTS test tasks were based on an analysis of the ways in which language was used in academic contexts and were intended to reflect the use of language in the 'real world'. Ian Seaton (personal communication 2014) summarises the new approach for ELTS:

> There was broad agreement about what features any new testing system should have. It should reflect the recent developments in communicative language teaching, have high face validity both for those taking it and those receiving its 'scores' and should have a positive feedback into language learning situations. It should try, in its content and skills specifications, to replicate the language used in different academic and training subjects. It should not use only a multiple-choice format, but 'authentic' performance in both writing and speaking should be measured as directly and reliably as possible in a test situation. And all this should be backed up with a properly resourced and staffed central administration that could not only carry out all the necessary initial specification, construction and

reliability/validity studies but then ensure that quality was maintained and crucially, on the basis of permanent monitoring and the provision of new versions, improved. You might call it a British ETS, on a smaller scale yes, but with the vital difference that it measured language performance directly and was referenced to the language needs in British study and training contexts.

So, the new ELTS test would have an innovative format that reflected changes in language learning and teaching theory and developments in language testing. In particular, ELTS would be influenced by the growth in 'communicative' language learning and 'English for specific purposes'. Under the auspices of the British Council and the UCLES, ELTS was introduced in January 1980 after the five-year period of development described above. It reflected a new paradigm of communicative language testing in its concern to assess ability to use language rather than simply test knowledge about language. Test tasks in ELTS were based on the ways in which language was actually used in academic contexts, i.e. in the various modes of study on university courses (see details of these in Chapter 3) with the tasks intended to reflect the use of language in that 'real world'.

The categories in Munby's communication needs processor had been matched to the profiles of six hypothetical participants, corresponding to the divisions used by the British Council for selection purposes overseas in relation to the broad subject areas of those coming to study in Britain: Life Sciences, Social Studies, Physical Sciences, Technology, Medicine and General Academic. The six participants typified the most frequent areas in which overseas students applied for scholarships from the BC (see Carroll 1981 for details). The six profiles took account of the ways in which language was used in the six academic contexts and were intended to reflect the use of language in the 'real world'. For example, in 1977 Roger Hawkey developed a profile of typical candidates in business studies who might sit for the test and Shelagh Rixon a profile of what students would need for social survival (see Carroll 1981 for a full set of these specifications).

Roger Hawkey was posted to the Council's Spring Gardens ELCD in 1976, following three years 'outposted' to the Kano State, Nigeria, Ministry of Education In-service Training Centre. Here he had, with typical support from the then British Council Regional Director, Graham Ness, and the Assistant Director, Arthur Sanderson, set up and led the 'Joint English Project' (the partners being the Nigerian Ministry of Education, British Council and Voluntary Service Overseas (VSO)), trialling and producing three cycles of students' and teachers' EL materials. Hawkey was thus already involved in a certain amount of learner needs analysis, syllabus and materials design and trialling, and progress assessment, all in the still early days of more communicative approaches to teaching, learning and assessment. When he was asked by Brendan Carroll to do a Munby Profile for a potential business English student, it is not surprising that Hawkey selected 'Audu Suleiman', schooled in Kano, where Hawkey had recently worked, putative age 22 and looking to study for his Higher National Degree in the UK. Hawkey's previous experience writing a Business English course in his earlier Council-supported post at the Ministry of Education Thailand would also have been relevant as he worked on his Audu Suleiman communication needs profile. So would the ESP needs analysis and course design consultancies he was doing while in ELC/SD, in close contact with Director John Munby himself, and with Consultant Testing colleague, Brendan Carroll.

Brendan Carroll (Alderson and Hughes 1981: 69–70) describes how these communication needs profiles were written:

> To ensure the best insights possible…we adopted the following procedures;
> The compilers of the profiles were chosen according to their special interests and backgrounds….
> All staff concerned made contact with institutions and/or individual lecturers in the disciplines concerned…. The Civil Engineering profile was prepared by an officer who had earlier done a study of Engineering courses and teaching methods in Britain who was advised by two colleagues in Education and Science Division with appropriate degrees and experience. It is intended that close and continual contacts of this kind will be maintained throughout the process of test development and validation.
> Continual reference was made to authentic documents in the disciplines such as college handbooks, course syllabuses and standard subject textbooks. We found the widely-used titles circulated under the Low-Priced Text Book Scheme to be of particular value in this respect.
> In general, we believe our data collection methods represent a reasonable compromise between what would be theoretically perfect and what could be done in an acceptable time-scale with resources to hand.

The six broad profiles specified by the British Council took account of many of the skills we identified as necessary for academic English in our literature survey of the EAP skills required in tertiary-level

English-medium study in Chapter 3 above (e.g. understanding lectures, participating in seminars, reading academic texts expeditiously and carefully and extracting relevant information for transformation in university writing tasks). A strong emphasis on communicative language demands in the study context meant that, as well as reading and listening components, sub-tests of writing and speaking ability were now included – in the form of the Writing module and the Individual Interview.

In 1980 each ELTS candidate was required to take three sections in their subject area or module and the two common tests in the General section:

M1 Study Skills (55 minutes) G1 General Reading (40 minutes)
M2 Writing (40 minutes) G2 General Listening (30 minutes)
M3 Individual Interview
(10 minutes)

Total test time 175 minutes

In addition to G1 and G2, a subject specific 'Modular Test' was offered to assess reading comprehension within a specific academic domain: M1 (Study Skills). The ELTS test initially offered a choice of six modules covering five broad areas of study in UK tertiary education, plus one non-specific area. The six M1 modules were:

- Life Sciences
- Social Studies
- Physical Sciences
- Technology
- Medicine
- General Academic for those whose areas of interest did not fit into any of the other domains.

There was also a Non-Academic test for vocational candidates.

These specialist modules would be cut to three in the 1986–1989 ELTS revision and then to only one General Academic module after the 1995 revision. The waning interest in ESP, as more commonalities were established between different subject areas (Dudley Evans 1988, Hutchinson and Waters 1987, Strevens 1988), coupled with the administrative complexities of producing multiple parallel forms would eventually lead to their demise.

In 1980 though, in addition to M1 for reading, there were also a writing test (M2) and an oral interview (M3), which were available across the six domains (see the Introduction in Taylor and Falvey 2007 for more details of the M2 and M3 modules). The Source Booklet for the three Modular tests – M1, M2 and M3 – which each ELTS candidate received (see above) as relevant to their chosen discipline from the six domains available, contained extracts from appropriate academic texts, including a bibliography and a typical index to allow for the testing of expeditious reading skills such as scanning. The three subject area modules (M1, M2 and M3) were thematically linked: candidates were required to write on a topic connected to one of the texts in the Study Skills paper, an early example of reading into writing to approximate to an academic reality, and in the Interview, following a general warm-up phase, the candidate would be asked to discuss a topic already covered in the M1 Reading module thereby establishing yet another intertextual link between academic modes (See Davies 2008 for copies of these ELTS modules *ex libris* Weir).

The testing of reading and listening in ELTS (1980–1989)

The assessment of reading and listening in ELTS between 1980 and 1989 can be summarised as follows:

Reading test (G1)

- 40 multiple-choice test items, divided into three sections included in a single Question Booklet together with the texts on which they are based
    - Section 1: sentence length texts; choosing option with closest meaning
    - Section 2: paragraph length texts (MCQ gap-filling)
    - Section 3: three related newspaper articles, with some test items on each text independently and some intertextual questions
- length = 40 minutes
- marks converted to a nine-band scale
- clerically marked using MCQ key and a template.

Listening test (G2)
- a tape and a Question Booklet with 35 multiple-choice test items in four sections
  - Section 1: choosing from diagrams
  - Section 2: listening to an interview
  - Section 3: replying to questions
  - Section 4: listening to a seminar
- length = approximately 35 minutes
- marks converted to a nine-band scale
- clerically marked using MCQ key and a template.

Study Skills test (M1) Reading
- linked to one of six academic domains (Life Sciences, Social Studies, Physical Sciences, Technology, Medicine and General Academic)
- based on a Source Booklet containing 5–6 textual extracts for input – taken from books, articles, reports etc. related to the specific subject area plus additional contents pages, bibliographies, appendices and indices
- an accompanying Question Booklet with 40 multiple-choice test items
- length = 55 minutes
- marks converted to a nine-band scale
- clerically marked using MCQ key and a template.

The testing of writing and speaking in ELTS (1980–1989)

The influence of needs analysis and communicative language demands in the study/work context described above, meant that sub-tests of writing and speaking ability were included in the new test – in the form of the M2 Writing and the M3 Individual Interview. In the M1 study skills paper, candidates received a Source Booklet relevant to their chosen discipline from the six domains available; the Source Booklets contained extracts from appropriate academic texts, and formed the basis for the writing tasks in M2 as well as for the main discussion in the M3 Interview.

The M2 Writing test consisted of two questions. The first was considered to be 'divergent'; although it was based on one of the reading texts in the Source Booklet, it still required the candidate to bring in their own experience and views. The second question was considered to be 'convergent', i.e. strictly limited to the information available in the input texts. Candidates had to write at least 12 lines for the first task and were advised to spend about 25 of the allocated 40 minutes on it. Hamp-Lyons (1986a, 1987b and 1991) describes the original ELTS M2 and the work she did with raters to develop the multiple trait scales and the Rater Training.

Taylor and Weir (2012b) describe how the M3 Individual Interview was conducted face-to-face between an examiner/interviewer and a single candidate and had three parts. In the first part the interviewer put the candidate at ease with non-standardised general questions, and on the basis of the candidate's responses selected an adjacent range of three (out of the possible nine) bands, which encompassed what the final oral proficiency band score for the candidate would be. Anecdotal evidence suggests that Part 1 sometimes produced a range of three possible scores that had subsequently to be modified in Part 2 or 3 because the candidate performed better or worse in these later parts. In the second part of the interview the candidate was asked about one of the texts from the Source Booklet, and the interviewer narrowed the band range assigned to two. In the final part of the interview, the candidate was asked to discuss his/her future plans; at the end of this phase the interviewer made the final band assignment. No interlocutor frame was available and the questioning was largely left to the discretion and the ability of each potentially idiosyncratic interviewer.

ELTS presented a number of practical and administrative challenges. Qualified EFL teachers had to be recruited and trained to mark the M2 essay; they also had to be trained to conduct and rate the M3 oral interview. Training for both components took several hours; in addition, each essay took around 10 minutes to mark and each oral assessment required about 15 minutes, making the whole test much lengthier to mark than its EPTB predecessor. Even though training manuals were created (see Hamp-Lyons 1985, 1986a and 1987a for details of the M2 manual), it was difficult to ensure effective training at all ELTS test centres since suitably qualified EFL staff were often in short supply, and in some more isolated centres there might be only one qualified individual to assume the role of writing/speaking assessor as well as test administrator. Practical constraints meant that marker training for M2 and M3 was largely carried out on a self-access basis, with the help of a set of exemplar candidate texts for M2 and an audio/video pack with exemplar candidate oral responses for M3.

The assessment of writing and speaking in ELTS between 1980 and 1989 can be summarised as follows:

Writing test (M2)

- linked to one of six academic domains (Life Sciences, Social Studies, Physical Sciences, Technology, Medicine, General Academic) based on a Source Booklet of textual extracts for input
- two writing tasks: 25 minutes advised for Task 1, 15 minutes for Task 2; total length = 40 minutes
- assessed on a nine-band scale
- required qualified EFL teachers trained specifically for marking M2.

Individual Interview (M3)

- linked to one of six academic domains (Life Sciences, Social Studies, Physical Sciences, Technology, Medicine, General Academic)
- based on a Source Booklet of textual extracts for input
- face-to-face, one-on-one interview
- three parts
- length = 15 minutes
- assessed on a nine-band scale
- required qualified EFL teachers trained specifically to conduct interviews and carry out M3 rating.

The above analysis shows clearly how ELTS at face value appears fit for purpose in terms of its content coverage at least. What was needed to determine whether a student was ready and able to study at tertiary level in Britain was a test which focused on the higher-order reading, listening, writing and speaking, language related study skills necessary to operate successfully in the academic context. ELTS was the first EAP test that sought to address these requirements.

Introduced in January 1980 with 3,506 candidates taking the test in 40 overseas countries and seven regional British Council offices in the UK, ELTS would replace the English Proficiency Test Battery (EPTB) completely by 1982. EPTB's demise was much regretted by a number of university admissions officers as it had given them the simple pass mark they craved for making acceptance decisions. However, Ian Seaton, one of the original ELTS team (personal communication September 2015)

168 *Assessing English on the Global Stage*

was positive about acceptance of ELTS by the majority of admissions teams because of its fitness for purpose:

> ...*some* admissions officers simply wanted a quiet life while *others* wanted to keep English peripheral to their decisions but, as I found out while introducing ELTS to them, *many others* wanted and appreciated the fuller information on English performance provided by the ELTS profile, both for admission and for pre-course language tuition.

The ELTS Validation Study (ELTSVAL), 1981–1986

The British Council Cambridge Joint Committee minutes of 3 July 1981 record the onset of the ELTS validation study:

> The Committee welcomed the validation exercise based on proposals from Edinburgh University. The Council and the [Cambridge] Test Development and Research Unit would be involved.

ELTS was an innovative approach to language testing and it is understandable that those involved wanted to share their evidence on how well it was working in comparison with more traditional test types (Westaway, Alderson and Clapham 1990: 241). It is likely that the study was initiated early on in the history of the ELTS test because the British Council/UCLES wanted to provide receiving institutions with more information they could use in relation to the interpretation of test scores at admission and also as regards the test's predictive validity of academic outcomes (Criper and Davies 1988: 11), i.e. the suitability of the ELTS test for its intended purpose. This would be one of the earliest attempts to generate 'validity evidence' on a large scale in language testing (see also Weir 1983).

In her interview for the history project on 10 December 1014, Lynda Taylor commented with regard to ELTSVAL:

> I think I would argue that is probably a good principle in language testing development and in the history of any language test as soon as it is up and running, that you would be wanting to think 'well what is the next iteration of the test going to perhaps begin to look like?' There should be an expectation: it will need updating, it will need revising, it will need reengineering or whatever phrase you would like to use to reflect particular aspects of a test that might need attention.

Others were less positive about the motives behind the study. In his 22 January 2015 interview, Alan Davies, when asked why the ELTS Validation Study (ELTSVAL) was set up so early in the test's life, offered a slightly different explanation:

> So ELTS was eventually put into action and very quickly there were so many complaints about it…because of the complaints I think it was recognised that there had to be a review of the test which had simply appeared as it were, without very much fanfare and so we put in a proposal for a review and were asked to do it and did so.

The ELTS test also came in for a lot of criticism at the inaugural meeting of what would become the annual *British Language Testing Forum* in Lancaster in 1980. The proceedings and commissioned papers from that weekend meeting can be found in the volume *Issues in Language Testing* edited by Alderson and Hughes (Alan Davies and Clive Criper were two of the eight participants at the meeting along with Charles Alderson, Caroline Clapham, Arthur Hughes, Alan Moller, Don Porter and Cyril Weir). The volume laid out sufficient theoretical and practical queries about ELTS to justify the validation study proposed by Davies.

Westaway, Alderson and Clapham (1990: 241) set out the specific aims of the Validation Project:

1   To examine the predictive validity of ELTS in relation to students' success in their academic studies.
2   To examine the face, content and construct validity of ELTS.
3   To examine the concurrent validity between ELTS, EPTB and University of Edinburgh English Language Battery (ELBA).
4   To assess the extent to which proficiency in English affects success in academic studies.
5   To evaluate the internal reliability and retest reliability.

Internal correspondence in the British Council archives (e.g. in Gen/591/7C) indicates there was some friction between the Council and Alan Davies in the early days, not least because of the attention Edinburgh paid to concurrent validity at the expense of other validities; 'the lack of a conceptual framework to the study, any thinking nor any wish to really understand ELTS'; the slow pace of the research and the failure to recruit adequate samples of students for data generation. The Council were happier after the appointment of Liz Hamp-Lyons as the part-time (25%) project coordinator 1982–1986 whilst working on her PhD, teaching EAP and training language teachers at the University of Edinburgh. A note from Ian Seaton (Gen/591/C 2 December 1982) records: 'She seems to have the calibre and commitment...to greatly improve the quality of the study; she seemed moreover, to understand the rationale of ELTS...'.

Hamp-Lyons' responsibilities were (personal communication March 2015): 'test materials handling; test arrangements and administration; travel arrangements; data preparation, handling, assembling; contacts with ELTS Unit in London; administration of questionnaires; data retrieval from previous records'. She became heavily involved in the ELTS writing component, and designed the new writing scales for ELTS as a consultancy for the British Council as well as producing an innovative and well received marker's manual for scoring the M2 test. Her PhD (1986) provides a wealth of detail on research concerning ELTS in practice in the 1980s particularly in relation to the Writing module.

Hamp-Lyons, in her interview (May 2015), as well as commenting on the slow progress of the project (as previously noted, a source of much irritation to the British Council), points to a fundamental flaw in the ELTSVAL research design. She argues that a mass of data were collected, but given the antediluvian computing facilities available in that era of mainframe computing, it was too immense a task to process expeditiously, let alone analyse all the data. In the event much of the data proved not to be particularly useful for validation purposes. Her comments are very revealing on the extent of the problem in processing huge data sets in the early 1980s, which inevitably slowed the study down and consumed much of the human resource time available:

> We collected this vast amount of data, test score data to be matched with demographic data, huge amounts of test score data...and every single thing had to be hand-entered into.... So when you entered it all, it was just a string, like that, and then you go to the next line and it was just a string, very small and very hard to see on the dark green/light green contrast screens of the time.... And I could only do it for two hours or so, because literally, you know, I started to feel sick, and I couldn't tell what cell I had got to, and I just made so many mistakes. And then you'd have to go somewhere and put in your chit and come back four or five days later, and they'd give you the print, 'greenbar' it was called, the paper that it came on. And it was a concertina that went on forever, probably a mile of stuff.... And then you've got to data check, for hours and hours and hours.
>
> And so, I mean it just sounds absolutely ludicrous, but probably two years was spent just entering all of this raw data. This would never happen in any project any more. And that was because nobody, probably in

the Council or in Edinburgh, had any concept of the processes that would need to be involved. Because nobody was trained, as far as I could tell, in research methods that involved large data....

She then draws attention to a more serious problem with the research design which had not paid due attention to the size of the samples of different student groups required to make reporting and comparison meaningful:

> And then there was a larger set of questionnaire data which was on a bigger level, that British Council sent us, selected from volunteers that they got in each country, so sometimes you'd have, you know, two people from a British Council centre somewhere and 50 from a centre somewhere else, so this was a terrible grind, but the real tragedy was when I realised it was all useless,...what can you do with these data? Nobody grasped at that stage, until we got to the point, that big data is useless unless you can cluster it together in meaningful clumps, and we didn't have a database set up to do that.... So, when you look at the report, it says almost nothing about patterns, because most of the data was a discard, so we probably had enough Chinese, there were some Spanish, Greek probably was one where we had a fair amount of data. But there were only really a very small number of countries where there were enough data, enough items in the cell that you could make a statement of any generalisability. And nobody understood that until we were at least halfway through my time, at least two years in.

Hamp-Lyons concludes on the pressing need in any future studies of this type to address the issue of validity head on *ab initio*:

> I mean, OK, nobody had done anything like it before, fair enough, it was a ground-breaking attempt, but a lot more of the time needed to have been spent on conceptualising what the test was, what the goals were and what it would be necessary to know in order to be able to say, 'OK, so, we've got a valid test.' Valid for what? Valid for whom? etc. But when I walked through the door, when the ELTSVAL project was nearly a year old...everything was already set up, I had no say at all in any aspect of the validation study design.

Findings

The ELTS Validation project (ELTSVAL) 1982–1986 was intended to provide information on the test's fitness for purpose. It set out to explore aspects of the practicality and validity of the English Language

Testing Service (ELTS) test. The authors of the *ELTSVAL Report*, Criper and Davies (1988: 1), argue that despite the 'hasty and unpiloted construction' of the test, they found '… much to value in ELTS' and refer to the many comments from supervisors and students on the 'test's positive face validity'. They concluded prophetically for the future directions ELTS would take: 'what is chiefly at fault with the test is a certain impracticality'.

Practicality

ELTS was more communicative than EPTB or TOEFL in covering the range of productive and receptive skills required in an academic environment, but was thereby more unwieldy and less efficient. It presented a number of administrative and practical challenges from the start.

In the Joint Committee meeting minutes for July 1980 there were early signs that the administration of the tests was proving somewhat unwieldy.

> Minute v
> There had also been some discussion of a possible reduction and simplification of the tests to a more easily manageable and economic scale but this was a matter of policy, which must now await reports on the monitoring and evaluation programme undertaken by the Test Development and Research Unit.

Davies (2008: 38–40) notes that ELTS was a much longer test than EPTB, three times as long, and was more complicated to administer given the multiple and 'tailored' components involved. Westaway et al. (1990: 243–244) go into more detail:

> There were found to be considerable practical difficulties in administering *ELTS* owing to the length of the test, the need to set up an interview for each individual candidate, the need to find and train examiners for the M2 Writing test and the M3 Interview, and the amount of time spent dealing with the wealth of test booklets comprising the G and M components in the different modules.

In the 1980s the ELTS test candidate numbers were quite low, but it was clear that there were still serious practical difficulties with the administration of the test, for example the number of different booklets and answer sheets with six potential modules; and the time taken to administer the test securely, complete and mark, package and return the test (Criper and Davies 1988: 20). Hamp-Lyons (personal communication 14 October 2014) notes:

> These points were made repeatedly and from the beginning by the ELTSVAL Progress Reports and this was one reason for the real clash between AD/CC [Alan Davies/Clive Criper] and the British Council cadre of former ELOs.

In the interview with him in January 2015, Davies reflects back on these practicality concerns:

> ...one of the problems of ELTS was that it wasn't deliverable. You know you had all these different possibilities that a student could take, so you had bundles of papers, of exam papers, and that was a real problem actually, and people complained about it quite seriously.

As early as the British Council/Cambridge Joint Committee meeting in July 1979 there had also been concern about a further practical issue, the production of parallel forms to replace existing test versions, the responsibility of the *British Council*:

> (vi) Concern was expressed by the Chairman at the lack of detailed information before the Committee about the specification and forms of the tests, validation and supply of reserve material.

It was concluded in the Validation Study that generating sufficient comparable test forms across multiple testing domains posed significant challenges for test production and sustainability (Criper and Davies 1988), especially as the British Council was responsible for producing new and parallel versions of multiple modules and all the pre-testing and administrative procedures this entailed, not least in commissioning items from external personnel. Unfortunately, no mechanisms were in place for a rolling programme of test production and instead a rather haphazard system for commissioning further modules prevailed (such as the second Social Studies module from Cyril Weir in 1984 and one from Pauline Rea in 1985).

Even by 1986 there were only two versions of G1, G2, M2 and M3 and one version of the complete range of M1 tests. Production of additional or replacement versions did not seem to be a priority when candidate numbers were relatively small in the early 1980s and staff resources were stretched in both UCLES and the British Council. An early letter from

Patricia Smith at the UCLES Test Development Research Unit (TDRU) dated 26 October 1979 to Cyril Weir, who was involved in an external editing role of the early ELTS draft modules, suggests no plan was in place from the beginning:

> We have not yet been able to think how we shall set up a more permanent team to deal with this material. We shall probably have to set up the next round of editing in the New Year and we may or may be not be bothering you again at that point.

Alderson and Clapham (1992a: 6) comment on the absence of a policy on new versions for ELTS. There seemed to be no idea when a new version would be necessary and self-imposed deadlines were allowed to slip 'and the preliminary work did not proceed with sufficient speed or method'. This compared unfavourably with UCLES's systematic schedule of producing a new version of FCE and CPE twice a year.

Davies (2008: 40) too is critical of the lack of progress in the 1980s in developing additional parallel forms of all the ELTS modules. This he ascribes to deficiencies on the practical and administrative side of the testing operation due to the absence of a professional testing body to manage the project. He argues that it was entirely appropriate for Cambridge to take over this side of the operation and accept full responsibility for production and pre- and post-test analysis as ELTS morphed into IELTS. Davies (2008: 109–110) in fact sees the administrative side as being the key weakness of both EPTB and ELTS. Because production, delivery and administration were only part-time activities, first for a university department (EPTB) and then for the British Council (ELTS), there was no rolling programme for the production of new versions and when the numbers began to increase there was no infrastructure to provide efficient training of the personnel involved, expeditious delivery and administration of the tests, or comprehensive analysis of test results.

Content validity

In the ELTS Validation Study, Criper and Davies (1988: 89–96) are critical of the content validity basis on which ELTS was created:

> ...ELTS was constructed with something of a needs analysis blueprint but in what was, it appears, a highly unsystematic way and also in a thoroughly non-empirical manner...since needs analysis stands or falls by the empiricism it demands, it is regrettable that the needs analysis used for the construction of this first version of ELTS was not in itself the result of an

empirical investigation but rather, as far as we can see, the result of best guesses of various language teachers. This activity may well have helped in the construction of a good language test but in no way can it be regarded as an exercise in needs analysis.

Brendan Carroll (1978, 1980 and 1985) might well have taken some exception to this version of events and presumably would have argued that the considerable experience of ELCD staff in EAP projects in the 1960s and 1970s, the extant literature of necessary EAP study skills (see Chapter 3), contact with EAP providers in British universities, e.g. SELMOUS, and the systematic model available in the Council for the specification of learner needs analysis (Munby 1978) were collectively sufficient to prepare trial versions of the test.

Carroll in his 1980 book *Testing Communicative Performance* provides an extensive description of the systematic needs-based approach adopted in the development of ELTS. He provides this model for test development, which they followed (1980: 13):

Phase 1: *Design*	(1) description of participants(s); (2) analysis of communicative needs; (3) specification of test content.
Phase 2: *Development*	(4) realisation of tests; (5) trial application; (6) validation and test analysis.
Phase 3: *Operation*	(7) full-scale application; (8) operational use; (9) revision of test system.

Carroll (1980: 14) confirms that the needs-based approach to content specification adopted was based on the comprehensive and systematic model of Munby, who, as noted above, laid out his techniques fully in *Communicative Syllabus Design* (1978). Munby provided the framework which enabled Carroll and his colleagues in the British Council to outline the communicative needs of learners in a number of profiles. This facilitated the specification of the content of a test in terms of language skills and functions, which were then translated into appropriate language forms. Carroll provides a detailed analysis of the systematic language skills and units of meaning selection behind an ELTS module (1980: 22). He argues that *the taxonomy of 260 micro-skills in 54 skill categories,* based on Munby (1978), was the most immediately useful aspect of the needs specification model.

The skills are grouped into the following:

- oral and aural skills
- graphic skills
- language patterns within the sentence
- discourse features
- reference study skills.

Carroll (1980: Appendix 1, pp. 106–122) provides an example of the application of Munby's model in the full specification for a Business Studies student adapted from Hawkey (1977). In his interview for this project (2014), Hawkey describes how the close proximity of ELT specialists working in ELCD/ELSD in British Council headquarters in Spring Gardens led to such specifications:

> Brendan would literally turn and say, I remember him saying, 'Roger, you were in Nigeria, weren't you? Can you give me a...Munby model for, you know, a real student.' In other words, profile of an imagined, typical student from a country like Nigeria, who wanted to study in Britain, analysed in terms of his communicative needs profile.... That's how it happened, and other people were asked for help too, so no wonder the ELTS is very much a test based on the Munby model.

Carroll's detailed account of the needs analyses (1981: 66–110) appears again in the *Issues in Language Testing* volume (ed. Alderson and Hughes) based on the proceedings of a meeting of a small group of experts in Lancaster (including Davies). It contains details of all six profiles.

The ELT cadre at the British Council was well aware of the typical demands made on students in UK tertiary education. The extant literature on EAP in the 1970s, which we referred to in Chapter 3, Hawkey's ongoing PhD research on overseas students' needs and Moller's on previous tests used with overseas students, and British Council contact with the SELMOUS organisation (meetings held on the test with SELMOUS as early as 21 May 1977) provided the test developers with a clear picture of where the demands and problems with regard to testing language related study skills lay. Carroll's substantive experience of developing study skills materials for English-medium universities in India in the 1960s should not be discounted either.

Furthermore, as Carroll points out (1980: 3 and above) the British Council had considerable experience of Academic English testing projects in tertiary-level institutions round the world from the 1960s onwards. Roger Hawkey in his interview describes how:

> the British Council got very heavily involved in major developmental projects, which were potentially hugely money making, in countries such as Saudi Arabia, setting up of a brand new university, where English for specific purposes was going to be a key feature. The Council was constantly sending its own people from London out there, to advise on this, for a week or two, including Brendan, and of course, one of their major needs was tests and English, you know, English medium type tests. So,...there are two projects, one was at the King Aziz University anyway, two major universities, two major projects [the Aim Shams project in Egypt was the other].

It would in any case be a mistake to apply today's rigorous and sophisticated procedures for the test development process (see Saville 2003) to the British Council in-house ELTS operation conducted within a very tight shoestring budget in the late 1970s. It should be noted that test development systems, including explicit test specifications, were not in place anywhere at this early stage; even Cambridge only gradually introduced these in the late 1980s (see Weir 2013). Hawkey (2009: 94) puts the Council's efforts into perspective when he describes how in 1986, an internal UCLES EFL memorandum noted:

> The Syndicate has announced its intention to develop an examination tentatively called the Second Certificate in English [one of several names for what is now the Certificate in Advanced English (CAE)], 'to be at a level between FCE and Proficiency (CPE)'. Neither of these exams, it was admitted, however, had 'a clearly defined syllabus', since 'both examinations were developed long before the existence of models for syllabus description such as the Council of Europe's Threshold...we cannot introduce an examination which claims to be between two other levels, without defining these levels!' A Working Party would thus analyze past papers in order to produce a 'retrospective syllabus which will serve as a basis for the syllabus in the new exam'.

In his interview for this history in May 2015, Mike Milanovic looked back on how ELTS was constructed by Carroll, and reinforced the point that we need to judge a test in the context of the time at which it was developed:

> ...the definition of real research is limited to the time that it takes place so one person's real research in 1975 is another person's speculation in 2015. I wouldn't say it wasn't real research, I would simply say it approached the problem in a different way from the way that we would approach it today. But, that in approaching the problem as it did at the time; it was a perfectly legitimate way of approaching it.
>
> In fact, most of the work in language testing that took place in relation to understanding for example the factor structure of an assessment really didn't take place until later. All the ground-breaking work that people like Bachman were doing, was taking place in the eighties....
>
> What made it better than anything else that was around was that it took into account language as communication, what made it ultimately worse was it seemed to have no way, no mechanism in place to validate its pre-suppositions. But neither did anything else, in the way that we understand it today, at that time.

Nevertheless, despite the limited resources at Carroll's disposal, it must be said that the basic procedures used for ELTS test development were sound, and the commissioning of test materials was carried out under the watchful and experienced eye of the Test Development and Research Unit (TDRU) led by David Shoesmith who had an organisation-wide brief at UCLES. For each special Reading module, 55 four-option MCQ items were required from the item writer, out of which 40 would be selected after editing and piloting. Notes for the guidance of item writers were supplied, which contained: test specifications, advice on text selection and item writing, and an analysis of the texts in the existing Social Studies module (word length, subject matter, purpose of text, genre, principal text types, graphics, style, target audience). Of particular value for Cyril Weir when he was producing a back-up Social Studies module in the early 1980s, was a breakdown of the skills tested by each item in the first version of the Social Studies module, cross-referenced to Munby's (1978) categorisation of reading skills, and a total for each category across the whole 40 items. This gave item writers an idea of the range of skills to be covered and the relative proportions. The skills in the M1 (Social Sciences) Mark II version included understanding explicit information, cohesion devices, discourse indicators, distinguishing main from subsidiary matter, summarising, coordinating information, basic reference skills, scanning and transcoding. Item writers were asked to specify skill(s) being tested à la Munby for each of the draft items they submitted. Items covered a range of processing levels from sentence level to whole text level, from decoding to discourse comprehension.

Ten questions were set on each of the four passages previously vetted by the TDRU, five questions on a bibliography, five questions on an index and five general questions covering all texts (an interesting and worthwhile early example of assessing intertextuality in a high-stakes test).

Staff at the British Council screened the items, e.g. Clive Bruton and colleagues in the English Language Services Department reviewed Weir's new draft Social Studies module. After pre-testing, data were also provided on each question showing its facility value and discrimination between the different ELTS band levels, and how each distractor in the multiple-choice items was working. Attendance at a one-day editing meeting was then required. The feedback was useful in indicating where further revisions or excisions might need to be made. Revised items were submitted again and monitored by British Council and UCLES staff. All in all, this constituted a *more structured process* than the one described below for the writing of the new IELTS in 1989, where no advice was given on specifications or task content to item writers and an emergentist approach to test development was adopted.

Despite a clearly principled ESP approach to test development in the construction of the six ELTS modules, it was nevertheless sometimes thought difficult to match the prospective test candidate to the most appropriate subject domain (Weir 1988). Should a candidate take a module s/he had studied or one s/he was going to study? What if previous studies overlapped the discipline boundaries of a module?

Clapham's (1996) doctoral research confirmed that it was difficult to classify students by subject knowledge and to choose reading passages which covered all specialisms in a particular area. For example, in engineering one would have to cater for chemical, physical, aeronautical, biological, marine and many other types of engineer, 34 in all according to Davies (2008). Once on the slippery slope of ESP it seems you inevitably ended up with individual students taking different configurations of courses on the same degree programme. Davies saw a reduction in the 'needs sensitivity' of ELTS as inevitable. Yet, the modules were, if anything, too general rather than too specific and did not cater for the heterogeneous varieties even in the same academic domain.

Criper and Davies (1988: 108) were aware of the serious difficulty that matching presented, given the underlying rationale for the complex test design:

> The principle underlying *ELTS* is that true English proficiency is best captured in a test of specific purposes. If it is the case that matching student

to module (or testee to test) is so uncertain, the ELTS loses the very advantage it was designed to maximise.

In her PhD thesis (1986a: 188 et seq.) Liz Hamp-Lyons raised two related problems she had found with regard to the M2 writing component:

> ...the possible totality of disciplines is incorrectly parcelled out; or, the writing required in the text is not sufficiently like the writing required in the disciplines.

She found limited support for a strong ESP construct (p. 370), but she was unable to make:

> ...a strong argument for the use of SAP [specific academic purpose] rather than GAP [general academic purpose] writing tests in the assessment of writing of postgraduate students seeking entry to British tertiary education.... There was no case in the study where the data fit a pattern which could be predicted by an ESP construct. (p. 371)

She throws doubt (p. 376) on whether the M2 modules as then constituted were 'truly SAP writing tasks':

> No consistent design parameters can be constructed from the M2Q1 tasks...there is no evidence that the constructors had any design principles or parameters in mind at all apart from the appeal to experience...and the need to link the writing task to an input text chosen for another purpose, i.e. a text used previously to test reading comprehension. Some tasks show SAP characteristics but this is haphazard and unpredictable, appearing to be more due to luck, or good intuitions, than to judgement.

Construct validity

Varimax rotated factor analysis (Criper and Davies 1988: 100–102) of the ELTS test results suggested a general factor and a reading and listening factor for the test providing some support for a multi-factorial model.

As regards construct validity, Criper and Davies (1988) concluded that G1 tested components of reading but G2 lacked entirely 'any of the skills in the specification list which relate to "listening" as an activity independent of a generalised language ability'. Listening seemed to equate in G2 with decoding elementary input only.

The authors also found that outside General Academic (GA) and Social Studies (SS) in the other comprehension modules 'many items are potentially answerable without any reference to the text', bringing into question the nature of the construct being measured. Henning (1988) also pointed out that many of the MCQ items were answerable from background knowledge alone. Indeed, at a validation study meeting in Edinburgh in 1986 participants were invited to take various modular reading tests without the passages and most of us were able to achieve a Band 6 or above without ever seeing the texts themselves. Comparability was also an issue (1988: 97): 'as different modules seem to be drawing on different skills in different proportions'.

Concerns were also expressed (Criper and Davies 1988: 103–104) about the limited time of 40 minutes available for the M2 writing, which precluded much task representation, planning, monitoring and editing, the hallmarks of the construct of academic writing. The restricted range of cognitive processing that was initiated by the tasks casts doubt on their validity as tests of academic writing.

Predictive validity

With regard to predictive validity Criper and Davies (1988: 112–113) found:

> The general conclusion of our predictive validity studies is that the ELTS test predicts as well (no more than/no better than) other English language proficiency tests accounting in the main, with r's of about 0.3 for about 10% of the variance. However while that is the general conclusion we are also able to show that there is considerable variation in predictive power in that ELTS does show in some disciplines (e.g. medicine) and in some skills (e.g. oral) much closer approximation to a criterion.

These predictive validity studies in ELTSVAL were affected by the limited samples available. Many students volunteered but few turned up, according to the authors of the report. Liz Hamp-Lyons (personal communication 2014) confirmed the enormous amount of time taken up in trying to get test subjects. Furthermore, the sample was already truncated as matriculation had hopefully already sorted out the weakest students. This may have lowered correlations, a feature of comparisons made with truncated samples.

The use of academic success as the criterion, the dependent variable, is also open to some criticism. Language tests are never designed to predict course grades, only language abilities. The plethora of potential intervening variables, e.g. subject capability, motivation etc., in studies that use course grades as the dependent variable testify to the problems involved. In any case few students fail their courses even though their language 'performance may not be up to the required standard' (Westaway et al. 1990: 241).

Reliability

In ELTSVAL questions were raised (Criper and Davies 1988: 105) about the low levels of inter-rater reliability in the writing tasks evidenced by the study, at 0.54 to 0.78, with most around 0.64. The authors point out that this must impact on the validity of the writing results. Subsequent to these studies, it should be noted that considerable work was carried out to improve reliability including the production of detailed assessment guides.

Hamp-Lyons carried out an extended study of the scoring procedures of the ELTS writing component in her PhD thesis *Testing Second Language Writing in Academic Settings*. She notes (1986a: 187, 208):

> ...within two years of the introduction of ELTS, objections were being raised to the writing test based on anecdotal evidence and impressions of its poor reliability....
>
> The lack of precise guidance, the imprecision of the criteria and performance descriptions, and an awareness of the tremendous constraints imposed by the operational context had already caused concern among British Council English Language Officers and other ELT professionals involved with ELTS.

Hamp-Lyons was concerned whether ELTS M2 scores were 'operationally sufficiently reliable for ethical decisions to be made about testees'. Her research shows that (1986a: 202):

> On no occasion does the single rater reliability reach the criterion level for operational reliability of .80.... An average single score reliability of .689 indicates that any two raters are only agreeing 36% of the time on the value of a piece of writing: on a single-rater test such a small amount of agreement is of some concern.

She argues that her study highlighted (1986a: 208):

> An existing awareness of the urgent need for a new scoring procedure and a method of training which would improve the reliability of scores of single raters....

and then goes on in Chapter 5 to explore empirically through three iterations how this might be done.

Her doctoral studies contributed greatly to the IELTS assessment guides for writing (Hamp-Lyons 1985, 1987a, 1987b and 1989). She describes (1987b: 79) how:

> The Assessment Guide took the criteria which had been implicit in the original general explanation of what should be valued in M2 answers and made these explicit. Each criterion was extensively characterised and some key problems raised by raters...were tackled. The Guide took a self study standardisation approach, and included a set of 'criterion' papers for trial scoring, with discussion of how the standardisation team handled them, and a further set for refresher scoring.

The new rating scale she developed also produced marked benefit to ELTS writing test reliability under operational conditions.

Weir (1988: 24) also raised questions over the comparability of so many different modules available; their parallel forms reliability. Referring to the Criper and Davies 1988 ELTSVAL report Weir (ibid.) commented:

> In Section 5.2.5 the correlations between parallel versions of some of the objectively scored modules are investigated. The results are disturbingly low and this brings into question whether supposedly parallel versions of the same test are in fact measuring the same construct. At the very least it argues for greater effort in future test construction to ensure that supposedly parallel versions are more obviously so....

Hamp Lyons (1986a: 245) had earlier argued:

> Even a cursory examination of the M2 questions revealed that they were not parallel; this became obvious during the attempt to construct 'parallel' questions for the second SAP essays. Questions were not parallel linguistically, cognitively or rhetorically; they were not parallel in terms of the demands they made on interpretation of the source materials or on knowledge in the specialist field. ...there seemed to be no way to measure the discipline specificity of questions.

Conclusions of the ELTSVAL study

In conclusion Criper and Davies (1988: 107) state:

> In our view, the single most important contribution of the project has been to collect data on ELTS testees over several years. This makes the project of unique value because of its wide-ranging and in-depth study of all aspects of validity. It is perhaps the case that as a result of this study ELTS has been better reviewed than any other EFL test with the possible exception of TOEFL.
>
> [p. 114]: ...In its own terms it is a satisfactory test of English proficiency because of its reliability and certain claims on validity. Its face validity is high but its content validity is less so. In terms of construct validity our evidence from the predictive and concurrent studies suggests specialists do ideally require different sub-tests or combinations of subtests but that the model presented in the present ELTS test of specialist modules is not effective.
>
> Similarly, in practical terms, our concurrent and predictive studies indicate that a shorter and more easily administered test would be equally effective.

The issue of practicality would be addressed by the 1986–1989 Revision Project though that of differential constructs would not.

The ELTS Revision Project, 1986–1989

In an interview for this British Council history project in May 2014, Mike Milanovic explained the background to the ELTS revision project:

> ELTS suffered from the fact that it was complex and essentially unvalidated. While ambitious and interesting, the project did not conform to any recognised standards of applying measurement principles to language assessment, or measurement techniques to assessment, really. Actually for the whole of its existence from '76 to when it was withdrawn in '89 or 1990 only two versions of the exam were ever produced. There was no serious attempt to consider issues of equating between different subject modules and so on.
>
> It was recognised therefore that while ambitious and interesting and somewhat valid, it really wasn't a sustainable model and so around the mid-eighties the Council actually contracted to Lancaster [University] the job of revising ELTS.

Personnel

The completion of the report on the ELTS Validation Project was the starting point for the *ELTS Revision Project*, a three-year project (1986–1989) set up by the ELTS Management Committee in late 1986, to be carried out under the lead of Professor Charles Alderson and his colleagues at Lancaster University. The British Council paid a research grant of £220,000 to Lancaster for the study.

A steering committee, including representatives of both the British Council and UCLES, and with Dr Charles Alderson as Project Director, was set up in late 1986 to be responsible for the ELTS revision:

- Chairman: Dr Peter Hargreaves, British Council (until 1988, then UCLES)
- Secretary: Gill Westaway, British Council
- Project Director: Dr Charles Alderson, Lancaster University
- UCLES representative: Dr John Foulkes, UCLES
- Research coordinator: Caroline Clapham, Lancaster University.

British Council management support for the project came from a team headed by Dr Peter Hargreaves, and included Gill Westaway, and Richard Webber from ELSD, who worked closely with staff at Lancaster. Once Hargreaves transferred to Cambridge, Gill Westaway took over the lead role in providing British Council management support to the Project and became actively involved in the professional development of the new test. She worked closely on the development of the new Writing and Speaking Band Descriptors (along with Grahame Cawood, a British Council consultant) and the early examiner training packages, supervised much of the pre-testing overseas in countries as diverse as Malaysia, Bangladesh, Algeria and Rwanda, and jointly wrote and delivered conference papers with Alderson and Clapham on the project. She was also instrumental in convincing the Australian authorities to join the ELTS Revision Project rather than going down the road of developing their own test or using TOEFL; all options that were being actively considered at the time. Before IELTS was launched she was seconded to IDP for a month to help train Australia-based examiners to conduct and mark the writing and speaking tests. An Australian perspective was provided by Professor David Ingram of Griffith University, seconded to the ELTS revision project in Lancaster from 1987 with support from the International Development Program (IDP) of Australian Universities and Colleges. David Ingram's work focused mainly on the development of the new Speaking test. Hawkey and Milanovic (2013: 103) record that Cambridge's limited involvement in the ELTS revision came largely through the participation of John Foulkes, who was working as a researcher in the newly formed Council for Examination Development (CED) headed by Ron McLone, later Chief Executive of the Oxford, Cambridge and RSA (OCR) exam board.

The consultation phase

Taylor and Weir (2012b) describe how first, from the mid-1980s onwards, a large-scale, questionnaire-based consultation exercise was conducted by the project team under the direction of Charles Alderson with various ELTS user groups (receiving institutions, British Council staff, overseas administrators, EAP teachers, language testers and applied linguists) in order to determine the perceived strengths and weaknesses of the existing test and the desirable characteristics of a revised test (see Alderson and Clapham 1992a for results and copies of the multiple survey instruments employed). User views were also gathered via focus group meetings in one-day workshops.

Westaway et al. (1990: 246) describe a second strand of the research:

> ...papers on the nature of language proficiency relevant to the testing of English for Academic Purposes were requested from a number of well-known applied linguists.

However, the 22 *applied linguists* consulted could offer no consensus or alternative theoretical model to Munby (1978) on which the test might be based. Alderson and Clapham (1992a: 9) admit that no new orthodoxy to replace target situation needs analysis had been found.

Davies (2008: 61) notes that according to the survey data there was a good deal of satisfaction expressed with the existing ELTS and a clear desire to retain the overall format. In general, responses from the 46 receiving institutions indicated they were happy with the ELTS service as were pre-sessional teachers and overseas test administrators (see Alderson and Clapham 1992a: 3–9).

There was also a good deal of support for subject modules among all the responding groups. With this level of institutional support and the evidence that bias might occur if candidates were taking a test too far removed from their own discipline, it was felt that some degree of modularity should survive the revision.

The *British Council* was worried that that 90% of overseas centres were running the test at a loss because of its complexity to administer (Alderson and Clapham 1992a: 4) and favoured a simpler test. However, Gill Westaway (personal communication November 2015) stresses that they were equally concerned with:

> ...producing a test with good construct and content validity which would have strong predictive validity and address reliability concerns especially over the Writing and Speaking tests.

In *UCLES* the main concern was with the lack of comprehensive specifications for the test, which created problems for the development of parallel forms. UCLES was very conscious of quality assurance issues with regard to test maintenance, delivery, administration and the marking of so many different modules. There was felt to be lack of provision for satisfactory piloting of pre-tests or the construction of parallel forms.

Taylor and Weir (2012b) report how those responsible for *administering the test at centre level* expressed concerns about the test's length and its logistical complexity, in particular the difficulty of selecting appropriate subject-specific modules for candidates. *EAP teachers*, though generally favouring the tests, also commented on the difficulty in deciding on the most suitable subject modules. As noted above, Davies (2008) cites 34 different branches of engineering, according to those listed in the completed report forms collected during ELTSVAL, bringing into question whether one module (technical) could ever be fit for purpose for all of these engineering students. Criper and Davies (1988: 108) did, however, make the point that the number of actual mismatches as perceived by testees or administrators was in fact very few.

At a meeting with *language testers*, Alderson and Clapham (1992a: 8) found support for a reduction in the number of modules but also acknowledgement that the high face validity of the test was partly due to its subject specificity.

The questionnaire responses in the consultation phase had acknowledged the importance of the direct Speaking and Writing components but the difficulty of achieving standardised marking was also recognised. The *UCLES* view on this issue was expressed in their brief report to the Project Steering Committee; it commented:

> ...although the Assessment Guides used to train markers for M2 (Writing) and M3 (Interview) were being constantly improved, and sample monitoring of M2 scripts was being implemented, with the revised ELTS 'this

> monitoring needed to become more rigorous and systematic and needed to be supplemented by the monitoring of sample recordings of the oral interviews'.
> (Alderson and Clapham 1992a: 6)

Alderson and Clapham (p. 2) also established data concerning the unreliability of the M2 Writing module. Financial constraints and logistics, however, dictated that the Speaking and Writing modules would continue to be single marked and this serious deficit with regard to reliability evidence from double marking has remained to this day.

With regard to the Listening module, most stakeholder respondents felt that it would be better to convert the general Listening test (G2) into a specialised M component, thus making it domain-specific and modular alongside the M1 Reading (see Hughes, Porter and Weir 1988: 101, Alderson and Clapham 1992a: 16–17). An integrative test was envisaged, perhaps involving candidates listening to a lecture, making notes and then carrying out a writing task as in the contemporaneous TEEP test developed by Weir (1983) for the Associated Examining Board, Aldershot. Alderson and Clapham (1992a: 17) pointed out that overwhelming, practical and logistical constraints made such an authentic approach impossible. Most test centres arranged for all candidates to take the existing ELTS G2 Listening test in one room so they could not be listening to different texts from multiple modular recordings being played out loud at the same time when individual headphones were not available to candidates. To operate with multiple versions would require a separate room for each version, or for the different Listening test versions to be run at different times. The administrative demands this would impose on test centres were deemed unacceptable. Alderson and Clapham comment as follows: 'Until the day when candidates could have individual headphones it looks as if it would be impossible to have Listening in the M component' (1992a: 17). The assessment of listening skills was therefore to remain general rather than subject-specific.

Interestingly, the original M3 Interview would now be located alongside G2 Listening as a non-specific test of Oral Interaction (G3) (see Alderson and Clapham 1992a on the rationale for this). One of the main reasons was the lack of subject expertise of the examiners who were expected to conduct a subject specific oral interview.

For further details of the consultancy side of the ELTS Revision Project, the reader is referred to Westaway, Alderson and Clapham (1990), Alderson and Clapham (1992a), Clapham and Alderson (1997), Davies (2008: Chapter 4) and Taylor and Weir (2012b).

So in all a good deal of satisfaction with the test was expressed by informants but there were serious concerns relating to modularity, reliability and practicality.

The ELTS Validation Consultative Conference, 17–19 October 1986

Early on in the revision project an invited ELTS Validation Consultative Conference organised by the British Council, under the aegis of Roger Bowers, Deputy Controller, English Language and Literature Division, was held in London in October 1986. The conference brought together language testing researchers from Britain, Australia, Canada and the USA to review Criper and Davies' ELTS Validation report (finished in 1986 but not published till 1988); to consider the early outcomes (see above) of the consultation exercise conducted by Alderson and his colleagues (eventually published as Alderson and Clapham 1992a); and to discuss possible options for the revision of the test. Papers on various aspects of test validity in relation to ELTS were commissioned from a number of the participants and circulated among the group prior to the meeting and then formally presented and discussed.

The Conference agreed that the test needed shortening, the number of subject-specific modules should be reduced, its administration needed simplifying and scoring validity had to be improved through double marking (Hughes, Porter and Weir 1988). But the main message from the assembled testing experts was: 'changes to the test should not be too radical.' Various contributors at the Conference criticised the construct validity of the test or rather the lack of definition of the construct(s) it was intended to measure (ibid.). Weir, Hamp-Lyons and Skehan (in Hughes et al. 1988) all argued forcefully that in any revision, construct validation was essential. Weir and Skehan felt that much more could have been done in the earlier ELTSVAL study of Criper and Davies (eventually published 1988) to explore the nature of the constructs being measured for example by think aloud protocols and Weir argued that notions of validity posited mainly on predictive and concurrent studies may not be enough. The lack of an adequate theoretical or empirical basis for the validation of the original ELTS was seen as a major flaw. Weir commented (Hughes et al. 1988: 18):

> Carroll's earlier view (1981) that: 'the ultimate validation of our methods would be in the effectiveness of the test based on their results', pushed serendipity too far.

Skehan (1988: 30) was concerned about the close relationship between ELTS and tests such as ELBA and EPTB in the concurrent validation studies that were carried out:

> ELTS correlates surprisingly highly with other tests based on radically different rationales, and there is a worrying level of test instability (poor test-retest correlations). Further we do not have evidence on the internal correlations of ELTS, and therefore we cannot come to any conclusions as to the wide range of constructs that are implied.

Hughes is similarly critical of the concurrent validation carried out and does not see the value of correlating against more limited discrete point micro-linguistic tests. He does not see how this validates ELTS. He is also concerned about the correlations with supervisors' judgements, as they had to invent their own scales thereby making the results of any comparison difficult to interpret. He concludes (Hughes et al. 1988: 54): 'little that is useful can be learned from the study about the test's concurrent validity'.

Most criticism of the subject modules came from language testers who in the main wanted the number of modules reduced and in some cases favoured a return to a single general test for all. Language testing specialists were more sceptical about the need for modularity than end users (Weir 1983, Alderson and Urquhart 1985a, Henning 1988 and Alderson and Clapham 1992a: 12).

Weir (1983: 549–550) had concluded the following after extensive trialling for his Test in English for Academic Purposes (TEAP):

> In our investigations of the language events and activities overseas students have to deal with in British academic environments and the difficulties they encounter therein, we discovered much that was common between students of different disciplines and at different levels. This did not remove the possibility though that the subject content of texts employed in our test tasks might unduly affect performance. Whilst we attempted to take account of this in our sampling, we were unable to produce any conclusive evidence that students were disadvantaged by taking tests in which they had to deal with texts other than those from their own subject area. The case for a variety of E.S.P. tests therefore remains unproven.

Grant Henning (1988: 91) was also critical of the modular approach in his paper commissioned to provide an American perspective for the *1986 ELTS Validation Consultative Conference*. He commented that in all the validation analyses the test was uni-factorial where principal component analysis had been employed, but figures supporting a multi-factorial view were obtained with Varimax Rotation. Henning suggested (1988: 92) that a revised version should consist of:

> Generalised sub-tests for reading, listening and possibly writing while retaining the specialised speaking modules, since that module appeared to show the best predictive and face validities among the specialised modules, and since it would be the least redundant of the competing specialised modules.

As regards modularity, a compromise was reached in 1988, which it was hoped would satisfy the majority of stakeholders. Following analysis of thousands of report forms from participants in the consultation process, it was decided that a tripartite split into Arts and Social Sciences (ASS), Physical Sciences and Technology (PST), and Life and Medical Sciences (LMS) provided the best practical solution to a conflation of the candidates' intended subjects (Alderson and Clapham 1992a: 14). The original six subject specific modules were reduced to three to help simplify the module selection process. As we will see below this is the direction of travel which ELTS' successor IELTS would assume in 1989 and pursue even more radically in 1995. A fourth non-academic module was also envisaged to meet the needs of vocational students. This was later referred to as the General Training Module.

It was thought that further efforts might be made to reduce the size of ELTS to enhance efficiency whilst at the same time maintaining a commitment to profiling across the four language skills. The similarity of sub-skills being tested in the G1 and M1 reading components suggested that one of these could be dropped in order to avoid duplication and overlap and to reduce test length. The decision would be taken to retain reading in M1 (rather than G1) since this linked reading directly to the M2 writing component, creating a reading-into-writing proficiency measure which closely reflected real-life academic literacy demands. Reading and Writing would remain integrated so that, to some extent at least, candidates' written output depended on the reading input in the Reading sub-test, though separate scores would be reported for the two skills as in Weir's TEAP test (1983).

Revising ELTS: From consultation to test implementation

Draft specifications and tasks for the new revised ELTS were first developed in 1988 by item writing teams selected by Lancaster University for each of the three sub-tests. No 'prescriptive' guidance was given by the Lancaster project group to these teams with regard to what should be included in either the tasks or the specifications. This lack of control was to have consequences for the resulting tests, which suffered from a lack of comparability across the different domain papers.

The general briefing provided by Lancaster to team members/item writers provided descriptions of the overall content of the revised test, the target population, general idea of level expected, time table for stages of test, plus the following core instructions:

1 **The Task**
a) Each team should draw up draft specifications and draft sample items for their component of the test. Each team needs to decide on its own construct and design item types which will reflect this
b) The specifications should be drawn up so clearly that parallel versions can be based on them

...

6 **Test constraints**
Test constructors need to:
a) maintain continuity with the present test
b) reduce administrative costs
c) make the test administratively simpler
d) make the test applicable to non UK situations.

Given the lack of guidance regarding specifications and test content, a team at Reading University, consisting of Don Porter, Arthur Hughes and Cyril Weir, reluctantly chose not to accept the invitation to participate in writing the Arts and Social Sciences (ASS) reading module. Their objection was to a methodology where each team would come up with their own idiosyncratic specification and tasks with little hope of equivalence between the three and then be told whether they had done a good job or not with no criteria of success established in advance. Three separate teams nevertheless went ahead and prepared their own specifications and tasks. Given the strictures above of Criper and Davies in the ELTSVAL concerning the lack of an empirical base for the original ELTS test development and the pointed criticisms of Carroll's light-touch approach to needs analysis in Alderson and Hughes (1981), this course of action might be considered to have been a tad 'adventurous'.

In July 1988 three external experts were asked to comment on the three sets of initial draft reading and writing materials (the tasks and specifications the three teams produced), both in general terms and specifically item by item. Only general advice was given by the Steering Committee to the experts moderating the draft tests:

- The M tests should discriminate best at Band level 6
- The M tests should provide more information for pre-sessional courses about candidate abilities than does current ELTS
- M1 and M2 should be to some extent integrated...care must be taken to avoid the knock-on effect whereby students who are weak in reading are penalised in the writing section
- It is not necessary for the M1s in the different subject modules *to test the same skills in the same proportions or the same formats* [emphasis added]
- M1 should be objectively marked but at least some of the questions should not be MCQ. Answers should be markable by clerical staff
- The test must be no longer than 1 hour and should preferably last 45 minutes
- Questions should not be answerable before the text is read
- M2 must not take longer than 40 minutes and should preferably last 30 minutes
- There should be two writing tasks
- A criterion scale should be used for marking
- The assessment of scripts should not take longer than 5 minutes and should tie in with existing bands
- It is up to the team to choose item types (although some suggestions were provided from the consultative conference, language testers meeting and pre-sessional teachers meeting).

The experts moderating the draft tests were also asked to comment on: the suitability of the different proposals for their target audiences; the desirability of having different formats for different audiences; any overlap between G1 and the subject modules; the compatibility of the tests with each other; the extent to which the teams' draft items reflected current constructs of reading and writing; whether significant components of academic skills in reading and writing have been left out; the similarity of the constructs being measured across the three modules and the level of each.

Perhaps not surprisingly, the external moderators found a number of clear differences between the three modules in terms of construct being measured and formats employed, even within the same team (those in the replacement ASS module team produced three separate tests). Liz Hamp-Lyons, a member of a subject module team commented in her interview on the process of redesigning ELTS:

> ...within our team we didn't agree very well, and across the team there was a huge amount of disagreement as to how this whole problem should be solved.

Different timings were used for writing tasks; different numbers of tasks were used in the modules; different interpretations of the need to be thematic were applied; lack of specification of text characteristics was common, varying text characteristics were evident, e.g. level and length of texts, cultural inappropriateness; the integration or lack of it of the reading to writing part differed from module to module; and there were differences in degree of control in the writing tasks, in the rigour and precision of the specification provided for the tasks, and as regards how they were to be marked: some modules sticking to tasks that could be clerically marked other modules not.

In October 1988 the panel of moderators were sent a new set of specifications and tests for critical comment. Alderson and Clapham (1992b: 163) reveal that:

> More than half the applied linguists wanted candidates to be given tasks which were as similar as possible to those they would meet during their future courses. *Since several analyses have been carried out into the language needs of tertiary level students (in particular, Weir 1983), we used these for the test specifications and tests....* [emphasis added]

The specifications were then revised by the team at Lancaster, taking on board the comments of the moderators, and 'a range of specialists in different disciplines' (ibid.). But at the end of the day it is clear that the team at Lancaster fell back on the needs analyses of the UK academic target situation already done by others as the means of deciding what to include in their final version of the test and specifications. Their earlier attacks on Carroll's Munby-driven specifications for ELTS (Alderson and Clapham 1992a: 151) and Weir's use of Munbyan needs analysis in the TEEP project (Alderson 1988: 223–224) seem to have been conveniently forgotten.

As Weir (1983) had noted earlier, there was much in common in the study skills deployed across disciplines. The specifications had become 'remarkably similar' to each other according to a letter from Caroline

Clapham to the moderators (4 October 1988). The tasks across the three remaining academic subject areas were so similar that the specifications were virtually identical and only differed in respect of the reading texts they employed.

Cycles of piloting and main trialling were then conducted with these revised tests, with both L2 students and native English speakers, to check the statistical properties of the individual test items and the test components, as well as to confirm the maintenance of standards between the new test and the previous incarnation of ELTS. Some students were asked to sit more than one subject module so comparisons could be made.

Following analysis of the results of the piloting and comments from the moderators, proper trial versions of the test were prepared. Gill Westaway coordinated development and trialling of the revised new test modules in her role as British Council project head. Trials took place at various centres round the world, most of them in Britain and Australia, but also in Guinea (Conakry), Francophone West Africa, Malaysia, Singapore, Hong Kong, Bangladesh, Algeria and Rwanda. Among the data sets gathered were detailed observations on the clarity of test instructions and item rubrics based on test session observations, and interviews with selected candidates by Gill Westaway from the British Council (see Griffin and Gillis 1997 for results of the trialling exercises).

By 1989 the proposed structure of the 'new ELTS' envisaged:

- a general (G) component containing grammar (G1) and listening (G2) sub-tests, and a 15-minute speaking sub-test (G3)
- an academic (M) component linked to three subject-specific areas (Physical Sciences and Technology (PST), Life and Medical Sciences (LMS), and Arts and Social Sciences (ASS) later renamed Business Studies and Social Sciences (BSS), containing linked reading (M1) and writing (M2) sub-tests
- a non-academic (general training, i.e. vocationally-oriented) component containing linked reading (M1) and writing (M2) sub-tests.

The processes and procedures involved in the revision above are fully described in the *IELTS Research Report 3* (Clapham and Alderson 1997), which contains a dedicated chapter on each of the proposed sub-tests that resulted.

UCLES's John Foulkes (1997) wrote a chapter on the General Module Listening (G2), which was intended to cover understanding of social and then instructional situations common to all students. The G2 tapes were scripted but some effort was made to include real-life features such as hesitation, self-correction, asides and digressions and a partial attempt was made to move away from MCQ. Reliability was satisfactory at between 0.83 and 0.92, and correlated highly with the original ELTS G2 at 0.82, suggesting that it was not 'measuring anything substantially different from what was measured by the old one' (Foulkes 1997: 11). Foulkes also (p. 12) found high correlations with the grammar test and rather worryingly concluded:

> ...The developers of the listening test might be said to have fallen into the trap of developing a test which was a reliable measure, though it could not be said what it was a reliable measure of...further effort should have been made to use language designed to be heard and tasks which realistically related to it.

Clapham and Alderson (1997: 30–48) explain how the *G1 (Grammar)* testlet was not included as part of the final IELTS battery in 1989. Trialling results had provided evidence of such a strong correlation between the G1 sub-test and results for the test as a whole that it was considered to perform no distinct function and offer no useful additional information over the more communicative papers. One important finding was that: '...dropping the Grammar Test from the battery would not adversely affect test reliability' and given the strong relationship of the grammar test with the reading, with both loading heavily on the same first factor in the factor analysis, the construct would not be adversely affected either (p. 40). They commented:

> ...given the overlap between the Reading and Grammar and the minimal increase in reliability gained by retaining Grammar, it seems reasonable to conclude that dropping Grammar is unlikely to compromise seriously the test's predictive validity.... [p.44]

Face, washback and construct validity considerations were in favour of a more communicative exam, so the grammar test was abandoned. Weir (1983) had found similar relationships in his earlier research for the TEAP test, with his 60-item grammar test being the best predictor of overall performance when compared to a battery of EAP skills testlets. In the communicative teaching and testing era, the preference was for the more comprehensive EAP skills-based tests in TEAP and ELTS, the greater efficiency and predictive validity of the discrete-point grammar test notwithstanding.

Clapham (1997: 49–69) discusses the *Academic Reading Module (M1)* in its three domain-related versions. She is clear that: '...since no firm idea of a test construct had emerged during the consultative process (see Alderson and Clapham 1992a) the teams were asked to devise their own...'. The resulting suggestions were then modified by the views from: subject specialists on each of the three modules (pp. 51–52) and 30 language teachers and testers (pp. 52–54), though since many of these were not concerned with EAP, their answers were of restricted value; and three moderators felt in the BSS module, that 'the specifications lacked rigour and the text characteristics were not sufficiently specific.... None of the moderators were satisfied with the somewhat sketchy reading tasks' (p. 54). During the revision process, the revised M1 specifications (ibid.):

> gradually became more and more similar to each other.... Eventually the final list of academic tasks was identical for all three subject areas...the macro and micro purposes were modified according to subject specialists' comments and to the findings of needs analyses such as Weir (1983).

It seems strange that, given the degree of 'consensus' reached, such specifications could not have been developed and provided in advance for the item writers as would normally be expected in test development projects. The appendix to Clapham's chapter (1997: 141–145) gives extracts from the draft specifications developed for the M1 Reading Module for LMS. This provides more detailed insights into how the team conceived the test focus, the stimulus materials and the test tasks.

Comprehensive details of the *Speaking Test (G3)* developments can be found in Ingram and Wylie (1997: 14–29). The aim was to have a more structured format to enhance reliability and in addition assessor training should be improved and rating more closely monitored. There had also been concern in the consultancy phase that interviewers were not subject specialists and that this had impacted on their performance.

Hamp-Lyons and Clapham (1997: 69–80) describe the development of the *Academic Writing Module* (M2). Feedback from the consultancy phase encouraged the view that all three modules should have two similar writing tasks and that these should be based on a similar specification whilst differing according to topic and subject matter (p. 74):

> One writing task was to involve information transfer of the description of a process, and the second was to be an essay involving analysis and synthesis, and calling upon personal experience, knowledge and views. The former was to be based on a stimulus such as a graph, table or flow chart, and the latter was to be related to at least one of the Reading texts.

Liz Hamp-Lyons had been brought in during the revision process to improve the new test's writing tasks (pp. 75–76) and finalise the development of the rating scales (pp. 76–80). Her first job was to establish clearly the task types as none of the teams had produced a full specification; 'seat of the pants test specification' as she later described it (personal communication September 2015). She then set about the rating scales working within the requirement that they were to be as close to the old ones as possible to facilitate transition for administrators and markers. The *Assessment Guide for M2 Writing* (see Hamp-Lyons 1985, 1987a and 1989) was produced containing (Hamp-Lyons and Clapham 1997: 79) '…explanations of the marking criteria and Band Scales for each question and also contained marked sample scripts with comments as to why these marks had been given'. Hamp-Lyons later commented (personal communication September 2015):

> This was a much-revised version of the first Guide to M2 that I did in 1984 and that was in use by 1985, but kept the same basic structure. The tasks were the largest change.

Interesting issues emerged from the revision project in relation to scoring validity and usability. Griffin and Gillis (1997) present the data from the 1989 widespread trialling of the PST reading test (n=779) around the world with large samples taking the module in Australia and Britain. 'The purpose of the trials was to establish the properties of the components and to establish a basis for future reliability and validity studies' (p. 109). The tests demonstrated adequate internal consistency (0.90–0.91) and a wide range of item difficulties with generally good discrimination. For students entering universities at Bands 5.5 to 6, the test coped adequately and most items discriminated around these levels. The problem was that many universities required Bands 7 and 7.5, especially for linguistically demanding courses such as linguistics and law. Only two items were discriminating above 6.5, which was problematic in the case of these universities, which had almost no information on English language proficiency available for decision-making.

The formats introduced in 1989 for the IELTS Academic Test by the Project Steering Group were evidence based, drawing on stakeholder views in the ELTS Revision, the suggestions from the consultative committee and the earlier recommendations of the ELTS validation report. Full details of all the revisions can be found in the above volumes produced by the revision project (Alderson and Clapham 1992a, Clapham and Alderson 1997). Salient characteristics from these, covering test aims, content, dimensions, administration, scoring, rater-training are given in brief as follows:

IELTS Academic Writing Module (M2)

- linked to one of three academic domains: Physical Sciences and Technology (PST), Life and Medical Sciences (LMS) and Arts and Social Sciences (ASS later renamed BSS – Business Studies and Social Sciences). All three academic modules should contain two writing tasks and these should be based on similar sets of specifications, with any difference being related to topic and subject matter rather than to genre or task type
- length = 45 minutes
- assessed on a nine-band scale
- use of both analytical/profile and holistic/global criteria and descriptors. Fewer criteria to assist markers to come to a composite band/level more readily
- M2 would be marked by a trained ELT specialist at the local centre
- an enhanced *Writing Assessment Guide* was produced as part of the training programme for future examiners including explanations of the marking criteria and band scales for both questions and exemplar scripts
- for the first time, examiner training materials included a Certification Package, i.e. a set of writing performances which all examiners had to mark to standard within acceptable limits in order to become 'licensed' ELTS examiners
- introduction of sample monitoring for quality assurance.

IELTS Speaking Module (G3)

- the Oral Interaction component had been subject-specific but this proved unsuccessful in cases where the interviewer and candidate were from different disciplines or where candidates did not yet have a subject discipline to draw on. It was therefore decided to transform the Speaking component from a modular form (M3) to a general speaking ability test (G3) which would be taken by all candidates.

- more structured Speaking test format than previously – 'designed to measure general proficiency in speaking' and 'to interact in social, survival and training or academic contexts without focusing specifically on technical or academic features of the language' (Ingram and Wylie 1997: 14)
- include tasks that could discriminate at every band level
- include five phases requiring progressively higher proficiency levels as follows: Phase 1 (1–2 min) – Introduction, warm up; Phase 2 (3–4 min) – Extended Discussion, cue cards used for candidates to get information from interlocutors; Phase 3 (3–4 min) – Elicitation: opportunity to produce extended speech on a familiar topic; Phase 4 (3–4 min) – Speculation and Attitudes: dialogues on basis of short candidate cv; Phase 5 (1 min) – Conclusion: short round-up session
- length = 10–15 minutes
- the old ELTS Oral Interaction Band Scale was redeveloped to produce a new global, holistic nine-band scale
- examiner acting as interviewer-rater would be an ELT specialist at the local centre who would undergo a comprehensive training programme; a new examiner training package (face-to-face, and also in self-access mode for remote locations) was created for this purpose, and it included a standardisation video as part of the Speaking Assessment Guide
- introduction of certification procedures for examiners
- to confirm their ability to mark to acceptable standards, a sample monitoring process was set up according to which all live test interviews would be audio-recorded and one in ten of these would be returned to a centre in the UK or Australia for moderation.

IELTS Academic Reading Module (M1)

- linked to one of three somewhat diverse academic domains (Life and Medical Sciences (LMS), Physical Science and Technology (PST) and Arts and Social Sciences (ASS, later renamed BSS – Business Studies and Social Sciences)
- final list of academic tasks identical for all three subject areas but which differed with regard to topic, source and text type of

reading passage; content not closely related to particular branches of an academic discipline
- a Question Booklet containing 3–4 reading passages (a maximum total of 2,500 words), accompanied by around 40 items included gapped summary, information transfer, diagram completion, multiple-choice, multiple-matching, true/false/doesn't say and short constructed response formats; same types of item considered suitable for all three modules
- length = 55 minutes
- assessed on a nine-band scale
- clerically marked according to an objectively-scored marking key.
- the Academic Reading module (like the Listening) was intended to measure most sensitively at Bands 5 and 6 on the ELTS nine-band scale, but also to function above and below these bands
- Reading and Listening are reported on an 'overall scale', with general descriptions for each of the nine scale points (Ingram and Wiley 1997: 94) following the abandoning of attempts to generate descriptors that would describe the quality of a test taker's performance on the indirect tests of Reading and Listening for the purpose of score reporting.

IELTS Listening Module (G2)

- Overall aim in the test tasks was to provide a plausible purpose for listening and an appropriate response to make during the listening
- Though recordings were to be heard once only, stimulus material would contain some naturally occurring internal repetition
- Material was scripted rather than authentic speech; attempt to simulate 'plausible spoken language' by including normal features such as hesitation phenomena, shifts of register and asides
- Time was to be given to test takers for prior reading and for review of answers afterwards
- Tape and Question Booklet containing around 40 test items, divided across two stages each containing two sections
- Stage 1: language skills needed in social situations, typically involving informal and semi-formal transactional situations, e.g. obtaining accommodation, form-filling; one monologue and one dialogue, to include some accent variation

- Stage 2: a test of general listening ability but based within study-related contexts and situations common to the experience of all students, e.g. introduction to library, lecture on a general topic; one conversation with up to four speakers, one monologic lecture – formal and informal styles
- Four-option multiple-choice, multiple-matching, true/false and assorted short constructed response items, including gap filling, providing short answers to questions or 'guided note-taking' such as completing a form or a grid and summary completion
- Length = 30 minutes
- Reading and Listening are reported on an 'overall scale', with general descriptions for each of the nine scale points (Ingram and Wiley 1997: 94) following the abandonment of attempts to generate descriptors that would describe the quality of a test taker's performance on the indirect tests of Reading and Listening for the purpose of score reporting
- Clerically marked at the test centres in-country according to the MCQ key (this inevitably impacted on the scope of test-taker responses)
- All completed answer sheets were returned to Cambridge for monitoring and data capture.

Endnote

In the event, what is perhaps most striking is that so few real changes were made to the content of the original ELTS test by the 1986–1989 ELTS revision project, beyond the reduction in the number of ESP modules from six to three for reasons of efficiency (Davies 2008: 89–90). Overall time was reduced from the 180 minutes that ELTS had taken, down to a new total time of 110 minutes to meet the criticisms of practicality that had haunted ELTS. There was no apparent improvement though in the measurement of underlying constructs. The shift to IELTS after the revision study 1986–1989 thus did little, if anything, to improve the validity of what was being measured, though clearly it made IELTS a more efficient test to deliver than its predecessor.

Distinctions between the surviving three 'ESP' modules related largely to text types and topics: few genre-based differences had been established between the skills the test developers attempted to assess in each. Clapham (1997: 66) emphasised the appropriateness of cross-disciplinary as against subject-specific EAP tests, when she described the purpose of the drafting, redrafting and trialling process as to:

> make the IELTS reading modules as suitable as possible for students in the three broad areas of BSS, LMS and PST. This was a difficult task because each broad subject area covered two not so perfectly compatible narrower ones, so that PST, for example, had to be suitable for both chemists and engineers although the texts required in their two disciplines are different both in subject matter and style. However, this is only a problem when selecting text types and topics; from our content validation study it appears that the academic reading skills required are the same in all three areas, and the test types, although not on the whole typical of the sorts of tasks students would do, are equally appropriate for all three subject areas.

Davies (2008: 111) would later pose the question 'what is academic language proficiency?' in the final pages of his book on testing English for academic purposes. In that monograph (p. 113), he puts forward the argument for a single IELTS test based on cross-cutting EAP skills. Academic proficiency is seen to involve *performing the appropriate discourse*, which is in his view generalisable across all disciplines. He identifies the components of this skilled literacy of the educated as:

- argument,
- logic,
- implication,
- analysis,
- explanation,
- reporting

and argues for a *general* language factor relevant to all those entering higher education, whatever their area of specialism. Davies (2008: 71) also offers a complementary definition of communicative language testing further supportive of the arguments against modularity. He argues that what should be tested are the skills and features underpinning communicative behaviour, i.e. the abilities rather than the behaviour itself.

This was the direction of travel, established initially in the ELTS revision 1986–1989, that IELTS would eventually take (see Chapter 5).

Despite the considerable effort spent in surveying a wide range of stakeholders, the ELTS revision project did not come up with a more viable or superior alternative to test specification and development than the one adopted by Brendan Carroll and his colleagues in the British Council when the ELTS was being designed in the late 1970s. Most of the skills eventually decided on for the ELTS reading revision (Clapham 1997: 49–50), and a number of important ones that weren't, could be found in the appropriate sections of Munby's taxonomy of language skills (1978: 176–184) on which Weir's Test in English for Academic Purposes (Weir 1983), developed for the Associated Examining Board, Aldershot, was based and which indeed were largely present in the already existing forms of the ELTS test.

The British Council's needs analysis approach used in developing ELTS was perhaps not as empirically extensive as Weir's doctoral research which underpinned the TEAP development, but through interviews; the body of published research on EAP (see Chapter 3); the British Council's wider involvement in the EAP area in the 1970s (Carroll 1980: 1–3); Carroll's own work on academic study skills in India in the late 1960s which had resulted in him publishing an EAP study skills course (Carroll 1969) intended to bridge the gap between what college entrants knew and what they were expected to know in undergraduate programmes conducted through the medium of English in India; the doctoral work of Munby on language needs analysis; of Hawkey on study fellows' experiences in the UK; and Moller's on existing EAP tests, there was arguably enough target situation information available to the test developers on the requisite language related study skills appropriate for the test, backed further by the possibility of recourse to the wide-based experience and expertise of its world-leading ELT cadre.

The ELTS revision project 1986–1989 would produce nothing superior in terms of a methodology for test construction. In fact, despite an expenditure in excess of £200,000 on the ELTS revision and the involvement of countless stakeholders through questionnaire and interview, the data generated and the procedures employed to construct the test did not result in any major advances in test development or associated systems for effective test delivery and validation.

Clapham's verdict on the contribution of the applied linguists surveyed to the definition of a reading construct in the revision project to be measured is revealing:

> ...the applied linguists' responses were varied, contradictory, and inconclusive, and provided no evidence for a construct for EAP tests on which we could base the test.

Davies (2008: 90) is quite severe in his final judgement of the ELTS revision project and concludes that viewed from a negative perspective it might be considered a pointless activity. He argues that the time spent on consulting the focus groups and the unusable and unhelpful information generated through a wide variety of sources produced little of benefit to the revision and as a result the changes it recommended for ELTS were minimal.

Davies (ibid.) does note more positively, however, that what the revision project did achieve was to establish a consensus by consultation and empirical study, which favourably compared with the development of ELTS, where he felt neither of these sine qua non elements for test development had been present.

Westaway, Alderson and Clapham (1990: 255) in an article on the early stages of the ELTS revision project take a more benign view and emphasise the breadth of the consultation that took place:

> The Project has attempted to consult all those who could conceivably have opinions to offer on the current *ELTS*, and has endeavoured to involve testing specialists from the United Kingdom and beyond in the process of devising a revised test....

Gill Westaway (personal communication November 2015) provides a retrospective view differing slightly from Davies on the value of the ELTS revision project:

> Maybe it had its weaknesses but an enormous amount of good solid research was done, even if the eventual decisions taken on the form of the new test did not take ELTS in radically new directions.

In 1980 ELTS had certainly shown itself to be a significant change in direction in EAP testing from EPTB and with some justification could lay claim to the mantle of the first communicative test of English for Academic Purposes. Davies (2008: 90) emphasises that the revision project evidence confirmed that there was merit in the ELTS innovation, which would last. The problems lay on the practical side and these would be addressed in the later IELTS revisions.

Lynda Taylor in her interview for the history project concurs:

> ELTS...was a significant break with what had gone before...a radical reinterpretation of how language ability could be tested and it focused very much on a skills based approach to reading, writing, listening and speaking but in an integrated way so that reading and writing were integrated and the speaking was also integrated with other elements of the test. It reflected

the communicative era and an attempt to move into a much more functionally oriented testing of language, knowledge and ability, rather than just language knowledge. It also reflected a strong interest in language for specific purposes, the notion that language is tied to academic domains, and not just to a general academic context but to specific discipline oriented contexts. So the original ELTS had six different discipline areas that it sought to cover. It did involve a face-to-face speaking test which was a major positive feature. It involved a direct writing test, which was another positive feature. So in many respects I think you could say, ELTS rather set the frame of reference for later tests and IELTS was an attempt to build on the experience of ELTS, take account of some of the things that weren't perhaps working as well as they might; and the IELTS revision in 1995, which started almost the moment that IELTS came on stream, sought to ensure that the test would have a future, and that it would be sustainable. I think that one of the things we have learnt in the last 20 years is the importance of sustainability in language assessment systems. If you can't generate the amount of material that's needed, if you can't calibrate that material in the right sort of way, if you can't deliver your test in a reliable manner then you may produce a brilliant test but it's not sustainable in the long term and it has no long-term life to it.

Even after the ELTS revision project 1986–1989, there were still some residual problems with test development, administration and validation, which had not been addressed. The May 2015 interview with Mike Milanovic for our history project is revealing on what Cambridge inherited from the ELTS revision project when they took over the management of IELTS in 1989:

> Well, what was quite curious when the results of the ELTS revision were handed over to Cambridge to operationalise, was that what actually came over was little more than two versions of the test. There was no finalised set of test specifications, other than some work that had been done on the relationship between writing and other modules in order to band them, some form of equating that was done. No procedures were laid down for ongoing test equating or calibration at all. So there were no specifications, no item writer guidelines, no statistical procedures proposed for the ongoing maintenance and creation of equivalent test forms etc. No structures that were recommended, so it was basically a revision project which ended up leaving Cambridge with two full IELTS tests, but very little else and so the task initially was to put all of those other things in place....
>
> ...I wasn't privy to whatever the rationale was for just having the two versions, but I was quite surprised to find that so little came across with the test, so little, that was, formally. It's not fair to say there was nothing, there

were bits, but the way in which they were compiled or not compiled or put together was essentially *ad hoc* as far as I could tell and really provided absolutely minimal, if any, support for how we were going to go forward.

So our first challenge was to recognise that, and to put in place procedures, which would allow you to create multiple forms and that you could equate those forms, calibrate them to a common scale etc. The scale existed and we accepted the nature of that scale,…. I worked closely with Alastair Pollitt, who was then working with the Exams Syndicate and one of his specialist areas is Rasch analysis. So we decided that what we needed to do was create a scale using the IRT variant called Rasch and that we needed to pre-test materials and that we would then calibrate those materials to the common scale we'd effectively created. But the notion of pre-testing in relation to IELTS was meanwhile still a largely unknown and unaccepted notion; the mechanisms to do it were very limited so we had to find a couple of places where we could actually get people to do these pre-tests, and were able to work with people in Hong Kong and Singapore to at least get us to a point where we had pre-tested the material, calibrated the material, put it on to a common scale.

In the next chapter we explore in more detail the continuing development of the IELTS test from the 1990s onwards, where, as indicated in the above quotations from Lynda Taylor and Mike Milanovic, the majority of changes relate to making it a more efficient test administratively by the introduction of systematic, comprehensive and rigorous testing procedures to meet the shortcomings detailed above, rather than to any real change in measuring its underlying constructs.

Chapter 5

The International English Language Testing System, 1989–2016

> The aged love what is practical while impetuous youth longs only for what is dazzling. – Petrarch

We saw in Chapter 4 how, after the 1986–1989 revision, a more practical, efficient version of the highly innovative ELTS, the International English Language Testing System (IELTS) emerged. In this chapter we will consider the enhanced systems that were put into place to: develop IELTS; promote it; deliver it; ensure its security; guarantee the quality of its examiners and the marking; and develop a research base to underpin the argument for its evidence-based validity. We examine how each of the three IELTS partners (Cambridge English, the British Council and IDP: IELTS Australia) shared these critical responsibilities, and examine in detail the contribution each partner made to the systems in IELTS.

Then in the second part of the chapter we will look at the changes that were made to the test itself in this period. This will include a consideration of any alterations to the way the test was attempting to measure the underlying Academic English construct(s) we looked at in Chapters 3 and 4.

Then there were three

The Cambridge Executive Committee 57th meeting, November 1986, is interesting for its discussion of a number of important developments in relation to the spread of the IELTS in Asia and possibly Australia:

86/24 English Language Testing Service
...A considerable growth of interest in overseas areas was reported, with the possibility of ELTS replacing the Scholarship Selection Test at present being phased out in Australia, and of linking ELTS testing to secondary schools in Malaysia.

These developments were indeed a harbinger of future directions for ELTS. In the late 1980s a third partner, the International Development Program (IDP) of Australian Universities and Colleges, was to emerge from the Southern hemisphere. Anne-Marie Cooper (2009), formerly Director IELTS Australia, provides us with invaluable background detail on the Australian context in this period:

In March 1985 the Australian Government announced a new overseas student policy...to develop Australia's role as an educational provider in the Asia/Pacific region, expand certain sectors of the education community and market education as an export commodity. As a result of this new policy there was an expansion in the marketing of Australia as an educational destination and a connected increase in enrolment of overseas students....

In relation to the then current matriculation requirements for entry to Australian tertiary education, Cooper describes how:

...a number of concerns were being raised about the level of English language proficiency required for entry into Australian universities.... A significant number of students (in fact the majority) were required to sit the Australian Government Short Selection Test (SST) either in their own country or in Australia. The SST had a number of concerns associated with it, not the least of which was the issue of reliability...there were only six or seven versions of the test and as a major component of the test was multiple-choice it was found that students were able to memorise each version; the test was not held regularly throughout the year hence it was often difficult to arrange for a student to sit at a convenient time.

Cooper explains how IDP first became involved in an alliance with Cambridge and the British Council:

In late 1986, Dr Ed Burke, of Griffith University was commissioned by the then Department of Employment, Education and Trade (DEET) to investigate other tests being used around the world to assess English language proficiency and to report back with recommendations on the test/tests which were appropriate for the Australian context...it was decided that the best way forward for Australia was to embark on a collaborative study with the British Council and UCLES....

Australia's involvement in IELTS began in 1988 with discussions at IDP between the late Dr Elton Brash and Dr Denis Blight, then head of IDP's core program (Development) and Deputy Executive Director respectively. Dr Brash had been approached by a contact in the UK to see if IDP might be interested in joining a research project on language testing being undertaken at Lancaster University. This was to fit in with DEET's criteria for an appropriate Australian organisation to manage the process of a new test...Dr Blight agreed to IDP's involvement with the concurrence of Professor Ken Back, IDP's Executive Director at the time. IDP was required to contribute some AUD$150,000 to fund participation in the research by Professor David Ingram, from the Centre for Applied Linguistics and Languages, Griffith University.

...A team of testing experts was put together in England [for details of the ELTS Revision project see Chapter 4]. Australia was represented by Professor David Ingram who was based at Lancaster University for a period of more than a year...[Ingram] contributed significantly, particularly in ensuring that the test was genuinely international in character.

Cooper makes clear the scale of IDP's investment in this fledgling test:

> Over a period of about two years, IDP's investment in test development exceeded AUD$350,000. Most of these funds were borrowed thereby extending IDP's overdraft...a structured business arrangement was agreed upon, governed by a Memorandum of Understanding.

and outlines the division of responsibilities and territorial rights:

> Cambridge would assume responsibility for test development and central administration, under the purview of a joint technical advisory group, and the British Council and IDP would oversee test administration including delivery.

Thus the International Development Program of Australian Universities and Colleges, now known as IDP Education Australia (IDP), joined the British Council and UCLES in 1988 in an international partnership, reflected in the new name for the test: The *International English Language Testing System* (IELTS). The inclusion of a third partner, as well as providing a welcome financial boost, gave a wider perspective and helped guard against any Eurocentric bias, whilst at the same time enhancing access to markets in the Far East and Australia.

Mike Milanovic (personal communication March 2014) described their joining the partnership as a 'major stimulus to growth'.

In her interview for the British Council history project in August 2015, Anne-Marie Cooper stressed the importance of the international dimension:

> I think from the very beginning it was agreed that if Australia was to participate on a global scale, the test needed to be very clearly identified as an international test...there were discussions within the Australian university sector and there would not have been the same level of recognition and support if it were known as a British test.... The option was if it couldn't be known as an international test, then Australia would go it alone and develop their own, which we really didn't want to do.

Nick Saville provides further insight into the implications of the change in name to **IELTS** in his interview for the history project:

> ...the importance of having an international dimension to what was offered, and not simply a parochial one, was an idea that came out of the ELTS revision; one of the significant differences between ELTS and IELTS. So the two bits of that acronym that changed was firstly 'S', the 'System' bit at the end...recognition that what you were offering was a *system* and not a *service*. It led people, it certainly led me to believe that there would be more needed in the behind-the-scenes concept of the system....
>
> ...Of course at that time they were looking for a North American partner as well. Not from the US, but from Canada, so there were some discussions in that ELTS revision period where you were looking for an Australian, and a Canadian, so a South and North partner, and that bore fruit with the IDP relationship, but didn't come to fruition with the Canadian one. So you ended up with 'I' being, on one level a manifestation that the relationship wasn't just a UK partnership, but also that English was an international language. So the 'I' had, in my view, two connotations: the nature of the partnership had changed, but also the nature of the idea of 'English is not just out of England any more'. It was international English that we were beginning to think of, or English for international mobility, not just coming to the UK.
>
> The *system model* is mostly stuff that the public doesn't see. It's how you go about writing tests; how you go about producing the number of items you need; how you standardise that; how you calibrate that; how you administer it in ways that don't lead to inadvertent problems, like cheating or non-standardisation of the administration, and so on and so forth. And that is a system in a different sense: it's not just putting together different components that make up the academic or general training, that makes up this module, that module; it's the underlying system which allows you to

make it fair, make it reliable, make it practical, and to ensure that it has the right kind of impact.

Gill Westaway (personal communication November 2015) also commented on earlier attempts to break through in the USA:

> ...we were also consciously wooing the U.S. through the involvement of some of their testing experts like Grant Henning and regular conference presentations at TESOL and NAFSA meetings around the States. Back in the 1980s, though, there was very little receptiveness to the idea of the U.S adopting such a test as ELTS/IELTS, and concerns were frequently expressed as to its reliability which were only properly addressed once responsibility for the test development and maintenance had passed to Cambridge.

Overall partnership responsibilities

The period 1989–2016 would witness major change in the *modus operandi* of what had hitherto been known as the English Language Testing Service (ELTS). The new test partnership of the British Council, UCLES and IDP Education Australia, placed the responsibility for *test production, marking standards* and *examiner standards* with UCLES, and the responsibility for *delivery* and *promotion of the test worldwide* jointly in the hands of the British Council and IDP (see below for detail). This was seen by the IELTS partners to be playing to the strengths of the three organisations.

Cambridge assumed greater responsibility than hitherto for the new IELTS. The number of well-qualified and experienced staff in its newly formed *EFL Evaluation Unit* grew rapidly in this period whilst at the same time the professional cadre in the British Council was reduced. As regards the latter, Les Dangerfield (personal communication September 2015, following his interview in May 2015) emphasised:

> ...the UK based professional testing cadre was deliberately reduced once the professional aspects of ELTS had been handed to UCLES – there was no longer the same work for the BC people to do in the UK.

In contrast Dangerfield also noted:

> The British Council overseas resource in professional and administrative support for the delivery of the test grew substantially in the years that followed.

As we will see below, the British Council would no longer play the leading role in English language test development and validation, which it had enjoyed for nearly 50 years. Its influence on the IELTS test waned as changing priorities led to large-scale reductions in the ranks of the professional cadres in Spring Gardens and many of its testing specialists left.

In his interview for the history project in February 2015, Mike Milanovic, Chief Executive, Cambridge English Language Assessment until 2014, draws attention to the growth of a critical mass of language testers in UCLES in the late 1980s (see the subsection *The Cambridge contribution to IELTS, 1989–2016* below for full details). In particular he identifies the critical importance of the appointment by Cambridge of Peter Hargreaves from the British Council and highlights the role that Peter Falvey, then British Council English Language Officer seconded to Cambridge, played in the Cambridge reorganisation:

> Cambridge under John Reddaway needed advice on how to structure English Language Assessment at Cambridge. Recognising that it was potentially important for the future they turned to the British Council for help and the British Council seconded Peter Falvey to Cambridge. That was the first significant event and it was through the combination of John Reddaway and Peter Falvey that the concept of an English Language Division was established and it was then the job [of heading the division] was advertised. Various people applied, Peter Hargreaves being one of them with a background in evaluation and assessment and he came to Cambridge in around May 1988. So as significant as Peter coming to Cambridge was the work that was done to create the position.

While still in the British Council, Peter Hargreaves, the new Director of UCLES EFL, had taken overall responsibility for the ELTS Revision Project. After 1988 there were still people like Gill Westaway in the Council managing the IELTS development process, but it was a clear decision that once IELTS was operationalised in 1989, all responsibility for its continuing development and maintenance would lie with Cambridge. Alan Davies (2008: 92) argued that this was the right direction of travel. He contended that policy matters were rightly the concern of all three partners, but the management of the consortium required a full-on test delivery agency like UCLES.

Mike Milanovic (personal communication 2014) provides further detail on the general responsibilities of the partners in the 1990s:

> Neither the British Council nor IDP played any part in item production. This was always the exclusive domain of Cambridge and is recorded as such in all written agreements. Cambridge was responsible for all aspects of test production, calibration and defining quality assurance processes in the delivery of examinations. The contribution of the British Council came in the areas of test administration and marketing, which all improved over the years.

So, the production of test materials was coordinated by Cambridge and they would manage the development and validation of the test overall. Item writers were recruited both in the UK and Australia and Lynette Murphy O'Dwyer, then the head of the TEFL unit at UCLES following the move of the RSA ELT qualifications to Cambridge in 1988, administered the process. Test materials were designed under the scrutiny of an International Editing Committee chaired by Professor Chris Candlin of Macquarie University, Australia with Dr Sandy Urquhart from the College of St Mark and St John, Plymouth, UK and Professor David Ingram from the Centre for Applied Linguistics and Languages, Griffith University, Australia as Chief Examiners. Examiner and Item Writer committees normally met two or three times a year. Cambridge had the responsibility to ensure that there were sufficient IELTS versions available to ensure the integrity of the exam, and the stock of exam materials would be revised once every six months. All three parties had a responsibility for carrying out pre-testing and standard fixing as required by UCLES in order to provide reliable and equivalent versions and a quality product. The British Council or IDP would make no alterations to the exam, but both partners would make clear any improvements or developments to the exam they thought desirable.

Cambridge made available training materials for use in standardising the marking of the productive skills tests as well as an administrator's manual. The assessment procedures, including rating scales, and the validation process were now Cambridge's responsibility. The oral and written components, however, were always administered and marked by the two partners.

A Policy Committee met annually to oversee financial matters, test structure, research and validation. The initial representatives were Michael Milanovic from UCLES, Les Dangerfield from the British Council and Anne-Marie Cooper from IDP (all three were interviewed for the history project).

A formal agreement relating to the IELTS examination was signed between the Chancellor, Masters and Scholars of the University of

Cambridge and the British Council and IELTS Australia Pty Limited on 10 November 1999. The three partners were to have joint responsibility for managing and marketing IELTS, UCLES responsibility for its production and technical support and the Council and IDP Education Australia (IDP) (acting under a management agreement with IELTS Australia) responsibility for its local administration and the supervision of their own IELTS exam centres.

The agreement makes clear that the exam would be used for assessing English language competence for admission to courses of study conducted in the English language; provide information on the competence of candidates seeking immigration to New Zealand and Australia and elsewhere as agreed by all three parties; provide information on the English language competence for those intending to undertake work experience or training programmes; and provide information on the English language competence of candidates to professional organisations which have chosen to use the exam.

The Cambridge contribution to IELTS, 1989–2016

Implementing a systemic approach to test development and validation

The rapid professionalisation of testing at Cambridge, and the British Council handing over to Cambridge the responsibility for IELTS test construction and validation, would be significant for the development of IELTS. Test content would not alter much but there would be significant changes to the test systems as Cambridge took control of production and technical support. As in Cambridge Main Suite Examinations, IELTS would be improved through the methodical development of procedures to ensure test validity and in particular scoring validity. Administrative practices would be overhauled to enable the test to cope with use on a global scale. IELTS had started as a cottage industry in 1989. It would become an industrial behemoth.

The catalyst for the modernisation of approaches to testing in Cambridge was the visionary study commissioned by John Reddaway into the validity of the Cambridge and TOEFL examinations. The Cambridge-TOEFL comparability study of the First Certificate in English exam (FCE) and TOEFL took place from 1987 to 1989 with Professor Lyle Bachman, former President of the American Association for Applied Linguistics and of the International Language Testing Association, as Principal Investigator. ELTS might have made a more appropriate comparator exam as, like TOEFL, it was an EAP test. But, given the fact that FCE was taken by over 200,000 candidates worldwide (as against 10,000–15,000 for ELTS at the time) making the sampling of FCE candidates more feasible (ELTS was barely taken in Europe or South America), and given the far superior financial return on each FCE test administered, FCE was purposefully chosen by Secretary Reddaway instead. The comparability study systematically investigated the construct validity of each of these examinations through content analysis and a comparison of candidate performances on each test. The study encouraged Cambridge in the pursuit of scoring validity and the embedding of systematic test development and validation procedures in the organisation's processes (see Bachman et al. 1989 for a full discussion of the study, and Weir 2013).

The appointments by UCLES of Peter Hargreaves in 1988, Mike Milanovic, formerly British Council and Hong Kong Examinations Authority, together with Nick Saville from the British Council in Japan in 1989, Neil Jones following doctoral study at Edinburgh in 1992, and later in 1996 Lynda Taylor with extensive experience of the private English language sector and a PhD in the testing of reading comprehension, would be critical for the improvement of language testing practice at Cambridge. A new *Evaluation Unit* was created within the EFL Division under the direction of Mike Milanovic, staffed by this professional team of applied linguists/language testers. Their job was to focus on matters of validation and research for all the English language proficiency tests produced by Cambridge at that time. The creation of this Unit (later retitled the Cambridge English *Research and Validation Group* and, since 2015, *Research and Thought Leadership Group*) demonstrated an increasing recognition of the importance of psychometric respectability and a growing professionalism within the organisation. With these significant additions to its professional capacity, Cambridge was able to address directly the ongoing requirements for establishing the construct and scoring validity of its tests and a concerted effort was made to systematise English language testing at Cambridge, including IELTS, from the late 1980s onwards.

The increase in capacity for test development and validation at Cambridge was in stark contrast to a scaling down of these activities in the British Council (see the subsection *The British Council contribution to IELTS* for the rationale behind this). Mike Milanovic, formerly Chief Executive of Cambridge English Language Assessment, pointed, in his interview for this book, to some difficulties arising out of the disappearance of the professional testing cadre in the British Council:

> I think their [the British Council's] philosophy was that if you want expertise, particularly in assessment, you buy it in, you outsource it, you don't have it in house...so no one really who worked on IELTS from the Council at this time would have thought of themselves as a professional tester per se. They would have seen their role as almost entirely administrative and they would have seen it as protecting the bottom line....
>
> ...It was very disappointing because in the seventies and eighties the British Council had been much more oriented towards professional excellence in test development and validation.... But by the nineties that had pretty much disappeared and I don't think anyone in the British Council took any technical interest in any piece of assessment from 1990 through to whenever Barry [O'Sullivan] started working there [2012]....
>
> ...The first version of IELTS, launched in 1989, wasn't really fit for purpose from the measurement perspective. At the time it was pretty clear that maintaining three academic modules wasn't really feasible, but what made working on IELTS very difficult at this time was negotiating all the reforms that needed to take place such as getting the Academic component down to a single form that you could replicate, that you could calibrate, that you could put on a common scale, that was reliable and valid, secure etc.... The discussions about revision of the exam were often bizarre; we at Cambridge would say: 'Look, realistically you cannot produce these multiple modules for different skill areas: a) because they're ill-defined, b) because you can't calibrate them, c) because you can't equate them, d) because you can't produce enough of them, etc. And our Council colleagues would say things like, 'But we've asked the network what they want and they want three modules'.... Of course, the 'network' had little or no understanding of the significant measurement issues posed by the way the test was structured. Having said that, where IELTS was very strong was in its construct and face validity. We recognised this at Cambridge and so much of the way IELTS looked and what it sought to measure has remained very similar to the 1989 version. What needed to change related to how it operated and how we could demonstrate that it was a fair and appropriate measure.
>
> ...When you're talking about something that's actually highly technical and has a very significant impact on peoples' lives, then it really does need to be accurate, reliable, valid etc. So if you look at the 1995 version of IELTS, you will see that the nature of the tasks and focus of the test didn't change very much, other than reducing three academic modules to a single one. What did change very significantly was how the whole system operated behind the scenes. It became a much better test from the measurement point of view.

So IELTS needed to be reformed but what was disappointing and extremely challenging and very difficult overall was trying to engage in a discussion about the reforms needed with people in the British Council or indeed IDP, because there was little common ground to have a discussion.

Nick Saville, currently Director of Thought Leadership and Research in Cambridge English, commented in a similar vein (personal communication September 2015) on the downside of a lack of testing expertise in the other partners in the early 1990s:

The introduction of pre-testing to feed the needs of item banking and calibration of test forms was a major challenge in the period between 1990 and 1995. The main problem was that the partners thought it was our responsibility and were reluctant to get involved. There was lack of understanding that the pre-test candidates had to be sourced from the target test-taking population which only they [the partners] had access to.

Mike Milanovic (personal communication November 2015) claimed it was really left entirely to Cambridge to handle the specialist side of IELTS test development and validation. He critically initiated a project at Cambridge in 1990 to look into the future of IELTS, whereby the organisational and production requirements of a large-scale international test were reconciled with advances in knowledge about language, language testing and applied linguistics.

Taylor and Weir (2012b: 17–18) detail how, in the professionalisation of testing at Cambridge, particular attention was paid to improving procedures for producing test materials, and analysing item-level and task-based responses. This included increased pre-testing of materials for item and task calibration and the creation of an electronic item-banking system to enable more effective test construction and equating.

More detailed information about the test-taker populations for Cambridge EFL tests was collected to establish background factors and test-taker characteristics such as age, gender, first language, level of education. OMR technology was used for capturing not only candidate responses (to reading, listening and use of English test items) in order to analyse data for test facility, discrimination, and other technical measurement issues, but also for gathering key information on candidate background variables via a scanable Candidate Information Sheet (CIS) which was routinely completed by test takers as part of the test administration (see Saville 2003: 57–120 for a full treatment of the procedures and systems initially developed at Cambridge during this period, and

Khalifa and Weir 2009: 269–280). With these data, research triangulating test content, candidate background and test performance was now possible. This research inevitably impacted on the continuing evolution of IELTS, given the central roles now played by Cambridge in test construction, management and validation.

Taylor (2011: xi–xiii and Chapter 5) describes how the early 1990s also saw an increased interest at Cambridge in investigating performance assessment, particularly in relation to the nature of oral interaction and describing features of spoken/written language across proficiency levels. Nick Saville acted as coordinator of speaking test research in the 1990s and worked closely with overseas experts such as Anne Lazaraton, an experienced US researcher in teaching oral language skills (see, for example her *A Qualitative Approach to the Validation of Oral Language Tests* (2002)). A lot of effort was put into improving control features especially procedures for enhancing test scoring validity including rating scale development, marking strategies, the appointment, training, standardisation and monitoring of examiners, and most crucially a quality assurance and management system to support the growing numbers of examiners. The building and exploitation of corpora of learner written and spoken language were initiated, for example, the development of the Cambridge Learner Corpus began in collaboration with Cambridge University Press in 1993. Conversation and discourse analysis were used to examine the language and behaviour of Oral Examiners and aspects of test-taker language and behaviour (Lazaraton 2002); these informed understanding of criterial features of spoken language performance and were later to help validate and revise assessment scales.

Work on standardising the formats used in the oral test and the development of the interlocutor frame would be of major importance and instrumental in improving the scoring validity of the Speaking tests across the Cambridge Main Suite examinations (see Weir and Milanovic 2003: Chapter 7 for details of revisions in CPE 2002, Taylor 2011: Chapter 5, and Weir, Vidakovic and Galaczi 2013). Research confirmed the value of using a highly specified interlocutor/examiner frame for the standardisation of oral examiners; this work also led to the development of an Oral Examiner Monitoring Checklist for training and feedback purposes.

The Team Leader (TL) system introduced by Peter Hargreaves in 1994 would contribute to examiner standardisation and management. The TL system comprised a hierarchical network of professionals with various levels of overlapping responsibility and a set of procedures covering minimum levels and standards for examiner recruitment, induction, training, standardisation, monitoring and evaluation (see Taylor 2011: Chapter 5 for details).

Similar professional advances had been made in the comprehension papers. Weir (2013) reports that by the 1990s, the processes used by Cambridge ESOL to produce examination papers in Reading and Listening had been greatly enhanced through employing item-banking as the method for calibrating pretested items onto a common scale using the Rasch model, tagging test materials for known properties and constructing test papers with known measurement characteristics. Question paper production was based on Cambridge's Local Item Banking System (LIBS), which was a computer-based management and analysis tool developed by Cambridge ESOL to handle the entire production cycle. IELTS materials were the *first* to be pre-tested and calibrated to this common scale on the basis of the Rasch model.

However, the technical and theoretical issues involved in the process of calibrating and equating forms across even three IELTS subject-specific modules still proved highly problematic. By reducing the reading and writing component to a single Academic Reading and a Writing module (see *IELTS test content* section below), the linking procedure would be simplified and the parallel form reliability of IELTS improved. Caroline Clapham's 1996 research *The Development of IELTS*, published by UCLES/Cambridge University Press as *Studies in Language Testing 4*, was taken to indicate that such a reduction might not affect the validity of the test adversely.

The history of IELTS after 1989 is really all about how the original ELTS was turned into a valid, psychometrically respectable, high-stakes test that could be administered globally on an industrial scale. Mike Milanovic, in his interview for the history project, stressed the need for IELTS to match what he considered the psychometrically superior US TOEFL test:

> ...we were constantly being compared to TOEFL, which had always been a very professionally produced exam so there was an important comparator on the field that we could not ignore. ETS has essentially, always been and remains an organisation that values research, recognises the importance of psychometrics, recognises the importance of measurement, recognises many of the key elements of assessment that really do matter....

Meeting this challenge was one of the major achievements of IELTS in the 1990s.

John Gildea, Head of IELTS at the British Council, in an interview (June 2015) offers a contemporary view on Cambridge's contribution to the partnership:

> Cambridge's role in validating and producing the IELTS tests is pretty clear; it's not something we can see changing really.... I can see us having conversations about the future look and feel of the test...and I don't think Cambridge have any problems with having those conversations but ultimately the test production, validation and construction of the test is Cambridge's role....
>
> I think IELTS has been quite successful partly because the organisations involved in it brought different things to it. I think we have to respect the fact...Cambridge are probably one of the world's leading English language assessment authorities and to have that behind IELTS is a huge asset...they do bring all that expertise with them.

The British Council contribution to IELTS, 1989–2016

Lynda Taylor (interview December 2014) offered the following interpretation of the changing role of the British Council in the 1990s:

> ...maybe that was an era where outsourcing was beginning to take off so if you didn't have the expertise or didn't want to focus what expertise you had in that direction then the question is, what could you outsource? And it's not as if there weren't other people who could do some of that work and perhaps the British Council was looking at, was focusing more on how to grow the tests in its various market areas around the world and what that would mean. So if you are thinking and I am speculating here, because I don't know, that maybe the priority was to grow the tests on the ground as it were, in the field which was demanding enough because it meant finding examiners and training them and monitoring them and ensuring that you have a test centre that is up to scratch and so on so it might be that the Council felt that it was important to invest in those directions strategically.

Les Dangerfield, who served for 34 years with the British Council in Germany, Portugal, Italy, the UK, Singapore, India and the Western Balkans, and is now an independent consultant, working mainly in the field of education, was Director of Examination Services in the British Council from 1994 to 2000. In a personal communication to the authors in September 2015, Dangerfield supports Taylor's conjecture, arguing that it was:

> a deliberate decision to hand the test development to UCLES and for the British Council and IDP to focus on delivery and promotion of the test overseas. This meant there was no longer a need for so much in-house test writing expertise in the BC, so its resources were refocused to reflect this change....
>
> The British Council decided, with some reason, that it was not/should not be a test production organisation and handed the responsibility for this to an organisation that was/is a test production organisation.

It would not be until 2012, with the appointment of Professor Barry O'Sullivan as Senior Advisor in Assessment, together with a supporting assessment research team including Jamie Dunlea and Vivien Berry, that the nucleus of a professional language-testing cadre was available once more within the British Council and they became involved in test development again (for details of these tests: ILA (*International Language Assessment*) and Aptis, see Chapter 6).

During the 1990s and the 2000s the Council's former ELT Division was fundamentally reformed and its size in the UK reduced but the British Council's centres abroad were steadily strengthened in this period, often through the strong demand for British Council Direct Teaching of English Overseas (DTEO) centres, and this provided, amongst other things, a global infrastructure to support the professional delivery of IELTS worldwide.

Developing a testing system, which produces valid test scores, is clearly a fundamental requirement of any successful testing operation and, as we have seen, Cambridge took the leading role in this during the period under discussion. However, without secure and efficient test delivery and marking systems, the validity of IELTS would have been severely compromised and without the worldwide infrastructure provided by the British Council and IDP, IELTS would never have grown to the size it is today. Data from the IELTS media centre (http://www.ielts.org/media_centre.aspx) for 2014 are as follows:

> In 2014, more than 2.5 million IELTS tests were completed, with almost three quarters of candidates seeking to prove their English language ability for academic purposes. IELTS also caters for those seeking an English language test to prove their English communication skills for the workplace or for migration by offering the IELTS General Training test. Around a quarter of IELTS candidates prefer this option.
>
> IELTS continues to be the world's most popular English language proficiency test for higher education and global migration, and is accepted

by over 9,000 organisations worldwide, including schools, universities, employers, immigration authorities and professional bodies.

A comparison with the Test in English for Educational Purposes (TEEP) developed by Weir (1983) in the same period as ELTS is salutary. TEEP was a heavily researched, highly regarded, innovative development in assessing academic English in the early 1980s, but after it was sold by the Associated Examining Board (AEB) to the University of Reading in the 1980s it was hardly ever administered outside of the University itself. Only about 1,000 tests have been delivered annually, a fraction of those taking IELTS, of course. Unfortunately for TEEP there was no organisation like the British Council or IDP to promote the exam on the global stage or deliver it effectively overseas through an efficient and widespread infrastructure.

The British Council's contribution to IELTS in the 1990s can be considered under the following headings:

- Managing the IELTS examiners and assuring quality
- Test security
- Efficient test delivery
- Research
- Promoting IELTS including extending recognition to a range of UK and overseas educational and other bodies (such as the UK's General Medical Council).

Managing the IELTS examiners and assuring quality

Nick Charge, Assistant Director over many years at Cambridge English Language Assessment, comments, in his interview for the history project, on one of the British Council's major contributions:

> ...it was to do with the management of examiners. So we had a system here [in Cambridge] that we used to manage our examiners worldwide, which I think we tried to get the Council to adopt. And they looked and said 'No that's not right'. The Council and IDP took that idea forward and put together a comprehensive system to train, monitor and quality check their writing and speaking examiners. We were involved in it, we contributed to it, but they [the Council and IDP] were the drivers because they were their examiners. And that system is called the PSN system, the professional support network.... It developed into a very robust system of quality assurance for speaking and writing examiners globally and they took the lead on that and we contributed.

John Gildea commented further on the PSN in his interview for the project:

> It falls to British Council and IDP to mark the tests so we recruit, train and employ the examiners; it's a BC and IDP role, not a Cambridge role...the marking itself is all done by British Council and IDP who invested major time and resources in that area specifically through the introduction of the Professional Support Network for examiners or PSN for short. This is a comprehensive piece of work, which sets out all of the standards and processes for recruiting, training, managing, and standardising examiners.
>
> PSN is something which BC and IDP produced, there was some very limited Cambridge involvement but it was essentially a piece of work produced by IDP and British Council. It augments the official administrative manual, which describes how IELTS should be managed at test centres.
>
> The PSN Manual is available on different platforms, but all test centres have access to it...ourselves [the British Council] and IDP have professional teams within our own corporate organisations that are responsible for PSN on a day-to-day basis for overseeing the monitoring of examiners globally and dealing with any matters from test centres that are escalated upwards.

In the interviews with Anne Staniforth, head of IELTS Strategy and Development at IDP Education Australia, and Anne-Marie Cooper, formerly Director of IELTS Australia (September 2015), they added how:

> The [PSN] project was led and funded by British Council and IDP and saw the development of the processes and standards for examiner management and monitoring. As British Council and IDP managed the examiner network, it became clear to them that the processes and standards were no longer sufficient for the scale and stake of the test. This project represented a considerable long-term investment, and was driven by recognition that the quality and professional integrity of the test were critical to its future success.

John Gildea provided a further example of the contribution to exam consistency/reliability in marking the IELTS writing tasks introduced by the partners:

> ...there are two writing tasks and until about two years ago both tasks were marked by the same examiner and now task one goes to one examiner and task two goes to a different examiner so there's distributed marking of the writing that goes on now so that when you look at IELTS as a whole you've got multiple markers doing the clerical marking of the reading and

listening, supported by a sample monitoring process, and the two different examiners who mark the writing. In addition to this there is another examiner delivering the speaking module.... In short there are several markers and examiners involved in scoring each test.

Nick Saville commented, at his February 2012 interview, on the additional benefits arising from the division of labour within the partnership:

>...if your job is to train and monitor examiners, you also have to be involved in feeding back what examiners are doing or not doing well, so they are, if nothing else, a data collection point, which means you're a participant in the activity of research. You're not simply a conduit; you're a contributor to the endeavour. So having the partners involved in both understanding what might need to change, feeding into how it might need to be re-done, and then trying out the new ideas.... So if the people in the [British Council and IDP] Centres are professionals in delivering the test, they really don't want to necessarily have the hassle of coming up with rating scales; that's not what they know about. But they will tell you if the rating scales work or not. Or if you change them and they don't work, it's going to make their life more difficult. As we see in the idea of the *stakeholder model of testing*, it's a question of division of labour, rather than separation of interests. So you can have a conjoined interest, but separation of responsibilities, and that's how I would characterise the partnership really.

Test security

In his interview for the project, Mike Milanovic, former head of Cambridge English, was fairly scathing of the test security for ELTS in the 1980s. He described a less than satisfactory scenario he experienced in Hong Kong:

>...when I worked at the British Council in Hong Kong I observed some fairly relaxed behaviour on the part of the test centre. For example, they only had a limited number of test booklets and so they would re-use them.... Of course, candidates would write in the test booklets in pencil and at the end of the test teachers would be rubbing out what the candidates had written. Of course, you can't rub it out completely. So candidates would be getting these test booklets, there were only two versions in existence anyway for about ten years, and people had written in them and they'd been rubbed out. So possible answers were actually in the test booklets. Half the time, you'd be able to pick the one that you wanted. It was laughable, but it was a different world and no one really seemed to recognise just how inappropriate that was.

Nick Charge (personal communication August 2015) added another 'case':

> A rather nice example of 'lax' test security was the IELTS 'Postal Version' in use till around 1997. Basically for candidates who lived too far from a centre we posted a listening, reading and writing test to the candidate to complete and post back to us!

In his interview for the history project, John Gildea commented on how the vital issue of test reliability/security had improved immeasurably by the 21st century:

> ...the whole security around the test is on a different level now. Demands from the immigration authorities, mainly in Australia, provided the impetus for the introduction of test day photography, that is, a photograph of the candidate taken by us on the test day. We take the photograph and that photograph goes on to the test report form. The test report form is to some degree less important. It's what is on the web-based validation service that's important, so we know that the photograph on the validation service is of the person who took the test.
>
> The other thing we introduced along with the photograph was a finger scanning process, which sounds a bit over the top but basically given that IELTS is broken down into modules and the modules are taken at different times and sometimes at different halls, in the same building or sometimes in different buildings you have to be absolutely sure you're dealing with the same test taker for each module. A finger scan allows us to check people in and out quite easily, and the same process is used to monitor test taker toilet breaks. There are now multiple layers [of security] that have been introduced in recent years.

Nick Saville also noted the close cooperation needed to ensure security and efficient systems:

> If you're using question papers, which we do, not just an online system, which is another ball game completely, you have to print those question papers in an environment where nobody can steal any. You have to bag them up in an environment where they're put into bags that can't be tampered with. You have to dispatch them through a delivery system where you can rely on them getting there, and then, when they get to the other end, they have to be received, accounted for, and, eventually, opened in such a way that nobody has been able to steal any or see them in advance. So window envelopes, [like] where you have your bills, are no good, because people can peek. So you have to have peek-proof bags, rip-proof

bags. You have to have all these things, which modern technology can do. Then you have to have a machine that can put hundreds of papers into these bags at the same time, in very quick time, in order to keep up with the demand of two and a half million candidates a year taking the tests, with lots of question papers.

So the scalability of the system is, has been, one of the successes, and Cambridge has been able to scale up what we do, and obviously the centres dimensionally have had to scale up, so the improvement of the way centres are set up, managed, and the professional support network to ensure the people locally who do the assessment are coordinated the same, that's been a great success. It's been a *partnership* success. As you see the four things to do with security for example are shared, there are key points where Cambridge can't do anything about it, like the people recruited at the level of the centre and how they behave, and you know, human behaviour is probably one of the weak points in all security systems; if honesty is not there, then even your best systems can be defrauded. We've kept up with that as the stakes have gone up, but we have a system, a forensic system now, of being able to spot unlikely patterns of behaviour, [a system] which we developed in Cambridge and deploy now. This can help us to point the finger at someone and to look for the smoking gun, because you can't really accuse someone of cheating unless you can find out how they did it, but you can find different ways of raising suspicions, and then you can find out whether a person was culpable and take necessary actions to protect the integrity of the system. Those sort of collaborations work very well, but again it's had to be scalable, and I think having a specialist organisation who does some of it, like we do, and having consumer-oriented organisations doing the other, which is leading the marketing and customer support, has been a very successful model. The division of labour has turned out pretty well.

Taking the entries, giving the entries, giving the results, ensuring that person is treated fairly, is what the Council and IDP do, but the information they have to give about the tests, the way in which the test is managed to give good customer service, that's a partnership issue. So the overall package is the result of the partnership, but in the IELTS context, Cambridge doesn't have the direct contact with the customer.

So that's the model, and it's been very successful.

In response to a question concerning the development and retention of high standards on processes like this being a joint responsibility for all including Cambridge, the Council and IDP, John Gildea replied:

> ...we jointly manage risk and at a day-to-day level this is managed by a three- partner risk management group which meets frequently. So it's an

ongoing process of review and mitigation, which is ultimately responsible to the IELTS partners global strategy group.

Efficient test delivery systems

Lynda Taylor identified the importance of efficient IELTS delivery and team building in our interview with her:

> I was familiar with the delivery systems that are needed and it's not just about the systems in terms of logistics. It's about the teams of people that you need to identify and recruit and train and bring on in terms of professional development and monitor so that you have a professionalisation of the whole system that enables you to have a test that is sustainable and has potential for growth without losing the quality or without entailing risks.

When he was interviewed for the project, Les Dangerfield, the first Director of Examination Services in the British Council from 1994 to 2000, emphasised the importance he attributed to developing exam delivery within the British Council:

> ...the greatest thing I achieved, I think, in that period of the nineties was creating a body of exam staff around the world who felt really proud of what they were doing and really motivated in what they were doing.
>
> Each country with a certain degree of exams in terms of volume or income had a Country Exams Manager. This might be a whole post in big countries or it might be part of a role within someone's job description. Then the person who deals with exams on an everyday basis, making sure they actually happened, was called the ESM, Exams Services Manager.
>
> ...So creating this structure, getting these people trained and organising annual meetings for the Country Exams Managers, or whoever the relevant people were, sometimes Country Exams Managers, sometimes ESMs, planning meetings where they would stress-test their respective plans, [to see] if they're realistic or not, whether they should be, whether they're over-ambitious or under-ambitious or what. So we did a lot of training and that training, as well as developing people's skills, developed a sense of *esprit de corps* amongst that team as well.

Mike Milanovic, in contrast to his earlier reservations noted above, regarded this period of Cambridge's relations with the British Council as working well:

> So the Council set up the Central Exams Unit, which was headed by Les Dangerfield and that was actually very helpful because for the first few years, I think it was '94, '95 they recognised that exams were different

from teaching, that probably if you had people who could focus on exams that would be helpful and all of a sudden a dialogue was able to take place between Cambridge and the British Council by people dedicated to thinking about running exams...for a while at least there were people who recognised that you actually had to do quite a lot to make this thing work well. But, like most things with the British Council, it had a life of five years or six years and then it got disbanded and some other way of managing things emerged. And when that new structure emerged it was more difficult to communicate again with them.

The demise of the Examinations Services team in the UK made important and necessary exam reform more difficult, according to Milanovic:

So when the next major reform in IELTS was needed – the introduction of fixed dates in 2002/2003, we found ourselves yet again in a massive battle, primarily with the British Council, who argued that it was much better to keep the test forms in the centre and we keep on using them because it gave the centre a lot of flexibility. Flexibility perhaps but no security...if we hadn't introduced fixed dates, IELTS security would have been massively compromised and might even have ceased to exist. As I said, the battle was primarily with the British Council, and it took just took years to convince them. They were concerned about cost, margins, reaction from centres and so on.

Of course, now no one would ever dream of not having fixed dates and unique set versions but at the time convincing them that you couldn't possibly grow this exam and operate it to the necessary high standards unless you did that because your security would inevitably get compromised, was quite a challenge. By then we had two hundred thousand candidates and it was already pretty much on the edge. Thankfully, we did change, because within the year following the introduction of fixed dates, all seventeen versions of the previous listening tests, which had been kept in centres, were on the Internet. So the whole thing would have collapsed the following year had we not made the change, it was that close, at a critical point. I have to say, however, that once the decision had been made, the process of making it happen was possibly one of the most rewarding and most effective periods for the people running IELTS in the three organisations.

Nick Charge, in his interview, also identified this move to a fixed-exam-dates model as being a key critical factor in the success of IELTS and argued that after the initial reluctance on the part of the British Council to accept the shift, all parties cooperated fully to implement this change:

Okay, the biggest thing we [Cambridge] did was convince the British Council and IDP of the need to move to a fixed-base model. Up until that point, IELTS was on demand as you know...all the centres had a stock of papers with different versions. They decided when they ran and we didn't know. And that was very client-friendly and very centre-friendly. It gave centres complete freedom [on] when they scheduled their tests.... Now, of course, the downside to having an on-demand test is security. Mike [Milanovic] realised that unless we changed, IELTS was going to die because particularly in China, there are people who once they had broken the test, they had broken the system. They knew the versions and they knew the answers. It wasn't enough to keep producing new versions every six months and replacing them, because within a month they would have those as well. So the system needed changing and I think the biggest thing we did was convince the partners to do things the way we wanted them to: tell us about who they are testing before the event. We can send out papers and we agreed then to have 36 *fixed* dates a year throughout the world and to time-zone the paper to avoid knowledge creep from different time zones.... And once we had convinced the British Council it was the right thing to do – and it took some doing because they didn't want to move away from this very successful system.... They were saying the centres will hate this, they will stop doing it, the numbers will nose dive. The opposite was true long-term. If we hadn't done that, the test wouldn't have survived. It wouldn't have survived more than two or three years. It would have been discredited. So from a Cambridge point of view, I think that was one of the most important things we did.

And once we had convinced the partners and they were on board with the idea, they were fine and that was a very productive working relationship to deliver this project on time.... Where the Council came in, was [the need] to convince their centre network that this was the right thing to do because we had no direct relationship with them...it was the first time we had set up a cross-partner project to deliver this. And we worked incredibly closely together for about a two-year period to deliver that project on time and it was very rewarding. So I would say that was what one of the most important things we did.

Nick Saville (personal communication September 2015) also referred to the critical importance of this major re-engineering of the test production and delivery system in order to allow for fixed dates rather than stick to the on-demand model. In Saville's view it accounted for the growing success in terms of rapid growth in numbers which the test has experienced since 2003.

John Gildea explained the current British Council contribution to efficient test delivery in his interview (June 2015):

> ...the delivery of the test falls entirely to BC and IDP. Cambridge do not deliver IELTS and British Council and IDP compete on the ground in many markets around the world. British Council has its network of test centres and IDP have theirs. I think there are over 900 locations where candidates can take the test so it's a pretty extensive network by any measure.

John Gildea is also informative on the IELTS test centre audit:

> Certainly the inspection procedures at test centres, the audit programme as we call it now is a British Council and IDP responsibility and it's pretty extensive, every test centre in the IELTS network is audited regularly and all of the test centres associated with UK visas are audited every year.

Research

As regards the British Council's contribution to research on IELTS, Gildea notes as follows:

> For many years up until about 2012 the British Council was a very passive presence on the IELTS joint research committee basically providing funding for research. More recently we feel we're able to make a much more substantial and constructive input to that group through Barry O'Sullivan who represents IELTS on the Joint Research Committee. At some point in the past there were credible academics from the British Council involved in the research committee or what was preceded by it. [But] certainly from as long as I've been involved since 2003 there wasn't until Barry O'Sullivan took up that role.
>
> Now I think it's important that we have a say in the research and which projects are funded and so on, and then I think Barry helps by providing that level of professional input to the Joint Research Group from British Council.

Since 1995, more than 90 external studies by over 130 researchers around the world have attracted funding under the IELTS joint-funded research programme which is sponsored jointly by IDP: IELTS Australia and British Council with support from Cambridge English Language Assessment. Copies of each research study are available on the ielts.org website in a searchable database. The site explains that:

> The IELTS research programme ensures:
> - ongoing usefulness and contemporary relevance of the test for organisations that use IELTS results

- IELTS contributes more broadly to the growing understanding of the nature of language proficiency and its place within linguistics and language education.

The IDP website idp.com adds:

> Every year IDP: IELTS Australia and the British Council fund and support IELTS-related research that reflects current issues around IELTS in the international context. Such research makes an important contribution to the monitoring and test development process for IELTS; it also helps IELTS stakeholders to develop a greater understanding of the test.

IDP's role in promoting research on IELTS is discussed in the next subsection *IDP's contribution to IELTS, 1989–2016*.

It is interesting to note that the research on IELTS is *funded* by the British Council and IDP and not by Cambridge, though the latter have had a big say on which research projects are approved for funding.

Promotion and distribution

John Gildea was also asked in his interview why IELTS had been so successful. He attributes some of the success of IELTS to the advantages of the global networks available to the BC and IDP:

> BC and IDP made IELTS available and accessible on an enormous scale. We have networks of test centres and so IELTS is made available through all of those. So I think the test fitted a need and just at the time managed to get a foothold in the market and became integrated with and probably entrenched within the systems of organisations which use IELTS scores. In Higher Education in the UK IELTS has almost become a default word for the English test you need as an international student seeking entry to higher education in the UK. So IELTS has become entrenched within the education sector in the UK, Australia and increasingly in the US as well, and this has taken IELTS to where it is at the moment. I think what IDP brought to the piece really was significant recognition in Australia and IELTS became the test you needed to support a student or employment related visa in Australia…without IDP we would never have had that.

Les Dangerfield (personal communication October 2015) pointed out:

> One important thing is the decision by the three partners to jointly develop a separate visual identity for IELTS – incorporating the three organisational

logos beneath the IELTS identity. This helped greatly to establish a unified identity for IELTS as a global product.

He drew attention to the part played by the British Council and IDP in the promotion of the test:

> ...gaining recognition by significant players was an important feature of BC and IDP work in the '90s: such as the UK General Medical Council (achieved by the BC team) which led to large numbers of doctors, and, later, nurses, who wished to work for the NHS in the UK, taking the test; also by the government bodies deciding on qualification for immigration, particularly in Australia, the UK and Canada...

and was keen to stress the critical breakthrough in the USA:

> we did a lot of work collectively to set up an operation in the USA to extend recognition of IELTS and develop a network of IELTS centres there. For legal reasons this was set up under a jointly owned 'Delaware corporation'...the head of this unit was employed by Cambridge, but managed via the IELTS policy group. As we recognised at the time, this change was critical to the future development of IELTS markets – essentially IELTS would never be truly global without recognition and testing infrastructure in the USA.

IDP's contribution to IELTS, 1989–2016

The interview with Lynda Taylor (December 2014) provides valuable insight into IDP's role, comparing it interestingly with the British Council's.

> I think it [IDP] is very different to the Council and I think that is part of the creative tension in a way, just as the Council and IDP are very different from Cambridge, the third partner. I think IDP was always very entrepreneurial in my experience and British Council perhaps came later to that mind-set and I think IDP was always very, very committed to quality and to doing a good job. I am not saying that British Council wasn't, but I think it's probably fair to say that IDP had a narrower portfolio than maybe the British Council, and was able to concentrate more on this important phenomenon and this particular test, and was operating within, at that time, a narrower domain, Australia, New Zealand maybe some bits of the Far East. Obviously, it has grown since but you had a smaller number of universities, if you like, which were its own partners, compared with the British Council, which extended worldwide, and IDP was a much younger

organisation. So there are lots of factors that differentiate the two organisations and in a sense perhaps some of those factors meant that IDP could be fairly fleet of foot and was open to change in a way that perhaps the British Council struggled to be because it was much more established and much more entrenched, and I don't use that critically, I just mean it had been around in a particular sort of way for a long time. It's a big organisation, presumably subject to some government regulation. All of these things meant that it was perhaps harder to make some changes or certain types of decision when you look at the two organisations [the British Council and IDP] side by side.

Note, as Lynda Taylor continues her revealing description of working for Cambridge and with its language testing partners, the British Council and IDP, the effects on their work for IELTS of the regular posting, every few years, of Council career staff to jobs in new places:

I think, ironically for me, it was the British Council that lacked the continuity of personnel, whereas IDP maintained continuity of personnel working on IELTS, which meant that at meetings you never had to go back over something because people were there at the previous meeting. And I know both Nick Charge and I found that quite often it was frustrating that you would get to two years of working with someone and then you knew they were going to be leaving in a few months' time and there was never really any chance of a proper handover, so you anticipate that someone new was going to be here who won't have any IELTS history. Whatever you have given them to read, you can't acquire that from reading and it's going to be another year before they feel confident enough to do certain things or to understand those things and why certain things are important. So, and I always find that slightly interesting, that it wasn't an IDP problem; for me that was more of a British Council problem. But then if you have a system where you have rotation that tends to be what happens.

Test promotion and distribution

Mike Milanovic, in his interview, made similar remarks about IDP's involvement with IELTS and it is interesting how he found it differed from the British Council:

IDP engaged Professor David Ingram, who was then seconded to Lancaster [University]. So David Ingram worked on behalf of IDP to develop the first IELTS speaking test. IDP did take an interest in the professional side. Similarly, IDP recognised the importance of research and from quite early on they're the ones who effectively initiated the research papers and the funding of research in universities and recognised the value of engaging the academic community and in looking at, studying, analysing, critiquing the test in order to improve it. IDP, in particular its CEO Denis Blight, genuinely saw its potential from very early on and as a consequence in the first two or three years of the new IELTS, IDP numbers grew much faster than British Council numbers because essentially British Council didn't put the effort into it. But then they saw, as IELTS grew and IDP were selling more and more tests, that actually this test had real potential. This probably happened by the mid-1990s.

Anne-Marie Cooper in her interview for the project (September 2015) shed some light on the early successes of IDP in the promotion of IELTS in Australia, including some comparison with early British Council approaches to marketing the Test:

> I think it was through sheer effort in IDP's marketing and the recognition that we gained for the test. We started off from an absolute zero base in Australia with no one even knowing about the test, so part of my role in those very early days was to just go out and meet with all the Australian universities over and over again. Not begging them, but almost begging, but strongly suggesting that this was the test to be used for international students coming to Australia. And it was up to them then to recognise IELTS and then ask the students to take IELTS before coming to Australia. Because prior to that all the students would take TOEFL, but we had to move from TOEFL to IELTS and of course all the students found it more difficult. But it was absolutely sheer effort in that the first step of gaining recognition by the Australian universities and once the universities accepted it, I then went down to the TAFE level, which is the Technical and Further Education, and they really didn't know a lot, but they just said oh well if the universities accept it, we will. So that was the very first step. Getting that Australian recognition and our international student market was growing quite significantly, so we were able to encourage all the students coming to Australia to take IELTS. That's why we had very significant growth. Whereas from the British Council's perspective, I guess they weren't so heavily into marketing at that time, it was more just whoever came through the door did the test without significant promotion.

In the same interview Anne Staniforth commented:

> One of the things that really struck me when I first started working for IDP was the relationship that IDP had with its stakeholders and how proactive the management of that relationship was and how they collaborated with government and other stakeholders. That struck me as being something that was completely different in approach to the way that the British

> Council worked. And I do think that this work that was done right from the outset was critical. For many years it was Australia that was driving the IELTS volumes and the formal recognition of Australian, and later New Zealand immigration authorities, hugely contributed to the success of IELTS.

Anne Staniforth then paid tribute to the efforts of Les Dangerfield in the British Council adopting a more commercial approach:

> Les was always someone who really understood the role and value that exams could play for the British Council. Many of the overseas teams struggled to understand the point and benefit of exams. I think it was easier for them to relate to English language teaching because there was such huge demand for the English language and at every meeting they would have gone to they would have been asked for help with teaching. It's only very much more recently in the British Council that they have really understood the role and value that exams can add and Les was the pioneer I suppose of that.

The British Council, under the leadership of proactive Council English language teaching and testing staff like Les Dangerfield, took up the challenge in the 1990s. Les Dangerfield commented in his interview:

> One of the results of the Council's entrepreneurial approach during the mid to late '90s was that, as well as both organisations expanding their own IELTS candidature, the Council's share of the total candidature grew from 53% in 1994 to 70% in 1999, with, of course, IDP's share falling from 47% to 30%.

Test security

On the issue of test security Anne Staniforth of IDP commented:

> ...historically we've had an excellent and very professional team that have developed our approach. We really have bought industry expertise to developing the processes and systems to support this area. More recently IDP led on the development of the test day photography and finger scanning system – IAM (Identity Authentication Management) – for IELTS. Similar systems have now been introduced by competitors. IELTS has constantly tried to lead on innovation in this area.

Research

Lynda Taylor, interviewed in December 2014, comments on the important role IDP played in contributing to research on IELTS:

> ...in 1995, the joint-funded research programme was set up. It may not have been even joint funded at that stage. I think 1995 was the point at which IDP agreed to move to a slightly more managed grant-funded programme, which aligned itself with the needs of the tests, validation and needs of the test. Rather than a slightly more *ad hoc* arrangement which had happened during the early 1990s, where I think some projects were funded but perhaps a bit more arbitrarily rather than as part of an overall research strategy for the test.
>
> ...I think the very fact that IDP had seen the value of setting aside funding for research in the early 1990s was significant. They researched; they encouraged research in some quite important areas, particularly Speaking. But I think it's also true to say that they perhaps – and I don't think the British Council did either – they didn't necessarily have the in-house knowledge and understanding of how to manage that grant-funded activity. So it's one thing to set that money aside and give it to people to go away and do things you think are going to be useful, but it's another to know how that fits within a bigger strategic research agenda. But my impression is, and it is only my impression, that Mike Milanovic, particularly when Chair of the Joint Research Committee, was very persuasive and convincing in his arguments about how this could have been done better, to the benefit of the partners and IELTS as a test; and that's why in 1995 it wasn't difficult, I think, to embark on a new approach, which in principle did some of the same things. It still gave money to independent external researchers but it encouraged a framework of strategic research within which that happened.
>
> It took the British Council a few more years to be able to partner in that and I have to say I think one of IDP's major contributions was that it saw the priority of getting that research published and it supported quite a lot of the publication of the early research that was done. So it was done for things like Alderson and Clapham and Clapham and Alderson prior to the 1995 revision. But also particularly the IELTS volumes 1, 2, 3, 4 and 5 I think were all published by IDP. 6 was the first joint publication, so in that sense I think IDP were more proactive. And they saw the research obviously as valuable, not just for the test but from a marketing perspective. It was a mark of quality of the test, I think, so it had commercial value.
>
> ...In fairness to the British Council, all the grant applications that came in were reviewed both by IDP and by the British Council, so those that were submitted to IDP were reviewed by IDP teams, which may have included internal as well as external people, and by Cambridge and all the proposals

that were submitted by the BC were reviewed by BC people, who may have included internals and externals and by Cambridge. So Cambridge saw all of them and the British Council and IDP saw the ones that they received.

In the first part of this chapter we have explored the various roles and responsibilities of the three partners in IELTS from 1989 to 2016 and how these developed over time. We next turn to the actual test itself to examine closely how IELTS changed during this period.

IELTS test content

The IELTS Revision Project, 1993–1995

The early 1990s saw a review of test content and format, and perhaps more critically, as previously described, a far greater emphasis on key aspects of test delivery, administration and processing. The aim was to ensure that IELTS would be able to cope with the increasing demands being placed on it by growing numbers of students seeking higher education in English-speaking countries.

Mike Milanovic conceptualised, coordinated and closely managed the revision process that culminated in what is referred to as *IELTS 1995*. In a document entitled *IELTS Revision Specifications Draft Version 7 May 1993*, we find a comprehensive account of the proposed RIELTS, the revised IELTS test, including details of test purpose, rationale for development, formats, the Reading test, the Listening test, the Language System test, the Writing test, the Speaking test, the General Training module, a code of practice, specimen material, an item-writer checklist, overall ability descriptors and RIELTS assessment. *IELTS Specifications for Item Writers* (Taylor 1998) provides a clear picture of the modified test in its final form and some explanation of the revisions made.

In the interview in December 2014, Lynda Taylor expanded on the importance of clarifying what was being tested in this revision phase:

> I think one of the things that became particularly important through the 1995 revision was that there was very clear specification of what the test contained, should contain, in reading and writing, listening and speaking components and also across the academic and general training distinctions. So it became important to do what I think Cyril Weir has referred to in *Measured Constructs*, which is the pressing need to specify more explicitly features of the test components. Partly so that it would be easier

to communicate those to the people who needed to generate the materials, and provide content for item-writer training so that the item-writer team could bring together their expertise from English language teaching and learning and from testing and applied linguistics, and channel that through a mechanism to a specification for the test which allowed them to have confidence in producing the material that was needed to feed the test, to grow a number of tests. And I have to say, from my perspective some of the best times that I had in the mid-1990s were working with teams of item-writers, building confidence, you know, growing their knowledge and understanding, helping them to gain satisfaction in their work as well as generating good quality tests. A part of that had started in the early 1990s, about 1991, when a couple of us felt it would be really helpful if item-writers were encouraged to see their work within a bigger frame of reference. So we ran basic item-writer training courses. The first one that we ran was for three days. Peter Hargreaves [ex-British Council, then Head of UCLES ELFL exams] was very supportive of developing the expertise of item-writers to the extent of paying the expenses for [them] to have a three-day course in Cambridge. ... The aspiration was that people should feel that they were professionalising, they were growing their knowledge and expertise and skills in order that they could do a – I wouldn't say a better job, but have a more fulfilling role in their being item-writers. And I think if you talked to some people about the IELTS item-writer training courses and days that we had in the 1993, 1994 period, you will find they remember those very positively because they have told me that. They remember those as being very professionally fulfilling but also gaining a sense of *camaraderie* or collegiality in working on something that was really important, you know. And for me those are the more important things and I feel I took training very, very seriously,...so we developed a whole item-writer training manual which included examples not just of the exemplar materials that we were striving to produce, that came from the specification, but also examples of materials that hadn't made it, with a commentary about why it missed the mark or why it hadn't worked in pre-testing. So there was a genuine interest, I think, in trying to understand how materials work in the testing context and how we can learn from that.

Charge and Taylor (1997: 379) explain that the changes made to IELTS in 1995 were made in response to four factors:

- practical concerns
- administrative problems
- technological developments
- theoretical issues/recent research and development in applied linguistics and language testing.

With considerable experience of delivering tests on an industrial scale, Cambridge was aware of the complex infrastructure, which was needed for a large-scale, high-stakes assessment endeavour. Lynda Taylor in her interview for the history project (December 2014) argued that the 'long-term usefulness and sustainability of any test will inevitably depend as much on the successful design of the systems and procedures for producing, delivering and evaluating it in a sustainable way, as on the initial design of test content and format'.

The partners introduced a number of significant improvements, but these were for the most part to do with what Davies (2008: 98) described as: 'producing, administering, processing and maintaining the test' (see also Saville 2003 for additional details of Cambridge systems). These included:

- enhancement of the IELTS question paper production methodology for purposes of quality assurance, a Question Paper Production cycle meeting established qualitative and quantitative standards;
- enhancement of routine systems for capturing data on test-taker performance and background to improve test processing, validation and research;
- improved security measures relating to despatch, management and retirement of IELTS test forms;
- a new test centre administration package (ESOLComms) and training for staff at all BC and IDP test centres;
- the introduction of computerised item-banking for all reading and listening passages and their accompanying test items so as to enable accurate test equating.

Davies (2008: 99) sees the 1995 revision as being as much about remodelling the infrastructure necessary for developing and delivering a global high-stakes test like IELTS as it was about test validity matters such as content and format.

Comprehensive systems were set up to capture data about test performance and candidate background which could be reported routinely as and when required and provided a rich data set for research purposes. Leaving these administrative improvements aside, the developers did also propose one radical move, which signalled the final demise of the ESP and intertextual approaches introduced by the British Council back in 1978. 1995 saw the removal of subject-specific modules and their replacement by a single Academic module and a non-academic General

Training module (Clapham 1996); in addition the thematic link between the Reading and Writing modules was removed.

Taylor and Falvey (2007: 16–17) note that, despite the earlier reduction in 1989 from six to three subject-specific modules, administrative problems for test centres and receiving institutions had persisted and there was a growing demand for a further reduction in the number of sub-tests. Test candidates and their teachers, along with test centre staff, were sometimes unclear about the appropriate ESP module for different academic courses, and whether to match a candidate to a module based on their *previous* or their *intended* discipline area.

In her 2014 interview for this history project, Taylor observes the growing problems with making multiple versions for the increasing number of disciplines students were opting for:

> Through the late '80s and into the '90s, I suspect, and especially once you had 1992 Universities coming on-stream and also the internationalisation of higher education through the Australian Universities development programme and possibly in other parts of the world, it became almost inconceivable that you could expand the multiple options that had been mandated by the original ELTS test to accommodate all the multiple possibilities of higher education in multiple contexts around the world. So it is perhaps not so surprising that there was a regression to the middle ground to develop, by 1995, a *single* test. It's not *entirely* single because there's an academic and also a general training strand, if you like, in IELTS, you know, that would serve the purpose. That would be fit enough for purpose for most higher education needs and contexts, otherwise how would you have coped with multiple specific-purpose options in multiple contexts?

In any case, as Taylor and Weir (2012b: 20) report, around 75% of IELTS test takers were already accounted for by the Module C (Business Studies and Social Sciences) alone. Results from Cambridge's internal research into a single-module option versus a choice from a range of ESP modules (see Davies 2008: 95–96 for details of the trialling of the one-module version of the test), together with results from Caroline Clapham's doctoral research on second language reading and ESP testing (Clapham 1996), suggested that one test for all academic candidates would not discriminate for or against candidates of any particular discipline area. For such reasons, the 1995 IELTS Revision Project decided on one Academic Reading module and one Academic Writing module in place of subject-specific modules.

However, Sandy Urquhart (personal communication November 2015) points out that the argument about there being no evidence of a need for ESP modules was of course premised on the ESP texts in the existing specialist modules being representative of real-life texts in those subjects. There is limited evidence in Clapham (1996) to suggest that they were. Practicality won the day, however, and the pursuit of specificity disappeared from the field of language testing, at least as far as IELTS was concerned.

The strong thematic link between the Reading and Writing modules was removed on the grounds that such a link, though desirable in some respects, increased the potential for muddied measurement: confusing the assessment of writing ability with the assessment of reading ability (Anon. 2004). A poor performance in the Writing Module might have been occasioned by lack of comprehension in the Reading module. The same article points out that there were substantial differences in the way candidates approached the task. Some depended heavily on the reading passage, others relied mostly on their own knowledge of the topic, often with little reference to the text. For Cambridge this created issues relating to fairness at the marking stage. By removing the link, a more equitable task design was felt to be possible and this also made it easier to achieve comparability of task difficulty across versions. In her 2014 interview, Lynda Taylor emphasised the practical reasons behind the decision to remove the integrated reading into writing task:

> ...if you tie your reading paper, your reading component or sub-test very closely, topically or thematically, to your writing tasks, then in effect you make it more difficult to generate that material because your Item-Writers need to be producing not just reading texts and tasks but reading texts and tasks that are capable of generating writing tasks. It means that you are treating the whole material production process in terms of production units which are integrated and tied together. But it makes it harder to have the volume of material that you might need to generate multiple versions that are combinable, and the net result is [that] if you do adopt that approach then if there's a security compromise on either the Reading paper or the Writing paper. Invariably you have to withdraw part of the paper. So these are practical real-world considerations in large-scale language testing that cannot be ignored.

Reading and Writing have remained separate in IELTS ever since, despite the fact that, since 1995, integrated reading-into-writing tasks have seen something of a renaissance among language testers. It is revealing that TOEFL iBT (the TOEFL internet-based test) has recently incorporated integrated reading/writing tasks, as has Cambridge in its CAE and CPE exams. This 'revival' in using integrated reading/writing tasks has been the focus of recent research, in particular in relation to the new TOEFL (e.g., Cumming et al. 2004; Cumming et al. 2005). Chan (2013) and Pollitt and Taylor (2006) also make a convincing argument for this type of task, as do Grabe and Stoller (2002: 14) and Hughes (2003).

Weir (2013) argues that if one applies the parameters of socio-cognitive validity when developing writing tests of academic English, there is a good case for providing input in writing tests where the provision of stimulus texts reflects an important aspect of performance in the real-life situation (e.g. the writing of university assignments through integrating information from multiple texts). Moore et al. (2010) see the lack of an intertextual reading-into-writing task as a serious deficit in IELTS. The highest level of processing, i.e. one suitable for university students, in Weir's model of reading (Khalifa and Weir 2009), is where candidates have to integrate information from a variety of texts to develop a combined representation of the texts they have read (see also Weir et al. 2012a and 2012b for a detailed account of two IELTS research projects on undergraduate reading habits and the relationship with the IELTS reading test). Students entering university would normally be expected to cope with such tasks *ab initio*. Latham (1877: 282) similarly advocated the use of such integrated reading-into-writing tasks.

The existing face-to-face IELTS oral interview was both financially and logistically demanding, but the 1995 IELTS Revision Project was unable to determine how to make the Speaking test more efficient while retaining the emphasis on *validity*, which was always a key feature of the Cambridge approach to test validation, including for IELTS. No acceptable solution to the IELTS Speaking test problem presented itself from extant research or through internal discussion among the partners. Limited consensus emerged on the approach to take and although a number of research studies were in progress, no definitive conclusions were yet available to the IELTS partners. We learn from Taylor and Falvey (2007: 20), that the logistics were daunting as considerable time and resources would need to be allocated to retraining the cadres of examiners and to remodelling test delivery systems, test content and test format. There was a desire on the part of the three partners for the 1995 revisions to bed down and to hold fire on revisions to the Speaking test until they could be adequately resourced and sustainability ensured.

Taylor's interview for the history in December 2014 throws further light on why little changed with the Speaking examination in 1995:

> We did not revise the Speaking test. It was as much as we could do, I think, to revise the Academic Reading test, and General Training Reading, Academic Writing and Listening, and we were also looking possibly at a 'language knowledge' paper: that was part of the original 'Need Project' that I think we abandoned after some point because it didn't have any added value really. So Speaking wasn't in the frame, partly because when you revise a speaking test it is such a major endeavour if it is face-to-face speaking just because it means you have to re-train all your examiners worldwide and I think that was a bridge too far at that stage. But also because there were a number of speaking research projects which were still being completed, which we wanted to take account of and some of this was funded research by IDP. So it was felt better to delay the revision of the Speaking test and to allow the revised IELTS test to bed down in 1995, which it did.

Thus, no changes to the IELTS Speaking test format were made in 1995 but would be left until further research and development came up with viable options (see subsection *The IELTS Speaking Test Revision Project* below).

Table 5.1 presents a summary of the Academic modules introduced in IELTS 1995. In the event, all that really was lost from the original ELTS blueprint was the ESP element of the communicative approach, seen in the availability of specialist modules pre-1995. The original ELTS focus on academic skills was maintained, but this time it would be trans-disciplinary academic skills that would be tested. It was to be a 'general' specific-purpose EAP test; in the event, an evolutionary compromise rather than the revolution the ELTS test had been in comparison with EPTB (the 'Davies test'), the first English language proficiency assessment used by the British Council (see Chapter 3).

The IELTS Impact Study Project, 1995–2003

After a validity study by Samuel Messick (1989), increased attention was paid by the IELTS partners to the macro-issues of social impact and test use, the consequential aspects of test validity. Concern about the impact of large-scale tests on educational processes, and on society more generally, stimulated the British Council, IDP and Cambridge to consider how these effects might be investigated in a rigorous and systematic manner

Table 5.1 Details of the final formats of the Academic modules introduced for IELTS in 1995 (based on Taylor and Falvey 2007)

IELTS Academic Reading module	IELTS Listening module
• replacement of the three academic subject specific modules with a single Academic module • removal of the thematic link between the Reading and Writing modules • three reading passages of 750–1,000 words • total word-count = max 2,500 • 40 items across the whole test, approx. 13–14 items per reading passage • a variety of objectively scored item-types: multiple-choice, short answer, sentence completion, notes/summary/diagram/table completion, multiple-matching (e.g. headings to paragraphs) • reading passages and test items appear together in the Question Booklet • candidates record their responses on OMR Answer Sheets • length of module = 60 minutes • assessed on a nine-band scale	• four sections: Stage 1 – Social situations (Section 1 – dialogue, Section 2 – monologue); Stage 2 – Course-related situations (Section 3 – conversation; Section 4 – monologue, e.g. extract from lecture/talk) • 40 items across the whole test, approx. 10 items per section • a variety of objectively scored item-types: multiple-choice, short answer, sentence completion, notes/summary/diagram/table completion, multiple-matching (e.g. headings to paragraphs), classification • test items printed in Question Booklet • listening material recorded on cassette and played once • candidate instructions on cassette and in Question Booklet • length = approximately 30 minutes, including time to read questions and write answers in Question Booklet, additional 10 minutes to transfer answers from Question Booklet to Answer Sheet • assessed on a nine-band scale
IELTS Speaking module	**IELTS Writing module**
• face-to-face, one-on-one interview • five phases • length = 10–15 minutes • assessed on a global, nine-band scale • Speaking Assessment Guide for examiner training • continuation of certification procedures for examiners • continuation of sample monitoring for quality assurance	• replacement of the three academic subject-specific modules with a single Academic module • removal of the thematic link between the Reading and Writing modules • increase in length of output required from test takers: Academic Writing module – Task 1: 150 words instead of 100 and Task 2: 250 words instead of 150 • length of each module – extended from 45 minutes to 60 minutes • common assessment criteria across the Writing module: Task fulfilment; Coherence and Cohesion; Arguments, Ideas and Evidence; Communicative Quality; Vocabulary and Sentence Structure

and then to establish a long-term research programme exploring the concepts of test impact, including the socio-ethical consequences of test use. When the revised IELTS test went live in April 1995, following initiation by the Test Development and Validation Group in Cambridge, work began in collaboration with a team at Lancaster University to develop a suitable methodology for monitoring the effect of the test in four key areas:

- the content and nature of classroom activity
- the content and nature of teaching materials
- the views and attitudes of user groups
- the test-taking population and the use of results.

An account of IELTS impact research is published in Volume 24 (Hawkey 2006) in the Studies in Language Testing (SiLT) series. Hawkey provides a valuable overview of the methodological and theoretical issues of such research, taking into account the roles and viewpoints of a range of stakeholders: test takers, teachers, textbook writers, testers and institutions. Hawkey's extensive account of the Cambridge IELTS impact study takes us beyond a narrow focus on features of the test itself to cover the broader impacts that it has, and demonstrates that, in addition to its well-known proficiency measurement attributes, IELTS can impact positively on language learning and teaching.

The IELTS Speaking Test Revision Project, 1998–2001

Taylor and Falvey (2007: 20) record how early in 1998 the partners (BC, IDP and Cambridge) identified a number of key issues which needed addressing in the IELTS Speaking test. Past candidate score and test performance data for the operational IELTS Speaking test were re-examined, and theoretical and empirical studies on IELTS (e.g. Brown and Hill 1998, Merrylees and McDowell 1999, both examples of research done under the joint-funded British Council, IDP, Cambridge ESOL research programme) were considered, together with the available research literature on speaking assessment, speaking test design and delivery (e.g. Lazaraton 2002). The issue areas identified were:

- test format
- task design
- rating scales
- examiner/rater behaviour
- processes for test monitoring and validation.

At the IELTS Policy Group meeting in June 1998, the IELTS partners agreed to proceed with a formal revision project. Cambridge ESOL's test development and revision methodology would guide the study (see Saville 2003 for details). A number of Speaking test parameters would remain unaltered: the face-to-face, one-on-one format, audio-recording; the overall test length (maximum 15 minutes); and the multi-phase approach.

Alan Tonkyn and Juliet Wilson (2004: 191–192) describe how two types of revision were considered necessary by the revision team, viz. the rating scale and the test tasks. They discuss the key guiding principles guiding the revision: the creation of theoretically defensible criteria and tasks, the need for tasks and criteria to enable relevant distinctions between levels to be made, and finally that those features delineated for assessor attention should be salient and readily available to the single interviewer/assessor.

They conclude (2004: 201):

> ...the tasks in the IELTS speaking test have been designed with a bias for best for examiners, who now have a more user-friendly and standardised brief, and for candidates who will have more opportunity to speak at length and display the full range of their ability in English.

Taylor and Falvey (2007: 21–22) describe how the revision project focused on areas, which would improve the scoring validity of assessment in particular:

- developing a clearer specification of tasks to aid in the development of parallel forms
- introducing an examiner frame to guide examiner language and behaviour and so increase standardisation of test management
- re-developing the assessment criteria and rating scale to ensure that the descriptors matched more closely the output from the candidates in relation to the specified tasks
- re-training and re-standardising a community of around 1,500 IELTS examiners worldwide using a face-to-face approach, and introducing ongoing quality assurance procedures for this global examiner cadre.

No change was envisaged to the underlying construct/s of spoken language proficiency being measured by the IELTS Speaking test. The Speaking Test Revision Project's progress was regularly reported in the *IELTS Annual Review* between 1998 and 2002, but a more detailed account can be found in Cambridge ESOL's quarterly publication *Research Notes* (for example see Taylor 2001a and 2001b, Taylor and Jones 2001).

Taylor and Falvey (2007: 22–23) describe how the IELTS Speaking Test Revision Project was completed on schedule and the revised test became operational from 1 July 2001 in the following format:

- face-to-face, one-on-one interview (unchanged)
- three parts: Part 1 – Introduction and interview; Part 2 – Individual long turn; Part 3 – Two-way discussion (earlier five-way split had not produced 'richer' performance as intended in parts 3–4)
- length = 11–14 minutes (unchanged)
- assessed using four analytical criteria and subscales – Fluency and Coherence; Lexical Resource; Grammatical Range and Accuracy; Pronunciation
- new induction and training programme for examiners
- new certification programme for examiners
- continuation of sample monitoring for quality assurance.

In order to establish the validity of the new format for the speaking test, Brooks (2003) developed an observational checklist based on the earlier work of O'Sullivan, Weir and Saville (2002). Brooks used the modified checklist to identify the intended language functions (informational, interactional and managing interaction) of particular tasks and then built a functional profile from language elicited across these tasks in a live Speaking test. The checklist was applied to more than 70 IELTS Speaking tests in two research studies (Brooks 2003). The studies confirmed that the revised format was capable of eliciting a broad range of speech functions across the informational, interactional and interaction management range thereby offering validation evidence in support of the revised test's effectiveness.

In the interview with Taylor (December 2014) she commented on the speaking and writing revision as follows, and noted also the constructive relationships across the three IELTS partners, the British Council, IDP Australia and Cambridge ESOL:

> But by 1998 it was time to think about how we could, if necessary, revise the Speaking test and so we undertook a review between 1998 and 2001, which looked in detail at this and most of it is documented in *Research Notes* articles from the early days, the early 2000s. We looked at the content of the

test and format, we looked at the assessment criteria and the rating scales and we looked at examiner training and moderation. And so there were major changes to the IELTS Speaking test which are documented quite well in the SiLT 19 IELTS collected papers volume and the same is true for the Writing in the same volume and that involved training, re-training about 25,000 examiners worldwide I think we had at that stage in however many countries it was. Well, there had to be a good partnership between the three partners to sustain that and the new test went online in April 2001. The Writing revision was slightly more constrained in scope because we had significantly revised the writing tasks in test format in 1995 so that really focused on the assessment criteria, the rating scales and the training of examiners.

In terms of test content and format and the assessment criteria and scales I think probably Cambridge – the Cambridge team and various researchers, independent researchers – were strongly involved, and consultants as well, item writers, examiners, so, for example, in the Speaking assessment revision we had Alan Tonkin from Reading University [also heavily involved in the writing revision see below] and Paul Thompson, who was also at Reading at that stage, and they were both specialists in that area so they had a significant role. But I think much of what we decided was subject to the agreement of the partners. But the major role played by the two partners was in the development of new examiner guidelines and training packages because it was the partners [the Council and IDP] who cascaded the re-training down through their systems.

The IELTS Writing Revision Project, 2001–2005

Shaw and Falvey (2008: 9) describe how the project began with the formation of the IELTS Writing Assessment Revision Group first proposed at a meeting of the IELTS Joint Policy Group in June 2001 when approaches to assessing writing, in particular methods of analytic and holistic scoring, were discussed in depth.

The IELTS Writing Revision Project had three main objectives:

- the development of revised rating scales including a definition of assessment criteria and revised band descriptors
- the development of materials for training trainers and examiners
- the development of new certification/recertification sets and procedures for examiners.

No changes were made to the content or format of the Writing test as this had been substantially modified in 1995. The focus instead was squarely on improving the test's scoring validity and the practicality of the assessment procedures. The assessment criteria and rating scales were revised based on internal and external commissioned research, the current literature and feedback from stakeholders. The work was impressive in scale with hundreds of people involved and many thousands of hours committed to it. The writing assessment bands and descriptors went through 16 formal drafts before they became operational in 2005. Also of note was the extensive training that took place involving the training and retraining of all Writing examiners. We should perhaps expect such commitment of expenditure and human resources to constant iterative processes, large-scale validation and wholesale retraining of examiners where such a high-stakes examination is concerned. Full details of how the project progressed through its five revision phases are provided in an extensive report by Cambridge ESOL (Shaw and Falvey 2008: 1–295).

Taylor and Falvey (2007: 24–25) provide a useful summary of how the project was completed on schedule and the revised assessment criteria and band descriptors became operational from 1 January 2005. The revised approach for the Writing module is shown below:

- enhanced examiner training, certification and monitoring procedures for quality assurance
- two writing tasks: Task 1 – minimum 150 words; Task 2 – minimum 250 words
- Task 1 assessment criteria: Task Achievement; Coherence and Cohesion; Lexical Resource; Grammatical Range and Accuracy
- Task 2 assessment criteria: Task Response; Coherence and Cohesion; Lexical Resource; Grammatical Range and Accuracy
- length = 60 minutes
- assessed on a nine-band scale
- use of analytical/profile criteria and descriptors
- enhanced examiner training, certification and monitoring procedures for quality assurance.

Although extensive revisions were made to the IELTS Speaking and Writing modules in 2001 and 2005, Taylor and Weir (2012b: 23) comment that relatively few significant changes were made to the content of the Reading and Listening modules. The time is perhaps approaching for the IELTS partnership to consider whether a review of the *receptive* components is now long overdue, given the increase in our knowledge concerning comprehension over the last 25 years, especially in relation to meaning and discourse construction, and given the advances made in automated text analysis in that period.

Taking stock in 2016

Academic English language skills are essential if overseas students are to perform effectively in university/college contexts, and to engage in study with relative independence and adequate comprehension. Educational institutions need to be able to predict students' performance on academic courses accurately from test results. IELTS has made a useful contribution to the prediction of overall performance on academic courses. Weir et al. found that in general, the better the IELTS score the more likely the student is to perform well academically (Weir, Chan and Nakatsuhara 2013: 28).

Correct use of individual IELTS profile scores for target institution acceptance purposes invariably contributes to a fall in the number of students underperforming in their degree courses because of language deficiency (Banerjee 2003). Based on returns from 100 staff in 27 departments in 13 UK universities, Hyatt and Brooks (2009: 16) report that 88% of respondents felt the IELTS test to be a useful indicator of Academic English proficiency, enabling them to reject students with inadequate English language proficiency and target appropriate remedial instruction for those who fall just below an acceptable threshold.

Table 5.2 shows that the numbers taking IELTS grew rapidly from 1989 to 2015 as the test became better known and increasingly accepted by receiving institutions around the world. In 2015, more than 2.7

Table 5.2 IELTS candidature

1989	14,000
1991	25,000
1993	34,000
1995	43,000
1997	78,000
1999	106,000
2001	200,000
2003	475,000
2007	1,000,000+
2009	1,400,000
2011	1,700,000
2013	2,000000
2015	2,700,000

million IELTS tests were completed by candidates in around 140 countries. (http://www.ielts.org/media_centre.aspx). Almost three-quarters of IELTS candidates are seeking to prove their English language ability for academic purposes, but the test is also used to meet English language qualification requirements for professional and immigration purposes (Merrifield et al. 2012). The growth in test numbers also reflects the strong growth in the number of organisations turning to IELTS to meet their needs for language proficiency assessment. As of 30 August 2016, more than 9,000 education institutions, faculties, government agencies and professional organisations around the world recognise the IELTS test.

The exponential growth is most likely a result of multiple factors: increasing numbers of international students taking the test for entry to educational institutions in Australia, Canada, the United Kingdom and USA, among many other destinations (see Chapter 3); its successful marketing by the IELTS partners (see above), for example to professional bodies such as the GMC in UK and Nursing Councils in UK, Australia and the USA as well as to academic institutions; its establishment as a requirement for migration to Australia, New Zealand, Canada and the United Kingdom; the increased availability of IELTS testing centres around the world with 1,100 current locations in 140 countries; and perhaps not least for the individuals taking the test and receiving institutions using the results: a trust in IELTS scores as an accurate and secure indicator of a person's ability to communicate in English.

Of particular significance in recent years is the success of IELTS in the USA. IELTS is now accepted by over 3,000 institutions in the USA, including boarding schools, associate, undergraduate, graduate, professional and law programmes. Approximately 99% of American four-year colleges and universities that enrol more than 1,000 international students now accept IELTS as proof of English proficiency for their international applicants. Stephen Carey, Marketing Manager for IELTS at the British Council, said: 'The US is both a driver of growth in number of tests and in itself is also IELTS' fastest growing market for tests. The number of international students enrolling in US higher education is rapidly increasing. At the same time, the number of US higher education institutions accepting IELTS scores is also rapidly increasing.' (http://thepienews.com/news/us-pushes-ielts-demand-above-1-7million/)

The success of IELTS is, as we have seen, also very much a result of a close and professional relationship between the three partners: British Council, Cambridge English Language Assessment and IDP (Taylor and

Weir 2012b: 30). Cambridge currently provides most of the professional expertise, looks after test design and production and post-test analysis; and the British Council and IDP provide the global centre network, contribute local knowledge and manage the worldwide marking and examiner cadre.

In his interview (see above), Nick Charge of Cambridge reflects on the long period of time he was involved with IELTS, and stresses the value of the relationship between the three partners:

> But I think the relationship has always been key to IELTS. It has always been very important; it's vital and I think one of the things that was very good about the time.... I left IELTS in 2006 and moved on to other products in Cambridge. So I was with it for 12 years and the partner relationships in those 12 years were really interesting you know...I would call it a very *productive* relationship. Very productive and a very positive relationship and a relationship where you know when you could be very honest with each other, you could call a spade a spade. Not rude but honest – and out of that came a lot of very good things.

Anne-Marie Cooper echoed the value of the IELTS partnership in her interview:

> I'd really just like to stress the importance of the close working relationship that has been part of this partnership and I think above all respect. Respect for each other's organisations, respect for the differences and respect for the differences in expertise as well.

Anne Staniforth concurred:

> I think for me it is the strength of that relationship between the three partners and the contribution of each of those partners that has actually been critical to the success of IELTS. We've all contributed slightly different things and slightly different strengths in different places, but the combination of all of those is what has created the success of IELTS. I really don't think you could have removed any one of those partners.
>
> ...the other really important thing I think that we were able to bring was an actual international footprint for IELTS and I think no other test has been able to achieve what we have, because they don't have the infrastructure that we have, they don't have the relationships that we have to develop and deliver those tests at the local level. So for me that has been hugely important and that's all about the nature of the partnership for me. It's having three different companies that bring their individual expertise and that expertise was absolutely the right and relevant expertise to be bringing.

Mike Milanovic, who was uniquely involved with the IELTS project for 25 years, personally pushing through many of the reforms, stressed that for him the factor of greatest importance for the success of IELTS was how the test was actually managed by the partners in its manifold committees, groups and meetings (personal communication 21 August 2015):

> While the professional aspects are important, we need to remember the massive amount of back up needed to make the thing work, be that the thousands of examiners, test centres, printing and dispatch processes, IT systems etc. ...many of these areas are where the Council and IDP actually made the difference.

Section 3

Developing Language Tests for Other Purposes

Chapter 6

Language test development in the 21st century: The return to a product centred approach

In this chapter we look to more recent developments at the British Council. As will be seen in the text following, senior managers within the organisation, particularly those with interests in the area of examinations, realised the need for the British Council to reassess its position as primarily a global *service provider*. The need to consider a move back to *product development* was prompted by an increasing awareness of the changing face of the language testing market especially the desire on the part of consumers for greater localisation in tests themselves; more flexibility in terms of a variety of choice across test options; and greater accessibility in terms of test availability and mode of delivery. The British Council was encouraged in this direction by the perception that there was a lack of attention to these requirements amongst the major examination boards at that time. This was not all that surprising as their primary focus was, and continues to be, on large-scale standardised testing.

One specific catalyst for this change in direction was the perceived need for a new placement test which would be carefully tailored specifically for use in the organisation around the world and would help the British Council respond to the growing consensus on the importance of the standardisation of teaching and learning right across the Teaching Centre Network (TCN).

As we will see below, the placement test project, conceived in-house but carried out by external consultants, would also be the last time that a new test development project has been delivered for the organisation by outsiders. Out of the project emerged distinct plans for a return towards the British Council taking a major role itself in language test development and a concomitant awareness of the need for a renewal of testing and assessment expertise within the British Council itself. It would see a return to the situation pre IELTS 1989, when the British Council, from 1941 in its work with Cambridge (see Chapter 1); its work with Alan Davies on the British Council's EPTB 1963–1980 (see Chapter 3) and its development of ELTS 1975–1989 (see Chapter 4), had taken a leading role in British approaches to English language testing. A new type of test, designed to be flexible and accessible, a group of language testing professionals and a renewed willingness to support governments (such as in Vietnam and Azerbaijan) in creating independent and sustainable national language testing systems epitomised this new era.

The International Language Assessment (ILA)

By the turn of the 21st century, there were some early signs that the British Council was revisiting the strategy it had adopted in the 1990s of focusing on service provision rather than on product development. A large-scale international exploration of the potential for product development in support of e-learning was undertaken between 2002 and 2005 across 16 countries (Paul Sweeney, Manager, British Council Placement Test Project, personal communication September 2015). Of the resulting long list of products identified, it was found that the most commonly cited need was for a more accurate assessment of where learners were in their learning. As a result, discussions were held with Professor Charles Alderson at the University of Lancaster with regard to the possible adoption of DIALANG – an online diagnostic test of reading, writing, listening, grammar and vocabulary developed through a European Commission funded Socrates programme in a project led by Alderson. These discussions ultimately came to nothing, and at the same time the British Council decided to move away from e-learning since there was little evidence from the considerable British Council market research undertaken at the time of an appetite for a paid-for product. While there was no move towards the development of a specific assessment product, the exercise had brought into view again the whole question of assessment and in particular diagnostics and placement.

As the e-learning research was winding down, an interest in developing global products was emerging. A team led by Barbara Hewitt (Director Research and Consultancy for English) was tasked with scoping out potential products. This team recognised the existence of considerable expertise across the British Council and set up a series of workshops in which experienced language teaching professionals from across the organisation explored ideas for potential areas of development. It was in the context of this initiative that the need for a high-quality placement test was mooted.

The decision by the British Council to commission a new placement test was prompted by a broad dissatisfaction across the TCN with the accuracy and appropriateness of the existing tests. Centres were using either the Mini Platform test (see Chapter 4) or other, often locally produced tests. Teaching centres reported that they wanted a more up-to-date test, which could help them streamline the 'customer journey', from initial show-of-interest to paid participation in learning activities. A report commissioned by the British Council Exams team and carried out by Rita Green (2006) at four teaching centres confirmed that there was a significant issue with the lack of standardisation in placement testing across the four centres (which had been selected to reflect the typical teaching centres profile worldwide). In a later report on the situation across the TCN at that time, Sheehan (2007b: 1), indicates that

> Fewer than half of the centres in the network are using the official written placement test.... Concerns have been expressed about its accuracy and the usefulness of the information it provides about the test taker. The test has never been properly validated, therefore, it will never be known if the previously mentioned concerns were accurate. Centres were given little guidance as to how to interpret test scores. This led to centres adjusting the bands and this may account for the lack of accuracy of the test results.
>
> Some centres are using locally created solutions which undermine the value of the network.

She goes on to point out that some of the teaching centres were unhappy with the accuracy of the placement decisions, particularly at the higher and lower ends of the ability level. There was also a feeling that many learners came to their placement test with a strong idea of its content, while in other cases, local changes to the Mini Platform test had appeared to have been made on an *ad hoc* basis by staff with little or no training in assessment. The other significant issues with the placement test related to time. While some centres stuck rigidly to the time designated by the test developer, others offered their candidates as much time as they needed to complete it. This significantly undermined the meaning of the resulting scores and the placement decisions based on these scores. A common complaint made by teaching centres was that placement simply took far too long to process. The 90 minutes required for the different parts of the test broke the British Council's own regulations as it extended the 'customer journey' through the registration process beyond the 60 minutes then considered appropriate.

Following the Green (2006) report, Paul Sweeney was appointed as Project Manager to deliver the new project – in fact his participation in the role covered the creation of the preliminary product specification and tender documentation. Susan Sheehan was appointed to the role of Testing Manager and was tasked 'to identify the key features of a new placement test and ways of procuring tests' (Sheehan 2007a: 1). The different options explored included 'developing the test in-house, organising a tender and assembling a team of experts' (ibid.). Following discussion within the Exams team and based on Sheehan's recommendation, the British Council 'decided that the quickest and most efficient way to develop the test was to organise a tender' (ibid.).

The need for standardisation across the teaching centre network had, by this time, been recognised by the Exams management team at the British Council headquarters at Spring Gardens, London. In terms of the learning offer, this was driven to some considerable extent by a recently completed project to map language courses to the Common European Framework of Reference for Languages (CEFR). Prior to the CEFR mapping project, there was little or no standardisation across the programmes offered by different British Council teaching centres and the combination of the project and the new placement test was expected to help bring this about.

The systematic exploration of the British Council's needs in this area was driven by a number of senior British Council Exams team members, including Barbara Hewitt and Caroline Moore, with Susan Sheehan taking on the role of project leader. Within this role, she undertook a series of focus groups, workshops and interviews with key internal stakeholders, including teachers, Teacher Centre Managers (TCMs) and regional Business Development Managers (BDMs). As might be expected in any large organisation, the needs of these stakeholders were often competing, and so a significant element of Sheehan's work involved an attempt to balance the different needs and expectations. Finally, the drive for change, which had come from the testing and teaching arms of the organisation and was supported by senior management, led to the publication, in August 2006, of a pre-qualification questionnaire for a tender to provide to the British Council a new placement test.

The tendering process

A number of expressions of interest in developing the test were received and eventually two of the resulting tenders were found by the British Council team to be very close in quality and cost. The final decision of the British Council was, however, set aside in response to a disagreement between the two bidders concerned and the process began again.

The new pre-qualification questionnaire was almost identical to the original. It was focused on establishing the capacity of the completing organisation to deliver on a major project and did not ask specifically for any original design ideas. However, the introductory section contained an overview of the requirements identified in the preliminary work:

> The project is the development and supply of written level test or tests to assess the English language level of new customers for the network of British Council teaching centres in 58 countries (see https://www.britishcouncil.org/jobs/careers/english/global-network). The test(s) is for adult learners and teenagers. Around 100 000 tests are currently administered per year. The test(s) should reflect the Common European Framework levels and the British Council's approach to teaching and learning. The test should take around 30 minutes to complete. An oral placement interview is being developed internally and will be used along-side the written test to ensure correct placement. The test supplier will be expected to develop the test over its useful life in collaboration with British Council to ensure the continuing usefulness of the test. In addition, the test supplier will be expected to offer a support service, assistance with the roll-out and supporting documentation.
>
> Trials should be carried out in a good range of countries, covering a variety of learners from different language groups. The analysis should be completed within an agreed timeframe and a validation report. Piloting and trialling should be conducted in as many different centres as possible. The British Council is willing to offer support and co-ordination for trialling but the responsibility for it remains with the test supplier. The test provider should determine the most appropriate approach to research and validation and demonstrate its suitability.
>
> The test results will need to be linked to the CEFR based on recommendations in Council of Europe Manual.
>
> The test(s) has to be suitable for use throughout the network of teaching centres which means it has to cover a range of levels from below A1 to C2. The test will be used by the British Council for its courses held on-site, off-site or organised with partner organisations.
>
> The test will be pen-and-paper based in the first instance but it is expected to move to a computer-based test in the future and the supplier

will be expected to demonstrate a capability to produce a computer-based test.

Test scores should be reported in a form which is compatible with British Council systems such as CAMPUS. Copyright for the test will belong to the British Council. British Council undertakes not to sell the test to third parties.

(From The British Council Pre-Qualification Questionnaire 2007)

The response to the questionnaire resulted in three organisations being selected to tender for the new test; these included the same two bidders that had qualified previously along with a third institution, the Centre for Language Assessment Research (CLARe) at the University of Roehampton, London. The invitation to tender which was presented to the three qualifying organisations for completion by May 2007 reflected the original, but with the inclusion of a brief specification:

Specification of goods or services to be supplied
- a written level test(s) which is appropriate for the network of teaching centres and which places students with a suitable degree of accuracy
- test(s) will be rolled out to the network of teaching centres in September 2008 after a period of trialling and piloting which the test supplier will take responsibility for organising and ensuring sufficient numbers of participants are involved to have confidence in the results obtained
- test supplier will collaborate with British Council to provide wrap-around products to train, support and guide test administrators
- test supplier to update where necessary test content and to consider an online test if this should become appropriate (subject to a separate contract)
- a Service Level Agreement (SLA) will be reached to ensure test supplier meets agreed quality management targets
- the test should be appropriate for all levels from pre A1 to C2
- the test(s) should be a positive experience for the customer and offer an appropriate level of challenge
- British Council should have copyright for the test(s) and the test(s) will be used to place students into courses held on-site, off-site or courses conducted with partner organisations

(From The British Council Pre-Qualification Questionnaire 2007)

According to the tender document, the test supplier is expected to develop the test over its useful life in collaboration with the British Council to ensure the continuing usefulness of the test. In addition, the test supplier is expected to offer a support service, assistance with the roll-out and supporting documentation.

As a result of the tendering process, the British Council decided that the most appropriate tender had been supplied by the CLARe team, led by Professor Barry O'Sullivan, in partnership with the Centre for Research in English Language Learning and Assessment (CRELLA), under the leadership of Professor Cyril Weir at the University of Bedfordshire.

Preliminary negotiations

Since the tender supplied by CLARe had included quite a detailed test design, the discussions with the two partnering research groups and the British Council around the final design of the test were relatively short.

The responsibilities for the research and development of the ILA were to be shared by the two research groups, with CRELLA taking responsibility for the Reading paper (levels A1 to C2) and CLARe taking on responsibility for the Grammar and Vocabulary sections, together with the scaling and the CEFR linking work. CLARe would also take responsibility for the development of a series of easy-to-use pre-tests, which Teaching Centres would be able to select from in order to help identify which level ILA paper a prospective customer should attempt. The relevance of these pre-tests is made clear in the following subsection.

A project report from the period (British Council 2007a) indicates that the early thinking on the British Council side included an awareness of the importance to the TCN of developing 'a new, credible test which meets the needs of both internal and external customers'. It is also clear that the British Council had plans to broaden the impact of the new test by developing its web presence and wraparound products. By the following month the name had been agreed and preliminary work on the different elements of the test had begun (British Council 2007b). The new test would be called the International Language Assessment (ILA).

Design of the ILA

The original design called for a series of three overlapping test papers, covering Grammar, Vocabulary and Reading. The idea, as can be seen in Figure 6.1, was that prospective customers would first respond to a preliminary instrument (a 'Can Do' questionnaire) which would then offer an indication of which test form they should be offered.

264 *Assessing English on the Global Stage*

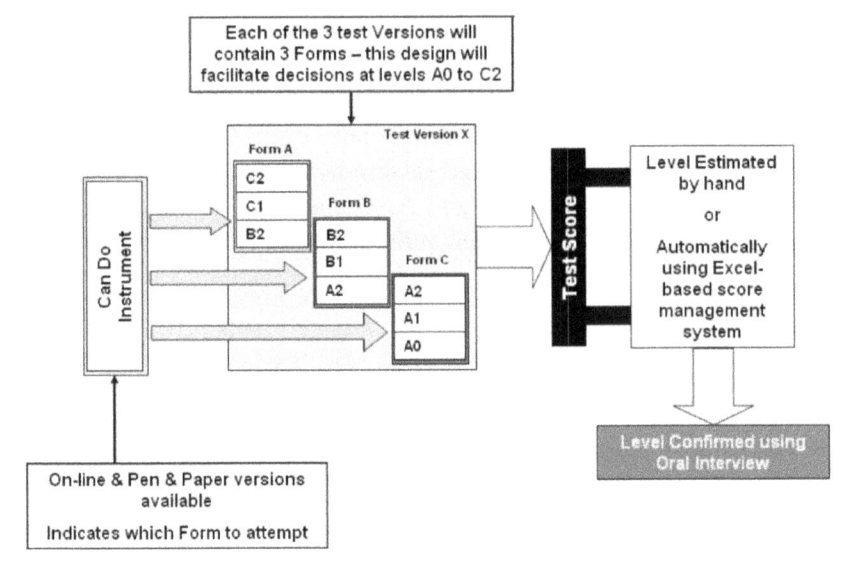

Figure 6.1 Original design suggested for the ILA

In the words of the developing teams (O'Sullivan 2007):

> We propose developing a self-assessment instrument based on the Common European Framework of Reference for Languages (CEFR) and presented in the form of a series of 'can do' statements, an approach used in the successful DIALANG project (www.dialang.org). We recognise that this type of instrument is useful in gaining a broad overview of the language level of an individual but it is unlikely to offer a very accurate picture. For this reason, we will use the instrument to help centres decide which form of the test candidates should sit. As can be seen in the above design, we propose an innovative approach which entails the development of three forms within each test version, each form will be anchored (or linked) using item response theory (IRT), as will each of the three test versions. We believe that this design is more likely to offer the British Council a solution that will accurately place learners in one of the six CEFR levels than the two forms suggested in the test specifications document, while also allowing for items designed to suit learners below the A1 level (referred to here as A0 level).

Since it was expected that, at least in its initial rollout phase, the ILA would be delivered using pen-and-paper only, the responses would be clerically marked. While there were to be some changes to this plan as the project materialised, the essential design was to remain the same.

Developing the ILA

The Project Status Reports from November and December 2007 (British Council 2007c, 2007d) indicate that the development teams had deliberately chosen to work very closely with British Council staff members on the preliminary work to give them a sense of ownership and facilitate change management. A working group within the British Council Exams team and a second group consisting of a group of internationally based senior teachers were asked to respond to a whole series of questionnaires which related to things such as test topic, item and task format as well as response formats and design parameters. In total, these groups responded to 27 questionnaires during the course of the project. The involvement of these British Council staff members was to have a lasting impact on how assessment was viewed within the organisation and appears to have, at least to some extent, reinforced the growing perceptions within the organisation of the need to build internal expertise and capacity in the area.

From early on in the process, it became clear to the teams at CLARe and CRELLA that the decision to include three sections in the test (Grammar, Vocabulary and Reading) was supported by the senior teacher group and by additional feedback from the TCN. However, it also became very clear that the proposed A0 (a pre-A1 level) was proving very difficult to operationalise. This was because the profile of such a learner was quite inconsistent across the TCN – learners at this level had very little language and what they had tended to be somewhat idiosyncratic and dependent on a very limited exposure to the language. It was therefore decided to abandon work on this level.

The development teams faced a number of challenges. In terms of the grammar paper, it was clear that an operational model of grammatical progression would need to be developed, as no such model currently existed. Similarly, for reading, no practical model of reading progression existed at the time. The theoretical model deemed most appropriate was that of Khalifa and Weir (2009), which was felt by the team at CRELLA to offer a significant step forward in operationalising a cognitive model of reading progression. With regard to the vocabulary paper, it had become widely accepted (e.g. Read 2001; Tamayo 1989) that the frequency of occurrence in daily use of vocabulary items is significantly correlated with their difficulty. Therefore, frequency was adapted by the CLARe team as underpinning the design of the vocabulary paper. However, since there had been dissenting voices from early

266 *Assessing English on the Global Stage*

Table 6.1 Development of the ILA papers

Paper	Developer	Format	Development Process
Grammar	CLARe	3 option MCQ	Theoretical Model elements ranked by Senior Teacher Advisors (STAs) Responses analysed using Multi-Faceted Rasch Final grouping and level agreed Items written and trialled Versions linked using IRT
Vocabulary	CLARe	Matching – definition, usage, synonym	Nation's word lists used Research to link frequency to CEFR level Item types identified and piloted Items written and trialled Versions linked using IRT
Reading	CRELLA	MCQ, Matching, Cloze	Khalifa and Weir's model operationalised Task types designed with feedback from STAs Test versions written and trialled Versions linked using IRT

on in the vocabulary literature (e.g. see Kirkpatrick and Cureton 1949) it was felt that additional research would be required, specifically into item and task focus.

The version of the ILA presented in the summer of 2008 for final trialling contained the three sections referred to above. These had been developed by the two groups working on the test. The process is briefly summarised in Table 6.1.

ILA final trials and roll-out

The final trials of the now complete ILA began in the summer of 2008. Over a period of three months, data from three test versions were collected from a range of British Council centres around the world. In addition to the score data, feedback was elicited from a number of teachers across the organisation. The results of the final formal trials suggested that the ILA was working well. The different versions had been linked statistically, while the semi-adaptive design had succeeded in generating test scores right across the six CEFR levels that were considered by teachers to be accurate and replicable.

One change to the original design was to offer teaching centres a range of options to use as pre-tests – i.e. to help identify which of the three papers a prospective client should be pointed towards. This was due to the fact that the Can Do questionnaires were not always appropriate, with learners unfamiliar with self-assessment often inflating their scores. A lack of understanding or experience with self-assessment is the likely cause of this issue. In all, a series of five pre-test tasks were devised and made available for use:

- Reading – self assessment of comprehension of reading passages aimed at increasingly higher CEFR levels
- C-test
- Quick grammar test
- Can Do Reading
- Can Do Writing.

Teaching centres were encouraged to select the pre-test, or tests, that would be most likely to suit the candidate profile of their teaching centre. Feedback on the tests and on the pre-tests suggested that, with minor updating, all were now ready to be finalised and rolled out.

The ILA was launched between September and November 2008 with a series of events in London, Cairo and Kuala Lumpur. These events, attended by a large group of senior teachers and teaching centre managers from the surrounding regions, were designed to introduce the tests and the delivery process while also stressing the fact that the ILA had been co-developed by the CLARe and CRELLA teams in partnership with British Council teaching centre staff. A number of those who attended these launch events became strong advocates of the new test and were to later go on to join the assessment team in various capacities.

ILA Administration Review Project

In order to gain evidence of how the ILA was perceived by teaching centre staff and ascertain the accuracy of the placement decisions, a project was agreed with CLARe to formally review the test through its first two years of administration. This work was undertaken from 2009 to 2011, with two formal reports presented to the British Council (O'Sullivan and Rugea 2011a, 2011b).

The main report (O'Sullivan and Rugea 2011a) on the operational performance of the test was based on over 15,000 candidates at 26 Teaching Centres worldwide. Analysis of the data indicated that the test was working well from a technical perspective, with few, if any problematic items, and certainly no significant issues with individual papers. In addition, analysis of task types in the vocabulary and reading papers, which were both task-based as opposed to discrete item-based, indicated that the hypothesised theoretical task difficulty was reflected in the test data. In an additional study, O'Sullivan and Rugea (2011b) report that the test was in use by almost 90% of the teaching centres sampled and that the Quick Grammar Test was the most commonly used filter. The report found that the mean number of changes per year to placements made as a result of the test results were:

- ILA Papers A   2.32%
- ILA Papers B   3.11%
- ILA Papers C   5.96%

The findings of the review project were, on the whole, positive. The ILA appeared as being used effectively in most teaching centres where it was used. There was still a considerable issue, of course, with the significant lack of competence in the area of assessment and testing across the organisation. Many of the problems reported with the ILA were actually related to a misunderstanding of how assessment worked or an unwarranted negativity towards assessment. This issue caused considerable concern for the British Council senior management team and was to be one of the key factors behind the later decision by senior management to consider re-building the technical expertise which had, until a few decades earlier, characterised the British Council.

The final word on the ILA should go to Susan Sheehan (interview 15 June 2015), the person who did so much work on behalf of the British Council to ensure that the project happened:

> Overall, the test did what we wanted it to do...and it became the springboard for this sea-change in attitude to testing and now there are huge numbers of testing projects going on which I don't think would have happened if the ILA hadn't been developed and developed in the way that it was.

At the time of writing, the ILA remains the most commonly used placement test across the British Council Teaching Centre network.

Back to the future: Professionalisation and innovation

The earliest discussions around the possibility of the British Council again developing global assessment products occurred in the year 2005/6, though the prioritisation of actual ownership of assessment instruments was not addressed until the end of the decade. Richard Sunderland (personal communication August 2016) states:

> After a period of rapid growth in the mid-to-late 2000s, which had seen the British Council's exams operations more than triple in size in many parts of the world, there was a need to look ahead, study future trends in assessment and outline how such growth could be sustained. Following a broad-ranging strategic review, which looked at a range of options for development, one direction of future growth was identified as further developing the organisation's ownership and development of assessment products, building on the experience of IELTS and others. The review prompted a strong interest to work in partnership with a UK exam board, either through co-ownership, co-development or some other form of joint venture. However, approaches to a number of UK awarding bodies about a genuinely jointly owned product or products came to nothing.

The observations made by Sunderland (at the time Regional Manager for two regions and also the Project Lead for the strategic review) are confirmed in an internal report on the project that emerged from the review by the Exams team (British Council 2009a: 22), which suggested that the organisation should consider

> Working in partnership with Cambridge ESOL or with other UK examination providers to develop new examinations, and move up the value chain, by creating a suite of English exams for the general market and certain niche sectors e.g. Oil and gas/ diagnostic tests that will be co-owned by the British Council and branded (or jointly-branded) with our name.

As Sunderland recalls, the partnership strategy was never likely to come to fruition. While in the event it proved impossible to identify an appropriate partner, there was also a recognition at the time that entering a relationship with another examination board 'relies on taking share from Cambridge ESOL which would result in significant change in the current relationship' (British Council 2009a: 22) and that this relationship was too important to the British Council to jeopardise.

Also in that report (ibid.: 18) was a suggestion that the IELTS partners 'leverage the IELTS brand by creating a suite of sub-products that deliver high volume and revenue over the period'. The test that was suggested in the report was to be 'aimed at higher education institutes and organisations who would use it to assess English proficiency at the point of entry/exit to undergraduate programmes'. It would be differentiated from the IELTS Academic and General Training tests by limiting its recognition 'to the institution (not international) and as such would not have the same number of checks and balances or security features'.

The specific suggestion (ibid.) was for a test that:

- Covers all 4 skills (speaking, listening, reading, and writing)
- Has both computer based (CB) and pen and paper versions
- Can be delivered by staff in the institution
- Is mapped to the Common European Framework (CEF)
- Is recognised by the institutions that adopt it (and any supervisory bodies in-country, e.g. Ministry of Education, University Grants Commission)
- Is Ofqual accredited (desirable).

The audience for such a test was seen as:

- Test takers: learners with an international outlook who seek globally recognised qualifications and career opportunities
- Receiving institutes: national higher education institutes who want to assess English proficiency at the point of entry/exit to graduate programmes (internal use).

This was just one of a number of project concepts that were suggested in the report. A three-skill version of a similar product also featured (with no Speaking paper) and, interestingly, a test of what we might now refer to as academic readiness – though none of these other instruments were ever pursued. These three ideas were all seen to relate to extending the IELTS brand by creating a suite of examinations. The report recognised that the success of any such initiative rested on the 'successful resolution of governance issues at partner level' (British Council 2009a: 20). While these initiatives never resulted in operational products, the thinking that lay behind them clearly reflected the growing desire within the British Council to expand their work into the area of test development.

The report is also of interest as it contains the first discussions of an entity referred to as 'BC-Tests'. The imperative to move towards British Council owned test products was driven, according to the report, by the

Language Test Development in the 21st Century 271

perception of a need to '*mitigate the risks inherent in the current distributor model*' (ibid.: 23). By this the report refers to the potential threat to the British Council business model of relying solely on the distributing of products which might either be withdrawn by their owners or fail. Clients might also decide to move to another delivering body or to a new (e.g. web-based) delivery system.

The British Council Exams Strategy report of April 2009 (British Council 2009b) was based very much on the strategic review report (British Council 2009a). It explicitly stated that the Council 'must move up the value chain into ownership to mitigate risk'. This was the final of three 'strategic headlines' highlighted in the plan overview. The plan recognised that '[British Council] core business is distribution but changes in the external environment mean this is unsustainable in the long term'. The solution offered in the plan was to move to a position which saw the 'BC as owner/operator of exams'. In the final slide of the plan, there is a hint as to how the senior management team saw the way towards achieving this goal when they identify 'Building a professional global team' as a key short-term [two-year] initiative 'to deliver the plan' (Figure 6.2). The strategy was endorsed by the Executive Board later that year (British Council 2010a: 39).

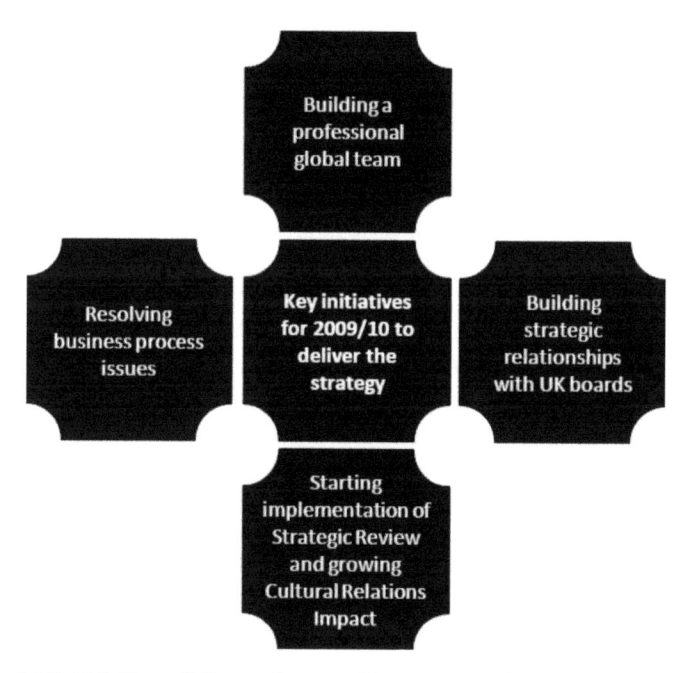

Figure 6.2 British Council Exams Strategy: Key initiatives for 2009/10

Despite the fact that this approach was clearly set out in a formal strategy report, later that same year a document entitled 'A Global Vision and Framework for English' contained no reference to BC-Tests. This suggests that there was still some confusion or even resistance to moving in that direction. However, by the time the Teaching and Exams Strategic Business Unit (SBU) presented their business plan for 2010–2012, there seems to have been a substantial shift in the position. Among the examples given of how the business plan might be operationalised from the perspective of the Exams team was 'British Council tests' (British Council 2010a: 3). The potential threat to the relationship with Cambridge ESOL in pursuing product development was recognised (ibid.: 31) and outline contingency plans were proposed. This suggests quite a strong commitment to what was being referred to in the plan as the 'British Council tests project'.

Another very interesting aspect of the plan was its reflection of the underlying commitment to building what was referred to as 'World Authority Status' across teaching and assessment. This included a recognition that

> In our expansions up the value chain from not only test deliverer to also include test owner/business development partner/consultant, we need to have a properly articulated strategy and supporting tactical plan.

One of the key elements proposed for inclusion in this strategy was the

> Identification of and approach to testing researchers/academics that could represent us in the more immediate future in terms of IELTS (and in the medium term for British Council tests?).

The diversification into test ownership which formed the central part of the global strategic plan for the Exams business, was, at this time, perceived as being most likely to succeed if the British Council entered into in partnership with a UK examination board. The decision to take this path was made following discussion between the senior management team from Exams and the then Chief Executive (Sir Martin Davidson) in February 2010. This decision was taken in response to the perceived risk of the major English language examination providers reacting negatively to the British Council's decision to pursue an exams ownership policy. However, in the business plan a two-pronged approach was suggested, again an indication of the determination of the senior management team to push ahead with the initiative. The proposal (British Council 2010a: 39) was:

- Strand 'a' – Begin to build 2 initial British Council test products which can be launched in October 2010 and Feb 2011
- Strand 'b' – Simultaneously to explore a possible joint venture with an exam body (addressed in separate paper)

The purpose of 'a' is to mitigate the risk that 'b' does not progress at all or takes an extensive period of time, allowing us in any event to bring a product to market in the autumn. It also enhances the value of the offer we bring to the table in pursuit of strand 'b'.

The business plan finished (ibid.: 55) by reiterating the fact that the main teaching and assessment initiative to be undertaken in 2010–2012 was the '[D]evelopment of British Council tests'. It also concluded that

> By the end of the 5-year period the British Council will be a large scale player in UK exams and qualifications. We will have significantly grown our business, completed our transition further into co-ownership and delivered significant cultural relations and economic impact for the UK.

It should be noted what lay behind the strategic review. By the time of the project, the grant received by the British Council from the British government had been drastically reduced from its earlier levels. The radically reduced grant meant that the organisation was forced to either reduce its critical work in areas such as Society and the Arts or increase its income to support these initiatives (see the British Council website for links to these areas of the organisation and for an overview of current projects: https://www.britishcouncil.org). The strategic review, therefore, was essentially designed to focus attention on how to ensure that the work of the organisation in these areas could continue. It continues to be the case at the time of writing, that at least some of the projects that are described on the British Council web pages 'are made possible by funds generated by our work with IELTS, teaching centres and Aptis' (John Knagg, personal communication September 2016).

Clearly, by mid-2010, the British Council had decided to re-engage in English language testing. There is a definite commitment in the language used in the documents discussed above to building a group of professional language testers within the organisation. The reference above to researchers/academics representing the British Council on the IELTS front indicates an awareness of the need for high-quality professional advice and support when dealing with partners and clients. The fact that the reference goes on to suggest that these same people might offer support to the British Council tests project 'in the medium term' is the clearest signal yet that the longer-term plan was to build such a group within the organisation – very much reflecting the situation that had been in place until the exodus of the expert testing cadre in the late 1980s and early 1990s (see Chapter 5).

As we shall see in the following subsection, the move to make this happen was already under way by the time the 2010 business plan was presented.

Realising the vision of BC-Tests

The British Council was now left to discuss this proposal internally in order to decide on the most appropriate approach to pursue. This discussion led the Exams senior management team to the conclusion that the time had come for the organisation to re-enter the language testing world, which it had vacated as a major player 20 years earlier (see Chapter 5), by bringing in to the organisation a group of individuals expert in the area of testing and assessment. This latter decision meant that the test was to be developed internally rather than being outsourced. To create the proposed test internally, a professional team would be needed and at this point such a team did not exist within the British Council. It is to this phase of the process that we now turn.

Identifying and training internal assessment talent

A report entitled *Business Area Summary: English* (British Council 2010b) suggested that

> A lack of investment in UK BC expertise leads to perception that BC acts only as a broker, not a world authority.

It is clear from the document that the writer is referring both to English/Teaching and exams. However, what the writer was clearly unaware of was the fact that movement in that direction had already started. The plan to train a cohort of British Council staff in the basics of language testing theory and practice was actually instigated in late 2009. At that time, the senior leadership team responsible for exams decided to return to the person who had led the ILA project, Professor Barry O'Sullivan then the director of the Centre for Language Assessment

Research (CLARe) at the University of Roehampton, with the view to provide such training. As a result of this approach, CLARe proposed an online continuing professional development programme entitled *Principles of English Language Testing*.

This programme introduced approximately 120 experienced British Council staff to the socio-cognitive framework (Weir 2005, O'Sullivan and Weir 2011, O'Sullivan 2011c) and was to run until 2013. The framework marked an attempt to identify a practical model of test validation by showing how the key elements of a test (i.e. the test taker, the test task and the scoring system) must all be related. It focused on both the cognitive processes of language use and on the social context of that use. O'Sullivan had worked extensively with the model since 2001, almost exclusively in applying it to test development projects such as QALSPELL (Baltic States) and EXAVER (Mexico) where it was used for the first time to form the theoretical basis for test specifications. Therefore, the programme offered by him at CLARe was very much based on his interpretation of the model. This differed slightly from the version proposed by Weir in 2005 in that it was heavily motivated by O'Sullivan's attempts to put the model into practice in test development (rather than in post-development validation). The CPD programme was designed, therefore, to offer to British Council staff a coherent and theoretically sound introduction to the area of language testing from a particularly practical perspective. It was delivered online over a period of 10 weeks. As an additional incentive to participants, the programme was validated by the University of Roehampton and as such carried with its successful completion 20 postgraduate academic credits.

By the time a second cohort had successfully passed through the CPD programme, senior staff within the British Council Exams section were beginning to see the value it was bringing to the organisation in that it was the first time that a professional development initiative had been aimed at the area of assessment. Proponents of the idea of 'BC-Tests' such as Mark Robson (Director English and Exams), Mark Walker (Head of Operations) and Martin Lowder (Deputy Director Operations) began to consider how this training might be built upon to strengthen the organisation's assessment capability. Informal discussion with Barry O'Sullivan led to the recommendation to identify those successful candidates from the CPD programme who might be interested in further training in the area of assessment, this time taking an even more overtly practical approach by looking at the area of item writing, though maintaining a clear focus on construct definition and task specification.

The first item-writer training course took place in the summer of 2010. The goal of this training was initially to build a bank of items which would be made available to teaching centres so that the burden on teachers of continually creating tests might be minimised. An additional goal was to ensure that the quality of all tests generated at local British Council schools would be improved. Work focused initially on the development of a grammar item bank, the first iteration of which was ready to be populated with items trialled in November 2010. During the first of what was to become a series of week-long courses, participants worked on item development, specification and exemplification. While some of this work was based on the design of the ILA, new item types were proposed and worked on – the objective being to create a range of exemplar items, complete with specifications based on the socio-cognitive model, for each CEFR level. This first course was followed in the summer of 2011 by a second, this time looking at the other language skills.

A number of the individuals who successfully completed the first set of item-writer training courses would later form the core of what was to become the Assessment Research Group (ARG) and would contribute hugely to the re-emergence of the British Council as a leading player in the field of assessment.

During a second training course, Mark Walker and Martin Lowder approached O'Sullivan with a view to exploring how the work done to date might contribute to a test or tests. Discussions were had regarding the nature and format of the test they had in mind. It is now clear that the British Council pair were thinking in terms of the four-skills test mentioned in the various reports discussed above. This links the decision to consider building a test to the initial BC-Tests discussions from two years earlier. Mark Walker, by now promoted to the role of Director, Exams, had been a keen proponent of BC-Tests and was one of the key drivers in this new initiative. O'Sullivan's response was that it would certainly be possible to do this as the training work to date had been based on this possibility. O'Sullivan went on to describe how he had designed the whole approach to the training as conducive to a new type of test, one which would be built on the basis of accessibility, flexibility and quality underpinned by a socio-cognitive approach to language test development.

An outline plan for the proposed test was presented to the British Council during the summer of 2010 and was to lead quite quickly into the development process for the test that was to be called Aptis. Additionally, it led to the creation of the Assessment Research Group, a critical mass of internal experts who would rebuild the British Council's reputation as a leading innovator in the area of language testing and assessment. The basic plan was to replicate much of the work undertaken for the ILA with a paper testing grammar and vocabulary and for a reading paper. A listening paper would be based on an existing set of items which had been developed for a different project. These items would be formally trialled and IRT (item response theory)-based difficulty probabilities calculated. Additional items would then be developed where needed and an item bank created for a listening paper. For the productive skills of writing and speaking, O'Sullivan offered two documents in which the full design of each paper was presented – these designs remained unchanged in the development process (O'Sullivan 2010, 2011b).

Building a test development team

A formal proposal to recruit a high-level academic leader was brought to the British Council's Executive Board by Mark Robson and was approved in early 2011. The recruitment process started within months and by the end of the year the decision had been made to offer the role of Senior Advisor, English Language Assessment to Professor Barry O'Sullivan of Roehampton University, London. The primary remit that came with the post was to lead on the development of the new test, based on the ideas brought to the role by O'Sullivan himself. In addition, O'Sullivan was asked to build, over the coming years, a team of well-qualified professional testing and assessment experts. This latter aim was to be achieved by a combination of bringing experts into the British Council and ultimately by building a team from the people who already worked for the organisation.

O'Sullivan formally joined the British Council at the beginning of February 2012 and set to work with Andrew Mackenzie (Head of Assessment Services) and Martin Lowder (by now Aptis Product and Test Development Manager) to identify potential team members from within the organisation. In addition, he set out a detailed development plan and began the process of creating a medium- and longer-term strategy that would focus on professionalising the organisation in the area of language assessment. By this time, the British Council, through the senior management team in English and Exams had committed to the creation of a viable testing and assessment research team to support this goal. The Assessment Research Group (ARG) was inaugurated with the appointment of Barry O'Sullivan, though it was not until additional appointments were made (Vivien Berry and Jamie Dunlea in 2013) that the group began to take on a more formal structure.

The aim of the ARG was formally defined in early 2016:

- To work to establish the British Council as a global leader and product innovator in the field of English language assessment.

Further to this, the purpose of the ARG was

- to push the boundaries of theory and practice in language assessment research;
- to contribute assessment expertise to British Council initiatives in large-scale education reform globally;
- to develop and support British Council assessment products.

The creation of the ARG was very clear evidence of the commitment of the British Council to the process of replicating the levels of professional expertise that had existed in the organisation prior to the late 1980s. Of course, only time will tell if this initiative results in the same level of success exhibited by the British Council's earlier history (see Chapters 1–4 for details of this).

The first major activity engaged in by O'Sullivan was to work with the recently trained internal team to develop and help launch the Aptis test system.

Making Aptis a reality

As we have seen, the outline structure and much of the design work for the new test had already been completed by O'Sullivan before he joined the British Council. O'Sullivan (2010, 2011b) had already presented the British Council with the designs for the speaking and writing papers, while the grammar, vocabulary and reading papers were all built on the design of the ILA which had been validated in the evaluation study (O'Sullivan and Rugea 2011b). This left O'Sullivan to work with his new development team to create the listening paper and further develop the other test papers.

Underlying principles

The key underlying principles that underpinned the whole development process were those of flexibility and accessibility. These principles were operationalised in the following ways:

Accessibility   The test was to be made available across a range of delivery platforms, starting with computer, and then moving to pen-and-paper and to tablet. It should also be affordable and should be clear and easy to understand and complete. The delivery platform should also conform to recognised standards for test accommodations (special measures for test takers with specific disabilities).

Flexibility   The test should comprise five elements – a grammar and vocabulary paper and individual papers focusing on the four key skills (listening, speaking, reading and writing). The grammar and vocabulary section would form a core *language knowledge* paper to be taken by all test takers, while clients would be allowed to choose which of the four skills to include in their test package, from a single-skill to a full four-skills package. In addition, the test should report on a numerical scale but with an option to also report in terms of the CEFR. The grammar and vocabulary paper would be used to inform decisions on any borderline CEFR grades. In addition, the concept of *localisation* would contribute to test flexibility by allowing for systematic alterations to elements of the test for use with specific populations or in specific contexts or domains.

Localisation

O'Sullivan (2011c) argued for the recognition in assessment systems of the need for *localisation* where the conditions were found to be appropriate. Essentially, localisation is required when a test is used to make specified claims about a specified population that relate to their specified context. So, if we are using a test to make claims that are not meant to be generalised beyond a specified context (e.g. a company or university) then it is likely that the test itself should be designed to reflect features of that context (e.g. in the use of visuals, specific language or cultural references). In practice, localisation (of which flexibility of content is

280 Assessing English on the Global Stage

a significant part) requires the development of a practical operational approach.

Table 6.2 shows how this was achieved for this project. The idea of laying out the system as a series of levels was inspired by the need to communicate what was possible when clients expressed a need for some

Table 6.2 Levels of localisation in the Aptis test system (O'Sullivan and Dunlea 2015: 8)

Level	Description	Examples
Level 0	Aptis General (or other existing variant) in a full, four-skills package.	User selects a four-skills package of any Aptis (General or variant) available for use.
Level 1	Options for localisation are limited to selection from a fixed range of pre-existing features, such as delivery mode and/or components.	User is able to select the skills to be tested and/or the mode of delivery that is appropriate. For example, the Reading package (Core component + Reading component) of Aptis General, taken as a pen-and-paper administration.
Level 2	Contextual localisation: lexical, topical modification.	Development of specifications for generating items using existing task formats but with topics, vocabulary etc. relevant for specific domains (e.g. Aptis for Teachers).
Level 3	Structural reassembly: changing the number of items, proficiency levels targeted etc., while utilising existing item-bank content.	Developing a test of reading targeted at a specific level, e.g. B1, using existing task types and items of known difficulty calibrated to the Aptis reading scale.
Level 4	Partial re-definition of target construct from existing variants. Will involve developing different task types to elicit different aspects of performance.	Developing new task types that are more relevant for a specific population of test takers, while remaining within the overall framework of the Aptis test system (e.g. Aptis for Teens).
Level 5	The construct and/or other aspects of the test system are changed to such an extent that the test will no longer be a variant within the system.	Developing a matriculation test for uses within a formal secondary educational context; developing a certification test available to individuals rather than organisations; etc.

'local' aspect to the test they wished to use. As such it proved to be an effective tool for local British Council staff to use when discussing the possibilities around localisation to prospective clients and allowed for a consistency of approach between the regional/local and central British Council teams. The table outlines a series of possible changes that are available to the client. Details of how these changes might be operationalised in terms of time, effort and resources will most likely be different for contexts of use, but the general approach remains the same.

Changes to the Aptis test at levels 2–4 in Table 6.2 result in the generation of new variants of Aptis tests within the existing system. Examples of how such a process has worked include Aptis for Teachers (which was developed at a level 2 degree of localisation), and Aptis for Teens (which involved developing new tasks appropriate for learners younger than the typical test users of Aptis General, and thus required a level 4 localisation). Since level 5 is dependent on large-scale changes to the test, it would not lead to a variant, instead a whole new test would be generated.

In many ways, localisation is one of the key innovations included in the Aptis system. Traditionally, major tests have been designed and developed either with no specific population in mind or with a broad and necessarily diffuse population. This was due to the fact that it would be next to impossible to deal with population or test-taker appropriateness in a large-scale international test. Aptis, on the other hand, was designed to be used in specific contexts, and was referred to metaphorically as an ID card, valuable within the context, but not appropriate for international travel which required a test which resembled an international passport, such as IELTS or TOEFL. This meant that the likelihood of clients requesting some level of localisation was recognised from the beginning and as such, had to be hardwired into the system. As Table 6.2 suggests, the range of potential choices open to a client can prove difficult for sales staff to cope with and can also place additional pressure on the development team.

Sales staff have a steep learning curve when coming to work on Aptis for the first time as they rarely bring with them a knowledge of testing. This was recognised early in the process as being a likely source of concern and was one of the drivers behind the Language Assessment Literacy project (see the relevant subsection later in this chapter). Development staff are likely to be taxed by the extra work in first undertaking a small-scale research study, in cooperation with the client, to identify points of concern. This usually involves a critical review of the test with a panel of local experts and/or an administration and follow-up with test takers nominated by the client. This study typically leads to decisions being made regarding the test content, scoring and reporting systems (all of which may be affected in a localisation of the test). Changes to existing tasks or the development of new tasks will mean changes to the specifications, to item-writer guidelines and to the quality assurance system. This will then lead to additional trialling, updating and tagging within the item bank and finally to test production itself.

The development approach

As outlined in the *Aptis Test Development Approach* (O'Sullivan 2015a) the Aptis test system was designed to meet the needs of a modern, online test which would be sold on a business-to-business (B2B) basis. This model, where the responsibility for test scheduling and delivery was to be in the hands of the buying client, was new to the industry. It was also planned that the client would work with the British Council 'to generate evidence in support of the use of the system for the purpose intended by that user' (ibid.: 5).

The development process was based on two clearly articulated models, one of test development and the other of test validation. These can be seen in Figures 6.3 and 6.4. The original development model is based on the classic approach to test development suggested by scholars such as Bachman (1990) and Taylor (2000). Interestingly, the fact that the test to be developed was designed from the beginning to be a commercial product meant that the design model (Figure 6.3) was quite inadequate, as it failed to recognise that the test itself was just one cog in the whole

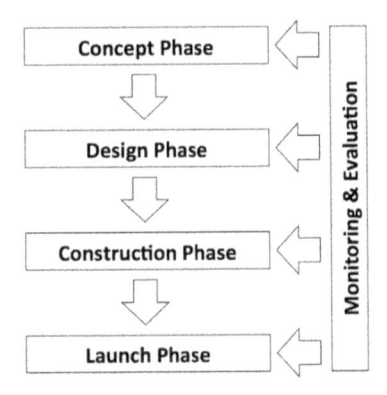

Figure 6.3 Initial theoretical Aptis test development model

Language Test Development in the 21st Century 283

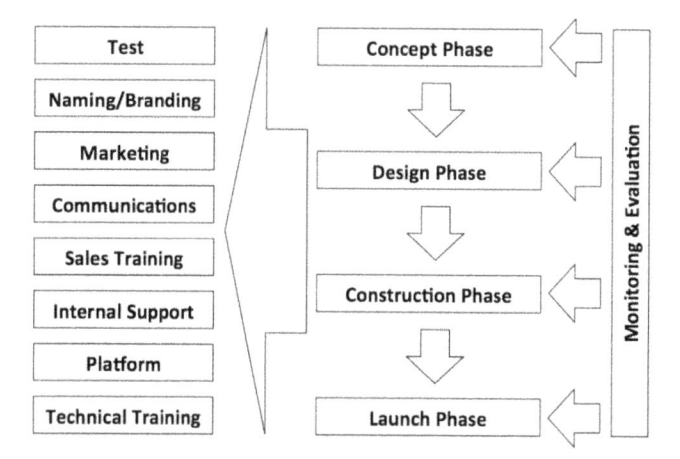

Figure 6.4 Actual Aptis test development model

development apparatus. The reality of having to deal with a large project such as this meant that a number of additional concerns had to be taken into consideration. These are indicated in Figure 6.4 and discussed below.

Test development theories and academic publications have, to date, largely failed to take into consideration the need for a broad understanding of the business that has grown up around language testing. When we develop a test in a commercial setting, there are a host of elements that are not normally considered relevant by academic theoreticians, but which are actually critical to the whole development cycle and equally critical to our understanding of the test development context:

Test Naming/ Branding   The naming and branding around the test will have a significant impact on its business success. Brands such as IELTS and TOEFL are globally known, but even these took some time to build. When launching a new product, it is important that it is given a clear identity, so in this project, we worked with the British Council's internal Brand team and also with an external agency (True North). The process itself was valuable in that it forced the development team to really think from a very early stage and in significant detail about the intended clients and the uses to which the test would be put. It has been our experience over the years that this is an aspect of the development process that is either left to a group outside of the development team or, in many cases, is not systematically undertaken at all. This has led to the use of unimaginative and uninspiring names which contribute little to the product or to the developing team. This latter point is important in this context as the objective was to create a new test and at the same time build a high-quality team. Giving the test a clear and unambiguous identity also meant giving the same to the new team.

Marketing The name given to the new test in 2012 was 'Aptis'. From the beginning of the project, the team included a marketing and communications unit. This was done in part to respond to any perception inside and outside of the organisation that we were not a test developer, and would not be able to produce a product of the same quality as some of the organisations we worked with. The focus of the marketing strategy was to identify opportunities to inform internal and external stakeholders of the growing expertise within the development team. The unit then worked directly with the development team to build an accurate and appropriate set of messages aimed at these stakeholders.

Communications The marketing and communications unit was also responsible for developing the communications strategy to support the test, pre- and post-launch. This strategy included regular internal updates and events, designed to build interest and confidence in the new test and in the development team. It also included a systematic analysis of the dissemination work that was to take place following the launch of the test – e.g. in academic conferences; local and regional launch events; internal webinars; etc.

It was this interaction between the teams that led O'Sullivan to begin to rethink his concept of validation and to revisit the socio-cognitive model. It became clear that developers do not work in a vacuum. In fact, they are expected to deal with and react to a number of overlapping contexts – the context of test development and the context of test use. Since contexts are primarily defined by people, it is critical that their specific concerns are taken into account when designing and delivering any messaging around a new test. In O'Sullivan's more recent work on validity (2014, 2016a, 2016b) he conceptualises test use in contexts defined by a range of key stakeholders, suggesting that the focus and messaging of validation arguments should be tailored to them, and not simply an academic or legal audience.

Sales Training Since Aptis was to be a different type of test to those traditionally delivered by the British Council, a new approach to selling the product was needed. This entailed bringing the development team into the whole sales training area, ensuring that the people designing the new system were fully aware of the test and of the underlying concepts of flexibility and accessibility. This work was to prompt a major project post-operationalisation. It became very clear during the training process that a whole range of individuals within the organisation were going to have to get up-to-speed on a range of assessment matters. The project aimed to identify the language assessment literacy and competency needs of British Council staff and to create products and materials to help them better understand the new expectations of their roles. This project is described later in the chapter.

Internal Support For Aptis to succeed, it was critical that the British Council as an organisation gathered behind it and the development team. At a senior level, this was not really a problem, with consistent and vocal support coming from the then CEO (Sir Martin Davidson) and the Executive Board in general. Others were less willing to add their support.

There was some internal resistance to the new test largely based around a concern that the organisation was entering 'new' territory. The fact that such a major test development project might encounter this type of reaction from teaching and exams staff was not envisaged by the development team, and without the work of marketing and communications staff the project itself might well have faltered – e.g. the development team relied to a large extent on the TCN to ensure the appropriateness of task types and later when piloting tasks and items.

Platform Since the proposed test was to be initially delivered by computer (with a pen-and-paper option coming soon after launch), a process was launched in early spring 2012 to find an appropriate delivery platform. This work was led by Martin Lowder and coordinated by the newly appointed project manager, Richard Munday. After a formal search procedure, the British firm BTL were chosen from a small field. The platform operated by BTL, called Surpass, was considered to be the most appropriate as it had almost all of the features identified by the British Council team – item bank, authoring system, delivery system, automatic/machine scoring of non-productive papers (core paper, reading and listening) and human scoring of the productive skills papers (writing and speaking). In addition, BTL were open to developing their system to meet the more exacting requirements of a modern language test. This was important as there were a number of quite significant issues that had to be dealt with by the Aptis development team. One such issue, for example, was the fact that the item bank was not actually structured around an IRT model. While this issue was quickly dealt with, others, such as access to test data at the item level took more time. The development team were also determined that the platform should not drive test content, as is often (though not always) the

Technical Training case with computer delivered tests. This meant working with BTL to ensure that the task types could be built within the system and then creating templates to allow for ease of task upload. Perhaps unsurprisingly, the complex nature of the test delivery and scoring system meant that the British Council needed to build a technical team capable of supporting local sales and delivery groups. This team was responsible for all aspects of the technical side of the project. They worked with the Aptis development team and with BTL to ensure that the product envisaged was finally delivered. They also managed the delivery of tests to clients until regional and local expertise was established – trained by the technical team.

As can be seen from the above overview of how the different groups within the Aptis team worked to help deliver the test on schedule, the organisation was forced to build from scratch a fully functioning assessment arm. That this was achieved in little more than half a year was remarkable.

The team that managed the Aptis development project was:

- Mark Walker: Director, Exams
- Andrew Mackenzie: Head of Assessment Services
- Barry O'Sullivan: Senior Advisor for Language Testing and Assessment
- Hannah Connell: Marketing and Communications
- Richard Munday: Project Management
- Martin Lowder: Aptis Product and Test Development Manager.

Test delivery mode

When the test was launched, the primary mode of delivery was computer. The system worked by the client downloading an application to each machine to be used for a test delivery. On opening the application, the test user is prompted to input a pre-ascribed key before accessing the test. Once open, the application locks down the test taker's computer and does not allow any access outside of the test. The test was designed to run offline, that is independent of an internet connection. A number of tests can be uploaded to a computer and the test taken without interruption. This has meant, for example, that the test could be used even in remote areas where there was no electricity, let alone internet connectivity, for example in a project with the Ministry of Education in Rwanda (Simpson 2013).

Within months of launch, a number of papers were made available in a pen-and-paper mode. These were the core, reading, listening and writing papers. Take-up on this delivery mode was never strong and as of 2016, just over 96% of all tests delivered used either a computer (desktop or laptop) or tablet (iPad or Windows equivalent). The introduction of new scanning technology is expected to see an increase in pen-and-paper delivery from 2017.

In addition to allowing for flexibility in test delivery mode, Aptis was also designed to offer clients flexibility in reporting: on a 0–50 numerical scale and currently as a CEFR level (see O'Sullivan 2015a) – with plans to extend this offer to local frameworks such as the Japanese localised CEFR-J (a version of the CEFR localised to the Japanese context by including Japan specific descriptors) and the CSE (the China Standards of English – a CEFR-like framework designed, researched and constructed from scratch entirely in China by a large team of Chinese researchers and due to be launched officially in late 2017).

Test cost

From its inception, British Council senior management agreed that the Aptis test was to be offered at an affordable cost. The cost of delivering the test online meant that the overall margin per test was to be quite low, but since the idea was to offer a high-quality service that would be accessible to as broad an audience as possible no other option was possible. Discounts were made available to allow clients some considerable benefit from buying in bulk – thus meeting the flexibility criterion.

Focus on the Aptis test system

In this section, we will focus on the Aptis test, highlighting its intended purpose, and taking a closer look at the different papers.

Purpose

O'Sullivan and Dunlea (2015: 9) see Aptis General as 'a test of general English proficiency designed for adult learners of English as a Foreign/Second Language (EFL/ESL)'. They then go on to identify a number of purposes for which Aptis might be used in an appropriate way. These are:

- Identifying employees with the language proficiency levels necessary for different roles
- Identifying language training needs for employees required to fulfil specific roles
- Streaming according to proficiency level within language learning and training programmes
- Assessing readiness for taking high-stakes certificated exams or to participate in training programmes
- Identifying strengths and weaknesses to inform teaching and support for learners
- Evaluating progress within language training programmes.

Aptis was designed to allow for generalisations to be made to a broad range of language use situations in three domains: educational, occupational and public. Some specific use contexts include language learners in upper secondary school (i.e. over 15 years of age) and adults either in work-related or study domains.

O'Sullivan and Dunlea (2015: 10) identify the following target language use domains as exemplifying Aptis usage:

… using English:
- to communicate with customers, colleagues and clients
- to participate in English-medium training and education programmes
- in the public domain while travelling for work or study
- to access information and participate in social media and other forms of information exchange online.

Typical test takers

Aptis General is designed to provide assessment options for adult and young adult (15+) ESL/EFL learners spanning proficiency ranges from A1 to C in terms of the Common European Framework of Reference for

Languages (CEFR). These learners may be engaged in education, training, employment or other activities.

The description of test-taker variables is necessarily generic for Aptis General, as it is intended to provide cost-effective, flexible testing options which can be made available as ready-to-use products (levels 0 and 1 of the localisation framework in Table 6.2) in a broad range of contexts. Prospective clients are expected to engage with the Aptis team to evaluate whether Aptis General is the most appropriate variant for the intended test-taker population. Where issues emerge they are dealt with either by the British Council advising the prospective client against the use of Aptis or by referring to the localisation framework in order to identify the level of localisation required. This approach has led to systematic changes to test papers to suit specific populations on several occasions, see below.

Operationalising the socio-cognitive model

As mentioned above, the test itself is comprised of five papers, the core (language knowledge – grammar and vocabulary) and four skills papers (listening, speaking, reading and writing).

Key features of the test include:

- Coherent structure
- Clear language focus
- Clear cognitive focus
- Clear social focus (particularly with regards to the productive skills)
- Task-related scoring system, also linked to underlying language model
- Scaled scores and CEFR levels are reported, with ongoing projects to establish links to both the CEFR-J and the CSE.

These features are realised through the use of the socio-cognitive model of test development and validation. Figure 6.5 shows a simplified view of the model. This version of the socio-cognitive model is built around the proposed update to the model suggested by O'Sullivan (2011a) and supported by O'Sullivan and Weir (2011) – this is the three-part model at the left of the figure. The belief is that the three parts (the test taker, the test system and the scoring system) contribute to the performance and its interpretation. As was previously mentioned, the stakeholders who formed the context (here seen as relating to the context of development and the context of use) form an integral part of the development process and are also taken into consideration when putting together any messaging around the tests. While some of these stakeholders will expect to see standard (or traditional) validation evidence, it was clear that others might either need different types of reassurance or simply different types of message – teachers, for example, are very unlikely to read a highly technical manual in which validation evidence is presented. The model is further explained in O'Sullivan's recent work (2015a, 2016a, 2016b), while the essential core of the approach is extensively explored in Weir (2005) and in the 'constructs' volumes in the CUP SiLT series (Shaw and Weir 2007, Khalifa and Weir 2009, Taylor 2011, Geranpayeh and Taylor 2013).

While O'Sullivan and Weir (2011) describe a number of test development and validation projects for which the socio-cognitive model formed the theoretical basis, the plan to use the approach to underpin Aptis marked its first use for a major international test development project.

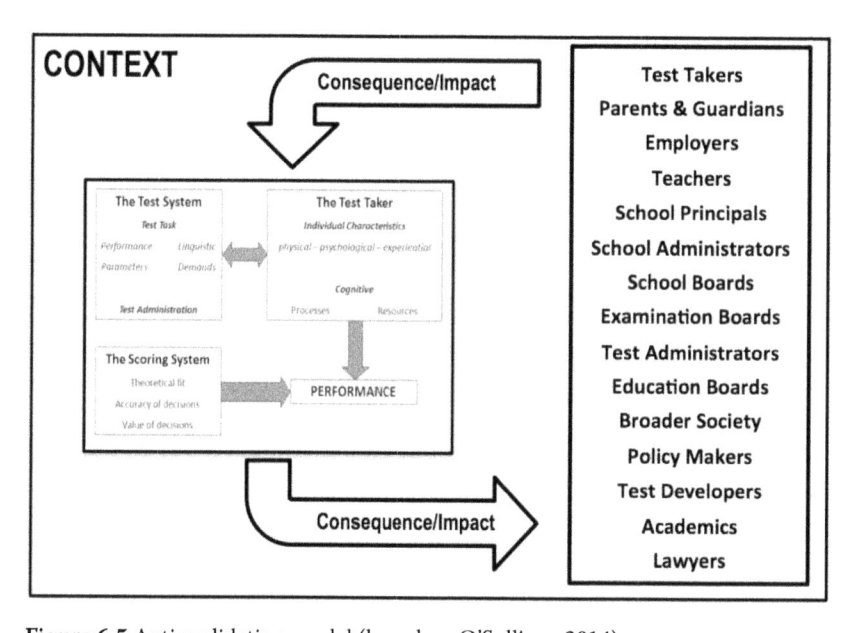

Figure 6.5 Aptis validation model (based on O'Sullivan 2014)

As O'Sullivan (2015a: 9) notes:

> the real strength of this model of validation is that it comprehensively defines each of its elements with sufficient detail as to make the model operational

Detailed descriptions of these elements can be found in O'Sullivan (2015a: 10–12). In practice, the socio-cognitive model is reflected in Aptis in the design of the underlying test and scoring systems. Detailed specifications, again based on the socio-cognitive approach, are then used to operationalise these elements; see Figures 6.6 and 6.7 for examples of the specifications for one task from each of the reading and writing papers. The specifications are supported by exemplar tasks and items (as reflected in the sample tests available on the Aptis website (www.britishcouncil.org/exams/aptis).

The specifications demonstrate how tasks are designed to reflect carefully considered models of language progression that incorporate cognitive processing elements explicitly into task design, for example, through the use of:

- the Khalifa and Weir (2009) model for reading
- the model suggested by Field (2015a) for listening
- the language functions derived from the British Council/EQUALS Core Inventory (North et al. 2010), themselves based on the lists for speaking developed by O'Sullivan et al. (2002) to form the basis of productive skill tasks.

At the same time, detailed attention is paid within the specifications to the contextual parameters of tasks across all components, with the interaction between contextual and cognitive parameters manipulated in explicit ways to derive tasks that are built to reflect specific CEFR levels. In the following subsections, we will take a further look at how the socio-cognitive model was used to specify the tasks contained in the test.

This was the first major test for which the developers used the socio-cognitive model. The great strength of the model is that it is not simply theoretical. It has a strong theoretical basis, building as it does on the work of Messick – in fact it represents the first fully practical model to successfully operationalise Messick's ideas (Dunlea 2016). However, it is the practicality of the model that is its most valuable asset. This is clearly seen in the way it can be used to inform the very basis of any test, the specifications.

Test structure

The Aptis test system was designed to allow for the client to decide which language skills to test. The test was divided into two parts, a 'core' paper testing knowledge of the language system (grammar and vocabulary) and a series of four papers, each aimed at a different 'use' or skill. All test takers are asked to sit the core paper, consisting of 50 grammar and vocabulary items. The results of this test are reported on a numerical scale (0–50) and are used to automate the decisions on borderline test takers. If a test taker achieves a score within one SEM of a CEFR border, then their performance on the core paper is referred to. Achieving a score above a set level means an automatic upgrade to the higher level, achieving a lower score means only that the original decision is confirmed.

Clients are free to decide which package to use in their particular situation, i.e. levels 0 and 1 of the localisation framework (Table 6.2). However, it has emerged over the past few years that the four-skills package is the most commonly used (Dunlea et al. 2016: 13).

Focus on the Reading paper

One criticism of many major standardised language tests is that they appear to be more concerned with measurement than with language. In fact, many tests fail to disclose the model or models of language on which they are based, leading to the suspicion that there is no clearly stated model underpinning the test. Items are written, trialled, analysed and placed on to a numerical scale. They are then included in a test based only on the numerical value. Of course, other tests have been criticised over the years (see for example Bachman et al. 1989) for having an insufficiently articulated measurement model – focusing too much on content as an indicator of validity.

From its conception, Aptis has focused on both language and measurement. The aim of the test developers was to create a test based on clearly articulated models of language that also met the highest standards of measurement consistency and accuracy. One example of how this works in practice is the reading paper.

The language focus for the reading paper is provided by the adaptation of the Khalifa and Weir (2009) model of reading progression. This model, which also served as the basis for the ILA, has been operationalised as shown in Figure 6.6. The test taker (and learner) progresses from short

294 *Assessing English on the Global Stage*

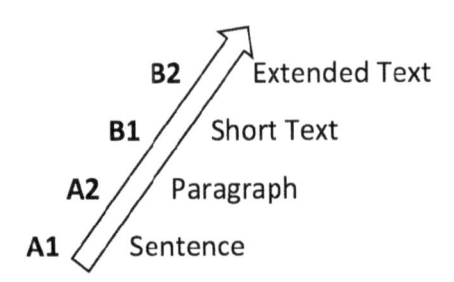

```
        B2 ╱╱ Extended Text
     B1 ╱╱ Short Text
   A2 ╱╱ Paragraph
  A1 ╱╱ Sentence
```

Figure 6.6 Operationalisation of the Khalifa and Weir (2009) Reading model

phrase- or sentence-level texts at A1, through to increasingly longer and more complex texts (in terms of lexis, syntax and structure) by the time they reach C1. The cognitive focus at each level is increasingly more complex as it changes from lower-order sentence-level comprehension to higher-order meaning construction at the text level. Tasks are developed to target a specific CEFR level. They are then trialled and the data analysed. The expectation at this point is that the newly developed task will 'fit' both with the language model (through the specifications) and the mathematical model (through fitting within a pre-determined range on the underlying mathematical scale).

Figure 6.7 shows an abridged version of the specification for Reading Task 4, from O'Sullivan and Dunlea (2015: 47). This can be read in the following way:

Column 1 Task parameters
Column 2 Details (operationalisation of parameters)
Section 1 Features of the task (general task description, detailed information on how each performance parameter is operationalised and details of how the cognitive model is operationalised)
Section 2 Features of the input text (in this case reading, but might describe a listening input text)
Section 3 Features of the response (detailed description of the expected test-taker response – critical to any scoring model).

It is clear from the specification pro-forma that there is a systematic attempt made in this approach to address all aspects of the task as it is operationalised and interpreted in Aptis. The performance parameters are the traditional focus of a specification, together with any input texts or images and, on occasion, a prediction of the expected output. With the socio-cognitive approach, this is extended to asking the developer to consider exactly what aspects of not only these but also of the cognitive processes are likely to be engaged in by successful test takers.

Test	Aptis General		Component	Reading	Task	Matching headings to text	
Features of the Task							
Skill focus	Expeditious global reading of a longer text, integrating propositions across a longer text into a discourse-level representation.						
Task level (CEFR)	A1	A2	B1	B2	C1	C2	
Task description	Matching headings to paragraphs within a longer text. Candidates read through a longer text consisting of 7 paragraphs, identifying the best heading for each paragraph from a bank of 8 options.						
Instructions to candidates	Read the passage quickly. Choose the best heading for each numbered paragraph (1-7) from the dropdown box. There is one more heading than you need.						
Response format	Matching headings to paragraphs in a longer text. Select 7 headings from 8 options.						
Items per task	7 (each heading is one item)						
Time given for part	30 minutes for the entire reading test (all tasks). Individual tasks are not timed.						
Cognitive processing Goal setting	Expeditious reading: local (scan/search for specifics)			Careful reading: local (understanding sentence)			
	Expeditious reading: global (skim for gist/search for key ideas/detail)			Careful reading: global (comprehend main idea(s)/overall text(s))			
Cognitive processing Levels of reading	Word recognition						
	Lexical access						
	Syntactic parsing						
	Establishing propositional meaning (cl./sent. level)						
	Inferencing						
	Building a mental model						
	Creating a text level representation (disc. structure)						
	Creating an intertextual representation (multi-text)						
Features of the Input Text							
Word count	700–750 words			Number of sentences		Not specified		
Avg sentence length	18–20 (This is an average figure. Individual sentences will span a range above and below the average.)						
Domain	Public		Occupational		Educational		Personal
Discourse mode	Descriptive		Narrative		Expository	Argumentative		Instructive
Content knowledge	General						Specific
Cultural specificity	Neutral						Specific
Nature of information	Only concrete			Mostly concrete		Fairly abstract		Mainly abstract
Presentation	Verbal			Non-verbal (i.e. graphs)				Both
Lexical level	K1	K2	K3	K4	K5	K6	K7	K8	K9	K10	(merged)
Lexical level	The cumulative coverage should reach 95% at the K5 level. No more than 5% of words should be beyond the K5 level. (See Guidelines on Adhering to Lexical Level for more information).						
Grammatical level	A1-B2 Grammatical exponents (See Guidelines on Adhering to Grammatical Level)						
Readability	Flesch Kincaid Grade Level of 9–12						
Topic	From topic list for B2.						
Text genre	Magazines, newspapers, instructional materials (such as extracts from undergraduate textbooks describing important events, the ideas, or movements). It should be possible to answer the questions: Where would a reader be likely to see a text like this outside the test? Is the genre relevant to TLU tasks important for Aptis General test-takers at B2 level?						
Intended writer/reader relationship	The relationship is not specified. The texts will typically be written for a general audience, not a specific reader.						
Features of the Response							
Targets	Length	Up to 10 words		Lexical	K1-K5	Grammatical	A1-B2
Distractors	Length	Up to 10 words		Lexical	K1-K5	Grammatical	B1-B2
Key information	Within sentence			Across sentences		Across paragraphs	
Presentation	Written			Aural		Illustrations/graphs	

Figure 6.7 Reading Task 4 specification (abridged, from O'Sullivan and Dunlea 2015: 47)

Table 6.3 Brief overview of key parameters (Reading)

Parameter	Gloss	Operationalised in Aptis
Response format	The type of response expected of the test taker – multiple-choice, matching, open-ended etc.	Task 1 – Multiple-choice gap fill Task 2 – Sentence re-ordering Task 3 – Banked gap fill Task 4 – Matching headings to paragraphs
Cognitive processing: Goal setting	Identifying the expected type of reading	Task 1 – Careful localised (sentence-level) reading Tasks 2, 3 and 4 – Careful reading of the whole text (main focus) Task 4 – Expeditious/speeded whole text reading (not explicitly tested but required if the test taker is to be successful)
Cognitive processing: Levels of reading	Word recognition; Lexical access; Syntactic parsing; Establishing propositional meaning As this task is aimed at B2, these processes are expected to have become fully internalised and are not explicitly focused on	
	Inferencing	The test taker is expected to infer: meaning within the text to allow them to make connections to the headings – i.e. the connections are not always explicit.
	Building a mental model Creating a text-level representation	In order to manipulate the different elements of the text and the heading, the test taker is expected to build a model of the entire text in their head. In addition, understanding and interpreting the discourse structure of the text is required if test takers are to successfully match the appropriate texts and headings.
	Creating an intertextual representation (multi-text)	This is seen as a higher-level skill – tasks targeting this are included in the Aptis Advanced, but not in Aptis General.
Domain and discourse mode	In the same way that it is important to vary the item and task types in a reading test, we also vary the language domain and discourse mode.	*Domain* Task 1 – Personal Tasks 2, 3 and 4 – Educational Task 2 – Occupational Tasks 2, 3 and 4 – Public *Discourse mode* Tasks 1 and 2 – Descriptive Tasks 1 and 2 – Narrative or Instructive Tasks 3 and 4 – Expository Task 4 – Argumentative

Content knowledge and cultural specificity	With a test such as Aptis General we would expect that the contents would be quite general and neutral in nature (localised tests may differ)	*Content knowledge* All tasks are very much on the General end of the spectrum (General to Specific)	*Cultural specificity* All tasks are very much on the Neutral end of the spectrum (Neutral to Specific)
Nature of information	We would expect that the information contained in a text would be quite concrete in nature at the lower levels and more abstract as the level increases.	This is reflected in the tasks: Task 1 – Only Concrete Task 2 – Only Concrete Task 3 – Mostly Concrete Task 4 – Fairly Abstract	
Key information	This refers to the work required by the test taker in locating information required to respond to specific items	As expected within the Khalifa and Weir model, the different tasks expect that the range will change according to the level of the task: Task 1 – Within Sentence Tasks 2 and 3 – Across Sentences Task 4 – Across Paragraphs	

Table 6.3 takes a closer look at some of the key parameters included in the specification as it is important to see the effect on the description of the contents of a test of basing the specification on the socio-cognitive model. It becomes immediately clear that the developer (and later the writer – since the specifications form the basis of an item-writer guide) is forced to consider not only the performance and response parameters, some of which are included here, but also the cognitive parameters that impact on task difficulty.

With the Listening paper, the model used was that proposed by Weir (1993) and Buck (2001) in which it is posited that listening items increase in complexity as the information to be comprehended moves from literal to inference. As with the other papers, the Listening paper continues to be scrutinised and a new model, conceived by Field (2015a) and operationalised by the ARG team (see Field and Tucker 2017), will mean some slight changes to the test when it comes to its revision in 2017. These changes are mainly at the higher levels, where ARG research suggests that few, if any, mainstream tests manage to effectively reach the C level with tasks that can be demonstrated to be appropriate from both the language and the psychometric perspectives.

The two, essentially cognition-focused, language models (reading and listening) ensure that there is a strong emphasis on understanding and operationalising appropriate cognitive processing across the receptive skills papers. It can be argued that the receptive papers are actually employing what we might call a *weaker* socio-cognitive approach in that they are more reliant on the cognitive than the social parameters of task description and design. It may well be that this is inevitably going to be the case with such test papers, as a more explicitly social element is more difficult to operationalise. Of course, there is still a social element to each paper, with an explicit concern in the Technical Manual (O'Sullivan and Dunlea 2015) with the contexts of language use and the concern with appropriateness of content in both the reading and the listening papers in terms of an explicit specification of contextual parameters at the different levels tested.

Focus on the Writing paper

In the productive skills papers, the abridged specification (Figure 6.8) again refers to the task and linguistic parameters that describe the test task in the socio-cognitive model. As can be seen in the 'Skill focus' section of the figure, this particular task is integrated, with the test taker expected to respond to a written description of a problem or variation on the topic of the paper (the detailed contextual parameters identified as appropriate for the input text are not included in the figure). Understanding the impact of decisions made regarding particular parameters to the likely cognitive demands of the subsequent writing task is critical to developing appropriate and consistent tasks. This is even more critical in productive skills tasks as they are rarely subjected to the same level of piloting as we would expect for receptive tasks.

Some of the key parameters included here relate to specific descriptions of the sort of performance parameters typically seen in test specification (e.g. task level, response format, length of input and expected output etc.). The specification is different in that it also focuses on things like audience (reader) and the typical functions that will be elicited from successful test takers.

In terms of the audience/reader, the test taker is confronted with a problem associated with the activity around which the writing paper is focused (e.g. specific club membership). They are then asked to write two emails, one to a friend telling that person about the situation, and then to a person in charge or responsible. The focus here is not just on content but on the different levels of formality called for. So, the critical focus of the task depends on the test taker fully understanding that two emails are to be written, and that this is operationalised by having two distinct readers. Therefore, the specification must be unequivocal in describing these readers.

Test	Aptis General	Component	Writing	Task	Task 4
Features of the Task					
Skill focus	Integrated writing task requiring longer paragraph level writing in response to two emails. Use of both formal/informal registers required.				
Task level (CEFR)	A1	A2	B1	B2	C1	C2
Task description	The candidate writes two emails in response to the task prompt which contains a short letter/notice. The first email response is an informal email to a friend regarding the information in the task prompt. The second is a more formal email to an unknown reader connected to the information (management, customer services, etc.)				
Instructions to candidates	The instructions will clearly identify the purpose by presenting a transactional email from the organisation which provides the background setting for all tasks (school offering online course, management of company, management of club/business etc.). The email will present a problem/issue/offer/opportunity which the candidate is expected to discuss in two different registers. The following is an example only: *You are a member of a travel club. You receive this email from the club. (text of short transactional email message). Write an email to your friend about your feelings and what you plan to do. Write about 50 words. Write an email to the secretary of the club. Write about your feelings and what you would like to do. Write 120–150 words.*				
Presentation of rubric	Aural	Written	Other non-verbal (e.g. photo)			
Time for task	50 minutes for Writing test. No time limit is set for individual tasks. (10 minutes recommended for first email, and 20 minutes for the second email).				
Delivery	Pen and paper	Computer				
Response format	Word completion	Gap-filling	Form filling	Short answer	Continuous writing
Intended genre	Emails, one informal, the other formal				
Writer/intended reader relationship	The readers are specified. The first reader will be known to the candidate as a participant in the same background activity as Tasks 1, 2, 3 (colleague, student studying on same online course, member of same club, etc.). Although the reader of the first email is known and the register is informal, the reader/writer relationship is defined by their roles as participants in the same activity in the public/occupational/educational domain. The intended reader of the second email will be specified but may or may not be personally known to the writer.				
Discourse mode	Descriptive	Narrative	Expository	Argumentative	Instructive
Domain	Public	Occupational	Educational	Personal	
Nature of task	Knowledge telling	Knowledge transformation			
Functions targeted	Expressing opinions, giving reasons and justifications, describing hopes and plans, giving precise information, expressing abstract ideas, expressing certainty/probability/doubt, generalising and qualifying, synthesising, evaluating, speculating and hypothesising, expressing opinions tentatively, expressing shades of opinion, expressing agreement/ disagreement, expressing reaction, e.g. indifference, developing an argument systematically, conceding a point, emphasising a point/feeling/issue, defending a point of view persuasively, complaining, suggesting (based on British Council Equals Core Inventory)				
Features of the Input / Prompt					
Description	A transactional email message is presented as the starting point for both email responses to be produced. A separate instruction of 1–2 sentences is given for each email response. The instructions will specify the intended reader and the purpose/function of the email (complaining, suggesting alternatives, giving advice, etc.).				
Length of input email	50–80 words				
Lexical level	K1	K2	K3	K4	K5	K6	K7	K8	K9	K10
Content knowledge	General	Specific				
Cultural specificity	Neutral	Specific				
Nature of information	Only concrete	Mostly concrete	Fairly abstract	Mainly abstract	
Relevant domain	Public	Occupational	Educational	Personal	
Information targeted	The information will be relevant to eliciting more complex and abstract functions described above.				
Features of the Expected Response					
Description	Two separate emails, one in an informal register, one in a formal register.				
Length of response	Approximately 50 words for the first email, 120–150 words for the second email.				
Lexis/grammar	K4–K5 lexis will be sufficient to complete both emails adequately. Responses must show control of B2-level grammar and cohesion across longer continuous writing texts.				
Rating scale for task	A task-specific holistic rating scale is used for the task. The rating scale is a 7-point scale from 0–6. A B2-level performance is required to achieve score bands 3–4. A score of 5 or 6 is awarded for performances beyond B2 level, with a 5 describing performance equivalent to a C1 level, and 6 for performances at a C2 level.				

Figure 6.8 Writing Task 4 specification (abridged, from O'Sullivan and Dunlea 2015: 59)

300 *Assessing English on the Global Stage*

Table 6.4 takes some of the key parameters in the model and indicates how they have been applied in the Aptis Writing paper. While it should be clear from the table exactly how these parameters are operationalised in Aptis, it is useful at this point to focus on the other key parameter, the functions expected of successful test takers' performances on the different tasks as laid out in Table 6.5.

Table 6.4 Brief overview of key parameters (Writing)

Parameter	Gloss	Operationalised in Aptis
Response format	This refers to the type of written output expected from the test taker. We would expect to see a variety of formats in a multi-level test such as Aptis.	Task 1 – Form Filling Tasks 2 and 3 – Short Answer Task 4 – Continuous Writing
Intended genre		Task 1 – Simple form for providing personal details Task 2 – Section of a simple form for providing personal details Task 3 – Interaction in a social-media context Task 4 – Emails, one informal, the other formal
Writer–intended reader relationship	In any productive test we expect that the audience/reader should be specified as there is evidence that this may impact on test performance (Porter and O'Sullivan 1999, O'Sullivan 2002).	This is the case in the Aptis Writing (and Speaking) paper where the task includes a clear description of the intended audience: Task 1 – Not specified (transactional task – form filling) Task 2 – Not specified (transactional task – form filling) Task 3 – The reader will be specified, though not personally known Task 4 – The readers are specified.
Domain and discourse mode	As with the receptive skills, we also vary the language domain and discourse mode.	*Domain* Personal – Task 1 Educational Tasks 2, 3 and 4 Occupational – Task 2 Public – Task 2, 3 and 4 *Discourse mode* Descriptive – Tasks 2 and 3 Narrative – Tasks 2 and 3 Expository – Tasks 3 and 4 Argumentative – Task 4 Instructive – Task 2

Nature of task	We expect that the challenge within a task will move from straight information exchange (knowledge telling) at the lower levels to the transformation of knowledge or information from one format to another at the higher levels.	This is the case in the Aptis Writing (and Speaking) paper: Task 1 – Knowledge telling Task 2 – Knowledge telling Task 3 – Knowledge telling Task 4 – Knowledge transformation
Functions targeted	We would expect that the different tasks in any production-based test will be designed to elicit as wide a range of different functions as feasible (O'Sullivan et al. 2002)	This is the case in the Aptis Writing (and Speaking) paper, though the nature of Task 1 (basic form filling) means that no functions are elicited aside from the very basic giving of personal information. The nature of the other tasks means that they all focus on slightly different functions.
Content knowledge and Cultural specificity	With a test such as Aptis General we would expect that the contents would be quite general and neutral in nature (localised tests may differ)	*Content knowledge* *Cultural specificity* All tasks are very much on the General end of the spectrum (General to Specific) All tasks are very much on the Neutral end of the spectrum (Neutral to Specific)
Nature of information	We would expect that the information contained in a text would be quite concrete in nature at the lower levels and more abstract as the level increases.	This is reflected in the tasks: Task 1 – Only Concrete Tasks 2 and 3 – Mostly Concrete Task 4 – Mostly Concrete to Fairly Abstract

Table 6.5 Language functions in expected responses (Writing)

Task	Focus	Function
1	Form Filling (word)	Personal Information Exchange
2	Form Filling (text)	Describing (people, places, job), describing likes/dislikes/interests, describing habits and routines, describing past experiences
3	Social Media	Describing (people, places, job), describing likes/dislikes/interests, describing habits and routines, describing past experiences, describing feelings, emotions, attitudes, describing hopes and plans, expressing opinions, expressing agreement/disagreement
4	Emails	Expressing opinions, giving reasons and justifications, describing hopes and plans, giving precise information, expressing abstract ideas, expressing certainty, probability, doubt, generalising and qualifying, synthesizing, evaluating, speculating and hypothesising, expressing opinions tentatively, expressing shades of opinion, expressing agreement/disagreement, expressing reaction, e.g. indifference, developing an argument systematically, conceding a point, emphasizing a point, feeling, issue, defending a point of view persuasively, complaining, suggesting

Table 6.5 demonstrates the difference in expected function elicitation in the different tasks. It is clear from this table that the higher-level tasks are designed to encourage the test taker to use a far broader range of functions. This is a feature of the length of expected output and of the nature of that output. Item writers are expected to indicate which functions are likely to be elicited in successful performances of each task from these lists.

The social aspect of the productive papers is more explicitly stated than is the case with the receptive papers, with audiences clearly named for all relevant productive tasks. Again, this is not unusual, though the combination of an awareness of the social and cognitive elements of each task marks the Aptis productive papers as unique in the world of language testing. We see this as a *strong* operationalisation of the socio-cognitive model.

Key aspects of the scoring system are presented and discussed in the following subsection. A series of short videos and written description of the Aptis papers is available online (www.britishcouncil.org/exam/aptis/take), while a detailed overview of the entire test can be found in Appendix 1.

Focus on the Aptis Scoring System

The core, reading and listening papers are scored automatically within the platform and results are available once the test papers have been completed. The Annual Operating Report (Dunlea et al. 2016: 15, 17, 19) cites very appropriate reliability estimates for these three papers, summarised in Table 6.6. The slightly lower estimates for reading are related to the fact that the ARG took a very conservative position with regards to item independence. By treating each task, which came with a set of associated items, as an individual element, we were able to make a more defensible estimate of the contribution of each of the four tasks to the overall performance. While the KR21 estimates are lower than for the other papers, they are clearly at an acceptable level. Further research by the team into item independence may well result in a re-think around the approach. This in turn is most likely to result in higher estimates (if for no other reason than the additional data points).

Table 6.6 Reliability estimates 2015 – Core, Reading, Listening (based on Dunlea et al. 2016)

	1	2	3	4	5	6	7	8	9
Core	0.913	0.897	0.921	0.924	0.934	0.919	0.931	0.918	–
Reading*	0.853	0.868	–	0.855	0.849	0.844	0.833	0.839	–
Listening	0.86	0.89	0.90	0.88	0.86	0.91	0.90	0.89	0.87

* KR21 used as analysis undertaken using the task as the basis for analysis and not the item.

The productive skills are, in many ways, more interesting in that the system designed to ensure accuracy and consistency in rating is unique in the language testing world. The system involves:

- Online training and accreditation
- Individual task rating
- Task-focused rating scales
- Control Item (CI) system.

304 *Assessing English on the Global Stage*

The online rater training system was developed by Judith Fairbairn from the ARG. The system provides online training for both writing and speaking raters and concludes with an accreditation exercise, in which actual responses to retired test material are rated (again online) by the trainee. Once ready for operational duty, it was validated in a major research project undertaken jointly by the British Council and the Language Testing Research Centre (LTRC) at the University of Melbourne. The final report (Knoch et al. 2015: 19) found that the two groups of raters who participated in the project, one trained face-to-face and the other trained using the new system, demonstrated 'no major differences in the rating behaviour', no differences in the degree to which they felt the experience was enjoyable and little difference in feeling that they had been 'generally sufficiently trained'. The report concluded with the statement:

> Overall, we feel that the study has shown that the British Council could implement rater training using the online platform and feel confident that the raters trained in this mode will be competent Aptis raters.

A series of recommendations were also included in the report. These typically focused on the continued screening of all trained raters for computer familiarity and rating consistency as well as some slight modifications to the system. All of these recommendations were acted upon and the system has been in operation since that time.

Unlike most other major language tests, the Aptis system takes advantage of the computer platform to break up each test taker's responses to be marked individually (Figure 6.9). This means that individual raters will see batches of a single task type during any one session. For the candidate it means that their overall test performance is seen by four different raters. This effectively eliminates any rater effect and contributes to the very high levels of inter-rater reliability reported in the Annual Operating Report (Dunlea et al. 2016: 28); see Tables 6.7 to 6.9 and the discussion below.

The design of the Aptis productive tests included a recognition that for a criterion such as 'task fulfilment' to be operationally functional it must be very clear and directly related to the actual task performance being assessed. In order to achieve this, rating scales were developed by the ARG that reflected a common understanding of productive language and also a specific element that related to the task. As can be seen in Figure 6.10, the test taker is expected to respond appropriately to at

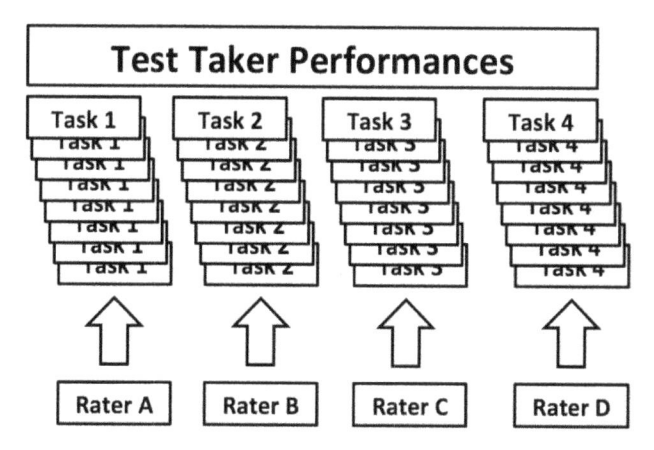

Language Test Development in the 21st Century 305

Figure 6.9 Aptis rating model

least two of the three questions asked as part of the task. All scales and all descriptors contain this reference to task fulfilment. The language focus is then consistent across all scales and focuses on grammatical range and accuracy, lexical range and accuracy, pronunciation, fluency and cohesion and coherence.

Feedback is constantly taken from raters on the effectiveness of the scales and their ease of use. This is vital to our understanding of how the scoring system functions operationally. The rating scales developed for the launch of Aptis have been refined based on this feedback and on analysis of score data. An extensive project was undertaken by members of the ARG to review the scales after their first year of use in live tests and the resulting scales have shown themselves to be quite robust in the period since that project.

3 B1.1	Responses to **two** questions are on topic and show the following features: • Control of simple grammatical structures. Errors occur when attempting complex structures. • Sufficient range and control of vocabulary for the task. Errors occur when expressing complex thoughts. • Pronunciation is intelligible but inappropriate mispronunciations put an occasional strain on the listener. • Some pausing, false starts and reformulations. • Uses only simple cohesive devices. Links between ideas are not always clearly indicated.

Figure 6.10 Aptis rating scale for Speaking Task 2 (extract)

306 *Assessing English on the Global Stage*

The final aspect of the scoring system to be presented here is the Control Item (CI) system.

Within Aptis, all task performances are scored by trained and accredited raters. The CI system was introduced in order to ensure that the ratings awarded by the markers (referred to in the system as raters) are consistent and accurate.

The way in which the CIs are selected and applied within the scoring system is outlined in Figure 6.11. As can be seen in this figure, CIs are actually live test performances that are identified by senior raters when new productive tasks go live. While a senior marker can recommend that a particular response should be classified as a CI, it is only when the response has received an 'agree' mark from at least three of these senior raters that it is included in the system as a CI. Any disagreement amongst the senior raters means that the response cannot be used as a CI. The CIs included in the system represent the whole range of ability levels assessed (A1 to C). In live scoring events, raters are exposed to a CI at the beginning of each rating session as a level check. A rater who is two or more marks away from the expected score (as agreed by

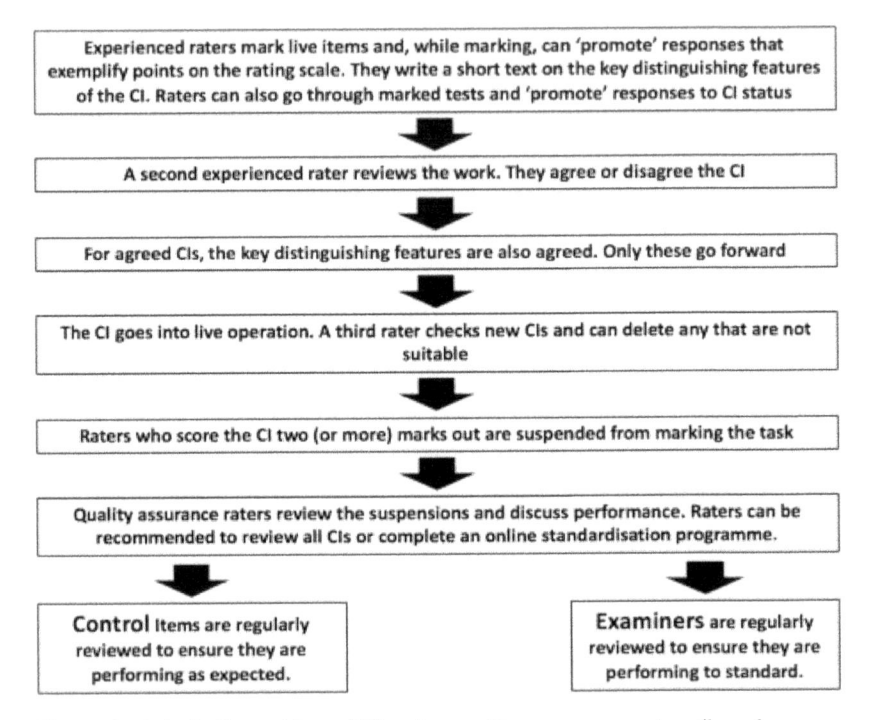

Experienced raters mark live items and, while marking, can 'promote' responses that exemplify points on the rating scale. They write a short text on the key distinguishing features of the CI. Raters can also go through marked tests and 'promote' responses to CI status

⬇

A second experienced rater reviews the work. They agree or disagree the CI

⬇

For agreed CIs, the key distinguishing features are also agreed. Only these go forward

⬇

The CI goes into live operation. A third rater checks new CIs and can delete any that are not suitable

⬇

Raters who score the CI two (or more) marks out are suspended from marking the task

⬇

Quality assurance raters review the suspensions and discuss performance. Raters can be recommended to review all CIs or complete an online standardisation programme.

⬇   ⬇

Control Items are regularly reviewed to ensure they are performing as expected. | **Examiners** are regularly reviewed to ensure they are performing to standard.

Figure 6.11 Aptis Control Item (CI) rating quality assurance system (based on Fairbairn 2015)

the senior raters) is promptly removed from the system and asked to re-standardise. Once in the system, between 5% and 7% of all performances rated are CIs. Repeated failure on the part of a rater to meet the agreed accuracy level first leads to suspension for re-training, and if the situation continues, raters are dropped from the system permanently. The CIs, in effect, introduce a system of continuous standardisation to the rating process.

The outcome of all of these measures is a very high level of rater agreement and of accuracy of judgements. Table 6.7 shows the mean correlations for the individual Writing tasks. As can be seen from the table, the correlations here are extremely high. It is perhaps unsurprising that the correlations with the CIs are high; after all these are meant to exemplify specific levels, with no ambiguous performances represented. The CIs are also the gatekeepers to the system, so individual raters failing to achieve very high levels of agreement with the CI ratings (i.e. within one band score) will not be allowed to continue rating. The success of the system can also be seen in the quotations from raters included in Fairbairn (2015):

> I make sure to check the Cl items before I start marking…I'm able to do the marking more confidently and accurately.

and

> When I saw it was a CI, I went back to the original to listen to it. It helped me standardise my marking….

Here, we can see that the raters pay attention to their rating and systematically refer to the CIs to self-standardise both before and during the rating event. This suggests that the effectiveness of the system is due not only to the extrinsic effect of constant monitoring, but also the intrinsic effect of self-empowerment – the rater can decide when to self-standardise. It is not surprising that raters feel that 'the CI System is very good and helps us standardise and mark within the accepted tolerance limit' (Fairbairn 2015).

Table 6.7 Mean correlations for Writing tasks (Dunlea et al. 2016: 28)

	Task 1	Task 2	Task 3	Task 4
Mean rater correlation with CIs	0.94	0.89	0.93	0.93
Mean correlation between all pairs of raters	0.93	0.90	0.92	0.92

As with the Writing ratings, there are very high correlations for the Speaking paper (see Table 6.8). These figures suggest that the entire system is working very well, though a more extensive research study is planned to expand the focus to both CIs and other live test data.

Table 6.8 Mean correlations for Speaking tasks (Dunlea et al. 2016: 28)

	Task 1	Task 2	Task 3	Task 4
Mean rater correlation with CIs	0.93	0.93	0.91	0.94
Mean correlation between all pairs of raters	0.92	0.91	0.86	0.91

Table 6.9 contains a summary of the Writing and Speaking correlation analysis. The figures contained in the table offer yet more support to the claim that the scoring system is functioning at a very high level.

Table 6.9 Mean inter-rater correlations across all tasks (Dunlea et al. 2016: 28)

	Inter-rater (all pairs of raters)
Mean of correlations across all Writing tasks	0.92
Mean of correlations across all Speaking tasks	0.90

The commitment to innovation by the British Council's team means that the scoring system is under regular review. It is expected that some additional work will be undertaken as part of the 2017 revision project to make the system even better, for example by looking to Task 3 (Speaking) to understand more about why the correlation coefficient is lower than for the other tasks and then working to rectify the situation.

Another aspect of the revision project involves working with academic partners in the UK to explore the potential value of automated scoring to the Aptis system. In a British Council commissioned review of the literature on automated scoring, Isaacs (2016) suggested a number of potential options for its use in both speaking and writing assessment, pointing out the potential gains (short term for writing and longer term for speaking) and risks. The work to further detail the strategic approach to be taken by the ARG on automated scoring is ongoing at the time of writing. Fairbairn (2016) presented to the ARG the preliminary thinking on such a strategy in a report undertaken with Dr Talia Isaacs at the University of Bristol.

Using Aptis

Following its launch on 20 August 2012 the numbers of people taking Aptis grew annually. During the financial year 2015/16 almost 150,000 Aptis tests were administered in 43 countries around the world. Almost two-thirds of these were Aptis General, with the other main variants (Browser, Teens, Teachers, Advanced) ranging from about 4% to 8% of the total number. The main localised variants, where test versions were produced for specific projects in countries in which clients felt that some degree of localisation was required, are shown in the final four entries in Table 6.10. These four variants resulted in almost 25% of all Aptis tests taken. While the focus in this book has been the development of the Aptis General test, much additional work was undertaken to create the variants described in Table 6.10 (see for example Zheng and Berry 2015).

From the beginning of the Aptis development project, the team was cognisant of the need to demonstrate the importance of establishing, with the full involvement of prospective clients, the validity of using Aptis for particular purposes in specific domains. While one aspect of this involved working directly with clients to collect evidence of appropriateness (or not) of use of the test system, another was the systematic recording of how the test was used by clients. Since its launch, local

Table 6.10 Aptis variants used in 2015/16 (based on Dunlea et al. 2016: 7)

Aptis variant	Level of localisation
Aptis General	None
Aptis General [Browser Version]	None
Aptis For Teens	Level 4 of Aptis General [new tasks]
Aptis For Teachers	Level 2 of Aptis General
Aptis Advanced	Level 4 of Aptis General [new high-level tasks]
Aptis General – Kerala Project	Level 2 of Aptis General
Aptis Advanced – Malaysia Pro-ELT	Level 4 of Aptis General [local/context specific]
Aptis For Teens – Kingdom of Saudi Arabia	Level 2 of Aptis for Teens [local/context specific]
Aptis General [American]	Level 2 of Aptis General [language and topic specific]

British Council staff have documented these uses and though earlier records tended to be relatively loosely structured, discussion within the ARG and additional input from the Assessment Advisory Board has led to the format seen in the series of studies included below. This format, which is informed by the socio-cognitive model, is designed to consider not only the usage of the test but also the impact of this usage. On one level, this offers British Council staff evidence for prospective clients of how the test can be used, and as such is a valuable marketing tool. On another level, the studies demonstrate how O'Sullivan's (2016a, 2016b) interpretation of consequence can be operationalised. In essence, each of these studies represents an individual validation study with intended audiences ranging from British Council staff to current and prospective clients. Although the studies focus on impact they also highlight the importance of localisation in ensuring that the test system is fit for purpose. The fact that localisation decisions are not made solely by the British Council, but are made in tandem with the client, contributes to the validity of using Aptis in these specific contexts. This approach has the added attraction of highlighting to the client the need for direct involvement in test selection and evaluation beyond their traditional 'buyer' role. By systematically documenting this involvement as well as the impact of using the test to inform specific decisions, the case studies contribute significantly to the ongoing validation of the test system.

The first case study exemplifies how the test has been used for the purpose of language benchmarking in the work context. The Sri Lanka Bureau of Foreign Employment (SLBFE) used the Aptis General speaking package to identify the language ability of migrant workers from Sri Lanka who were planning to travel abroad to work. In this case, Aptis was used to form the basis of decisions on the level of training and support required by these individuals to help themselves and their families to achieve a better quality of life.

In the second case study, we see a very different use of the test. In this case, the Punjab Education and English Language Initiative (PEELI) opted to take a four-skills package to assess the English language ability of teachers in primary and middle schools. In this case, no localisation was asked for and the test was found to be of real value as it met the critical requirements of the project – cost, ease of delivery and accuracy. These criteria are also very likely to be of high priority in many such projects, particularly in less developed countries. It also demonstrates the value of the empowering of clients to make decisions around test content (in this case they decided against making changes and the

CASE STUDY 1

Country: Sri Lanka

Client: Sri Lanka Bureau of Foreign Employment (SLBFE) – Ministry of Foreign Promotion and Welfare, Government of Sri Lanka

Test takers: Migrant workers

Purpose of the test: Benchmarking of spoken English language skills

Variant: Aptis General

Skills package: Core + Speaking

Localisation: Level 1 [client selects appropriate package] – No changes required by client

Mode of delivery: Computer

Administration: Headway School of Languages

Description: The Sri Lanka Bureau of Foreign Employment (SLBFE) is using Aptis as a summative assessment for a migrant workforce language development programme.

The programme focuses on the speaking skills of domestic workers and is run in collaboration with the International Organization for Migration (IOM), Headway School of Languages and the SLBFE.

The SLBFE, under the direction of the Ministry of Foreign Promotion and Welfare, is using Aptis (computer-based test) to benchmark the level of English language for migrant workers. Through setting standards and supporting the learning process, Aptis helps the migrant workforce to become better prepared for the expectations of work and life overseas.

Results/impact: The SLBFE has worked with the British Council to use Aptis for over a year and has expanded the use to its established centres.

Summative benchmarking using the Aptis assessment is viewed by the Ministry as driving up quality standards in English for the Sri Lankan migrant workforce. The hope is that these migrant workers will be able to secure better jobs and contribute to higher foreign exchange remittance in the years to come.

Testimonial: In support of this initiative with the British Council, Amal Senalankadhikara, Chairman, Sri Lanka Bureau of Foreign Employment, expressed confidence that

> this project would benefit migrant workers enormously, providing them with improved English language skills to increase their employability and earn a higher remuneration.

CASE STUDY 2

Country: Pakistan

Client: Punjab Education and English Language Initiative (PEELI)

Test takers: Teachers

Purpose of the test: Benchmarking language proficiency of teachers

Variant: Aptis General

Skills package: Core + Reading + Listening + Writing + Speaking

Localisation: Level 0 – No changes required by client

Mode of delivery: Computer

Administration: British Council

Description: Punjab Education and English Language Initiative (PEELI) is a five-year project that aims to train 180,000 primary and middle school teachers who teach English, Maths, Science and Computer Science to 15 million children aged 5–14 in over 56,000 schools across Punjab, Pakistan's largest province. Overall, PEELI will be helping 300,000 teachers across Punjab improve their English language and pedagogical skills. PEELI's contribution is targeted at providing training, resources and self-directed learning platforms for not only teachers and teacher educators but also district officials and head teachers. The project is working to improve the ability of primary and middle school teachers to teach English as a subject, and to strengthen the ability of middle school teachers of Maths, Science and Computer Science to teach their subjects through the medium of English. PEELI collaborates with development partners and other stakeholders to ensure that the project is integrated with ongoing reform initiatives and contributes strategically to the Government of Pakistan's ambitions for the general improvement of education in Punjab.

Results/impact: Aptis provided the PEELI team with insights and helped them develop strategies to carry the project forward. Pleased with the results, the PEELI report suggested that Aptis be used in the recruitment process for the teachers and in addition as part of a recognition system. The report states (British Council 2013b: 32):

> It is suggested that schools that meet the Directorate of Staff Development's minimum standards of English for teachers at each grade level would receive the badge of 'Aptis Certified School'. To encourage further development of English-medium teaching beyond this basic threshold, higher award levels might be created – schools that achieve higher than average Aptis results among students, for example, might receive 'Excellence in English Language Teaching' awards, while those scoring higher than average in assessments of subjects taught through the medium of English might receive an 'Excellence in English Medium' award.

> **Testimonial:** Matt Pusey, the Senior Trainer on the PEELI Project summarised the importance of Aptis as follows:
>
> Aptis was chosen by the British Council's largest English-medium educational project in Pakistan (Punjab Education and English Language Initiative, PEELI) to benchmark English language levels amongst teachers annually over [the] project's lifetime because it provides a reliable, easy to administer low-cost solution. PEELI aims to improve the language ability of all 300,000 teachers in the Punjab and with that in mind Aptis seemed the logical solution when it came to benchmarking of English language levels as the test format is easy to follow, relatively quick to administer and provides a very reliable indicator of current English language levels. Furthermore, another critical factor that set Aptis apart from many other exams was its ability to be administered almost anywhere which was and remains vital for the PEELI project as it works, trains and tests teachers in all 36 districts of Punjab.

decision appears to have been vindicated by the outcomes) and in deciding on what skills packages to use.

The third case study is of interest for a different reason. Here is an Aptis variant (Teens), which was developed by localising Aptis General at level 4. This effectively meant taking the Aptis General as the basis for a trial with test takers of the appropriate age and across a range of levels. The trial indicated that the test papers worked very well in most ways. However, the final task (aimed at level B2) proved to be too challenging from a cognitive perspective for students of this age group. With this in mind, new task types were developed that would be more likely to prove appropriate to this target age group. These were trialled and the most appropriate introduced into the test in place of the originals. The new tasks were monitored in the early administrations of the test and were shown to work as predicted.

In this case study, the Aptis Teens test was further localised to ensure that it was appropriate for the local (Kingdom of Saudi Arabia) context. Features identified for change included images, topics and cultural references. In order to ensure the probability that the new items could be successfully and smoothly integrated into the item bank, and later into the test, an additional quality assurance level was introduced into the system. The members of this QA panel were local education experts who tagged all items and tasks as being appropriate or not before they were included in item trialling and analysis.

CASE STUDY 3

Country: Saudi Arabia

Client: Ma'arif for Education and Training

Test takers: Students in Years 7–10 (13–16 years old)

Purpose of the test: Benchmark levels within school network and measure progress of students

Variant: Aptis for Teens

Skills package: Core + Reading + Listening + Writing + Speaking

Localisation: Level 2 [images, contextualisations and topics made locally appropriate]

Mode of delivery: Computer (Secure client version)

Administration: British Council

Description: A localised version of Aptis for Teens was successfully launched in Saudi Arabia in March 2015 with the testing of over 4,000 students at 13 different schools within the Ma'arif Schools network in various cities throughout the Kingdom. Localisation was undertaken in cooperation with Ma'arif specialists and focused on ensuring the suitability of content for local use.

Ma'arif wished to assess the English level of students studying in their schools. The flexibility to choose their own test dates and the availability of the test in a computer-based format were key factors in the decision of Ma'arif to use Aptis, along with the knowledge that Aptis for Teens had been specifically designed for students in their target age group. British Council support during exam delivery, and the results analysis provided after the testing was completed were also highly valued by Ma'arif, and Aptis is now a central component of their English language programmes in all of the schools in their network. Aptis high achiever awards are planned for students who attained top grades in the test and Ma'arif intend to analyse the results of all of the students and use this to inform future decisions on training and staffing.

Results/impact: All students from Years 7–10 will now be required to take a four-skills Aptis test each year and their scores will be uploaded to a central school database. The Schools intend to use Aptis to benchmark English levels within their school network and also use Aptis scores as an indicator of progress for students as they pass up through their system.

In the next case study (number 4), a similar approach was taken. Here, an advanced version of Aptis was developed for a major teacher training project in Malaysia. Up to this point in time, no advanced version of Aptis was available, though there were concrete plans to develop one. The development of high-level (C1–C2) tasks followed similar lines to those described above. The advanced tasks included, for example, the development of an intertextual comprehension task based on the research undertaken as part of the ILA reading test development. As was our experience with the ILA project, the tasks developed here worked appropriately on both the linguistic/cognition and psychometric perspectives. There were some issues with using this task type in the ILA, mainly in distinguishing clear differences between B2, C1 and C2. As these were felt to have been caused by over-exposure to the main reading text – in the ILA a single input text was used as the basis for the three tasks – the task type was considered for use in the Aptis Advanced test, but with different main input texts. The B2 version asked the test taker to read a 750-word text and to then match a series of headings with each of the seven paragraphs. The C1 version had a similar length main text but this time whole sentences were to be integrated into the paragraphs, while for the C2 task, a second text of approximately the same length (750 words) was to be integrated into the main text.

Another interesting feature of this application of Aptis is the fact that the stakes were high for the test-taking population. This meant that a very different level of additional measures had to be taken to ensure that the test offered a secure and appropriate measure of language ability. These steps included security, which was boosted to the level of an IELTS administration with stringent identification checks and invigilation for example. While in many cases, the client undertakes to manage the entire delivery system (from test allocation, to invigilation, to results generation), in this project, the work was undertaken by experienced British Council exams staff.

In the final case study, (number 5), the test was used by the client (Beijing Aidi High School) for two purposes. The first of these was to place students into appropriate language classes using a reading and listening package. As can be seen from the case study, the Vice-Principal of the school was very happy with the use of the test for this purpose. He was also impressed with a second use of the four-skills package as a predictor for IELTS and TOEFL and not least with its affordability. In this case, a non-localised version of Aptis Teens was used.

CASE STUDY 4

Country: Malaysia

Client: Ministry of Education

Test takers: English teachers

Purpose of the test: Benchmarking

Variant: Aptis Advanced

Skills package: Core + Reading + Listening + Writing + Speaking

Localisation: Level 4 [new advanced level tasks developed, topics and images locally appropriate]

Mode of delivery: Originally mixed, subsequently CB.

Administration: British Council

Description: The project, named Pro-ELT, began in 2012 when over 5,000 Malaysian English language teachers took Aptis. Test takers who achieved a score within the B band of the CEFR were placed into a 12-month training course, provided by the British Council, before taking an exit Aptis test to see if they had improved by one or more CEFR level. The project was part of the Malaysian Education Blueprint, a nationwide programme to reform the education system, itself part of the country's broader aspiration to become a 'developed nation' by 2020.

A new 'advanced' version of Aptis was developed to meet the client's need to have the test differentiate between C1 and C2 on the CEFR in order to get a better understanding of the teacher's level of English.

Results/impact: The first cohort resulted in a very high improvement rate, over 75%, based on the results from the exit tests. The project was subsequently renewed.

Aptis has become an important assessment tool for English language teachers in Malaysia, with large financial incentives provided by the state to those candidates who score in the C band. Candidates are subsequently given the opportunity to re-sit the Aptis test at the discretion of the Ministry of Education. Moreover, the benchmarking of teachers on this project has resulted in other organisations – including teacher training institutions – adopting Aptis to benchmark their staff.

Testimonial: Tengku Nurul Azian Shahriman, Director Education National Key Results Area, Performance Management and Delivery Unit (PEMANDU), Prime Minister's Office:

> We have a very interesting programme to up skill and upgrade our English teachers and (addressing teachers) 'We hope that under this programme you will use it as an opportunity to develop yourselves as English teachers and impart that knowledge to our children in the classroom.'

CASE STUDY 5

Country: P.R. China

Client: Beijing Aidi High School

Test takers: students

Purpose of the test: To assess the English ability of students and decide whether they are qualified to enter into the next grade; to assess whether the students are ready to take other tests such as IELTS

Variant: Aptis for Teens

Skills package: Core + Reading + Listening / Core + four skills

Localisation: Level 1 [client selects appropriate package] – No changes required by client

Mode of delivery: Computer

Administration: Beijing Aidi High School

Description: Beijing Aidi High School is an international school in Beijing. It offers international courses and prepares students with the knowledge as well as the language ability to go abroad for further studies. Since all the courses are taught in English for high school students, listening ability is especially important. Before the students enter into the next grade each year, Aidi needs a standard English test to assess the English level and decide whether they are qualified. The Aptis Reading and Listening package was chosen for a number of reasons:

- Aptis is developed by the British Council, which is an authoritative organisation in English teaching and testing.
- Aptis is very convenient and flexible. Aidi can decide the test time based on its needs and timeline, and at its own venue.
- The results can be obtained in a very short time. The Listening and Reading package can provide instant results, which is extremely helpful because Aidi can make decisions right after students finish the test.
- The test result is mapped to CEFR, which could be used to predict and estimate the score a candidate can get in other tests, such as IELTS and TOEFL.
- Aidi can show the results to parents. The report from a third party, especially an authoritative organisation, is more official and reliable.
- Competitive price compared to some other international English tests.

Results/impact: Aidi has organised students to take the Aptis Listening and Reading package in 2014 and 2015. Having had a very positive experience with the test, and having received positive feedback on Aptis, Aidi renewed its contract with the British Council.

> **Testimonial:** Wang Si, the Vice Principal of Beijing Aidi High School:
>
> The Aptis test can predict the IELTS score very accurately, and can reflect the strengths and weaknesses of students in different skills. For instance, if a student gets B1 in Aptis, most of the time they will get 4.5 or 5 in IELTS. This is very useful for us because almost all the students in our school would like to go abroad to study in the future (so will need to take tests like IELTS). They can now have a chance to practice and know their levels in all the skills before they take IELTS.
>
> We have been having very pleasant cooperation with the British Council. We think Aptis is not only a tool to test students, but a tool to help students better communicate in English. And we think Aptis can help us assess the English level of students more accurately.

These five case studies offer a glimpse of the range of applications to which Aptis and its variants have been put. They also offer an understanding of how the test has been localised at different levels. The variants which have been most changed (i.e. are level 4 localisations) are the Teens and Advanced. Both of these have had new task types added to replace original tasks. Less intrusive localisation has been undertaken in other cases, for example:

- Level 1 (where the client selects only the skills required for their context of use) for case studies 1 and 5
- Level 2 (where surface-level changes are made to tasks to ensure their appropriateness to the test use context) for case study 3.

The case studies exemplify the flexibility built into the Aptis system and highlight the great strength of the test. This is that it can be quite quickly and appropriately localised to meet the needs of individual clients operating in very different domains of use and at a reasonable cost. They also show the clear commitment of the Aptis system to measuring impact in a way that few other tests do as a matter of course.

Building professionalism in language testing and contributing to the field

In order to build the professionalism of the nascent testing cadre in the British Council and also ensure that Aptis was securely underpinned by a sustained and comprehensive research base, a preliminary strategic plan for assessment and testing was first set out in 2013 and later formalised in 2015 (O'Sullivan, 2015b). In this plan, a series of initiatives were conceived which were intended to support the British Council's drive towards greater professionalism in assessment and testing, while also supporting the field internationally. The first of these initiatives was the setting up of an Assessment Advisory Board in 2013.

The Assessment Advisory Board (AAB)

The purpose of the Assessment Advisory Board (AAB) is to support the assessment research and development work undertaken by the ARG as well as the broader work in exams delivery of BC-Tests. The AAB meetings, which take place twice every year, offer a platform for discussions between the Assessment Research Group of the English and Exams Department of the British Council, and a group of external advisers. The support offered by the AAB takes the form of high-level advice on strategic and operational affairs as well as detailed discussions around specific assessment-related topics, such as the content and focus of the Annual Operating Report and the Aptis Technical Manual. The AAB has also been instrumental in helping the ARG develop its other strategic initiatives, such as the Assessment Research Awards and Grants, and the increasingly important research matrix.

The AAB includes five external board members from various academic institutions worldwide. The initial members of the board were:

- Professor Cyril Weir (Chair), University of Bedfordshire, UK
- Professor Micheline Chalhoub-Deville, University of North Carolina at Greensboro, USA
- Dr Craig Deville, Measurement Incorporated, USA
- Dr Christine Coombe, Higher Colleges of Technology, UAE
- Professor Jin Yan, Shanghai Jiao Tong University, China
- Professor Barry O'Sullivan, Head of Assessment RandD, British Council, London.

Assessment Research Awards and Grants (ARAGs)

The first Assessment Research Awards and Grants (ARAGs) were awarded in 2013 following a competitive proposal review. In the period since then over £400,000 in grants and awards have been offered to researchers worldwide with the clear intent of further grounding the testing products offered by the British Council.

Research grants are designed to promote research in the area of language assessment which will have a significant impact on assessment practice specifically in relation to Aptis but also more generally in the field. They are offered every year through a competitive process and have attracted interest from across the globe. Themes for the annual call for proposals are decided by the ARG with input from the AAB and are based on the Research Matrix for Aptis, covering all aspects of test validity. Final reports are published online on the Aptis publications pages. Four of these reports have appeared as of July 2016 and have already begun to have an impact on the test (see Table 6.11). Since their introduction, 16 grants have been awarded to researchers in ten countries.

One of the important outcomes of the research undertaken on any test is the impact the work has on that test. The research reports are designed to offer an open and transparent process of assessment-related research and it is incumbent on the developer to react to any findings, whether these show the test, or aspects of the test, in a positive or negative light. As can be seen in Table 6.11 the four reports published to date have all had an important impact on the test in one way or another. The value of having a very flexible system means that British Council can react quickly to the kind of findings reported in these studies, improving both the test and the systems around the test.

Assessment Research Awards are offered to doctoral-level research students (PhD/EdD) to assist in their data collection and/or analysis activities or in presenting their work at an international conference where they have had a proposal accepted. As is the case with the Research Grants, the Awards have attracted growing interest from across the world. They have been used by research students for such purposes as purchasing software, training, buying time out of work to facilitate the writing up of a thesis and presenting papers and posters at major language testing conferences. Four of the final reports submitted by recipients have been published by the British Council.

In addition to the ARAGs, the British Council makes various types of grant available to overseas students and one very good example of how the organisation's work with IELTS contributes directly to the world of education is the British Council IELTS Global Study Award scheme. This scheme was launched in 2015 and is

Language Test Development in the 21st Century 321

Table 6.11 Published Assessment Research Grants (2013–2016) and their impact

Year	Researchers	Institution(s)	Research Topic	Impact on Aptis
2014	Khaled Barkaoui (published 2016)	York University, Canada	Roles of delivery mode and computer ability in performance on Aptis writing tasks	Review of task specification to more fully contextualise and describe the intended audience
2013	Tineke Brunfaut and Gareth McCray (published 2015)	Lancaster University, UK	Looking into test takers' cognitive process while completing a teading task: a mixed-methods eye-tracking and stimulated recall study	Development of alternative task to replace the current cloze-based task [to be included in the 2017 revision]
	Charlotte Mbali and Julie Douglas (published 2015)	University of KwaZulu-Natal, South Africa	Evaluating Aptis tests with initial teacher training students, in-service primary school teachers and hospitality job-seekers in Durban, South Africa	Review of test specifications and quality assurance guidelines to ensure removal or explanation of UK cultural references
	John Field (published 2015b)	University of Bedfordshire, UK	The impact of single and double play on candidate behaviour in tests of L2 listening	Retention of the current double-play approach. Prompted further research into the impact of test-taker proficiency level

aimed at students above 18 who plan to enrol in a full-time undergraduate or postgraduate programme in 2016, in any country worldwide. The £10,000 available for each of the six students will be primarily used to cover tuition fees, and will be directly provided to the students' university of choice. (British Council IELTS Press Release, 31 August 2016)

Recipients may choose to study in the UK or another country; for example of the six 2016 awardees, three decided to study in the UK while the other three opted for Greece, Germany and the Netherlands.

In addition to the awards and grants, the British Council launched two other initiatives in 2013. These were:

- The International Assessment Award. This award is made to an individual working for the promotion of excellence in language assessment on the international stage.
- The Innovation in Assessment Prize is designed to complement the existing British Council ELTons awards and celebrates innovation in the area of language testing and assessment.

The full list of grant, award and prize recipients from 2013 to 2016 can be found in Appendix 2.

The Aptis Research Matrix

The Research Matrix was first conceived in 2013. Based on the socio-cognitive model, the matrix is designed to do two things: inform a database of research projects and help the ARG to identify areas within the Aptis test that are less well-supported in terms of validation evidence.

It forms the basis of a database of all research activities, ARAGs, internal projects and external commissioned projects. Within this database, all details of the project are included as well as the tracking of project status. In addition, on recommendation from the AAB, any implications that the research might have for British Council test products (e.g. Aptis, IELTS) are recorded together with their impact on the test or tests.

The second application of the Research Matrix relates to helping the ARG identify quickly what aspects of the Aptis test papers might be in need of research. This is done by reviewing each element of the socio-cognitive model for each Aptis paper on a regular basis. By keeping a record of the specific focus and methodological approach for all research projects, we are able to cross-reference to the matrix to identify where particular approaches might be applied to other papers. An example of this is the eye-tracking approach taken by Brunfaut and McCray (2015) for reading, which was revisited for listening by Spöttl et al. (2015 Research Grant, forthcoming). At the time of writing, there are 39 projects listed on the matrix in varying states of readiness – ranging from completed to ongoing.

Conference Support

There has been a commitment from the British Council, through the ARG, to support language testing conferences and seminars both in the UK and internationally since 2012. The rationale for this support is threefold:

1. To help disseminate any important findings from innovative research to the field.
2. To highlight the return of the British Council to language test development.
3. To demonstrate the organisation's commitment to supporting research and development in the field internationally.

Examples of this support include backing for the Testing, Evaluation and Assessment special interest groups in the International Association for Teachers of English as a Foreign Language (IATFL) and the British Association for Applied Linguistics (BAAL), and for the UK Association for Language Testing and Assessment (UKALTA) and its annual conference, the Language Testing Forum (LTF). The ARG supports other conferences worldwide by sponsoring speakers (e.g. The Asian Association for Language Assessment conference) and providing speakers – ARG members make over 30 presentations annually. In addition to supporting other conferences, the British Council in East Asia inaugurated an annual conference in 2013 called New Directions in English Language Assessment. This event, the brainchild of Greg Selby of the British Council with the support of the ARG, focuses on locally and regionally specific assessment and testing issues. It has already been recognised as a key regional conference, attracting attention from teaching practitioners, academics and policy-makers at every event – Beijing (2013), Tokyo (2014), Seoul (2015), Hanoi (2016) and Shanghai (2017).

The most important event proposed and sponsored by the ARG is for a plenary address to be made annually to the Language Testing Research Colloquium (LTRC) on subjects related to the importance of *language* in language testing. The first of these lectures, then called the British Council Lecture, was given by Barry O'Sullivan to the LTRC in Seoul in 2013. The following year, Doug Biber was invited to speak at the LTRC in Amsterdam with the award that year named in memory of John Trim (1924–2013), who had contributed so much to language education and testing across Europe through his work on what was to become the CEFR. From 2015, the award was named in honour of Alan Davies (d.

324 *Assessing English on the Global Stage*

Table 6.12 British Council sponsored award at the LTRC, 2013–2016

Year	Award	Speaker	Title
2016	The Davies Lecture	John Norris	Reframing the SLA-Assessment Interface: 'Constructive' Deliberations at the Nexus of Interpretations, Contexts, and Consequences
2015	The Davies Lecture	Alister Cumming	Connecting Writing Assessments to Teaching and Learning: Distinguishing Alternative Purposes
2014	The John Trim Lecture	Douglas Biber	Predictable Patterns of Linguistic Variation across Proficiency Levels and Textual Task Types
2013	The British Council Lecture	Barry O'Sullivan	Accountability: Standards and Assessment in Learning Systems

2015), a hugely important figure in language testing and a major contributor to British Council testing, particularly in the 1960s and 1970s (see Chapter 3). Table 6.12 tracks the award since its inception in 2013.

Presentations and publications

As indicated in the previous section, ARG members currently make over 30 conference presentations every year. These conferences range across topics from measurement to assessment for learning to assessment literacy to language testing. They also range in geographical reach, from the UK to New Zealand to Asia to South America. The British Council sees this active conference participation as being vital to disseminating important findings from our research to our colleagues in the field, illustrating the work we do to support our assessment products (particularly Aptis and IELTS) and contributing to the reputation of the organisation as a leading player in the area of language testing. In addition to the impact of conference presentations, the ARG has more recently looked to the area of publication to further disseminate its work. One major project over the past few years has resulted in the publication of this current volume, while the ARG signed an agreement with the same publisher (Equinox) to deliver, over the coming four to five years, a series of up to 12 books on specific subjects related to language testing and assessment. The first of these (Hasselgreen and Caudwell) appeared in 2016. At the same time, ARG members have contributed to journals and books, for example see O'Sullivan (2013a, 2013b, 2016b), Berry and O'Sullivan (2016a, 2016b) and Knoch et al. (2016).

Language Assessment Literacy (LAL)

The area of Language Assessment Literacy is of critical interest to the British Council as an organisation as it is directly involved in a whole range of activities in which assessment plays a key role. Some of these activities are:

- Developing high-quality language tests (e.g. Aptis)
- Marketing, selling and supporting language test products (British Council and external)
- Delivering language and other tests across the world
- Advising on test development across the world
- Language teaching
- Teacher training.

In order to perform this work to the highest possible standard, it is vital that the various personnel involved have a high level of awareness and understanding of the areas of assessment and testing that relate to their work. With this in mind, the ARG has been working on an ambitious language assessment literacy project since 2013. Initially designed to build British Council in-house expertise by creating materials which would be of direct value to the British Council in its testing and assessment work, the project is currently providing considerable resources free of charge to language teachers and testers worldwide, thus also benefiting the field of language testing in general.

The project has a number of elements. These are outlined in Table 6.13.

Looking to the Future

By early 2016, the ARG had achieved a critical mass of researchers and support staff to contribute significantly to the British Council's objective of developing and supporting high-quality assessment solutions. The other key objective for the group, to build the reputation of the British Council as a leading language testing and assessment organisation was generally felt by the ARG to have become an achievable goal at this point.

While it is increasingly difficult to predict the future of any organisation, there are a number of interesting areas on which the ARG is

Table 6.13 British Council LAL project elements

Element	Material	Details
1	Non-technical Animations	These are 5- to 6-minute animations created by Igloo Animations (Dublin) based on scripts written by ARG members. Each animation focuses on a specific language testing topic and attempts to explain it without recourse to technical language.
2	Classroom Assessment Materials	These are a series of very practical 'how to' workbooks, looking at aspects of assessment that are relevant to language teachers. The topics range from item specification and writing to scoring productive skills.
3	Professional Development Materials	This is an MA-level course of study offered to British Council staff. The programme lasts for 10 weeks and is delivered online with synchronous and asynchronous discussion groups. The programme is offered in partnership with the University of Reading, though the contents are based on extensive notes written by Professor Barry O'Sullivan.
4	Glossary	A teacher-focused and teacher-sourced glossary of important testing and assessment terminology. This part of the project was conceived and lead by Dr Christine Coombe, UAE.
5	Opinion Videos	This part of the project consists of a series of videos of a range of test stakeholders (including test takers, teachers, administrators and developers) responding to a set of questions about language tests and testing. They are designed to capture the needs and concerns of a wide group of stakeholders, vital to understanding the context of test use and from that to developing appropriate validation arguments (see O'Sullivan 2016b).

working which suggest that the future of the group is very promising. These are IELTS research, the Core Curriculum project and work on developing level-specific tests to support the new curriculum, and finally the English Impact project.

Since 2012, the British Council has been represented on the IELTS Joint Research Committee (JRC) by members of the ARG. In that time, they have played a major role in shaping the future of IELTS research, for example by actively engaging with partners to drive the research agenda. This has been facilitated by the ARG's work on its own research matrix. As part of its commitment to the JRC, the British Council continues to sponsor, with IDP: IELTS Australia and with support from Cambridge English Language Assessment, the joint-funded research programme, which has supported over 90 external studies by over 130 researchers around the world since 1995 (see https://www.ielts.org/teaching-and-research/research-reports).

In addition to working with the JRC, the ARG has also initiated and led on projects that are contributing to the current and future IELTS test. A good example of this has been the work undertaken by Vivien Berry with colleagues at the Centre for Research in English Language Learning and Assessment (CRELLA) at the University of Bedfordshire and with support from Cambridge English Assessment. This group explored the impact on test taker and examiner behaviour and performance of mode of delivery for a speaking test. The modes examined were live face-to-face and live internet streamed. The research found no meaningful difference between the modes. This work was then followed up by a project designed to identify and deal with any technical barriers to this type of remote delivery (Patel 2016).

The combined projects have led to the decision to move forward with remote delivery of IELTS in areas where it is difficult or dangerous to place live examiners (e.g. parts of the Middle East, remote countries or islands with few if any qualified personnel). It is clear that this innovation, supported by high-quality research, will make a significant contribution to IELTS in the coming years. Of course, the research findings may also encourage other exam boards to explore the use of remote examiners in their tests. See Berry and Nakatsuhara (2015) and Nakatsuhara et al. (2017) for a detailed report, analysis and discussion of the project.

Between 2015 and 2016, the ARG managed a cross English and Exams Strategic Business Unit (SBU) project called the Common Core Curriculum. This project was designed to deliver to the organisation a curriculum that was based on the CEFR and that could be *localised* to suit a number of language use domains (e.g. work, study) across a number of key client groups (e.g. young learners, adult business people). This flexibility was to be guided, in that end users would be instructed on how to operationalise it in their own contexts. The ARG also set about designing a series of level-specific tasks to exemplify the different CEFR levels across all four skills. The long-term goal of this part of the project is to create a series of end-of-level tests that could be integrated into the learning platforms used to deliver the learning content (live or online).

These tests would help teachers to more fully understand the curriculum, from the content and value perspectives. They would also offer British Council language learners a truly appropriate assessment of their language learning.

Finally, we would like to briefly discuss the English Impact Project (EIP). This is perhaps the largest and most important project undertaken by the British Council in recent years. The EIP has been designed to create a multifaceted report on the English language capability of a country. Developed in response to the dearth of high-quality data or indices that might be of value to countries when developing or implementing language policy or strategy, the EIP was initiated in 2014. In the first year of the project, a major trial was undertaken in which almost 9,000 people were tested and questioned in 25 countries. Existing economic and social indicators as well as English policy implementation were analysed and a preliminary report drawn up for each country. Due to the lack of standardisation across the population sampling, it was not always possible to compare countries, though the data proved to be quite robust and were considered to be of value to those countries involved.

From early in the project, it was decided to involve partners for specific elements. The first partnership to emerge was with the National Foundation for Educational Research (NFER) in the UK. NFER was chosen due to the extensive experience within the organisation for research on educational policy. They worked with the EIP team (led by Liz Shepherd from the ARG) to create a set of systematic procedures for gathering, evaluation and ultimately quantifying the language policies of countries and the implementation (or not) of those policies. Based on the experience gained from the initial pilot project, it was decided by the EIP Board to work with sampling experts to create a formal procedure for this part of the project. The partner chosen was the Australian Centre for Educational Research (ACER), who, as the developers of the sampling plan for the PISA project, were considered to be world leaders in the area. A new sampling plan was proposed by ACER and agreed by the EIP team in early 2016. This was the trigger for a significant drive to identify a number of countries from the original 25 to launch a full-scale administration of the EIP starting in late 2016. The EIP team decided to limit the number of participating countries in order that a full monitoring and evaluation process be implemented after the data delivery phase of the project. The lessons learnt from this would then help the project expand over the coming years.

Table 6.14 English Impact Project evidence bases

Language measure (Aptis four skills)	Associated language motivation and opportunities questionnaire
Existing economic and social indicators (e.g. World Bank, IMF etc.)	English language policy and implementation analysis

As can be seen in Table 6.14, the strength of the EIP is the fact that the final outcome is based on a range of evidence. With input from all four quadrants, a group of experts local to each participating country or region interpret the outcomes for the final report. This is critical, as without this local interpretation, the value to each participating country is likely to be very limited. The EIP will result in a series of country-specific reports, which will be of particular value to ministries when planning language policy and implementation. The broad nature of the evidence base means that any resulting report will have significant diagnostic value, in that it will be possible to identify specific strengths and weaknesses within and between education systems.

Endnote

In this chapter, we have seen how the focus of the British Council has changed over the past decade, during which the organisation has made a strategic move from test delivery to a combined delivery and ownership model. In doing this, there has been a very definite commitment to rebuilding the organisation's former strength in the area of test development.

The Aptis development project most obviously exemplifies the move towards test development and ownership. However, while the strategic decision to take this journey marks a major milestone in the history of the British Council, this in itself is only part of the story. The decision to create a new highly professional research and development department within the organisation marked the realisation that only such a group could deliver the level of support that the strategy and the test required. The whole approach centred around innovation, some examples being:

- The commitment to flexibility and accessibility of the final product
- The localisability of that product

- The first successful operationalisation of the socio-cognitive model of test development and validation in a major international test
- Stakeholder inclusion in major development-related decisions
- An awareness of the need for a high level of language assessment literacy across the organisation and the creation of a major project to support this need.

In addition, the development team brought innovation into the heart of the system:

- Detailed, validation-driven online specifications and item-writer guidelines
- Online item-writer training system
- Online rater training and accreditation system
- Task-focused rating scales for writing and speaking
- Control Item system for quality assurance of rating process
- Use of the core language knowledge (grammar and vocabulary) paper to inform CEFR borderline decisions
- The successful operationalisation of cognitive models of reading and listening development (Khalifa and Weir 2009, Field 2015a).

Besides this product-centred work, the British Council has also in this period re-established its support for the language testing profession through the ARAGs and by backing a growing number of language testing conferences around the world.

For the first time in over 25 years, the British Council is in a position to contribute cutting-edge in-house expertise in support of language testing colleagues in universities and ministries across the world to develop systems that meet local needs in a professional and sustainable way.

Chapter 7

Conclusions and the future

The British Council and soft power

In Chapter 1 we saw how the British Council formed a close association with Cambridge in the 20th century and helped it become the leading global provider of EFL examinations during the lifetime of their joint agreement, 1941–1993. As well as promoting and administering Cambridge examinations in its centres abroad, the British Council, through its wealth of experience of ELT globally, provided professional input into the research and development of Cambridge English language examinations and was itself largely responsible for bringing into being one particular Cambridge English language examination, viz. the Diploma in English. In exploring the development of the partnership formed with Cambridge by the 1941 Joint Agreement, we established the British Council's role in building soft power for Britain through the explicit objective of spreading British influence through promoting English around the globe.

In Chapter 2 we saw how, from the 1980s onwards, the British Council enhanced this role through its work for British government (ODA/DFID) and other agencies by commissioning and supporting indigenous, national, English language testing projects around the world; by providing training in English language assessment in numerous countries overseas using British consultants; through its own teachers and lecturers and ELOs delivering support on the ground in these countries for local and national English language test development, and by bringing indigenous personnel from the assessment field to the UK for study and consultation. These projects had an immediate impact on locally developed national English examinations overseas and more widely on important areas of society such as the military, the civil service and access to, and success in, tertiary education. The research and development associated with a number of these projects contributed to the development of wider language testing theory and practice, thereby enriching the language-testing field as a whole.

British Council tests

An increasing responsibility for government sponsored overseas students coming to Britain in the 1960s led to direct British Council involvement in language test development particularly in the important area of assessing academic English proficiency. Between 1963 and 1989, British Council staff in Spring Gardens became directly involved in test development projects such as the English Proficiency Test Battery (EPTB) (Davies 1965a and 2008 and our Chapter 3) and the innovative English Language Testing Service (ELTS) test (Carroll 1978, 1980, 1981 and our Chapter 4). Through its significant involvement in these projects, the British Council became the leading authority in this period on how to assess the English proficiency of overseas students wishing to study through the medium of English at tertiary-level institutions in the UK. This marked an important adjunct to its long-term facilitative role in helping spread English examinations and more recently British approaches to language testing round the globe.

As illustrated in Chapters 3–6, the period 1954–2016 saw significant changes in both the content of language tests developed by the British Council and the systems that were built to construct, validate and administer them in a rigorous fashion. Table 7.1 summarises how the British Council's tests developed in this period. The changes up until 2003 match closely the three stages of test development in the 20th century originally proposed by Bernard Spolsky (1978). Though in later works he felt his 1978 division into the stages of pre-scientific, psychometric structuralist and psycholinguistic-sociolinguistic was perhaps too rigid and needed further nuancing, these labels seem nevertheless to fit neatly the stages of development in tests involving the British Council in the 20th century.

In the 1950s we have the British Council subjective interviews conducted in its operations abroad. These one-on-one interviews used the *Knowledge of English Form* and the *OSI 210 Assessment of Competence in English Form*. These forms typify the 'pre-scientific period' (Spolsky

Table 7.1 British Council involvement in English language testing, 1941–2016

Stage 1 (1941–1959)	Traditional approaches to language testing	
	1941	Joint Committee of the British Council and the Cambridge Local Examinations Syndicate
	1945	*The Diploma in English* developed with UCLES
	1954	*Knowledge of English Form* for screening applicants for UK universities by BC abroad
	1957	British Council membership of UCLES Executive Committee for the Syndicate's examinations in English for foreign students
	1958	*OSI 210 Assessment of Competence in English Form*
Stage 2 (1960–)	**Psychometric-structuralist approaches to language testing**	
	1960	The audio-lingual approach (Brooks 1960); *English Sentence Patterns, Understanding and producing grammatical structures* (Fries and Lado 1962)
	1960	*Language testing: the construction and use of foreign language tests* (Lado 1961)
	1962	British Council takes on responsibility for government funded trainees and students coming to Britain
	1965–1982	*English Proficiency Test Battery (EPTB)* (Alan Davies PhD University of Birmingham 1965)
Stage 3 (1975–)	**Communicative approaches to language testing**	
	1975	British Council approach Cambridge to develop an English Language testing service: *The Threshold Level* (Van Ek, Council of Europe 1975); *Notional Syllabuses* (Wilkins 1976); The notional-functional syllabus
	1978	British Council decide to develop ELTS themselves; English for Specific Purposes (ESP): Munby (1978) *Communicative Syllabus design* and Widdowson (1978) *Teaching Language as Communication*
	1980	*ELTS Test* (Carroll 1978) launched
	1982	*Mini-platform* (Moller, Seaton and McNeill 1982)
	1989	*IELTS Test* (Alderson, Clapham, Ingram and Westaway)
	2001	*The Common European Framework of Reference for Languages: Learning, Teaching, Assessment* (CEFR), Council of Europe (2001)

Stage 4 (2003–)		The Socio-cognitive approach to language testing
	2003 onwards	Cambridge 'Constructs' Project: a socio-cognitive approach. Shaw and Weir 2007 – *Examining Writing*, Khalifa and Weir 2009 – *Examining Reading*, Taylor (ed.) 2011 – *Examining Speaking* and Geranpayeh and Taylor (eds.) 2013 – *Examining Listening*
	2004	QALSPELL – COE funded project to develop generic specifications for ESP in the Baltic states – socio-cognitive approach used as basis for specifications (O'Sullivan)
	2004–2008	EXAVER – University of Veracruz/British Council test suite – socio-cognitive approach used for specifications (O'Sullivan)
	2009	*International Language Assessment* (*ILA*) (O'Sullivan and Weir)
	2012	Aptis (O'Sullivan 2015a) based on the socio-cognitive approach
	2016	75th anniversary of British Council's involvement in language testing

1978) in approaches to language testing, the 'Garden of Eden' as it was termed by Morrow (1979), where little concern was paid to scoring, let alone construct validity (see Chapter 3). No training or standardisation was provided for examiners and there was an unquestioning faith in the connoisseurship of the local British Council personnel conducting the test to make the right decision.

In the next stage of development we can see examples of what Spolsky (1978) described as the 'psychometric-structuralist era' and Morrow the 'Vale of Tears', the so-called 'discrete point' approach to testing (see Chapter 3). Despite an initial concern with work sample tests, the Davies Test/EPTB as it was used in its short form was essentially a test of micro-linguistic knowledge e.g. of grammar and vocabulary.

The communicative era, what Spolsky termed 'the integrative-sociolinguistic era': the age of the integrative test, labelled by Morrow as 'the promised land', is typified by the ELTS test first administered in 1980 (see Chapter 4) and to a lesser extent by the IELTS test, first administered in 1989 (see Chapter 5). IELTS retained a number of the communicative features of ELTS, but the main focus under UCLES stewardship was to develop a comprehensive and rigorous testing system that would ensure each version was fit for purpose and comparable with all the others. It was one of the few tests in the UK that was underpinned by psychometrics.

The 21st century ushered in a fourth era in language testing, namely the socio-cognitive approach (Weir 2005, Shaw and Weir 2007, Khalifa and Weir 2009, O'Sullivan and Weir 2011, Taylor 2011, Geranpayeh and Taylor 2013 and O'Sullivan 2015a), what Keith Morrow might have termed *'beyond the promised land'*. Following a number of projects in which the approach was successfully used by O'Sullivan as the basis for developing test specifications (QALSPELL and EXAVER) the Aptis test, introduced by the British Council in 2012 (see Chapter 6), was the first test system to be based fully on the approach. Like IELTS it is similarly rigorous in its underlying systems but is in many ways different in that it is one of the most interactionally and situationally authentic tests available on the market today, having been constructed *ab initio* using the socio-cognitive framework. It takes full account of cognitive, contextual and scoring aspects of validity, making it truly a test for the 21st century.

As we saw in Chapter 6, the 21st century also marks a return by the British Council to in-house test development and a commitment to developing its own language testing expertise through a newly created Assessment Research Group (ARG); strengths it had let go in the 1990s when IELTS was just beginning to take off. The creation and expansion of the Assessment Research Group reflects a growing emphasis on research-led activity across the organisation since the arrival in 2014 of a new CEO, Sir Ciarán Devane. The commercial value to the organisation of once again involving itself prominently in English language testing is now recognised as IELTS candidature nears the 3 million a year mark and over 400,000 have already taken Aptis since it was introduced only four years ago.

Current Directions

The British Council's *current* EL-related purpose, as stated in its Corporate Plan for 2015, includes:

- more widespread and better quality teaching, learning and assessment of English worldwide.
- providing people worldwide with access to the life-changing opportunities that come from learning English and gaining valuable UK qualifications.

- to maintain the UK's profile and expertise in English language teaching and assessment worldwide.
- work with over 150 UK academic and professional examination boards and universities to help people around the world access UK qualifications, and the opportunities that derive from these.
- a global network of high quality teaching centres, with 83 centres in 50 countries and growth of over 30 per cent in the number of people learning English with us since 2011.
- delivery of examinations in over 850 towns and cities worldwide.
- extending our range of self-access English language learning products offered through digital and mobile technology.
- work with overseas governments to transform whole education systems and increase opportunity and employability through English.
(http://www.britishcouncil.org/sites/default/files/corporate-plan-2015-17.pdf)

The Plan documents how work in English and Examinations makes a major contribution to the UK's International Education Strategy, building recognition of UK expertise in this area and, through this, developing international opportunities for UK English Language Teaching (ELT) organisations and UK qualification awarding bodies. Through Accreditation UK the British Council supports the promotion of the UK as a leading destination for English language learners (a market worth in total £3 billion annually to the UK economy). It also supports the UK assessment and English language teaching sector, as well as academics, through research, publications and market intelligence.

Assessment clearly features much more in the current planning than it did at the outset of the British Council (it was not mentioned at all in the objectives set for Professor Ifor Evans, of London University when he became British Council Educational Director in December 1940, see Chapter 3), even though British Council engagement in assessment was in fact one of its earliest ELT activities.

In Chapters 1 and 2, we examined the role of the British Council in spreading British influence around the world through the export of British English language examinations and British expertise in language testing. In more recent years (1989–2008), though the British Council continued to support the export of British tests and British testing expertise, it ceased to carry out the critical role in language test development that we witnessed in Chapters 3 and 4. From 1989, the British

Council deliberately chose to focus its resources and expertise on the delivery of British examinations, in particular IELTS, through its global network (see Chapter 5). In Chapter 6, we have seen the re-emergence of professional expertise in language testing within the organisation and also the growing strategic influence of the organisation on assessment in English language education. This influence derives from a commitment to test localisation, the development and provision of flexible, accessible and affordable tests and an efficient delivery, marking and reporting system underpinned by an innovative socio-cognitive approach to language testing. This final period can be seen as a clear return by the British Council to using language testing as a tool for enhancing soft power for Britain: a return to the original raison d'etre of the organisation outlined in the Prince of Wales' speech in 1935 at the inauguration of the British Council.

Appendices

Appendix 1 Overview of the Aptis Test Papers

The Core component (based on O'Sullivan and Dunlea 2015: 12)

Part	Skill/Focus	Items per Part	Level	Tasks	Items per Task	Item/Task Focus	Description	Response Format
1	Grammar	25	A1	5	1	Syntax and word usage	Sentence completion: select the best word to complete a sentence based on syntactic appropriateness.	3-option multiple-choice.
			A2	5–7	1			
			B1	5–7	1			
			B2	5–7	1			
2	Vocabulary	25	A1	1	5	Synonym (vocabulary breadth)	Word matching: match 2 words which have the same or very similar meanings.	5 target words. Select the best match for each from a bank of 10 options.
			A2	1	5	Meaning in context (vocabulary breadth)	Sentence completion: select the best word to fill a gap in a short sentence. Understanding meaning from context.	5 sentences, each with a 1-word gap. Select the best word to complete each from a bank of 10 options.

B1	1	5	Meaning in context (vocabulary breadth)	Sentence completion: select the best word to fill a gap in a short sentence. Understanding meaning from context.	5 sentences, each with a 1-word gap. Select the best word to complete each from a bank of 10 options.
	1	5	Definition (vocabulary breadth)	Matching words to definitions.	5 definitions. Select the word defined from a bank of 10 options.
B2	1	5	Collocation (vocabulary depth)	Word matching: match the word which is most commonly used with a word targeted from the appropriate vocabulary level.	5 target words. Select the best match for each from a bank of 10 options.

The Reading component (based on O'Sullivan and Dunlea 2015: 13)

Skill/Focus	Total Items	Task	Items	Level	Task Focus	Description	Response Format
Reading	25	1	5	A1	Sentence-level meaning (careful local reading)	Gap fill. A short text with 5 gaps. Filling each gap only requires comprehension of the sentence containing the gap. Text-level comprehension is not required.	3-option multiple-choice for each gap.
		2	6	A2	Inter-sentence cohesion (careful global reading)	Re-order jumbled sentences to form a cohesive text.	Re-order 6 jumbled sentences. All sentences must be used to complete the story.
		3	7	B1	Text-level comprehension of short texts (careful global reading)	Banked gap fill. A short text with 7 gaps. Filling the gaps requires text-level comprehension and reading beyond the sentence containing the gap.	7 gaps in a short text. Select the best word to fill each gap from a bank of 9 options.
		4	7	B2	Text-level comprehension of longer text (global reading, both careful and expeditious)	Matching the most appropriate headings to paragraphs. Requires integration of micro- and macro-propositions within and across paragraphs, and comprehension of the discourse structure of more complex and abstract texts.	7 paragraphs forming a long text. Select the most appropriate heading for each paragraph from a bank of 8 options.

The Listening component (based on O'Sullivan and Dunlea 2015: 13)

Skill/Focus	Total Items	Skill/Focus	Items	Level	Task Input	Description	Response Format
Listening	25*	Lexical recognition	10	A1	Monologue	QandA about listening text. Listen to short monologues (recorded messages) to identify specific pieces of information.	4-option multiple-choice.
		Identifying specific factual information	5	A2	Monologue and dialogue	QandA about listening text. Listen to short monologues and conversations to identify specific pieces of information.	4-option multiple-choice.
		Identifying specific factual information	5	B1	Monologue and dialogue	QandA about listening text. Listen to short monologues and conversations to identify propositions. The information targeted is concrete and of a factual/literal nature. Requires integration of information over more than one part of the input text.	4-option multiple-choice.
		Meaning representation/inference	5	B2	Monologue and dialogue	QandA about listening text. Listen to monologues and conversations to identify a speaker's attitude, opinion or intention. The information targeted will require the integration of propositions across the input text to identify the correct answer.	4-option multiple-choice.

* The distribution of items across levels is an approximate target and may differ slightly across versions depending on content. The overall difficulty of each test version is constrained to be comparable.

The Speaking component (based on O'Sullivan and Dunlea 2015: 15)

Skill/Focus	Skill/Focus	Items	Task Input	Description	Time to Plan	Response Time	Scoring
Speaking	Giving personal information	A1/A2	Visual, aural and written	Candidate responds to 3 questions on personal topics. The candidate records his/her response before the next question is presented.	None	30 seconds to respond to each question	Separate task-based holistic scales are used for each task. Performance descriptors describe the expected performance at each score band. The following aspects of performance are addressed: 1) grammatical range and accuracy; 2) lexical range and accuracy; 3) pronunciation; 4) fluency; 5) cohesion and coherence.
	Describing, expressing opinions, providing reasons and explanations	A2	Visual, aural and written	The candidate responds to 3 questions. The first asks the candidate to describe a photograph. The next two are on a concrete and familiar topic related to the photo.	None	45 seconds to respond to each question	
	Describing, comparing and contrasting, providing reasons and explanations	B1	Visual, aural and written	The candidate responds to 3 questions/prompts and is asked to describe, contrast and compare two photographs on a topic familiar to B1 candidates. The candidate gives opinions, and provides reasons and explanations.	None	45 seconds to respond to each question	
	Integrating ideas on an abstract topic into a long turn. Giving and justifying opinions, advantages and disadvantages	B2	Aural and written	The candidate plans a longer turn integrating responses to a set of 3 questions related to a more abstract topic. After planning their response, the candidate speaks for two minutes to present a coherent, continuous, long turn.	1 minute	2 minutes for the entire response, integrating the 3 questions into a single long turn	

Appendices 343

The Writing component (based on O'Sullivan and Dunlea 2015: 16)

Skill/Focus	Skill/Focus	Items	Task Input	Description	Output	Scoring
Writing	Writing at the word level. Simple personal information on a form.	A1	Form completion	Basic personal information. All responses are at the word/phrase level, such as name, birthdate, etc.	9 gaps with 1–2 word responses	Separate task-based holistic scales are used for each task. Performance descriptors describe the expected performance at each score band. The following aspects of performance are addressed (not all aspects are assessed for each task): 1) task completion; 2) grammatical range and accuracy; 3) lexical range and accuracy; 4) cohesion and coherence; 5) punctuation and spelling.
	Short written description of concrete, personal information at the sentence level.	A2	Form completion – task setting and topic related to part 1.	Written. The rubric presents the context, followed by a short question asking for information from the candidate related to the context.	Single, short sentence-level response, personal information (20–30 words)	
	Interactive writing. Responding to a series of written questions with short paragraph-level responses.	B1	Social-media type written interaction on same task setting and topic as before.	Written. The rubric presents the context (discussion forum, social media, etc.). Each question is displayed in a sequence following the completion of the response to the previous question.	Interactive response to 3 separate questions. Each response requires a short paragraph-level response. (30–40 words each question)	
	Integrated writing task requiring longer paragraph-level writing in response to two emails. Use of both formal/informal registers required.	B2	Two emails in response to a short letter/notice on same task setting and topic as before.	Written. The rubric presents the context (a short letter/notice/memo). Each email is preceded by a short rubric explaining the intended reader and purpose of the email.	Email 1 (40–50 words) – informal to a friend. Email 2 (120–150 words) – formal to an unknown reader.	

Appendix 2 British Council Assessment Research Awards and Grants, 2013–2016

Assessment Research Grants 2013–2016

Year	Researcher(s)	Institution(s)	Research Topic
2016	Stephen Bax and Prithvi Shrestha	Open University, UK	Lexical thresholds and lexical profiles across the Common European Framework of Reference for Language (CEFR) levels assessed in the Aptis test
	Sally O'Hagan and Kellie Frost	University of Melbourne, Australia	Test-taker processes and strategies and stakeholder perceptions of relevance of the Aptis for Teachers Speaking test in the Australian context
	Parvaneh Tavakoli and Fumiyo Nakatsuhara	University of Reading, UK; University of Bedfordshire, UK	Scoring validity of the Aptis Speaking test: investigating fluency across tasks and levels of proficiency
	Xun Yan, Ha Ram Kim and Ji Young Kim	University of Illinois at Urbana-Champaign, USA	Complexity, accuracy and fluency features of speaking performances on Aptis across different CEFR levels
	Nguyen Thi Thuy Minh and Ardi Marwan	Nanyang Technological University, Singapore	Test-takers' pragmatic performance and cognitive processing in the Aptis General Writing test, Task 4
	Yo In'nami and Rie Koizumi	Chuo University, Japan	Factor structure and four-skill profiles of the Aptis test
2015	Jesús García Laborda, Marian Amengual Pizarro, Mary Frances Litzler, Soraya García-Esteban and Nuria Otero de Juan	University of Alcalá, Spain	Student perceptions of the CEFR levels and the impact of guided practice on APTIS oral test performance
	Carol Spöttl, Franz Holzknecht, Kathrin Eberharter, Benjamin Kremmel and Eva Konrad	University of Innsbruck, Austria	Looking into listening: using eye-tracking to establish the cognitive validity of the Aptis Listening test

Year	Author(s)	Institution	Title
2014	Khaled Barkaoui	York University, Canada	Roles of delivery mode and computer ability in performance on Aptis writing tasks
	Noriko Iwashita, Lyn May and Paul Moore	The University of Queensland, Australia	Features of discourse and lexical richness at different performance levels in the APTIS Speaking test
	Andrea Phillott and Rosalind Warfield Brown	Asian University for Women, Bangladesh	The influence of sociocultural context on tertiary students' understanding and performance on Aptis written tests
	Susan Sheehan, Peter Sanderson and Ann Harris	University of Huddersfield, UK	Identifying key criteria of written and spoken English at C1
2013	Tineke Brunfaut and Gareth McCray	Lancaster University, UK	Looking into test takers' cognitive process while completing a reading task: a mixed-methods method eye-tracking and stimulated recall study
	Charlotte Mbali and Julie Douglas	University of KwaZulu-Natal, South Africa	Evaluating APTIS tests with initial teacher training students, in-service primary school teachers and hospitality job-seekers in Durban, South Africa
	John Field	University of Bedfordshire, UK	The impact of single and double play on candidate behaviour in tests of L2 listening
	Steve Walsh, Dawn Knight and Paul Seedhouse	University of Newcastle, UK	Characterising interactional competence in higher education small group talk

Assessment Research Awards, 2013–2016

Year	Researcher	Institution	Supervisor(s)
2016	Maria Georgina Fernandez Sesma	University of Southampton, UK	Dr Ying Zheng
	Iftikhar Haider	University of Illinois at Urbana-Champaign, USA	Professor Emeritus Fred Davidson and Professor Melissa Bowles
	Benjamin Kremmel	University of Nottingham, UK	Professor Norbert Schmitt
	Suh Keong Kwon	University of Bristol, UK	Dr Guoxing Yu
	Heidi Han-Ting Liu	Teachers College, Columbia University, USA	Professor James E. Purpura
	Yueting Xu	The University of Hong Kong, SARPRC	Professor David R. Carless
2015	Tanzeela Anbreen	University of Bedfordshire, UK	Professor Stephen Bax
	Tony Clark	University of Bristol, UK	Dr Guoxing Yu and Dr Talia Isaacs
	Lin Fang	University of Bristol, UK	Dr Guoxing Yu
	Edit Ficzere	University of Bedfordshire, UK	Dr Fumiyo Nakatsuhara
	Elsa Gonzalez	University of Southampton, UK	Dr Ying Zheng
	Mikako Nishikawa	University of Bristol, UK	Dr Guoxing Yu
	Saerhim Oh	Teachers College, Columbia University, USA	Professor Jim Purpura
	Victor Santos	Iowa State University, USA	Professor Carol A. Chapelle
	Linxiao Wang	Northern Arizona University, USA	Dr Okim Kang
2014	Ahmet Dursun	Iowa State University, USA	Professor Carol A. Chapelle
	Suwimol Jaiyote*	University of Bedfordshire, UK	Dr Fumiyo Nakatsuhara
	Glyn Jones*	Lancaster University, UK	Dr Luke Harding
	Yumiko Moore*	University of Bedfordshire, UK	Professor Cyril Weir
2013	Stéphanie Gaillard	University of Illinois at Urbana-Champaign, USA	Professor Fred Davidson and Dr Annie Tremblay
	Ruslan Suvorov*	Iowa State University, USA	Professor Carol A. Chapelle
	Tami Aviad	University of Haifa, Israel	Professor Batia Laufer

* Published on the ARG Publications page: https://www.britishcouncil.org/exam/aptis/research/publications

International Assessment Awards, 2013–2016

Year	Awardee
2016	Sauli Takala, Professor Emeritus (University of Jyväskylä)
2015	Neus Figueras (Ministry of Education Catalunya)
2014	Randy Thrasher, Professor Emeritus (International Christian University, Japan)
2013	Dr Christine Coombe (Dubai Men's College, UAE)

Innovation in Assessment Prize, 2013–2016

Year	Winner	Innovation
2016	Abdul Halim Abdul Raof and his team (Language Academy, Universiti Teknologi Malaysia, Johor Bahru, Malaysia)	Development of an innovative validation programme for the revision of their assessment instrument, the Test of English Communication Skills for graduating students (UTM-TECS).
2015	Ricky Jeffrey (Centre for English Language Education, University of Nottingham Ningbo China)	A new, practical method of developing rating scales called the 'feedback content analysis' method
2014	Daniel Xerri, Patricia Vella Briffa, Joseph Gerardi, Odette Vassallo, Andrew Farrugia and Clyde Borg (Department of English, University of Malta Junior College)	Development and implementation of the Advanced English Speaking Examination – the first test of speaking at post-secondary level in Malta
2013	Carol Spöttl, Kathrin Eberharter and Doris Frötscher (University of Innsbruck, Austria)	Development of real-time marker support for national high-stakes school-leaving examinations

References

Abad Florescano, A., Dunne, R.A. and Grounds, M. (2004). A Local Alternative to International Proficiency Tests: The EXAVER Project. In J. Pender (ed.), *Ten Years of Collaboration in ELT: Accounts from Mexico* [CD-ROM edition] (pp. 156–166). Mexico City: British Council.

Abad Florescano, A., O'Sullivan, B., Sanchez Chavez, C., Ryan, D.E., Zamora Lara, E., Santana Martinez, L.A., Gonzalez Macias, M.I., Maxwell Hart, M., Grounds, P.E., Reidy Ryan, P., Dunne, R.A. and Romero Barradas, T. de E. (2011). Developing Affordable 'Local' Tests: The EXAVER Project. In B. O'Sullivan (ed.), *Language Testing: Theory and Practice* (pp. 228–43). Oxford: Palgrave.

Abbott, G. and Beaumont, M. (eds.) (1997). *The Development of ELT: The Dunford Seminars 1978–1993*. Wiltshire: Redwood Books.

Adam, C.F. (1948). *Life of Lord Lloyd*. London: Macmillan.

Alderson, J.C. (1988). New Procedures for Validating Proficiency Tests of ESP? Theory and Practice. *Language Testing* 5(2): 220–232. https://doi.org/10.1177/026553228800500207

Alderson, J.C. (ed.) (2009). *The Politics of Language Education: Individuals and Institutions*. Bristol: Multilingual Matters.

Alderson, J.C. and Clapham, C. (eds.) (1992a). *IELTS Research Reports 2: Examining the ELTS Test: An Account of the First Stage of the ELTS Revision Project*. Cambridge: The British Council/UCLES/IDP.

Alderson, J.C. and Clapham, C. (1992b). Applied Linguistics and Language Testing: A Case Study of the ELTS Test. *Applied Linguistics* 13(2): 149–167. https://doi.org/10.1093/applin/13.2.149

Alderson, J.C. and Clapham, C. (1997). The General Modules: Grammar. In C. Clapham and J.C. Alderson (eds.), *IELTS Research Reports 3* (pp. 30–48). London: IELTS Partners.

Alderson, J.C., Clapham, C. and Wall, D. (1995). *Language Test Construction and Evaluation*. Cambridge: Cambridge University Press.

Alderson, J.C. and Hughes, A. (eds.) (1981). *Issues in Language Testing*. ELT Documents 111. London: British Council.

Alderson, J., Krahnke, K. and Stansfield, C.W. (eds.) (1987). *Reviews of English Language Proficiency Tests*. Washington, DC: Teachers of English to Speakers of Other Languages.

Alderson, J.C., Nagy, E. and Öveges, E. (eds.) (2000). *English Language Education in Hungary, Part 11: Examining Hungarian Learners' Achievements in English.* Budapest: British Council.

Alderson, J.C., Nagy, E. and Pižorn, K. (2004). *Constructing School Leaving Examinations at a National Level – Meeting European Standards.* Ljubljana: British Council and Državni izpitni.

Alderson, J.C. and Urquhart, A.H. (1985a). The Effect of Students' Academic Discipline on their Performance on ESP Reading Test. *Language Testing* 2(2): 192–204. https://doi.org/10.1177/026553228500200207

Alderson, J.C. and Urquhart, A.H. (1985b). This Test Is Unfair: I'm Not an Economist. In P.C. Hauptman, R. LeBlanc and M.B. Wesche (eds.), *Second Language Performance Testing* (pp. 25–43). Ottawa: University of Ottawa Press.

Alderson, J.C. and Wall, D. (1992). *The Sri Lankan O Level Evaluation Project: Fourth and Final Report.* Lancaster: Lancaster University.

Alderson, J.C. and Wall, D. (1993). Does Washback Exist? *Applied Linguistics* 14(2): 115–129. https://doi.org/10.1093/applin/14.2.115

Alderson, J.C., Wall, D. and Clapham, C.M. (1987). *An Evaluation of the National Certificate in English (1986).* Volume 2: Final Report. Lancaster University: Institute for English Language Education.

Anderson, L. (2014). *The British Council and Support for Global Student Mobility.* Paper presented at the Council for Education in the Commonwealth Conference, Glasgow April 2014. Accessed 24 October 2014 from: http://www.cecomm.org.uk/images/stories/news/2014/lloyd%20anderson.pdf.

Anon. (2004). IELTS: Some Frequently Asked Questions. *Research Notes* 18: 14–18.

Atherton, L. (1994). Lord Lloyd at the British Council and the Balkan Front, 1937–1940. *The International History Review* 16(1): 25–48. https://doi.org/10.1080/07075332.1994.9640667

Bachman, L. (1990). *Fundamental Considerations in Language Testing.* Oxford: Oxford University Press.

Bachman, L., Davidson, F., Ryan, K. and Choi, I.-C. (1989). *An Investigation into the Comparability of Two Tests of English as a Foreign Language: The Cambridge TOEFL Comparability Study.* Cambridge: Cambridge University Press.

Banerjee, J. (2003). *Interpreting and Using Proficiency Test Scores.* Unpublished PhD Thesis, Lancaster University, UK.

Barkaoui, K. (2016). *Examining the Cognitive Processes Engaged by Aptis Writing Task 4 on Paper and on the Computer.* Research Report AR-A/2016/1. London: British Council. Accessed 14 September 2016 from: https://www.britishcouncil.org/sites/default/files/barkaoui_layout.pdf.

Barnes, D. and Seed, J. (1981). *Seals of Approval: An Analysis of English Examinations at Sixteen Plus.* Unpublished PhD Thesis, School of Education, University of Leeds, UK.

Belyaeva, Y. (2001). St Petersburg Examination Project (SPEX). *Language Testing Update* 29: 32–33.

Bentall, C. (2003). *Communication and Teachers' Learning during Training: A Case Study of the Secondary and Technical English Project, Mozambique.* Unpublished PhD Thesis, University of London, Institute of Education Lifelong Education and International Development.

Berry, V. and Nakatsuhara, F. (2015). *Exploring Performance across Two Delivery Modes for the IELTS Speaking Test – Face-to-Face and Computer Delivery Using Zoom – Report of Data Collection and Initial Score Analysis from the Follow-up Study in Shanghai, PRC.* Report delivered to the IELTS Partners, June 2015.

Berry, V. and O'Sullivan, B. (2016a). Language Standards for Medical Practice in the UK: Issues of Fairness and Quality for All. In C. Docherty and F. Barker (eds.), *Language Assessment for Multilingualism, Proceedings of the ALTE Paris Conference, April 2014*, Studies in Language Testing Volume 44 (pp. 268–285). Cambridge: UCLES/Cambridge University Press.

Berry, V. and O'Sullivan, B. (2016b). Setting Language Standards for International Medical Graduates. In J. Banerjee and D. Tsagari, *Contemporary Second Language Assessment* (Chapter 11) London: Continuum.

Berry, V., O'Sullivan, B., Schmitt, D. and Taylor, L. (2014). *Assessment Literacy: Bridging the Gap between Needs and Resources.* Panel discussion at IATEFL Conference, Harrogate, April 2014. Published in *Conference Selections IATEFL 2014.* Accessed 16 July 2016 from: http://edition.pagesuite-professional.co.uk/launch.aspx?pnum=9andeid=345a9f98-9589-491c-b93f-61b6d05c7ecf.

Bowers, R. (1983). Project Planning and Performance. In C.J. Brumfit (ed.), *Language Teaching Projects for the Third World* (pp. 99–120). ELT Documents 116. London: British Council.

Bozok, S. and Hughes, A. (eds.) (1987). *Proceedings of the Seminar, Testing English Beyond the High School, 9–11 May 1984.* Boğaziçi University Publications.

Brew, A. (1980). Responses of Overseas Students to Differing Teaching Styles. In G.M. Greenall and J.E. Price (eds.), *Study Modes and Academic Development of Overseas Students* (pp. 115–125). ELT Documents 109. London: British Council.

British Council (1950). *A Report on the British Council's Summer Conference held Between 3rd–13th May 1950 at the Government House, Mahableshwar, India.* London: British Council.

British Council (1975). *English for Academic Study with Special Reference to Science and Technology: Problems and Perspectives.* ETIC Occasional Paper. London: British Council.

British Council (1978a). *English for Specific Purposes.* ELT Documents 101. London: British Council.

British Council (1978b). *Pre-Sessional Courses for Overseas Students.* ETIC Occasional Paper. London: British Council.

British Council (1979a). *Seminar on ELT Course Design. Beyond Munby and into the Gap – Further Reflections on Course Design.* 30 July–10 August 1979 at Dunford House, Midhurst, Sussex. London: British Council.

British Council (1979b). *Testing Communicative Competence.* Report on a Workshop held at the British Council Centre, Hong Kong. London: British Council.
British Council (1980a). *Communicative Methodology.* Dunford House Seminar Report. London: British Council.
British Council (1980b). *Projects in Materials Design.* London: British Council.
British Council (1981a). *Survey of the Factors Affecting the Performance of O.D.A.-Sponsored Study Fellows.* London: English Language Division, British Council.
British Council (1981b). *Seminar on Design Evaluation and Testing in English Language Projects.* 27 July to 6 August 1981, Dunford House, Midhurst, Sussex. London: British Council.
British Council (1986). *Appropriate Methodology.* Dunford House Seminar Report. London: British Council.
British Council (1987). *ELT and Development: The Place of English Language Teaching in Aid Programmes.* Dunford House Seminar Report. London: British Council.
British Council (1989). *Dunford Seminar Report 1988: ELT in Development Aid: Defining Aims and Measuring Results.* London: British Council.
British Council (1991). *Dunford Seminar Report 1990: Training for Sustainability of ELT Aid Projects.* London: British Council.
British Council (1992). *Dunford Seminar Report 1991: The Social and Economic Impact of ELT in Development.* London: British Council.
British Council (1993). *Annual Report and Accounts 1992/93.* London: British Council.
British Council (1996). *Report of the Baseline Study: The Assessment of English in Secondary Schools.* London: British Council.
British Council (2007a). *Project Status Report: September.* Internal Mimeo. London: British Council.
British Council (2007b). *Project Status Report: October.* Internal Mimeo, London: British Council.
British Council (2007c). *Project Status Report: November.* Internal Mimeo. London: British Council.
British Council (2007d). *Project Status Report: December.* Internal Mimeo. London: British Council.
British Council (2008a). *Project Status Report: February.* Internal Mimeo. London: British Council.
British Council (2008b). *Project Status Report: July.* Internal Mimeo. London: British Council.
British Council (2009a). *Strategic Review: Exams Summary.* Internal Report, March 2009. London: British Council.
British Council (2009b). Exams Strategy (Kimberly Green). *EandE Briefing*, April 2009. London: British Council.
British Council (2010a). *Teaching and Exams: Business Plan 2010–2012 (Business Development Manager Team).* Internal Report. London: British Council.

British Council (2010b). *Business Area Summary: English*. Internal Report. London: British Council.

British Council (2013a). *The English Effect: The Impact of English, What It's Worth to the UK and Why It Matters to the World*. London: British Council. Accessed 20 September 2016 from: https://www.britishcouncil.org/sites/default/files/english-effect-report-v2.pdf.

British Council (2013b). *Can English Medium Work for Pakistan? Lessons from Punjab*. PEELI Project Report. Islamabad: British Council. Accessed 16 July 2016 from: https://www.britishcouncil.pk/sites/default/files/peeli_report_0.pdf.

British Council and ECLD (1978). *ESP Course Design Seminar*. Seminar Report, 28 June–8 July 1978, Dunford House, Midhurst, Sussex. London: British Council.

British Council IELTS (2016). I'm leaving to study abroad and packing my suitcase with... The Global Study Award!: Announcing the winners of Round 2 of the Global Study Awards. Press Release, 31 August 2016.

Brooks, L. (2003). Converting an Observation Checklist for Use with the IELTS Speaking Test. *Research Notes* 11: 20–21.

Brooks, N. (1960). *Language and Language Learning: Theory and Practice*. New York: Harcourt, Brace.

Brown, A. and Hill, K. (1998). Interviewer Style and Candidate Performance in the IELTS Oral Interview. In S. Woods (ed.), *IELTS Research Reports 1* (pp. 1–19). Sydney: ELICOS.

Brumfit, C.J. (1983). *Language Teaching Projects for the Third World*. ELT Documents 116. London: British Council.

Brumfit, C.J. and Johnson, K. (eds.) (1979). *The Communicative Approach to Language Teaching*. Oxford: Oxford University Press.

Bruner, J.S. (1975). Language as an Instrument of Thought. In A. Davies (ed.), *Problems of Language Learning* (pp. 61–68). London: Heinemann.

Brunfaut, T. and McCray, G. (2015). *Looking into Test Takers' Cognitive Process while Completing a Reading Task: A Mixed-Methods Eye-Tracking and Stimulated Recall Study*. Research Study AR-G/2015/001. London: British Council. Accessed 16 July 2016 from: https://www.britishcouncil.org/sites/default/files/brunfaut_and_mccray_report_final_0.pdf.

Brutt-Giffler, J. (2002). *World English: A Study in Its Development*. Clevedon: Multilingual.

Buck, G. (2001). *Assessing Listening*. Cambridge: Cambridge University Press. https://doi.org/10.1017/CBO9780511732959

Burns, D.G. (ed.) (1965). *Travelling Scholars: An Enquiry into the Adjustment and Attitudes of Overseas Students Holding Commonwealth Bursaries in England and Wales*. Slough: National Foundation for Educational Research.

Canale, M. and Swain, S. (1980). Theoretical Bases of Communicative Approaches to Second Language Teaching and Testing. *Applied Linguistics* 1(1): 1–47. https://doi.org/10.1093/applin/1.1.1

Candlin, C.N., Kirkwood, J.M. and Moore, H.M. (1975). Developing Study Skills in English. In British Council, *English for Academic Study with Special Reference to*

Science and Technology. Problems and Perspectives (pp. 50–69). ETIC Occasional Paper. London: British Council. Accessed 20 September 2016 from: https://www.teachingenglish.org.uk/sites/teacheng/files/F044%20ELT-19%20English%20for%20Academic%20Study_v3.pdf.

Candlin, C.N., Kirkwood, J.M. and Moore, H.M. (1978). Study Skills in English: Theoretical Issues and Practical Problems. In R. Mackay and A.J. Mountford (eds.), *English for Specific Purposes: A Case Study Approach* (pp. 190–219). London: Longman.

Carroll, B.J. (1969). *The Bridge Intensive Course for Indian Students of English*. Madras: Indian Branch, Oxford University Press.

Carroll, B.J. (1978). *An English Language Testing Service: Specifications*. London: British Council.

Carroll, B.J. (1980). *Testing Communicative Performance: An Interim Study*. Oxford: Pergamon.

Carroll, B.J. (1981). Specifications for an English Language Testing Service. In J.C. Alderson and A. Hughes (eds.), *Issues in Language Testing* (pp. 66–110). ELT Documents 111. London: British Council.

Carroll, B.J. (1983). Issues in the Testing of Language for Specific Purposes. In A. Hughes and D. Porter (eds.), *Current Developments in Language Testing* (pp. 109–114). London: Academic Press.

Carroll, B.J. (1985). Second Language Performance Testing for University and Professional Contexts. In P.C. Hauptman, R. LeBlanc and M.B. Wesche (eds.), *Second Language Performance Testing* (pp. 73–88). Ottawa: University of Ottawa Press.

Carroll, J.B. (1961/1972). *Fundamental Considerations in Testing for English Language Proficiency of Foreign Students*. Paper presented at the Conference on Testing the English Proficiency of Foreign Students, Washington, DC, 11–12 May 1961. Reprinted in H.B. Allen and R.N. Campbell (eds.), *Teaching English as a Second Language: A Book of Readings* (pp. 313–321). New York: McGraw Hill.

CBSE-ELT (1997). *Curriculum Implementation Study: Final Report*. Hyderabad, India: Central Institute of English and Foreign Languages.

Chan, S.H.C. (2013). *Establishing the Validity of Reading-into-Writing Test Tasks for the UK Academic Context*. Unpublished PhD Thesis, University of Bedfordshire, UK.

Chaplen, E.F. (1970). *The Identification of Non-Native Speakers of English Likely to Under-Achieve in University Courses Through Inadequate Command of the Language*. Unpublished PhD Thesis, University of Manchester, UK.

Charge, N. and Taylor, L. (1997). Recent Developments in IELTS. *English Language Teaching Journal* 51(4): 374–380. https://doi.org/10.1093/elt/51.4.374

Cheung, V.K.C. (1978). *Testing the English Language Proficiency of Overseas Post-Graduate Students – A Tentative Model*. Unpublished MA Dissertation, University of Exeter, UK.

Churchill, W.S. (1943). Common Tongue a Basis for Common Citizenship. *Vital Speeches of the Day* IX: 713–715.

Clapham, C.M. (1981). Reaction to the Carroll Paper (1). In J.C. Alderson and A. Hughes (eds.), *Issues in Language Testing* (pp. 111–116). ELT Documents 111. London: British Council.

Clapham, C.M. (1996). *The Development of IELTS, Studies in Language Testing 4*. Cambridge: UCLES/Cambridge University Press.

Clapham, C.M. (1997). The Academic Modules: Reading. In C.M. Clapham and J.C. Alderson (eds.), *IELTS Research Reports 3* (pp. 49–69). Cambridge: British Council/UCLES/IDP Education Australia.

Clapham, C.M. and Alderson, J.C. (eds.) (1997). *IELTS Research Reports 3, Constructing and Trialling the IELTS Test*. Cambridge: British Council/UCLES/IDP Education Australia; London: IELTS Partners.

Coleman, H. (2010). *The English Language in Development*. London: British Council.

Cooper, A.M. (2009). *Personal History of the Development of IELTS in Australia*. Unpublished Mimeo sent to authors November 2009.

Council of Europe (COE) (2001). *Common European Framework of Reference for Languages: Learning, Teaching, Assessment*. Cambridge: Cambridge University Press.

Cowie, A.P. and Heaton, J.B. (eds.) (1977). *English for Academic Purposes: Papers on the Language Problems of Overseas Students in the UK*. University of Reading: British Association of Applied Linguistics/SELMOUS.

Criper, C. and Davies, A. (1988). *ELTS Research Report 1(i): ELTS Validation Project Report*. Cambridge: British Council/UCLES.

Crossey, M. (2008). English for Global Peacekeeping, *Current Issues in Language Planning* 9(2): 207–218. https://doi.org/10.1080/14664200802139448

Crossey, M. (2009). The Role of Micro-Politics in Multinational, High-Stakes Language Assessment Systems. In J.C. Alderson (ed.), *The Politics of Language Education* (pp. 147–165). Bristol: Multilingual Matters.

Crossey, M. (2012). Peacekeeping English in Poland. In C. Tribble (ed.), *Managing Change in English Language Teaching* (pp. 93–97). London: British Council.

Crystal, D. (1997). *English as a Global Language*. Cambridge: Cambridge University Press.

Cumming, A., Grant, L., Mulcahy-Ernt, P. and Powers, D. (2004). A Teacher-Verification Study of Speaking and Writing Prototype Tasks for a New TOEFL. *Language Testing* 21(2): 107–145. https://doi.org/10.1191/0265532204lt278oa

Cumming, A., Kantor, R., Baba, K., Eedosy, U., Eouanzoui, K. and James, M. (2005). Differences in Written Discourse in Independent and Integrated Prototype Tasks for Next Generation TOEFL. *Assessing Writing* 10: 5–43. https://doi.org/10.1016/j.asw.2005.02.001

Daniel, N. (1975). *The Cultural Barrier*. Edinburgh: Edinburgh University Press.

Davidson, M. and Pollock, A. (2011). Foreword in *IELTS Research Reports 11*. Accessed 16 July 2016 from: http://www.ielts.org/researchers/research/volume_11.aspx.

Davies, A. (1965a). *Proficiency in English as a Second Language*. Unpublished PhD Thesis, University of Birmingham, UK.

Davies, A. (1965b). *English Proficiency Test Battery, Form 'B'*. London: British Council.
Davies, A. (1967). The English Proficiency of Overseas Students. *British Journal of Educational Psychology* 37(2): 165–174. https://doi.org/10.1111/j.2044-8279.1967.tb01925.x
Davies, A. (ed.) (1968). *Language Testing Symposium. A Psycholinguistic Approach.* London: Oxford University Press.
Davies, A. (ed.) (1975). *Problems of Language Learning.* London: Heinemann.
Davies, A. (1977). Do Foreign Students Have Problems? In A.P. Cowie and J.B. Heaton (eds.) (1977). *English for Academic Purposes* (pp. 34–46). University of Reading: BAAL/SELMOUS.
Davies, A. (1978). Language Testing. Survey Article Parts I and II. *Language Teaching and Linguistics Abstracts* 113(4): 145–159 and 215–231.
Davies, A. (1981). A Review of Communicative Syllabus Design. *TESOL Quarterly* 15(3): 332–338. https://doi.org/10.2307/3586758
Davies, A. (1983). The Validity of Concurrent Validation. In A. Hughes and D. Porter (eds.), *Current Developments in Language Testing* (pp. 141–146). London: Academic Press.
Davies, A. (1984). Validating Three Tests of English Language Proficiency. *Language Testing* 1: 50–69. https://doi.org/10.1177/026553228400100105
Davies, A. (2008). *Assessing Academic English: Testing English Proficiency 1950–1989 – The IELTS Solution.* Studies in Language Testing 23. Cambridge: Cambridge University Press and Cambridge ESOL.
Davies, A. and Alderson, J.C. (1977). *Report to the British Council on the Construction of the 'D' Version of the English Proficiency Test Battery.* Edinburgh: Department of Linguistics, University of Edinburgh, UK.
Davies, A. and Moller, A.D. (1973). *The English Proficiency of Foreign Students in Higher Education (non-University) in Scotland. A Report to the Scottish Education Department.* Edinburgh: Department of Linguistics, University of Edinburgh, UK.
De Quincey, T. (1907, originally serialized in *Tait's Edinburgh Magazine* 1848). *Reminiscences of the English Lake Poets.* London: J.M. Dent and Sons, Ltd.
Donaldson, F. (1984). *The British Council: The First Fifty Years.* London: Jonathan Cape.
Dudley-Evans, A. (1988). *Developments in English for Specific Purposes: A Multi-Disciplinary Approach.* Cambridge: Cambridge University Press.
Dudley-Evans, T. and St John, M. (1998). *Developments in English for Specific Purposes: A Multi-Disciplinary Approach.* Cambridge: Cambridge University Press.
Dunlea, J. (2016). *Validating a Set of Japanese EFL Proficiency Tests: Demonstrating Locally Designed Tests Meet International Standards.* Unpublished PhD Thesis, University of Bedfordshire, UK.
Dunlea, J., Dunn, K., Fairbairn, J. and Spiby, R. (2016). *Aptis 2nd Annual Operating Report: Overview and Commentary.* Internal Report. London: British Council.

Dunlop, F. (1966). *Europe's Guests, Students and Trainees: A Survey on the Welfare of Foreign Students and Trainees in Europe.* Strasbourg: Council of Cultural Cooperation of the Council of Europe.

Dunne, R.A. (2007). The EXAVER Project: Conception and Development. *MEXTESOL Journal* 31(7): 23–30.

Eastment, D. (1982). *The Policies and Position of the British Council from the Outbreak of War to 1950.* Unpublished PhD Thesis, University of Leeds, UK.

Edwards, P.J. (1978). *The Problems of Communication Facing Overseas Nurses in Training in England and Wales.* Unpublished PhD Thesis, University of London, UK.

Fairbairn, J. (2015). *Maintaining Marking Consistency in a Large Scale International Test: The Aptis Experience.* Poster presented at the EALTA Conference, Copenhagen.

Fairbairn, J. (2016). *Automated Rating Research Agenda.* Internal Report. London: British Council.

Fick, J.C. (1793). *Praktische englische Sprachlehre für Deutsche beyderley Geschlechts. Nach der in Meidingers französichen Grammatik befolgten Methode. [Practical English Language Textbook for Germans of Both Sexes. Following the Method Used in Meidinger's French Grammar].* Erlangen: Walther.

Field, J. (2015a). *Aptis Test of Listening: Final Report on Revision Project with Recommendations.* Internal Report. London: British Council.

Field, J. (2015b). The Impact of Single and Double Play on Candidate Behaviour in Tests of L2 Listening. Research Report AR-G/2015/003. London: British Council. Accessed 16 July 2016 from: https://www.britishcouncil.org/sites/default/files/field_layout.pdf.

Field, J. and Tucker, J. (2017). *Assessing Listening.* British Council Monograph Series. Sheffield: Equinox.

Fisher, A. (2009). *A Story of Engagement: The British Council 1934–2009.* London: The British Council.

Fries, C.C. and Lado, R. (1962). *English Sentence Patterns: Understanding and Producing Grammatical Structures.* Ann Arbor: University of Michigan Press.

Foulkes, J. (1997). The General Modules: Listening. In C.M. Clapham and J.C. Alderson (eds.), *IELTS Research Reports 3* (pp. 3–13). London: IELTS Partners.

Further Education Staff College (1971). *Study Conference 70/50A. Overseas Students in F.E. Colleges.* Further Education Staff College, Coombe Lodge, Bristol Report 4/4.

García Sánchez, M.E. (ed.) (2001). *Present and Future Trends in TEFL.* Almería: Universidad de Almería

Geoghegan, G. (1983). *Language Problems of Non-Native Speakers of English at Cambridge University.* Cambridge: Bell Educational Trust.

Geranpayeh, A. and Taylor, L. (2013). *Examining Listening: Research and Practice in Assessing Second Language Listening.* Studies in Language Testing 35. Cambridge: UCLES/Cambridge University Press.

Goonetillike, V., Samarasinghe, C., Senaratne, D. and Sinhalage, S. (1988). *An Evaluation of the National Certificate in English, 1987.* Colombo: National Institute of Education.

Grabe, W. and Stoller, F.L. (2002). *Teaching and Researching Reading.* London: Longman.

Graddol, D. (1997). *The Future of English?* London: British Council.

Graddol, D. (2006). *English Next: Why Global English May Mean the End of English as a Foreign Language.* London: The British Council.

Green, A.B. (2007). *IELTS Washback in Context: Preparation for Academic Writing in Higher Education.* Studies in Language Testing 25. Cambridge: Cambridge University Press.

Green, A.B. (2012). *Language Functions Revisited: Theoretical and Empirical Bases for Language Construct Definition Across the Ability Range.* Cambridge: Cambridge University Press.

Green, R. (2006). *Review of Placement Testing at Four British Council Teaching Centres.* Internal Mimeo. London: British Council.

Green, R. and Wall, D. (2005). Language Testing in the Military: Problems, Politics and Progress. *Language Testing* 22(3): 379–398. https://doi.org/10.1191/0265532205lt314oa

Greenall, G.M. and Price, J.E. (eds.) (1980). *Study Modes and Academic Development of Overseas Students.* ELT Documents 109. London: British Council.

Griffin, P. and Gillis, S. (1997). A Cross National Investigation. In C.M. Clapham and J.C. Alderson (eds.), *IELTS Research Reports 3* (pp. 109–124). London: IELTS Partners.

Haigh, A. (1974). *Cultural Diplomacy in Europe.* Strasbourg: Council of Europe.

Halliday M.A., McIntosh A. and Strevens, P. (1964). *The Linguistic Sciences and Language Teaching.* London: Longman.

Hamp-Lyons, L. (1985). *Assessment Guide for M2 Writing.* Cambridge: UCLES/British Council ELTS.

Hamp-Lyons, L. (1986a). *Testing Second Language Writing in Academic Settings.* Unpublished PhD Thesis, University of Edinburgh, UK.

Hamp-Lyons, L. (1986b). Testing Writing across the Curriculum. *Papers in Applied Linguistics*, Michigan (PALM), 2(1): 16–29.

Hamp-Lyons, L. (1987a). *Assessment Guide for M2 Writing.* Cambridge: British Council ELTS/UCLES.

Hamp-Lyons, L. (ed.) (1987b). Performance Profiles for Academic Writing. In K.M. Bailey, T.L. Dale and R.T. Clifford (eds.), *Language Testing Research: Selected Papers from the 1986 Colloquium* (pp. 78–92). Monterey, CA: Defense language Institute.

Hamp-Lyons, L. (1989). *IELTS Assessment Guide for the Writing Test.* Melbourne: IDP Education Australia.

Hamp-Lyons, L. (1991). *Assessing Second Language Writing in Academic Contexts.* Norwood, NJ: Ablex Publishing.

Hamp-Lyons, L. and Clapham, C. (1997). The Academic Modules – Writing. In C. Clapham and J.C. Alderson (eds.), *IELTS Research Reports 3* (pp. 69–80). Cambridge: British Council/UCLES/IDP Education Australia.

Hasselgreen, A. and Caudwell, G. (2016). *Assessing the Language of Young Learners.* Sheffield: Equinox.

Haug, U.A. (1981). *Student Selection with Particular Reference to Applicants Whose Native Language is Not English.* Unpublished PhD Thesis, Polytechnic of Central London in collaboration with London University.

Hawkey, R. (1977). Communication Needs Profile for an English for Business Studies Students. Reproduced in B. Carroll (1980), *Testing Communicative Performance: An Interim Study* (pp. 106–122). Oxford: Pergamon.

Hawkey, R. (1978). *English for Special Purposes.* London: British Council English Teaching Centre.

Hawkey, R. (1982). *An Investigation of Inter-Relationships between Cognitive/ Affective and Social Factors and Language Learning. A Longitudinal Study of 27 Overseas Students Using English in Connection with Their Training in the United Kingdom.* Unpublished PhD Thesis, University of London, UK.

Hawkey, R. (2005). *A Modular Approach to Testing English Language Skills: The Development of the Certificates in English Language Skills (CELS) Examinations.* Studies in Language Testing 16. Cambridge: Cambridge University Press.

Hawkey, R. (2006). *Impact Theory and Practice: Studies of the IELTS Test and Progetto Lingue 2000.* Studies in Language Testing 24. Cambridge: Cambridge University Press.

Hawkey, R. (2009). *Examining FCE and CAE: Key Issues and Recurring Themes in Developing the First Certificate in English and Certificate in Advanced English Exams.* Studies in Language Testing 28. Cambridge: Cambridge University Press.

Hawkey, R. and Milanovic, M. (2013). *Cambridge English Exams – The First Hundred Years. A History of English Language Assessment from the University of Cambridge 1913–2013.* Cambridge: Cambridge University Press.

Hawkins, J. and Buttery, P. (2010). Criterial Features in Learner Corpora: Theory and Illustrations. *English Profile Journal*, Vol. 1, Cambridge University Press. https://doi.org/10.1017/S2041536210000103

Heaton, J.B. (1975a). *Writing English Language Tests.* London: Longman.

Heaton, J.B. (1975b). *Studying in English.* London: Longman.

Heaton, J.B. and Pugh, A.K. (1974). *A Study of the Relationship between Scores Obtained by Overseas Students on a Test of English Proficiency and the Examination Results in Their University Courses.* Mimeo, University of Leeds, UK.

Hebron, C.C. (1967). *The Performance of Overseas Students in Rutherford College.* Mimeo, University of Newcastle-upon-Tyne, UK.

Henning, G. (1988). An American View on ELTS. In A. Hughes, D. Porter and C.J. Weir (eds.), *ELTS Research Report 1(ii) ELTS Validation Project: Proceedings of a Conference Held to Consider the ELTS Validation Project Report* (pp. 84–92). Cambridge: UCLES.

Hindmarsh, R.X. (1977). An Overview of English Language Testing Overseas. In A.P. Cowie, and J.B. Heaton (eds.), *English for Academic Purposes* (pp. 21–24). University of Reading: BAAL/SELMOUS.

Holden, S. (ed.) (1977). *English for Specific Purposes*. London: Modern English Publications Ltd.

Holes, C.D. (1972). *An Investigation into Some Aspects of the English Language Problems of Two Groups of Overseas Post-Graduate Students at Birmingham University*. Unpublished MA Dissertation, University of Birmingham, UK.

Home Office (Cmnd. 4298) (1970). *Instructions to Immigration Officers. Commonwealth Immigrants Acts 1962 and 1968*. London: HMSO.

Hornby, A.S. (1946a). *First Issue of English Language Teaching*. London: Oxford University Press.

Hornby, A.S. (1946b). Linguistic Pedagogy: I. The Doctrines of de Saussure. *English Language Teaching* 1(1): 7–11. https://doi.org/10.1093/elt/1.1.7

Hornby, A.S. (1946c). Linguistic Pedagogy: II. The Beginning Stage. *English Language Teaching* 1(2): 36–39. https://doi.org/10.1093/elt/1.2.36

Howatt, A.P.R. (1997). Talking Shop: Transformation and Change in ELT. *English Language Teaching Journal* 51(3): 263–268. https://doi.org/10.1093/elt/51.3.263

Howatt, A.P.R. and Widdowson, H.G. (2004). *A History of English Language Teaching*, second edition. Oxford: Oxford University Press.

Howe, P. (1980). *English Language Entrance Examination*. Mimeo, University College at Buckingham, UK.

Hughes, A. (1987). A Review of the English Proficiency Test Battery. In J.C. Alderson, K. Krahnke and C.W. Stansfield (eds.), *Reviews of English Language Proficiency Tests* (pp. 31–32). Washington, DC: Teachers of English to Speakers of Other Languages.

Hughes, A. (ed.) (1988). *Testing English for University Study*. ELT Documents 127. Oxford: Modern English Publications Ltd.

Hughes, A. (2003). *Testing for Language Teachers*, second edition. Cambridge: Cambridge University Press.

Hughes, A., Porter, D. and Weir, C.J. (eds.) (1988). *ELTS Research Report 1(ii) ELTS Validation Project: Proceedings of a Conference Held to Consider the ELTS Validation Project Report*. Cambridge: UCLES.

Hughes, M. (2004). *British Foreign Secretaries in an Uncertain World, 1919–1939*. London: Routledge.

Hunter, D. (2009). *Communicative Language Teaching and the ELT Journal: A Corpus-Based Approach to the History of a Discourse*. Unpublished PhD Thesis, Centre of Applied Linguistics, University of Warwick, UK.

Hunter, D. and Smith, R. (2012). Unpackaging the Past: CLT Through ELTJ Keywords. *ELT Journal* 66(4): 430–439. https://doi.org/10.1093/elt/ccs036

Hutchinson, T. and Waters, A. (1981). Performance and Competence in English for Specific Purposes. *Applied Linguistics* 2(1): 56–59. https://doi.org/10.1093/applin/2.1.56

Hutchinson, T. and Waters, A. (1987). *English for Specific Purposes: A Learning-Centred Approach.* Cambridge: Cambridge University Press. https://doi.org/10.1017/CBO9780511733031

Hyatt, D. and Brooks, G. (2009). *Investigating Stakeholders' Perceptions of IELTS as an Entry Requirement for Higher Education in the UK: IELTS Research Reports 10.* Melbourne: IDP, IELTS Australia and British Council.

Ingram, D. and Wylie, E. (1997). The General Modules-Speaking. In J. Clapham and J.C. Alderson (eds.), *IELTS Research Reports 3* (pp. 14–29). Cambridge: British Council/UCLES/IDP Education Australia.

Ingram, E. (1964). *English Language Battery (ELBA).* Edinburgh: University of Edinburgh, Department of Linguistics.

Ingram, E. (1973). English Standards for Foreign Students. *University of Edinburgh Bulletin* 9(12): 4–5.

Isaacs, T. (2016). *Automated Assessment of Speaking: Literature Review on Automated Rating Technology for Speaking Tests for the British Council.* Commissioned Report. London: British Council.

James, K. (1980). Survey of University of Manchester Overseas Postgraduate Students' Initial Level of Competence in English and Their Subsequent Academic Performance: Calendar Year 1977. In G.M. Greenall and J.E. Price (eds.), *Study Modes and Academic Development of Overseas Students* (pp. 126–132). ELT Documents 109. London: British Council.

Johns, A.M. (1981). Necessary English: A Faculty Survey. *TESOL Quarterly* 15(1): 51–57. https://doi.org/10.2307/3586373

Johns, C.M. and Johns, T.F. (1977a). Seminar Discussion Strategies. In A.P. Cowie, and J.B. Heaton (eds.), *English for Academic Purposes* (pp. 99–107). University of Reading: BAAL/SELMOUS.

Johns, T.F. (1980). The Text and Its Message: An Approach to the Teaching of Reading Strategies for Students of Development Administration. In H. von Faber (ed.), *Leserverstehen im Fremdensprachenunterricht* (pp. 147–170). Munich: Goethe Institut.

Johns, T.F. and Johns, C.M. (1977b). The Current Programme of Materials Development in English for Academic Purposes at the Universities of Birmingham and Aston. In A.P. Cowie and J.B. Heaton (eds.), *English for Academic Purposes* (pp. 127–130). University of Reading: BAAL/SELMOUS.

Johnson, K. (1977a). Why Are Foreign Students Incoherent? In S. Holden (ed.), *English for Specific Purposes* (pp. 68–72). London: Modern English Publications Ltd.

Johnson, K. (1977b). Teaching Virtuous Writing. In S. Holden (ed.), *English for Specific Purposes* (pp. 17–20). London: Modern English Publications Ltd.

Johnson, K. (1981). *Communicate in Writing: Teachers Book.* London: Longman.

Jordan, R.R. (1977a). Identification of Problems and Needs: A Student Profile. In A.P. Cowie and J.B. Heaton (eds.), *English for Academic Purposes* (pp. 12–20). University of Reading: BAAL/SELMOUS.

Jordan, R.R. (1977b). Study Skills and Pre-Sessional Courses. In S. Holden (ed.), *English for Specific Purposes* (pp. 24–26). London: Modern English Publications Ltd.

Jordan, R.R. (2002). The growth of EAP in Britain. *Journal of English for Academic Purposes* 1: 69–78. https://doi.org/10.1016/S1475-1585(02)00004-8

Jordan, R.R. and Mackay, R. (1973). A Survey of the Spoken English Problems of Overseas Post-Graduates at the Universities of Manchester and Newcastle-upon-Tyne. *Journal of Durham and Newcastle Institutes of Education* 25: 125.

Kaplan, R.B. (1966). Cultural Thought Patterns in Intercultural Education. *Language Learning* 16(1–2): 11–25.

Kay, T.R. and Russette, B. (2000). Progression Analysis (PA): Investigating Writing Strategies at the Workplace. *Journal of Pragmatics* 35: 907–921.

Kelly, R. (1978). *On the Construct Validation of Comprehension Tests: An Exercise in Applied Linguistics*. Unpublished PhD Thesis, University of Queensland, Australia.

Kessel (van), T.M.C. (2011). Cultural Promotion and Imperialism: The Dante Alighieri Society and the British Council contesting the Mediterranean in the 1930s. Unpublished PhD Thesis, University of Amsterdam, Holland.

Khalifa, H. (1997). *A Study in the Construct Validation of the Reading Module of an EAP Proficiency Test Battery: Validation from a Variety of Perspectives*. Unpublished PhD Thesis, University of Reading, UK.

Khalifa, H. and Weir, C.J. (2009). *Examining Reading: Research and Practice in Assessing Second Language Reading*, Studies in Language Testing 29. Cambridge: Cambridge University Press.

Kirkpatrick, J.J. and Cureton, E.E. (1949). Vocabulary Item Difficulty and Word Frequency. *Journal of Applied Psychology* 33(4): 347–351. https://doi.org/10.1037/h0063369

Knoch, U., Fairbairn, J. and Huisman, A. (2015). *An Evaluation of the Effectiveness of Training Aptis Raters Online*. VS/2015/001. Accessed 16 July 2016 from: https://www.britishcouncil.org/sites/default/files/knoch_fairbairn_and_huisman_0.pdf.

Knoch, U., Fairbairn, J. and Huisman, A. (2016). An Evaluation of an Online Rater Training Program for the Speaking and Writing Sub-Tests of the Aptis Test. *Papers in Language Testing and Assessment* 5(1): 90–106.

Lado, R. (1961). *Language Testing: The Construction and Use of Foreign Language Tests*. New York: Longman.

Laing, A. (1971). *Common Study Difficulties of Overseas Students*. Coombe Lodge: Further Education Staff College.

Lambert, G.M. (1979). *English Language Testing Service Letter in Notes to Registrars and Secretaries* (pp. 1–8). London: Committee of Vice Chancellors and Principals.

Latham, H. (1877). *On the Action of Examinations Considered as a Means of Selection*. Cambridge: Deighton, Bell.

Lawrence, J. (2004 reprint of 1998 edition). *The Rise and Fall of the British Empire* (pp. 386–427). London: Abacus,

Lazaraton, A. (2002). *A Qualitative Approach to the Validation of Oral Language Tests*. Studies in Language Testing 14. Cambridge: Cambridge University Press.

Lee, M.Y., Abdella, M. and Burks, L.A. (1981). *Needs of Foreign Students from Developing Nations at U.S. Colleges and Universities*. Washington: NAFSA.

Leeper, R.A. (1935). British Culture Abroad. *Contemporary Review* 148: 201.

Lott, B. (1984). ELT and the British Council – The First Fifty Years. *ELT Journal* 38(4): 283–285. https://doi.org/10.1093/elt/38.4.283

Luxon, M. and Luxon, T. (1996). *The British Council Curriculum and Testing (CAT) Project, Kazakhstan*. Project Design Consultancy. London: British Council.

Mackay, R. and Mountford, A. (1973). A Programme in English for Post-Graduate Students in the Faculties of Science, Applied Sciences and Agriculture in the University of Newcastle-upon-Tyne. *Bulletin Pedagogique: Langues Vivantes* 15 (November): 9–38.

Mackay, R. and Mountford, A.J. (eds.) (1978). *English for Specific Purposes: A Case Study Approach*. London: Longman.

Mackenzie, J.G. (1977). Some English Language Problems of Latin-American Post-Graduate Students. In A.P. Cowie and J.B. Heaton (eds.), *English for Academic Purposes* (pp. 41–43). University of Reading: BAAL/SELMOUS.

Martens, K. and Marshall, S. (2003). International Organisations and Foreign Cultural Policy. A Comparative Analysis of the British Council, the Alliance Française and the Goethe-Institute. *Transnational Associations* 4: 261–272.

Martin, N. (2014). *Cultural Value at the British Council and BBC World Service: A Comparative Examination of Annual Reports, 1952–1978*. www.open.ac.uk.

Martins, A. and Green, R. (2001). *An Examination Handbook: English Grades 10 and 12*. Ministry of Education, Mozambique.

Mason, C. (1971). The Relevance of Intensive Training in English as a Foreign Language for University Students. *Language Learning* 21(2): 197–204. https://doi.org/10.1111/j.1467-1770.1971.tb00058.x

Mathew, R. (1997). *Final Report (A Summary): CBSE-ELT Curriculum Implementation Study*. Hyderabad, India: CIEFL Department of Evaluation.

Mbali, C. and Douglas, J. (2015). Evaluating Aptis Tests with Initial Teacher Training Students, In-Service Primary School Teachers and Hospitality Job-Seekers in Durban, South Africa. Research Report AR-G/2015/002. Accessed 16 July 2016 from: https://www.britishcouncil.org/sites/default/files/douglas_layout_3.pdf.

McDonough, F. (1998). *Neville Chamberlain, Appeasement and the British Road to War*. Manchester: Manchester University Press.

McEldowney, P. (1976). *Test in English (Overseas). The Position after Ten Years*. Occasional Paper 36. Manchester: Joint Matriculation Board.

Mead, R. (1981). Review of J. Munby's Communicative Syllabus Design. *Applied Linguistics* 3(1): 70–77.

Melissen, J. (ed.) (2005). *The New Public Diplomacy: Soft Power in International Relations*. Basingstoke: Palgrave Macmillan. https://doi.org/10.1057/9780230554931

Merrifield, G., GBM and Associates (2012). *An Impact Study into the Use of IELTS by Professional Associations and Registration Entities: Canada, the UK and Ireland.* Accessed 16 July 2016 from: www.ielts.org/PDF/vol11_report_1_an_impact_study.pdf.

Merrylees, B. and McDowell, C. (1999). An Investigation of Speaking Test Reliability with Particular Reference to Examiner Attitudes to the Speaking Test Format and Candidate/Examiner Discourse Produced. In R. Tulloh (ed.), *IELTS Research Reports 2.* Melbourne: IELTS Australia.

Messick, S.A. (1989). Validity. In R.L. Linn (ed.), *Educational Measurement*, 3rd edition (pp. 13–103). New York: Macmillan.

Moller, A.D. (1977). A Case for a Crude Test Overseas. In A.P. Cowie and J.B. Heaton (eds.), *English for Academic Purposes* (pp. 25–33). University of Reading: BAAL/SELMOUS.

Moller, A.D. (1981a). Assessing Proficiency in English for Use in Further Study. In J.A.S. Read (ed.), *Directions in Language Testing* (pp. 58–71). Anthology Series 9. Singapore: SEAMEO Regional Language Centre.

Moller, A.D. (1981b). Reaction to the Morrow Paper (2). In J.C. Alderson and A. Hughes (eds.), *Issues in Language Testing* (pp. 38–44). ELT Documents 111. London: The British Council.

Moller, A.D. (1982). *A Study in the Validation of Proficiency Tests of English as a Foreign Language.* Unpublished PhD Thesis, University of Edinburgh, UK.

Moller, A., Seaton, I. and McNeill, A. (1982). *A Guide to the Mini Platform Placement Test.* London: British Council.

Moore, T., Morton, J. and Price, S. (2010). *Construct Validity in the IELTS Academic Reading Test: A Comparison of Reading Requirements in IELTS Test Items and in University Study.* Unpublished IELTS Research Report. London and Melbourne: British Council/IDP Australia.

Morris, B.S. and I.O. Ajijola. (1967). *International Community?* London: National Union of Students.

Morrison, J.W. (1974). *An Investigation of Problems in Listening Comprehension Encountered by Overseas Students in the First Year of Post-Graduate Studies in Sciences in the University of Newcastle-upon-Tyne and the Implications for Teaching.* Unpublished MEd Thesis, University of Newcastle-upon-Tyne, UK.

Morrow, K.E. (1977). *Techniques of Evaluation for a Notional Syllabus.* London: The Royal Society of Arts.

Morrow, K.E. (1979). Communicative Language Testing: Revolution or Evolution. In C.J. Brumfit and K. Johnson (eds.), *The Communicative Approach to Language Teaching* (pp. 143–158). Oxford: Oxford University Press.

Morrow, K.E. and Johnson, K. (1977). Meeting Some Social Language Needs of Overseas Students. In A.P. Cowie and J.B. Heaton (eds.), *English for Academic Purposes* (pp. 53–68). University of Reading: BAAL/SELMOUS.

Munby, J.L. (1977). *Designing a Processing Model for Specifying Communicative Competence in a Foreign Language: A Study of the Relationship between*

Communication Needs and the English Required for Specific Purposes. Unpublished PhD Thesis, University of Essex, UK.

Munby, J.L. (1978). *Communicative Syllabus Design.* Cambridge: Cambridge University Press.

Nakatsuhara, F., Inoue, C., Berry, V. and Galaczi, E. (2015). *Exploring Performance across Two Delivery Modes for the Same L2 Speaking Test: Face-to-Face and Video Conferencing Delivery – A Preliminary Comparison of Test-Taker and Examiner Behaviour. IELTS Partnership Research Papers 1.* Accessed 20 August 2016 from: https://www.ielts.org/~/media/research-reports/ielts-partnership-research-paper-1.ashx.

Nakatsuhara, F., Inoue, C., Berry, V. and Galaczi, E. (2017). Exploring the Use of Video-Conferencing Technology in the Assessment of Spoken Language: A Mixed-Methods Study. *Language Assessment Quarterly* 14(1): 1–18. https://doi.org/10.1080/15434303.2016.1263637

National Association of Foreign Students' Advisers (NAFSA) (1961). *Research in Programs for Foreign Students.* NAFSA Studies and Papers: Research Series 2. Washington: NAFSA.

Nicolson, H. (1939). *Diplomacy.* London: Thornton Butterworth.

Nicolson, H. (1955). *The British Council 1934–1955, Twenty-first Anniversary Report.* London: British Council.

North, B., Ortega, A. and Sheehan, S. (2010). *British Council – EAQUALS Core Inventory for General English.* London and Zurich: British Council and EAQUALS.

Nye, J. (2004). *Soft Power: The Means to Success in World Politics.* New York: Public Affairs.

O'Sullivan, B. (2002). Learner Acquaintanceship and Oral Proficiency Test Pair-Task Performance. *Language Testing* 19(3): 277–295. https://doi.org/10.1191/0265532202lt205oa

O'Sullivan, B. (2006). *Issues in Testing Business English: The Revision of the Business English Certificates.* Studies in Language Testing Volume 17. Cambridge: Cambridge University Press.

O'Sullivan, B. (2007). *British Council Placement Test Bid.* London: Roehampton University.

O'Sullivan, B. (2010). *Speaking Specifications, October 2010.* Internal Report. London British Council.

O'Sullivan, B. (2011a). Language Testing. In J. Simpson (ed.), *Routledge Handbook of Applied Linguistics* (pp. 259–273). Oxford: Routledge.

O'Sullivan, B. (2011b). *Writing Task Ideas, February 2011.* Internal Report. London: British Council.

O'Sullivan, B. (2011c). Introduction – Professionalisation, Localisation and Fragmentation in Language Testing. In B. O'Sullivan (ed.), *Language Testing: Theory and Practice* (pp. 1–12). Oxford: Palgrave.

O'Sullivan, B. (2013a). Assessing Speaking. In A. Kunnan (ed.), *Wiley Companion to Language Assessment* (pp. 156–171). Oxford: Wiley. https://doi.org/10.1002/9781118411360.wbcla084

O'Sullivan, B. (2013b). Assessing Spoken Language: Scoring Validity. In D. Tsagari, S. Papadima-Sophocleous and S. Iannou-Georgiou (eds.), *International Experiences in Language Testing and Assessment* (pp. 261–274). Frankfurt: Peter Lang.

O'Sullivan, B. (2014). *Stakeholders and Consequence in Test Development and Validation.* Plenary Address at the Language Testing Forum, University of Southampton, November.

O'Sullivan, B. (2015a). *Aptis Test Development Approach.* Technical Report: TR/2015/001. London: British Council. Accessed 16 July 2016 from: https://www.britishcouncil.org/sites/default/files/tech_001_barry_osullivan_aptis_test_-_v5_0.pdf.

O'Sullivan, B. (2015b). *Assessment Research Group: Strategies and Activities, 2012–2015.* Internal Report. London: British Council.

O'Sullivan, B. (2015c). *Linking the Aptis Reporting Scales to the CEFR.* Technical Report: TR/2015/003. London: British Council. Accessed 16 July 2016 from: https://www.britishcouncil.org/sites/default/files/tech_003_barry_osullivan_linking_aptis_v4_single_pages_0.pdf.

O'Sullivan, B. (2016a). Validity, Validation and Development: Building and Operationalizing a Comprehensive Model. *Japanese Language Testing Association Journal*, pp. 25–33.

O'Sullivan, B. (2016b). Validity: What Is It and Who Is It for? In Y.-N. Leung (ed.), *Epoch Making in English Language Teaching and Learning* (pp. 201–222). Taipei: Crane Publishing Company Ltd.

O'Sullivan, B. and Berry, V. (2015). *Introducing Language Assessment.* Animated video series. British Council Online: https://www.britishcouncil.org/exam/aptis/research/projects/assessment-literacy.

O'Sullivan, B. and Dunlea, J. (2015). *Aptis General Technical Manual, Version 1.0.* Technical Report, TR/2015/005. London: British Council. Accessed 16 July 2016 from: https://www.britishcouncil.org/sites/default/files/aptis_general_technical_manual_v-1.0.pdf.

O'Sullivan, B. and Rugea, S. (2011a). *Review of the ILA Placement Test Usage.* Internal Report. London: British Council.

O'Sullivan, B. and Rugea, S. (2011b). *ILA Administration Review Project: Final Report.* Internal Report. London: British Council.

O'Sullivan, B. and Weir, C.J. (2011). Language Testing and Validation. In B. O'Sullivan (ed.), *Language Testing: Theory and Practice* (pp. 13–32). Oxford: Palgrave.

O'Sullivan, B., Weir, C.J. and Saville, N. (2002). Using Observation Checklists to Validate Speaking-Test Tasks. *Language Testing* 19(1): 33–56. https://doi.org/10.1191/0265532202lt219oa

O'Sullivan, B., Weir, C.J., Yan, J. and Bax, S. (2007). Does the Computer Make a Difference? Reactions of Candidates to a Computer Delivered versus Traditional Hand Written Academic Forms of the IELTS Writing Component. *IELTS Research Reports* 7: 311–347. London: The British Council.

Overseas Development Agency (1985). *Guide to the Key English Language Teaching (KELT) Scheme.* London: Overseas Development Agency.

Patel, M. (2016). *The Technical Feasibility of Remote Speaking Test Delivery*. Internal Report. London: British Council.
Pearson, I. (1988). Tests as Levers for Change. In D. Chamberlain and R. Baumgardner (eds.), *ESP in the Classroom: Practice and Evaluation* (pp. 84–93). London: Modern English Publications Ltd in association with The British Council.
Pennycook, A. (1994). *The Cultural Politics of English as a Foreign Language*. Harlow: Longman.
Perren, G.E. (1963a). *The Construction and Application of Some Experimental Tests of English Ability for Overseas Students in Britain*. Unpublished report of work carried out at the University of Manchester, 1958–60.
Perren, G.E. (1963b). *Linguistic Problems of Overseas Students in Britain*. ETIC Occasional Paper No. 3. London: British Council.
Phillips, L.R. (1956). Professor E.V. Gatenby, C.B.E., M.A. (Obituary). *English Language Teaching* 10(3): 87–90. https://doi.org/10.1093/elt/X.3.87
Phillipson, R. (1992). *Linguistic Imperialism*. Oxford: Oxford University Press.
Pickett, D. (1980). *Aspects of the Cambridge First Certificate in English Examination, 1975–1980*. Unpublished MA Dissertation. University of London, UK.
Pilliner, S. (1965). *A Comparison of Two English Language Proficiency Test Batteries*. University of Edinburgh: Department of Linguistics.
Pincas, A. (1995a). China. Sino-British Co-operation in ELT 1970–1993: Joint Ventures in Education Development. In A. Pincas (ed.), *Spreading English: ELT Projects in International Development* (pp. 1–16). Hertfordshire: Prentice Hall.
Pincas, A. (ed.) (1995b). *Spreading English: ELT Projects in International Development*. Hertfordshire: Prentice Hall.
Pizorn, K. and E. Nagy (2009). The Politics of Examination Reform in Central Europe. In J.C. Alderson (ed.), *The Politics of Language Education: Individuals and Institutions* (pp. 185–202). Bristol: Multilingual Matters.
Political and Economic Planning (P.E.P.) (1965). *New Commonwealth Students in Britain: With Special Reference to Students from East Africa*. London: Allen and Unwin.
Pollitt, A and Taylor, L. (2006). Cognitive Psychology and Reading Assessment. In M. Sainsbury, C. Harrison and A. Watts (eds.), *Assessing Reading: From Theories to Classrooms* (pp. 38–49). Slough: NFER.
Porter, D. and O'Sullivan, B. (1999). The Effect of Audience Age on Measured Written Performance. *System* 27(1): 65–77. https://doi.org/10.1016/S0346-251X(98)00050-5
Price, J.E. (1977a). *Information on Pre-Sessional English Language Courses in Britain Today*. Paper prepared for a 1977 SELMOUS Seminar.
Price, J.E. (1977b). Study Skills – With Special Reference to Seminar Strategies and One Aspect of Academic Writing. In S. Holden (ed.), *English for Specific Purposes* (pp. 25–30). London: Modern English Publications Ltd.
Price, J.E. (1980). The Structure of Post-Graduate Taught Courses in Engineering: Some Implications for Language Course Design. In G.M. Greenall and J.E. Price (eds.), *Study Modes and Academic Development of Overseas Students* (pp. 50–68). ELT Documents 109. London: British Council.

Raban, S. (2008). *Examining the World; A History of the University of Cambridge Local Examinations Syndicate.* Cambridge: Cambridge University Press.

Rea, P.M. (1978). Assessing Language as Communication. *University of Birmingham M.A.L.S. Journal, New Series* 3.

Rea-Dickins, P. and Germaine, K. (1993). *Evaluation (Language Teaching: A Scheme for Teacher Education).* Oxford: Oxford University Press.

Read, J.A.S. (2001). *Assessing Vocabulary.* Oxford: Oxford University Press.

Read, J.A.S. (ed.) (1981). *Directions in Language Testing.* Anthology Series 9. Singapore: SEAMEO Regional Language Centre.

Richterich, R. (1974). *Language Needs and Types of Adults.* ELT Documents 74/3. London: ETIC – British Council.

Riddle, M.F. (1978). *Test in English Language Performance.* Mimeo, Middlesex Polytechnic, UK.

Roach, J.O. (1929). *Memorandum of Reform,* Mimeo1/1d i, Cambridge Assessment Archives: Roach Papers.

Roach, J.O. (1945). *Report on Policy and Future Development.* Mimeo, Cambridge Assessment Archives: Roach Papers.

Roach, J.O. (1956). *Examinations as an Instrument of Cultural Policy.* Mimeo, Cambridge Assessment Archives: Roach Papers.

Roach, J.O. (1983). *'My Work' with the Local Examinations Syndicate 1925–45.* Cambridge Assessment Archives: Roach Papers.

Robinson, P. (1991). *ESP Today: A Practitioners' Guide.* New York: Prentice Hall International.

Rogers, S. (1977). The Communicative Needs of Some Overseas Post-Graduate Students. In A.P. Cowie and J.B. Heaton (eds.), *English for Academic Purposes* (pp. 34–36). University of Reading: BAAL/SELMOUS.

Royal Society of Arts (RSA) (1980). *Examinations in the Communicative Use of English as a Foreign Language: Specifications and Specimen Papers.* London: Royal Society of Arts.

Ryan, D.E. (2014). *Consider the Candidate: Using Test-Taker Feedback to Enhance Quality and Validity in Language Testing.* Paper presented at the 5th International Conference on Teaching English as a Foreign Language, 21–22 November, Lisbon, Portugal.

Ryan, M. (1979). *English for Academic Purposes.* Unpublished MA Dissertation, University of Wales Institute of Science and Technology (UWIST), UK.

Saville, N. (2003). The Process of Test Development and Revision within UCLES EFL. In C.J. Weir and M. Milanovic (eds.), *Continuity and Innovation: A History of the CPE Examination 1913–2002* (pp. 57–120). Studies in Language Testing 15. Cambridge: Cambridge University Press.

Saville, N. (2004). *The ESOL Test Development and Validation Strategy.* Internal Discussion Paper, UCLES.

Saville, N. (2009). *Developing a Model for Investigating the Impact of Language Assessment within Educational Contexts by a Public Examination Provider.* Unpublished PhD thesis, University of Bedfordshire, UK.

Scott, A. (2011). *Public Relations and the Making of Modern Britain: Stephen Tallents and the Birth of a Progressive Media Profession.* Manchester: Manchester University Press.

Seaton, I. (1981). *Background to the Specifications for an English Language Testing Service and Subsequent Developments.* In A.P. Alderson and A. Hughes (eds.), *Issues in Language Testing* (pp. 121–122). ELT Documents 111. London: The British Council.

Self, R. (2005). *The Neville Chamberlain Diary Letters: The Downing Street Years, 1934–1940,* Volume 4. London: Ashgate Publishing.

Self, R. (2006). *Neville Chamberlain: A Biography.* London: Ashgate Publishing.

Sen, A. (1970). *Problems of Overseas Students and Nurses.* Slough: National Foundation for Educational Research.

Shaw, A.M. (1976). *Approaches to a Communicative Syllabus in Foreign Language Curriculum Development.* Unpublished PhD Thesis, University of Essex, UK.

Shaw, S.D. and Falvey, P. (2008). *The IELTS Writing Assessment Revision Project.* University of Cambridge ESOL Examinations Research Reports Issue 1. Cambridge: Cambridge Assessment.

Shaw, S.D. and Weir, C.J. (2007). *Examining Writing: Research and Practice in Assessing Second Language Writing.* Studies in Language Testing 26. Cambridge: Cambridge University Press.

Sheehan, S. (2007a). *Brief History of the Placement Test Project.* British Council Internal Mimeo, October 2007.

Sheehan, S. (2007b). *Placement Testing in British Council Network of Teaching Centres.* British Council Internal Mimeo. London: British Council.

Shohamy, E. (2001). *The Power of Tests: A Critical Perspective on the Uses of Language Tests.* Harlow, England: Longman.

Shohamy, E. (2008). Introduction to Vol. 7: Language Testing and Assessment. In N.H. Hornberger (gen. ed), *Encyclopedia of Language and Education,* 2nd edition (pp. xiii–xxii). New York: Springer Science+Business Media.

Simpson, J. (2013). *Baseline Assessment of English Language Proficiency of Teachers in Rwanda.* Project Report. London: British Council.

Singh, A.K. (1963). *Indian Students in Britain.* New York: Asia Publishing House.

Skehan, P. (1988). Construct Validity. In A. Hughes, D. Porter and C.J. Weir (eds.), *ELTS Research Report 1(ii) ELTS Validation Project: Proceedings of a Conference Held to Consider the ELTS Validation Project Report* (pp. 26–31). Cambridge: UCLES.

Smith, R. (2004). *An Investigation into the Roots of ELT, with a Particular Focus on the Career and Legacy of Harold E. Palmer (1877–1949).* Unpublished PhD thesis, University of Edinburgh, UK.

Smith, R. (2005). General Introduction. In R. Smith (ed.), *Teaching English as a Foreign Language, 1936–1961: Foundations of ELT, Volume 1* (pp. xv–cxx). Abingdon: Routledge. https://doi.org/10.1039/9781847550729-00001

Smith, R. (2007). *The Origins of ELT Journal*. Oxford University Press ELT Journal website. Accessed 24 September 2016 from: http://www.oxfordjournals.org/eltj/about.html.
Smith, R. (forthcoming) *The British Council and ELT: Milestones, 1946–2016*. London: British Council.
Spolsky, B. (1968). Language Testing: The Problem of Validation. *TESOL Quarterly* 2: 88–94. https://doi.org/10.2307/3586083
Spolsky, B. (ed.) (1978). *Approaches in Language Testing. Advances in Language Testing, Series: 2*. Arlington, DC: Center for Applied Linguistics.
Spolsky, B. (1995). Obituary: J O Roach 1900–1995. *Language Testing Update* 18: 75–76.
Spöttl, C., Holzknecht, F., Eberharter, K., Kremmel, B. and Konrad, E. (2015). *Looking into Listening: Using Eye-Tracking to Establish the Cognitive Validity of the Aptis Listening Test*. Assessment Research Grant, British Council (publication forthcoming).
Stansfield, C.W. (ed.) (1986). *Towards Communicative Competence Testing: Proceedings of the Second TOEFL Invitational Conference*. TOEFL Research Report 21. Princeton, NJ: Educational Testing Service.
Stern, H.H. (1983). *Fundamental Concepts of Language Teaching*. Oxford: Oxford University Press.
Stevenson, R.W. (1974). *Welfare Problems Facing Overseas Students*. Edinburgh: University Students' Association.
Strevens, P.D. (1961). *Objective Testing*. Unpublished Working Paper for the Commonwealth Conference, Makerere, Uganda.
Strevens, P. (1971). Alternatives to Daffodils, or – Scientist Thou Never Wert. In G.E. Perren (ed.), *Science and Technology in a Second Language* (pp. 7–11). CILT Reports and Papers 7. London: Centre for Information on Language Teaching.
Strevens, P.D. (1988). ESP after Twenty Years: A Re-Appraisal. In M. Tickoo (ed.), *ESP: State of the Art* (pp. 1–13). Singapore: SEAMEO Regional Language Centre.
Swales, J.M. (1988). *Episodes in ESP: A Source and Reference Book on the Development of English for Science and Technology*. New York: Prentice Hall.
Tajfel, U. and Dawson, J. (eds.) (1965). *Disappointed Guests*. Oxford: Oxford University Press.
Tallents, S. (1932). *The Projection of England*. London: Faber and Faber.
Tamayo, J.M. (1989). Frequency of Use as a Measure of Word Difficulty in Bilingual Vocabulary Test Construction and Translation. *Educational and Psychological Measurement* 47(4): 893–902. https://doi.org/10.1177/0013164487474004
Taylor, C. (1979). *An Assessment of the University of Cambridge Certificate of Proficiency English*. Unpublished MA Dissertation, University of London, UK.
Taylor, L. (1998). *IELTS Specifications for Item Writers*. Cambridge: UCLES.
Taylor, L. (2000). Principles and Practice in Test Development: The PETS Project in China. *Research Notes* 3: 2–4.
Taylor, L. (2001a). Revising the IELTS Speaking Test: Developments in Test Format and Task Design. *Research Notes* 5: 3–5.

Taylor, L. (2001b). Revising the IELTS Speaking Test: Retraining IELTS Examiners Worldwide. *Research Notes* 6: 9–11.

Taylor, L. (ed.) (2011). *Examining Speaking: Research and Practice in Assessing Second Language Speaking*. Studies in Language Testing 30. Cambridge: Cambridge University Press.

Taylor, L. and Falvey, P. (eds.) (2007). *IELTS Collected Papers: Research in Speaking and Writing Assessment*. Studies in Language Testing 19. Cambridge: Cambridge University Press.

Taylor, L. and Jones, N. (2001). Revising the IELTS Speaking Test. *Research Notes* 46: 9–12.

Taylor, L. and Weir, C.J. (2012a). Introduction. In L. Taylor and C.J. Weir (eds.), *Research in Reading and Listening Assessment* (pp. 1–36). Studies in Language Testing 34. Cambridge: Cambridge University Press.

Taylor, L. and Weir, C.J. (eds.) (2012b). *Research in Reading and Listening Assessment*. Studies in Language Testing 34. Cambridge: Cambridge University Press.

Taylor, P.M. (1981). *The Projection of Britain: British Overseas Publicity and Propaganda 1919–1939*. Cambridge: Cambridge University Press. https://doi.org/10.1017/CBO9780511562242

Taylor, P.M. (1999). *British Propaganda in the 20th Century: Selling Democracy*. Edinburgh: Edinburgh University Press.

Templeton, H.R. (1973). *Cloze Procedure in Aural Proficiency Tests for Foreign Students Studying in English*. Unpublished MEd Dissertation, University of Manchester, UK.

Tompos, A. (2001). *A Genre-Based Approach to ESP Testing*. Unpublished PhD Dissertation, The University of Pécs, Hungary.

Tompos, A. and Tóth, I. (1998). Developing a Framework for ESP Testing in Hungary. *novELTy* 5(3): 59–63.

Tonkyn, A. and Wilson, J. (2004). Revising the IELTS Speaking Test. In L. Sheldon (ed.), *Directions for the Future: Issues in English for Academic Purposes* (pp. 191–203). Bern and Oxford: Peter Lang.

Tóth, I. and Bánóczy, E. (2000). A Novel Approach to ESP Testing. In J. Dvoráková (ed.-in-chief), *LSP Forum '99: The Proceedings of International Conference on Teaching Languages for Specific/Academic Purposes* (pp. 14–16). Prague: CR-AUACR/ATECR.

Toulmin, S.E. (1958). *The Uses of Argument*. Cambridge: Cambridge University Press.

Tribble, C. (2012). *Managing Change in English Language Teaching; Lessons from Experience*. London: British Council.

UKCOSA (1974). *Guidance Leaflet 14*. London: United Kingdom Council on Overseas Student Affairs.

United Kingdom Trade and Investment (UKTI) Education (2014). *English Language Education and Training Capability*. Accessed 15 September 2016 from: https://www.gov.uk/government/uploads/system/uploads/attachment_data/file/356794/UK_capability_in_English_language_training.pdf.

Urquhart, A. and Weir, C.J. (1998). *Reading in a Second Language: Process, Product and Practice.* Essex: Pearson Education Ltd.

Van Ek, J. (1975). *Systems Development in Adult Language Learning: The Threshold Level, with an appendix by L. Alexander.* Strasbourg: Council of Europe.

Vollmer, H.J. (1981a). Why Are We Interested in 'General Language Proficiency'? In J.C. Alderson and A. Hughes (eds.), *Issues in Language Testing* (pp. 176–181). ELT Documents 111. London: The British Council.

Vollmer, H.J. (1981b). Response: Issue or Non-Issue – General Language Proficiency Revisited. In J.C. Alderson, and A. Hughes (eds.), *Issues in Language Testing* (pp. 195–207). ELT Documents 111. London: The British Council.

Walker, D. (1978). *The Integration of Overseas Students into a College of Education.* Unpublished MEd Dissertation, University of Sheffield, UK.

Wall, D. (1990). Update on Sri Lanka – The O Level Evaluation Project. *Language Testing Update* 8: 15.

Wall, D. (1996a). Introducing New Tests into Traditional Systems: Insights from General Education and Innovation Theory. *Language Testing* 13(3): 334–354. https://doi.org/10.1177/026553229601300307

Wall, D. (1996b). Baltic States Year 12 Examination Project. *Language Testing Update* 19: 15–17.

Wall, D. (2001). *Report on a Consultancy Visit to Six Countries in the Peacekeeping English Project.* Confidential Report for The British Council.

Wall, D. (2005). *The Impact of High-Stakes Testing on Classroom Teaching: A Case Study Using Insights from Testing and Innovation Theory.* Studies in Language Testing 22. Cambridge: ESOL and Cambridge University Press.

Wall, D. and Alderson, J.C. (1993). Examining Washback: The Sri Lankan Impact Study. *Language Testing* 10(1): 41–69. https://doi.org/10.1177/026553229301000103

Wall, D., Clapham, C. and Alderson, J.C. (1991). Validating Tests in Difficult Circumstances. In J.C. Alderson and B. North (eds.), *Language Testing in the 1990s* (pp. 209–225). London: Modern English Publications Ltd in association with The British Council.

Wallace, M.J. (1980). *Study Skills in English.* Cambridge: Cambridge University Press.

Walter, C., West, R. and Millrood, R. (2006). *Review of ELT Projects in Russia.* British Council Internal Document.

Wayment, H.G. (ed.) (1961). *English Teaching Abroad and the British Universities.* London: Methuen.

Weir, C.J. (1983). *Identifying the Language Problems of the Overseas Students in Tertiary Education in the United Kingdom.* Unpublished PhD Dissertation, University of London, UK.

Weir, C.J. (1988). Construct Validity. In A. Hughes, D. Porter and C.J. Weir (eds.), *ELTS Research Report 1(ii) ELTS Validation Project: Proceedings of a Conference Held to Consider the ELTS Validation Project Report* (pp. 15–25). Cambridge: UCLES.

Weir, C.J. (1990). *Communicative Language Testing*. Englewood Cliffs, NJ: Prentice Hall.

Weir, C.J. (1993). *Understanding and Developing Language Tests*. Oxford: Prentice Hall.

Weir, C.J. (2005). *Language Testing and Validation: An Evidence-Based Approach*. Oxford: Palgrave. https://doi.org/10.1057/9780230514577

Weir, C.J. (2013). An Overview of the Influences on English Language Testing. In C.J. Weir, I. Vidakovic and E.D. Galaczi, *Measured Constructs: A History of the Constructs underlying Cambridge English Language (ESOL) Examinations 1913–2012* (pp. 1–102). Studies in Language Testing 37. Cambridge: Cambridge University Press.

Weir, C.J., Chan, S.H.C. and Nakatsuhara, F. (2013). Examining the Criterion Related Validity of the GEPT Advanced Reading and Writing Tests: Comparing GEPT with IELTS and Real Life Academic Performance. *LTTC-GEPT Research Report 1*: 1–43. Accessed 16 July 2016 from: www.lttc.ntu.edu.tw/lttc-gept-grants/RReport/RG01.pdf.

Weir, C.J., Hawkey, R.A. and Green, A.B. (2012a). The Relationship between the Academic Reading Construct as Measured by IELTS and the Reading Experiences of Students in their First Year of Study at a British University. In L. Taylor and C.J. Weir (eds.), *Research in Reading and Listening Assessment* (pp. 37–119). Studies in Language Testing 34. Cambridge: Cambridge University Press.

Weir, C.J., Hawkey, R.A. and Green, A.B. (2012b). The Cognitive Processes Underlying the Academic Reading Construct as Measured by IELTS. In L. Taylor and C.J. Weir (eds.), *Research in Reading and Listening Assessment* (pp. 212–269). Studies in Language Testing 34. Cambridge: Cambridge University Press.

Weir, C.J. and Milanovic, M. (2003). *Continuity and Innovation: A History of the CPE Examination 1913–2002*. Studies in Language Testing 15. Cambridge: Cambridge University Press.

Weir, C.J. and Saville, N. (2015). Series Editors' Note. In R. Wilson and M. Poulter (eds.), *Assessing Language Teachers' Professional Skills and Knowledge* (pp. vii–xii). Cambridge: Cambridge English Language Assessment/Cambridge University Press.

Weir, C.J., Vidakovic, I. and Galaczi, E.D. (2013). *Measured Constructs: A History of the Constructs Underlying Cambridge English Language (ESOL) Examinations 1913–2012*. Studies in Language Testing 37. Cambridge: Cambridge University Press.

Weir, C.J., Yang, H. and Yan, J. (2000). *An Empirical Investigation of the Componentiality of L2 Reading in English for Academic Purposes*. Studies in Language Testing 12. Cambridge: Cambridge University Press.

West, R. and Tompos, A. (2000). From Generic to Specific: A Genre-Based Approach to ESP Testing. In M. Beaumont and T. O'Brien (eds.), *Collaborative Research in Second Language Education* (pp. 195–206). Stoke on Trent, UK: Trentham Books.

Westaway, G. (1993). Roles for Evaluation in the British Council's Management of ODA Funded Projects in the Kenyan Context. In P. Rea-Dickins and A.F. Lwaitama (eds.), *Review of English Language Teaching: Evaluation for Development in English Language Teaching* 3(3): 130–140.

Westaway, G., Alderson, J.C. and Clapham, C. (1990). Directions in Testing for Specific Purposes. In J.H.A.L. de Jong and D.K. Stevenson (eds.), *Individualizing the Assessment of Language Abilities* (pp. 239–256). Bristol: Multilingual Matters.

White, A.J.S. (1965). *The British Council: The First 25 Years 1934–1959*. London: British Council.

Wickham, B. (1995). Sino-British Co-operation in ELT 1970–1993: Joint Ventures in Educational Development. In A. Pincas (ed.), *Spreading English: ELT Projects in International Development* (pp. 1–16). Hertfordshire: Prentice Hall.

Widdowson, H.G. (1978). *Teaching Language as Communication*. Oxford: Oxford University Press.

Wijasuriya, B.S. (1971). *The Occurrence of Discourse Markers and Inter-Sentence Connectives in University Lectures and Their Place in the Testing and Teaching of Listening Comprehension in English as a Foreign Language*. Unpublished MEd Dissertation, University of Manchester, UK.

Wilkins, D.A. (1976). *Notional Syllabuses*. London: Oxford University Press.

Wilson, R. and Poulter, M. (2015). *Assessing Language Teachers' Professional Skills and Knowledge*. Cambridge: Cambridge English Language Assessment/ Cambridge University Press.

Wingard, P.G. (1971). English for Scientists at the University of Zambia. In G.E. Perren (ed.), *Science and Technology in a Second Language* (pp. 53–63). CILT Reports and Papers 7. London: Centre for Information on Language Teaching.

Yang, H. and Weir, C.J. (1998). *Empirical Bases for Construct Validation: The College English Test – A Case Study*. Shanghai: Shanghai Foreign Language Education Press.

Zheng, Y. and Berry, V. (2015). Aptis for Teens: Analysis of Pilot Test Data. Technical Report TR/2015/004. Accessed 16 July 2016 from: https://www.britishcouncil.org/sites/default/files/aptis_for_teens_layout.pdf.

Zou, S., Green, R. and Weir, C.J. (1997). *The Test for English Majors (TEM) Validation Study*. Shanghai: Shanghai Foreign Language Education Press.

Subject and Key Personnel Index

Approaches to English language testing
Communicative x, 29, 43, 44, 56–57, 76, 87, 102, 119, 121, 122, 133, 135, 136–140, 145, 146, 148, 152, 154, 155, 160, 161, 162, 163, 165, 172, 175, 176, 196, 203, 205, 206, 244, 333, 334, 350, 352, 353, 355, 358, 359, 362, 363, 367, 368, 371
Pre-scientific 64, 111–113, 332, 333, 334
Psychometric-structuralist 44, 63, 77, 116–119, 121, 122, 133, 135, 137, 138, 140, 332, 333, 334
Socio-cognitive 44, 79, 87, 91, 243, 275, 276, 285, 290–292, 293–303, 322, 330, 334, 335

English language examinations
Advanced English Reading Test (AERT) (1995) 46, 86–87
Aptis (2012–) 91, 273, 276–318, 322, 334, 335, 338–343, 349, 355, 356, 361, 362, 364, 365, 368, 373
  Aptis Advanced 296, 309, 315, 316
  Aptis General 280, 281, 289, 290, 296, 297, 301, 309, 310–313, 344, 365
  Aptis for Teachers 280, 281, 309, 344
  Aptis for Teens 280, 281, 309, 314, 317, 373
Certificate of Proficiency in English (CPE) (1913–) 13, 14, 17, 18, 23, 24, 25, 28, 29, 32, 101, 120, 145, 157, 174, 177, 219, 243, 309, 367, 372
College English Test (CET) (1987–) 46, 63, 67, 79–81
Diploma of English Studies (1945–1996) 25–30, 101, 331, 333, 334
English Language Testing Service (ELTS) (1980–1989) 22, 42, 102, 114, 123, 124, 129, 130, 131, 132, 135, 139–207, 209, 211, 212, 213, 215, 216, 220, 223, 225, 332, 333, 348, 354, 357, 358, 359, 368, 371
EPTB (the Davies Test) (1965–1982) 21, 102, 106, 114–121, 123, 129, 132, 133, 135, 137, 140, 141, 143, 146, 148, 157, 166, 167, 169, 172, 174, 190, 205, 244, 258, 332, 333, 334
First Certificate in English (FCE) (1975–) 36, 64, 101, 145, 150, 174, 177, 215, 216, 358
International English Language Testing System (IELTS) (1989–) 43, 47, 59, 64, 160, 174, 179, 183, 185, 191, 195, 196, 199–207, 208–254, 258, 269, 270, 272, 273, 281, 283, 315, 317, 318, 320, 322, 324, 326, 327, 333, 334, 335, 337, 348, 349, 350, 352, 353, 354, 355, 356, 357, 358, 359, 362, 363, 365, 367, 369, 370, 371, 372
International Language Assessment (ILA) (2009–) x, 149, 150, 151,

Subject and key personnel index 375

258–268, 274, 276, 277, 278, 293, 315, 334, 365
Knowledge of English 4-point scale (1953–58) 112
Lower Certificate in English (LCE) (1939–75) 14, 18, 23, 24, 25, 28, 36, 101, 120
Mini-platform (1982–2009) 42, 148, 149–151, 259, 333, 363
Overseas Spoken Interview (OSI 210) (1958–1965) 113, 332, 333
Test for English Majors (TEM) (1990–) 45, 46, 81–86, 87, 373
Test in English for Academic Purposes (TEAP) (1979–82) 76, 137, 138, 160, 190, 191, 196, 204
Test in English for Educational Purposes (TEEP) (1983–) 138, 188, 194, 223
TOEFL (1964–) 141, 157, 160, 173, 184, 185, 215, 216, 220, 235, 349, 368
TOEFL iBT (2005–) 77, 243, 281, 283, 315, 317, 354

Key concepts in the assessment work of the British Council
Accessibility 11, 69, 91, 232, 257, 258, 276, 279, 285, 288, 329, 337
Affordability 92, 279, 288, 315, 337, 348
Assessment literacy 281, 285, 324, 325, 326, 330
Assessment Research Awards & Grants (ARAGs) 319–322, 330, 344–347
Common European Framework of Reference for Languages (CEFR) 30, 35, 38, 91, 92, 156, 260, 261, 263, 264, 266, 267, 276, 279, 288, 290, 292, 293, 294, 316, 317, 323, 327, 330, 333, 344
    CEFR-J 288, 290
China Standards of English (CSE) 288, 290
Consequences 244, 246, 310, 324
Economic imperatives 5, 6, 9, 10, 11, 12, 54, 60, 61, 65, 76, 93, 109–111

English as a global language 10–12
English for Academic Purposes (EAP) 9, 21, 45, 46, 75, 76–77, 81, 86, 87, 110, 118, 119–135, 138, 141, 145, 152, 154, 155, 157, 158, 160, 167, 169, 175, 176, 186, 187, 190, 196, 197, 203–206, 216, 244, 332, 354, 355, 358, 360, 361, 362, 363, 367, 370, 372
English for immigration purposes 215, 223, 226, 233, 236, 252
English for specific purposes 43, 46, 53, 75, 78, 101, 140, 146, 161, 177, 179, 206, 333
English for work purposes 53, 101, 165
Examination reform 13, 44–52, 53–91, 278, 312–313, 316
Flexibility 48, 229, 257, 258, 276, 279, 285, 288, 290, 314, 317, 318, 320, 327, 329, 337
Impact 36, 39, 44, 45, 48, 50, 53–102, 212, 217, 244–246, 263, 298, 310, 311–318
Localisation 41, 45, 49, 59, 91, 94, 257, 279–282, 287, 288, 290, 293, 309, 310, 311–318, 323, 327, 329, 330, 331, 337, 348, 355, 364
Marketing 214, 215, 227, 235, 237, 252, 284, 286, 310, 325
Online rater training 303, 304, 330
Online rating 304–305
Online test taking 258, 282, 288
Partnership
    BC-Tests 269, 272
    Cambridge 101, 331
    English Impact 328
    Governments 67
    IELTS 210–211, 212–215, 221, 225, 227, 249, 250, 253
    ILA 263, 267
Product centred approach 257–330
Project management 47–102
Promoting British education 105–113, 139, 232, 331

Promoting culture 4, 5, 7, 13, 30, 31, 32, 109, 110
Promoting English 4, 7, 8, 10, 11, 12, 13–15, 30–32, 40–41
Real-life approach 56, 76, 79, 119, 136, 140, 155, 191, 196, 242, 243
Reliability 33, 56, 58, 81, 82, 87, 88–89, 113, 115, 118, 138, 151, 157, 161, 169, 182–183, 184, 187, 188, 189, 196, 197, 198, 209, 212, 220, 224, 226, 303–304
Research 21, 23, 31, 32–38, 41, 43, 54, 57–59, 71, 74, 80–81, 84–85, 86, 91, 99, 115, 125, 132, 136, 143, 153, 156–157, 159, 168–171, 172, 176, 178, 185, 186, 189–191, 204, 205, 210, 214, 216, 219, 220, 222, 223, 231–232, 234, 237–238, 239, 240, 243, 244, 246, 248–249, 250, 258, 261, 263, 266, 272, 276, 278, 281, 297, 303, 304, 308, 315, 319–325, 326–328, 329, 331, 332, 335, 336, 344–347
Responsibility for government funded trainees and students from overseas 9, 21, 102, 106–119, 154, 156, 161, 177, 251, 332, 358
Socio-cognitive approach (see under **Approaches to English language testing** above)
Soft power 9, 13–15, 67, 102, 331–332, 337
Stakeholder involvement 50–52, 62, 66, 88, 94, 95, 139, 188, 191, 199, 203, 204, 225, 232, 235, 246, 250, 260, 284, 285, 291, 312, 326, 330, 344
Sustainability
  Assessment/Test project 51, 65, 77, 82, 90, 91, 92, 173, 184, 206, 228, 240, 243, 258, 330
  Educational 48
  Financial 47, 48, 50, 107, 188, 214, 243, 271, 273
Test delivery 10, 40, 46, 55, 56, 61, 62, 65, 80, 150, 174, 187, 204, 210, 212, 214, 222, 223, 226, 228–231, 238–239, 243, 246, 257, 267, 271, 279, 280, 282, 286, 287–288, 310, 311–317, 319, 321, 327, 328, 329, 336, 337, 345
Test impact 36, 39, 44, 45, 48, 50, 53–54, 56–59, 62–63, 65–67, 68, 70, 72, 76, 85–86, 92, 93–101, 102, 212, 217, 219, 244–246, 263, 273, 310, 311–317, 318
Test specification 66, 68, 71, 73, 86, 88, 89, 90, 95, 147, 177, 178, 187, 194, 198, 203, 204, 206, 275, 298, 321, 335
Validity 34–35, 56, 57, 58, 80, 81–84, 87–89, 95–96, 138, 159, 160–168, 168–182, 184, 187, 189, 190, 196–198, 202, 208, 215, 216, 217, 219, 220, 222, 240, 243, 244, 247–249, 285, 293, 309, 310, 320, 334, 335, 344

Key English language testing projects
Advanced English Reading Test Project, China (1995–1998) 46, 86–87
Boğaziçi University English Proficiency Test, Turkey (1982–84) 45, 46, 76–77, 350
College English Test (CET) Validation Project, China (1991–1995) 46, 79–81, 83, 87, 373
Egyptian Universities' National Academic Reading Test (1990–1995) 45, 46, 78–79
English for Tourism Project, Venezuela (2007) 46, 101
English Language Assessment System for the Public Service (ELPA), Malaysia (1998–2000) 46, 94–96
Examination Reform Teacher Support Project, Hungary (1998–2002) 45, 46, 71–75, 348
EXAVER Project, Mexico (2000–2010) 46, 91–92, 275, 334, 335, 348, 355
Secondary and Technical Education Project (STEP) Mozambique (1997– 2002) 46, 67–70, 91, 349, 362

Subject and key personnel index 377

Sri Lankan National Certificate in English Evaluation (1986–1987) 44, 46, 54–56, 349, 356
Sri Lankan O Level English Language Evaluation Project (1989–1991) 44, 46, 56–60, 349, 371
St Petersburg Examination Project (SPEX) Russia (1996–2001) 46, 64–67, 349
Test for Civil Servants, Thailand (1991–2015) 45, 46, 93–94
Test for English Majors project, China (1993–1996) 45, 46, 81–86, 87, 373
UK Peacekeeping English Project (1996–2010) 46, 50–51, 96–100, 354, 371
University Entrance Test Development Projects, Uzbekistan (2004–2009) 46, 87–90
Year 12 English Examinations Project, Baltic States (1994–1997) 46, 59–64, 370

Key events

Agreement between Cambridge and the British Council (1941–1993) 14–18, 331, 333
Basic English movement (1920s–) 14, 23–24
Birth of the British Council (1934–) 3–10
Cambridge–TOEFL comparability study (1987–1989) 215–216, 349
Creation of the Assessment Research Group (2012–) 276, 277–278, 319, 335, 364
Department for Technical Cooperation (1961) 111
Drogheda Report (1953) 12, 30, 109
ELTS Revision Project (1986–1989) 184–189, 191–207
ELTS Validation Consultative Conference (1986) 189–191
ELTS Validation Study (1981–86) 168–184

English Language Teaching Journal (ELTJ) (1946–) 19, 20, 21, 22, 138, 353, 359, 361, 368
Hill Report (1957) 110–111
IELTS Impact Study Project (1995–2003) 244, 246
IELTS Revision Project (1993–1995) 238–244
IELTS Speaking Revision Project (1998–2001) 246–249
IELTS Writing Revision Project (2001–05) 249–250
Joint Committee of the Board of Trade and Board of Education (1933–) 5
Loraine's Despatch on Egypt (1933) 6
Overseas student scholarship scheme (1938–) 107
Publication of Canale and Swan (1980) article on communicative approaches x, 137, 352
Publication of *Communicative Syllabus Design* (1978) 146, 147, 156, 161, 175, 186, 204, 333, 355, 362, 363
Report of the Official Committee on the Teaching of English Overseas (1956) 110
Resident Foreigners Division (1939) 19, 105
Royal Charter of Incorporation (1940) 8
Tilley Report (1920) 5

Key organisations

Cambridge English Language Assessment (formerly UCLES and Cambridge ESOL) 10, 13–15, 41, 64, 78, 83, 84, 101, 120, 129, 139, 141–147, 148, 149, 152, 155, 157–159, 174, 177, 185, 186, 202, 206–210, 212–221, 227, 229, 230, 232, 233, 240–243, 246, 247–250, 253, 269, 272, 327, 331, 333–334, 349, 358, 361, 365, 366, 367, 368, 369, 372
ELTS Management Committee 147, 152, 156, 185

Executive Committee 19, 34, 36, 38, 333
Joint Committee of the British Council and Cambridge Local Examinations Syndicate 15–19, 21–39, 168, 169, 333
Department for International Development (DFID) 40, 45, 50, 69, 79, 102, 331
Department of Technical Cooperation (DTC) 111
Edinburgh University 20, 43, 156, 168
Educational Testing Service (ETS) 77, 141, 220
English Teaching Information Centre (ETIC) (1961) 21, 115, 125
Foreign Office (UK) 4, 5, 6, 7, 14, 16
IDP: IELTS Australia 185, 208–211, 212, 214, 215, 218, 222, 223, 224, 225, 227, 230, 231, 232, 233–238, 240, 244, 246, 248, 249, 252, 253, 254, 327
Lancaster University 43, 45, 52, 55, 56, 57, 61, 62, 63, 64, 65, 70, 71, 99, 139, 147, 169, 176, 184, 185, 191, 192, 194, 210, 234, 246, 258, 321, 345, 346
Overseas Development Administration (ODA) 40, 41, 43, 44, 45, 57, 78, 79, 93, 102, 126, 149, 331, 372
Reading University 43, 76, 80, 84, 86, 94, 147, 192, 223, 249, 326
Special English Language Materials for Overseas University Students (SELMOUS) group 120, 124, 125, 133, 152, 175, 176
University of Bedfordshire, CRELLA 59, 263, 265, 266, 267, 319, 321, 327, 344, 345, 346
University of Roehampton, CLARe 91, 262, 263, 265, 266, 267, 275, 277

Key players

Alderson, Charles 40, 43, 45, 55, 56, 58, 59, 65, 70, 72, 73, 117, 139, 156, 162, 168, 169, 174, 176, 185, 186, 187, 188, 189, 190, 191, 192, 194, 195, 196, 197, 199, 205, 237, 258, 333, 348, 349, 353, 354, 355, 356, 357, 359, 363, 366, 367, 370, 371, 372
Bachman, Lyle 77, 178, 215, 216, 282, 293, 349
Candlin, Chris 125, 128, 139, 214, 352
Carroll, Brendan 22, 41, 42, 102, 122, 139, 140, 141, 145, 146, 151, 152, 154, 155, 156, 161, 162, 175, 176, 177, 178, 189, 192, 194, 203, 204, 332, 333, 353, 358
Charge, Nick 223, 226, 229, 234, 239, 253, 353
Clapham, Caroline 43, 55, 56, 59, 63, 139, 140, 156, 168, 169, 174, 179, 185, 186, 187, 188, 190, 191, 194, 195, 196, 197, 198, 199, 202, 204, 205, 220, 237, 241, 242, 333, 348, 349, 353, 354, 356, 357, 359, 371, 372
Cooper, Anne-Marie 209, 210, 211, 214, 224, 235, 253, 354
Criper, Clive 43, 141, 168, 169, 172, 173, 174, 179, 180, 181, 182, 183, 184, 187, 189, 192, 354
Crossey, Mark 50, 97, 98, 100, 354
Csépes, Ildiko 73
Dangerfield, Les 62, 212, 214, 221, 228, 232, 236
Davies, Alan 43, 102, 113, 114, 115, 116, 117, 118, 119, 120, 121, 122, 123, 126, 127, 134, 140, 141, 142, 145, 146, 156, 164, 168, 169, 172, 173, 174, 176, 179, 180, 181, 182, 183, 184, 186, 187, 188, 189, 192, 202, 203, 204, 205, 213, 240, 241, 244, 258, 323, 332, 333, 334, 352, 354, 355
Evans, Ifor 17, 18, 24, 25, 26, 32, 107, 336
Fairbairn, Judith 304, 306, 307, 308, 355, 356, 361
Falvey, Peter 32, 38, 146, 164, 213, 241, 243, 245, 246, 247, 248, 249, 250, 367, 369

Subject and key personnel index

Foulkes, John 185, 186, 195, 196, 356
Gildea, John 221, 224, 226, 227, 230, 231, 232
Green, Anthony 35, 43, 59, 357, 371, 372
Green, Rita 43, 45, 51, 68, 69, 81, 83, 84, 85, 86, 87, 88, 89, 90, 93, 94, 95, 97, 100, 259, 260, 357, 362, 373
Hamp-Lyons, Liz 43, 139, 166, 169, 170, 171, 173, 180, 181, 182, 183, 189, 194, 197, 198, 357
Hargreaves, Peter 22, 42, 64, 84, 139, 141, 157, 158, 185, 213, 216, 219, 239
Harrison, Andrew 139, 142, 143, 155, 158, 366
Hawkey, Roger 14, 15, 19, 23, 30, 41, 42, 44, 106, 120, 121, 123, 124, 125, 126, 129, 139, 141, 145, 146, 151, 154, 156, 161, 162, 176, 177, 186, 204, 246, 358, 371, 372
Hewitt, Barbara 258, 260
Hindmarsh, Roland 22, 32, 36, 37, 38, 43, 139, 144, 147, 358
Hornby, Albert 14, 15, 19, 20, 359
Hughes, Arthur 3, 43, 44, 76, 77, 79, 117, 118, 139, 162, 169, 176, 188, 189, 190, 192, 243, 348, 350, 353, 355, 358, 359, 363, 367, 368, 370, 371
Ingram, David 185, 197, 200, 201, 202, 210, 214, 234, 333, 359, 360
Jones, Daniel 17, 18, 19, 24, 28, 33
Jones, Neil 141, 216, 248, 369
King, Arthur 22, 31
Lazaraton, Anne 219, 246, 361
Leeper, Rex 6, 7, 9, 361
Lilley, Tony 45, 78
Lloyd, Lord 6, 8, 105, 106, 348, 349
Lowder, Martin 275, 276, 277, 286, 287
Mackenzie, Andrew 277, 287
Maingay, Susan 49, 60
McEldowney, Pat 43, 122, 139, 362
McGovern, John 62, 64
McNeill, Arthur 43, 139, 141, 149, 333, 363

Milanovic, Mike 14, 15, 19, 23, 30, 35, 41, 64, 83, 84, 106, 141, 145, 146, 177, 184, 186, 206, 207, 211, 213, 214, 216, 218, 219, 220, 225, 228, 229, 230, 234, 237, 238, 254, 358, 367, 372
Moller, Alan 22, 42, 43, 117, 120, 121, 122, 126, 137, 139, 140, 141, 148, 149, 150, 155, 156, 157, 169, 176, 204, 333, 356, 362
Morrow, Keith 43, 122, 137, 138, 139, 334, 335, 363
Munby, John 121, 140, 145, 146, 147, 148, 151, 152, 154, 155, 156, 158, 161, 162, 175, 176, 178, 186, 194, 204, 333, 350, 362, 363
Nakatsuhara, Fumiyo 251, 327, 344, 346, 350, 363, 371
O'Sullivan, Barry 91, 217, 222, 231, 248, 263, 264, 267, 268, 274, 275, 276, 277, 278, 279, 280, 282, 284, 285, 287, 288, 289, 290, 291, 292, 294, 295, 298, 299, 230, 301, 310, 319, 323, 324, 325, 326, 334, 335, 338, 340, 341, 342, 343, 348, 350, 364, 365, 366
Palmer, Harold 14, 31, 368
Parkinson, Nancy 106
Perren, George 21, 113, 115, 365, 369, 373
Rea, Pauline 43, 139, 173, 366
Reddaway, John 15, 38, 213, 215, 216
Roach, Jack 13, 14, 17, 23, 33, 34, 106, 366, 367, 368, 369
Robson, Mark 96, 275, 277
Saville, Nick 29, 141, 177, 211, 216, 218, 219, 225, 226, 230, 240, 247, 248, 365, 367, 372
Seaton, Ian 43, 139, 140, 141, 149, 151, 152, 155, 157, 158, 160, 167, 170, 333, 363, 367
Sheehan, Susan 259, 260, 268, 345, 364, 368

Shoesmith, David 157, 178
Smith, Richard 13, 20, 21, 30, 31, 106, 110, 136, 149, 157, 174, 178, 359, 368
Spolsky, Bernard 13, 137, 332, 334, 368
Staniforth, Anne 224, 235, 236, 253
Sunderland, Richard 269
Taylor, Lynda 87, 133, 141, 164, 166, 168, 186, 187, 188, 205, 216, 218, 219, 220, 221, 228, 233, 234, 237, 238, 239, 240, 241, 242, 243, 244, 245, 246, 247, 248, 250, 252, 282, 291, 334, 335, 350, 353, 356, 366, 369, 371, 372
Urquhart, Alexander 131, 139, 190, 214, 242, 349, 370
Walker, Mark 275, 276, 287
Wall, Dianne 43, 52, 55, 56, 57, 58, 59, 60, 61, 63, 64, 65, 97, 98, 99, 100, 348, 349, 357, 370, 371
Weir, Cyril 14, 15, 18, 19, 21, 22, 24, 29, 32, 34, 35, 37, 43, 44, 54, 64, 76, 77, 78, 79, 80, 81, 83, 84, 86, 87, 91, 106, 123, 129, 130, 131, 132, 137, 138, 139, 146, 155, 156, 160, 164, 166, 168, 169, 173, 174, 177, 178, 179, 183, 186, 187, 188, 189, 190, 191, 192, 194, 196, 197, 204, 216, 218, 219, 220, 223, 238, 241, 243, 248, 250, 251, 253, 263, 265, 266, 275, 290, 291, 292, 293, 294, 297, 319, 330, 334, 335, 346, 358, 359, 361, 365, 367, 368, 369, 370, 371, 372, 373
West, Richard 43, 67, 371
Westaway, Gill 43, 47, 48, 141, 168, 169, 172, 182, 185, 186, 187, 188, 195, 205, 212, 213, 221, 333, 371, 372
Wickham, Barbara 48, 79, 80, 372
Yan, Jin 80, 81, 86, 87, 319, 365, 372
Zou, Shen 84, 85

Test Systems
Administration 14, 41, 55, 56, 62, 65, 69, 71, 87, 88, 90, 92, 96, 140, 152, 153, 170, 172, 174, 187, 189, 199, 206, 211, 214, 215, 218, 238, 240, 267–268, 280, 282, 311–317, 328,
Automated scoring 286, 308
Building test corpora 35, 219, 358
Delivery 10, 40, 53, 55, 56, 61, 62, 65, 80, 150, 174, 187, 204, 210, 212, 214, 222, 223, 226, 228–231, 238, 243, 246, 257, 267, 271, 279, 280, 282, 286, 287, 287–288, 310, 311–317, 319, 321, 327, 328, 329, 336, 337, 343
Examiner management: the professional support network 223–234
Examiner standardisation 33, 34, 71, 81, 83, 97, 183, 200, 211, 219, 220, 247, 334
Examiner training 73–74, 185, 199, 200, 245, 249, 250
Marker reliability: Control Item System 306–308
Post-test analysis 44, 174, 253 (see also Reliability under **Key concepts in the assessment work of the British Council**)
Product development
  Item writing 52, 63, 66, 71, 81, 89, 93, 159, 178, 191, 275
  Pre-testing 100, 173, 179, 185, 207, 214, 218, 239
  Standard fixing 214
  Item banking 72, 218, 220, 240, 276, 277, 280, 282, 286, 313
Promotion 40, 41, 148, 149, 212, 222, 232–233, 234–236
Quality assurance and management 50, 138, 187, 199, 214, 219, 223, 240, 245, 247, 248, 250, 262, 282, 306, 313, 321, 330
Rater training 71, 74, 166, 199, 304, 306, 330
Security 62, 65, 90, 97, 172, 208, 217, 222, 223, 225–228, 229–230, 236, 240, 242, 270, 275, 314, 315

Subject and key personnel index

Test-taker characteristics 81, 218, 270, 279, 289–290, 311, 312, 313, 314, 316, 317
Validation 32, 44, 45, 46, 56, 63, 78, 79–86, 92, 95–96, 100, 115, 140–141, 147, 151, 156, 158, 159, 162, 168–184, 189–191, 199, 203, 204, 206, 213, 214, 215–221, 226, 237, 240, 243, 246, 248, 250, 261, 275, 282, 285, 290, 291, 292, 310, 322, 326, 330, 347

Testing English language knowledge and skills
Grammar 19, 23, 27, 70, 88, 93, 116, 117, 118, 137, 140, 150, 195, 196, 197, 258, 263, 265, 267, 268, 276, 277, 278, 279, 290, 293, 330, 334, 338
Listening 55, 71, 72, 76, 81, 82, 87, 93, 116, 117, 118, 119, 120, 122, 127–130, 131, 132, 133, 160, 163, 165, 167, 180, 188, 191, 195–196, 201, 202, 205, 218, 220, 225, 226, 229, 238, 240, 244, 245, 250, 258, 270, 277, 278, 279, 286, 288, 290, 292, 294, 297, 298, 303, 312, 314, 315, 316, 317, 321, 322, 330, 334, 341, 344, 345, 352, 356, 363, 368, 369, 372
Phonetics 19, 27, 28, 33, 115, 116, 117, 128, 132
Reading 27, 33, 34, 45, 46, 55, 57, 69, 71, 72, 76, 78–79, 81, 82, 86–87, 88, 93, 94, 95, 115, 116, 117, 118, 119, 120, 122, 126, 128, 129, 130–131, 132, 133, 134, 160, 163, 164, 165, 167, 178–179, 180, 181, 188, 191, 192, 193, 194, 195, 196, 197, 198, 200–201, 202, 203, 204, 205, 216, 218, 220, 224, 226, 234, 238, 241–243, 244, 245, 250, 258, 263, 265, 266, 267, 268, 270, 277, 278, 279, 280, 286, 288, 290, 292, 293–298, 303, 312, 314, 315, 316, 317, 322, 326, 330, 334, 339, 340, 344, 345, 349, 352, 356, 361, 369, 370, 371
Reading into writing 118, 164, 191, 205, 242–244, 245, 353
Speaking 27, 28, 55, 66, 69, 71, 72, 77, 82, 87, 94, 95, 96, 112, 113, 118, 119, 122, 128, 129, 130, 132, 133, 134, 138, 140, 150, 160, 163, 165, 166, 167, 185, 186, 187, 188, 191, 195, 197, 199–200, 201, 205, 206, 219, 223, 225, 234, 237, 238, 243–244, 245, 246–249, 270, 277, 278, 292, 300, 301, 304, 305, 308, 310, 311, 327, 330, 334, 341, 342, 345, 346, 347, 359, 360, 362, 363, 364, 365, 369, 370
Vocabulary 13, 14, 19, 22, 23, 24, 37, 91, 112, 116, 117, 118, 128, 131, 132, 137, 140, 144, 178, 201, 245, 248, 250, 258, 263, 265, 266, 268, 277, 278, 279, 280, 290, 293, 294, 296, 302, 305, 315, 340, 330, 334, 338, 339, 341, 342, 343, 344, 345, 366
Writing 27, 28, 55, 57, 63, 66, 68, 69, 71, 74, 76, 81, 82, 85, 87, 89, 94, 95, 118, 119, 120, 125, 126, 128, 130, 131–132, 133, 157, 159, 160, 163, 164, 165, 166, 167, 170, 172, 180, 181, 182–183, 185, 187, 188, 191, 193, 194, 195, 197, 198, 199, 205, 206, 220, 223, 224–225, 238, 241, 242–243, 245, 248, 249–250, 258, 267, 270, 277, 292, 298–303, 304, 307, 321, 326, 330, 334, 343, 345, 349, 357, 368, 369